DATA PROCESSING LOGIC

DATA PROCESSING LOGIC

Laura Saret

Oakton Community College

McGraw-Hill Book Company

New York St. Louis San Francisco Auckland Bogotá Hamburg
Johannesburg London Madrid Mexico Montreal New Delhi Panama
Paris São Paulo Singapore Sydney Tokyo Toronto

DATA PROCESSING LOGIC

3 4 5 6 7 8 9 0 DOCDOC 8 9 8 7 6 5

ISBN 0-07-054723-8

This book was set in Times Roman by University Graphics, Inc.
The editors were Eric M. Munson and Jonathan Palace;
the designer was Rafael Hernandez;
the production supervisor was Charles Hess.
The drawings were done by Danmark & Michaels, Inc.
R. R. Donnelley & Sons Company was printer and binder.

Library of Congress Cataloging in Publication Data

Saret, Laura.
Data processing logic.

Includes index.
1. Electronic digital computers—Programming.
2. COBOL (Computer program language) 3. Flow charts.
I. Title.
QA76.6.S265 1984 001.6′1 83-24865
ISBN 0-07-054723-8

to Larry,

my husband and best friend

Contents

Preface

This book is one of the few available on structured data processing logic. The book was developed from lecture notes and handouts which have been used successfully in a course on data processing logic and programming techniques at Oakton Community College.

Although there are many books available on computer programming languages, most do not teach students how to program. The available books concentrate on a particular programming language, with a minimal amount of text being devoted to problem solving. This book concentrates on problem solving, with little emphasis placed on programming languages.

The approach of the book is to teach via examples. All the rules for programming can be listed, but unless a student can see how to apply the rules, he or she will not learn. There are 41 realistic business examples used in this book to illustrate the various topics. Unlike other logic books, all examples are completely solved, so the student can see the entire solution process. All examples in the book relate to business problems. Data names used in this book are COBOL names, because they are more "English-like" than the names allowed by other languages. All examples, however, can easily be converted to FORTRAN or BASIC by changing names to adhere to FORTRAN or BASIC rules.

The book is organized by topic. Chapters 1 to 4 should be covered in sequence. After Chapter 4 is completed, however, the remaining chapters can be completed in any order. After each chapter, exercises and logic problems are included for the student to reinforce the concepts introduced in the chapter.

The author has found that there is sufficient material in this book for a 3-hour 1-semester college course in programming logic. In addition, the book can be used:

1. As a supplement to a programming language course. Many programming students and instructors have indicated that the examples in this book relate to the types of problems assigned in a beginning programming class.
2. As a high school course in the fundamentals of computer programming.
3. In an industry course to train computer programmers.
4. In short courses for business and management people who desire an introduction to computer programming and how a computer works.
5. For programmers in industry desiring to improve their programming skills using structured techniques.
6. For the person desiring to purchase a computer for his or her business and who is interested in learning how to describe the solutions to problems in a way that makes them easy to program.

This book assumes no previous knowledge of data processing. It is expected that the reader can use simple arithmetic tools, but no previous formal training in advanced mathematics is required.

With almost all books, there are people who contribute thoughts, constructive criticism, time, energy, and emotional support to the author, and yet do not receive the recognition they deserve because of space limitations. This book is no exception. Nevertheless, I would like to thank Fran Perlman, a former student, who reviewed the book as a favor to me; my other reviewers; McGraw-Hill for seeing this as a worthwhile project and publishing the book; and my students at Oakton Community College whose questions, comments, and academic successes and failures did much to develop this book. Finally, I would like to thank my husband, Larry, my children, Marla and Jeffrey, my sister, Sheri, and my parents, Marilyn and Harvey, who always expressed substantial interest in the book and encouraged me to start and finish it, probably so that they could see their names in this preface.

Laura Saret

To the Student

You will find this book useful whether you are a beginning data processing student, a manager in a corporation, a data processing professional wishing to update your skills and learn structured programming techniques, or a person curious about how to get the computer to do what you want it to.

Learning programming logic is not easy. For many of you, this is your first experience in learning to "think like a computer." You must unlearn the complicated thought processes you have become used to in dealing with everyday life and learn to tell the computer, in simplified terms, exactly what to do step by step.

The intent of this book is to teach you how to program without emphasizing any programming language. You will find this book useful in any programming language class you take, since writing a computer program merely involves translating programming logic into a language that the computer can understand.

This book assumes no previous knowledge of data processing. It is assumed that you can use simple arithmetic tools, but no training in advanced mathematics is required. If you have had an introductory course or previous experience in data processing, many of the concepts in the beginning of the book will be a review.

I hope that you will enjoy learning to program, and whether you end up as a data processing professional, as a manager, or as a user of video games, word processors, and other packaged programs, that you will appreciate the time, effort, and creativity involved in generating the logic of a computer program.

Laura Saret

DATA PROCESSING LOGIC

CHAPTER 1

Data Processing Terminology

Data Processing
Hardware
Data Organization
Software
The Programming Process
Arithmetic and Logic Symbols
Questions and Exercises for Review

DATA PROCESSING

Data processing involves taking raw data as input to a system, processing the data, and producing information as output.

Input data → process data → output information

The basic requirements, therefore, of any data processing system (computerized or not computerized) are input, processing, and output. Consider, as an example, a system used to compute student grades at the end of a semester. Input consists of exam and assignment scores for each student in a class. The scores for each student are processed to compute his or her average and grade. Output will consist of a grade for each student.

Input exam and assignment scores → process scores to compute average and grade → output grades

HARDWARE

A computer is a machine used for data processing. It is a system of devices capable of processing data which has been entered and supplying the resulting information as output. As such, a computer system must consist of input devices, output devices, and a processing device. These devices are referred to as *hardware.* The processing device used by the computer is called the *central processing unit (CPU).* The CPU is what is usually thought of when you hear the term "computer." It consists of a control unit, an arithmetic logic unit (ALU), and a storage unit.

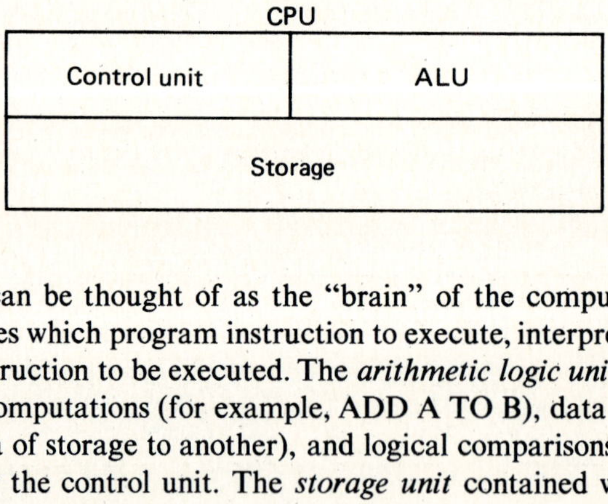

The *control unit* can be thought of as the "brain" of the computer. Among other things, it determines which program instruction to execute, interprets the instruction, and causes the instruction to be executed. The *arithmetic logic unit* is responsible for doing arithmetic computations (for example, ADD A TO B), data transfers (moving data from one area of storage to another), and logical comparisons (such as IS A = 3?) as directed by the control unit. The *storage unit* contained within the CPU is referred to as *primary* or *main storage.* It is used to store the data and instructions (programs) needed by the computer. Another term used for storage is *memory.* The memory size of a computer refers to the storage capacity of the CPU.

Because of space and cost constraints, main memory is not the only storage used by a computer. Imagine the size of the CPU that would be needed if the Internal Revenue Service, for example, stored all its programs and data in main memory! *Secondary* or *external storage* media are used as additional storage or memory for the computer. However, in order for the CPU to use data or instructions, they must be in main memory. The computer can't process data or use instructions that are on a secondary storage medium.

Examples of secondary storage media include punched cards, magnetic disks, and magnetic tapes. *Input/output (I/O) devices* are hardware used to get data and instructions from secondary to primary storage and vice versa. I/O devices include such things as card readers, magnetic tape drives, magnetic disk drives, and printers.

DATA ORGANIZATION

Data are organized as files in secondary storage. A *file* consists of a group of related *records.* Examples of files include payroll files, student files, and accounts receivable files. A payroll file, for example, will probably have a record for each employee of the company. A student file may have a record for each student in the school. Records are composed of fields. A *field* is a group of consecutive storage positions reserved for a specific type of data, e.g., name, address, or social security number. Fields are composed of *characters.* In the name field which contains the name JONES, there are five characters: J, O, N, E, and S.

Fields are said to be alphabetic, numeric, or alphanumeric (alphameric), depending on the characters stored in the field. An *alphabetic field* can contain the characters A through Z, and spaces or blanks. A *numeric field* can contain the characters 0 through 9, a decimal point (.), and an optional sign (+ or −). An *alphanumeric field* can contain alphabetic characters, numeric characters, and special characters such as a dollar sign ($), comma (,), quote ("), apostrophe ('), percent sign (%), hyphen (-), etc.

Consider again the earlier example of computing students' grades. Suppose we keep track of the scores on an index card file. We will have an index card (record) for each student (see sample below). The fields in the record include student name, social security number, Exam 1 score, Exam 2 score, Exam 3 score, Assignment 1 score, and Assignment 2 score.

Student name: Susan Smith			
Soc. Sec. No.: 325-84-1722			
Exam 1 score:	56	Assignment 1 score:	10
Exam 2 score:	73	Assignment 2 score:	21
Exam 3 score:	21		

The student name consists of letters and a blank between the first and last name. It is an alphabetic field. The social security number contains numbers and hyphens, and is therefore an alphanumeric field. Each of the "score" fields is numeric.

SOFTWARE

Software is the term used to describe computer programs. A *computer program* is a set of instructions written in a specific sequence to direct the computer to perform certain predetermined tasks. In the student grade example, we can write instructions that cause the computer to input a record for a particular student, compute the grade based on the contents of the exam and assignment score fields, and print (output) the student's name and his or her grade. Then we can write an instruction to have the computer process the next record and continue doing so until we run out of records.

THE PROGRAMMING PROCESS

In general, the systems analyst working on a particular project will provide program specifications to be used by the programmer. The specifications will include such things as a statement of the problem, a description of all inputs and outputs, and details of the processing that is to take place. The programmer can then write a program which will meet the specifications.

There are seven steps in the programming process:

1. *Understand the program specifications.* Before doing anything else, the programmer needs to become familiar with what the program is trying to accomplish and with the input and output files designed by the systems analyst.
2. *Plan the program logic.* Suppose you are going to drive from Chicago to New York on a trip. Most people would not just get into the car and start driving; they would plan an itinerary, figure out what to pack, phone ahead for reservations, etc. In much the same way, a programmer should not begin by coding. During the planning step, a programmer decides how best to meet the program specifications set forth by the analyst. The programmer usually divides the program into modules or subroutines and uses design techniques, such as flowcharts, pseudocode, and hierarchy charts, to help plan the solution.

   A *subroutine* or *module* is a set of instructions that will accomplish a specific function of the program, e.g., printing headings, doing totals, accessing a table, etc. The subroutine takes data from the main (calling) routine or program, executes the instructions of the subroutine, and sends the results back to the main program. The advantages of using subroutines include the following:

   a. A decrease in the cost and time of testing and modifying programs, because the programmer can test or change a subroutine without affecting the logic of the rest of the program.
   b. A programmer can write a standardized routine which can then be used in other programs. This reduces programming cost by eliminating the need to write duplicate code in every program.
   c. Several programmers are able to work on the same program simultaneously since each may be assigned a separate module to write.
3. *Code the program.* After the solution is planned, the next step is to code the solution in a programming language such as ASSEMBLER, COBOL, or FOR-

TRAN. Coding involves translating the solution into a language that the computer can understand. The coded program is called the *source program.*

4. *Get the program into machine readable form.* This is done by punching the program onto cards, entering it via a computer terminal, or using a key-to-tape or key-to-disk machine.
5. *Compile or assemble the program.* Computers cannot execute source programs. They work electronically and, therefore, must represent data and instructions in binary (on-off) form. Compilation or assembly involves the conversion of the source program to an *object* or machine language (binary) *program.* The conversion is done by a program called a *compiler* in the case of a high-level language such as COBOL or an *assembler* in the case of an assembly language program. The input to the compiler or the assembler is the source program. Outputs from the compiler or the assembler include the object program and a list of diagnostics (errors). The errors listed are *syntax* (or "language") *errors.* Examples of syntax errors include the use of a variable name that contains too many characters, writing GO TO STEP-10 when the programmer used the name STEP10 without a hyphen when labeling the instruction, and violating punctuation rules of a language. *Logic errors* are *not* listed during compilation. An example of a logic error is using an ADD instruction instead of a SUBTRACT instruction in a COBOL program. Even though both instructions are valid, very different results will be obtained during program execution. Logic errors can only be detected by testing the program.
6. *Test the program.* Once all the syntax (language) errors have been corrected, it is time to test the logic of the program. This involves using sample data as input, executing the program, and checking the results.
7. *Document the program.* Documentation is listed as the last step in the programming process, but documentation, i.e., providing a written commentary of steps 1 to 6, should be done as the steps are done. Some of the things to include in documentation are the specifications provided by the analyst, flowcharts and other planning aids, program listings, sample test data, and test results.

This book concentrates on the planning step. Program flowcharts, hierarchy charts, and pseudocode will be used to aid in the development of program logic.

ARITHMETIC AND LOGIC SYMBOLS

The following arithmetic and logic symbols will be used in this book:

Symbol	*Meaning*	*Example*
$=$	Equals	$A = B$ means A is equal to B.
$<$	Less than	$A < B$ means A is less than B.
$>$	Greater than	$A > B$ means A is greater than B.
$\leq$	Less than or equal to	$A \leq B$ means A is less than or equal to B.
$\geq$	Greater than or equal to	$A \geq B$ means A is greater than or equal to B.
$\neq$	Not equal	$A \neq B$ means A is not equal to B.

Symbol	*Meaning*	*Example*
:	Compare	$A : B$ means compare the value of A to the value of B.
+	Addition	$A + B$ means add A and B.
−	Subtraction	$A - B$ means subtract B from A.
*	Multiplication	$A * B$ means multiply A and B.
/	Division	A/B means divide A by B.
**	Exponentiation	$A ** B$ means A to the B power.

QUESTIONS AND EXERCISES FOR REVIEW

1. Define the following terms:
   a. Data processing
   b. Computer
   c. Hardware
   d. Primary storage
   e. Memory
   f. Secondary storage
   g. File
   h. Record
   i. Field
   j. Character
   k. Alphabetic field
   l. Numeric field
   m. Alphanumeric field
   n. Software
   o. Computer program
   p. Subroutine
   q. Source program
   r. Object program
   s. Compiler
   t. Documentation
2. What are the basic requirements of any data processing system?
3. What are the three parts of the CPU? Describe the function of each.
4. What are I/O devices?
5. Describe the relationship between files, records, fields, and characters. Give an example to illustrate.
6. What are the steps of the programming process? Describe each.
7. What is the difference between a logic error and a syntax error?
8. How does a source program become an object program?
9. How would you express each of the following using arithmetic and logic symbols?
   a. 5 is equal to C
   b. 7 is not equal to 12
   c. Add 3 and 6
   d. 4 is less than 11
   e. A is less than or equal to 15
   f. Subtract 11 from 23
   g. Raise 5 to the power of 2
   h. Divide 87 by 3
   i. Compare D to 6
   j. Multiply 4 and 15
   k. X is greater than or equal to 12
   l. 15 is greater than 3

CHAPTER 2

Introduction to Program Flowcharts

FLOWCHARTS (DEFINITION)

A program flowchart (logic diagram) is a tool used by a programmer to develop program logic. A program flowchart focuses on the sequence of data transformations from the input to the output. In other words, a program flowchart shows how the data on the input files become the output files and/or reports that you desire.

REASONS FOR FLOWCHARTING

1. Since a flowchart is a diagram or picture of a program's logic, drawing a flowchart gives the programmer a good visual reference of what his or her program will do.
2. Flowcharts serve as program documentation. They can be used to communicate among several programmers, between programmers and analysts, or between programmers and users. Since flowcharts are language-independent, a person doesn't need to know a programming language to understand and review the logic depicted in a flowchart.
3. Flowcharts allow a programmer to test alternative solutions to a problem without ever coding the program. Flowcharts provide a method for easy *desk checking*. That is, a programmer can use sample data as input and trace the data through the flowchart to see if the resulting output is what is expected. Although desk checking can be done in any step of the programming process, it is much easier to find and correct logic errors prior to program coding.

DRAWBACKS OF FLOWCHARTING

1. Constructing a flowchart is time-consuming. However, the time spent in constructing a good program flowchart is made up by a saving in coding and testing time.
2. A program flowchart shows *how* the input becomes the output, but it doesn't show *why* a particular step is done. It is quite useful, therefore, to include comments in your flowcharts.
3. Flowcharts are very subjective. One programmer's flowchart for a particular problem may not be the same as another programmer's flowchart for the same problem. Whenever possible in the examples in this book, rules have been given for the logic. In many cases, however, there are no rules to follow. In such cases examples serve as suggested ways to "attack" a particular problem. You may discover another method for solving a particular problem that is just as efficient and "logical."

FLOWCHART SYMBOLS

In constructing flowcharts, standard symbols are used. The American National Standards Institute (ANSI) symbols will be used throughout this book. These symbols and examples of their use are illustrated below.

I/O Symbol
Used for an instruction to either an input or an output device.

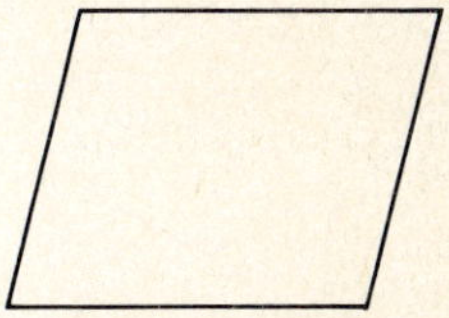

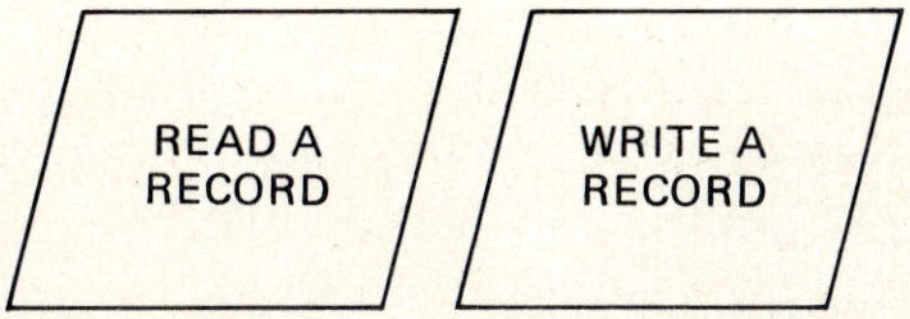

Process Symbol
Used to denote an operation involved in the actual processing of data. The process symbol is used for all arithmetic and data transfer (MOVE) operations.

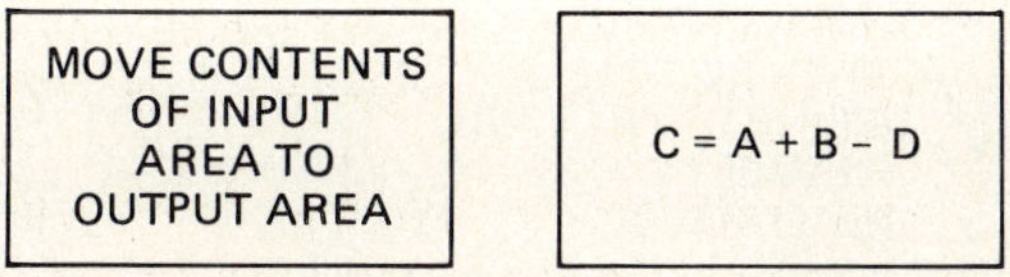

Flowline Symbol
Used to link symbols and to indicate the sequence of operations. The flowline symbol consists of a line (with or without an arrowhead) of any length. Normal flow is from top to bottom and left to right on the paper.

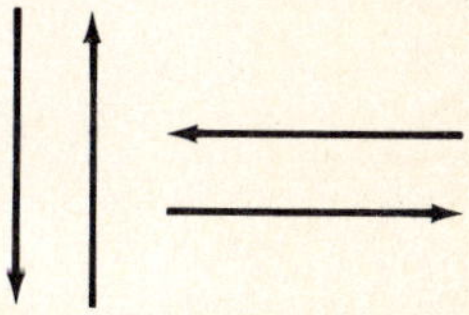

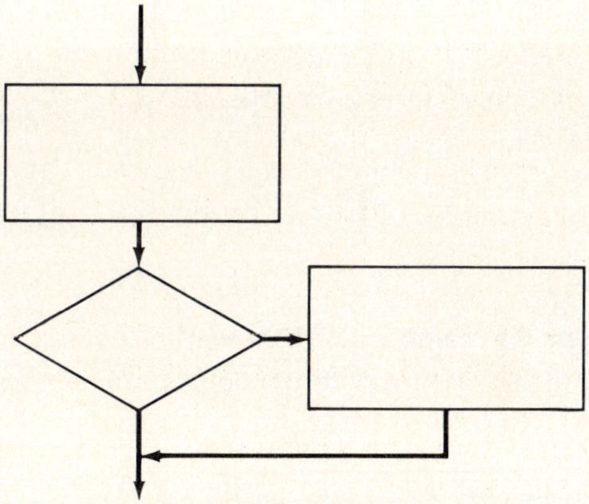

Terminal Symbol
Used to designate the beginning or end of a program or routine.

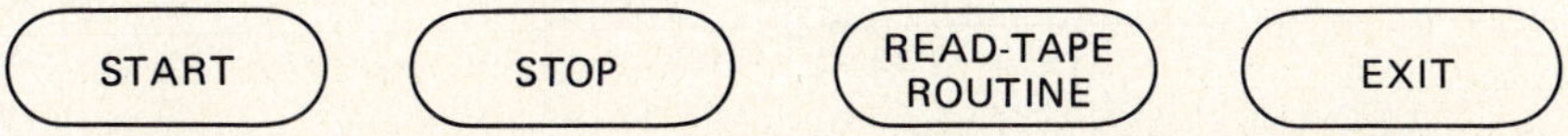

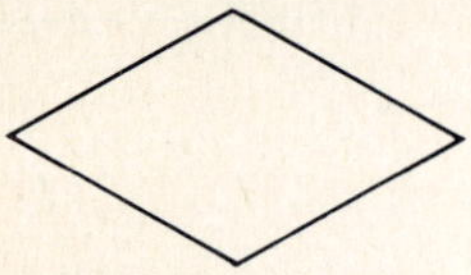

Decision Symbol
Used to designate that different logic paths will be followed based on a condition occurring within a program.

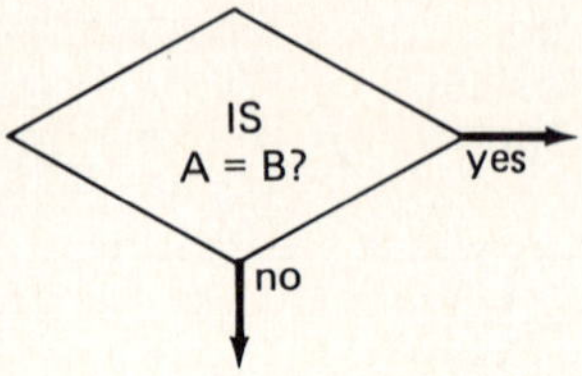

Preparation Symbol
Used to define data names and formats used in input, output, and work areas, and to assign initial values to work areas.

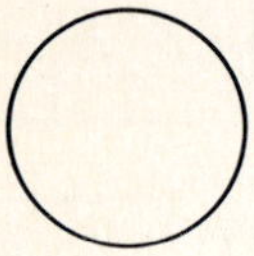

Connector Symbol
Used to connect parts of the flowchart when the use of flowlines would be confusing or otherwise undesirable.

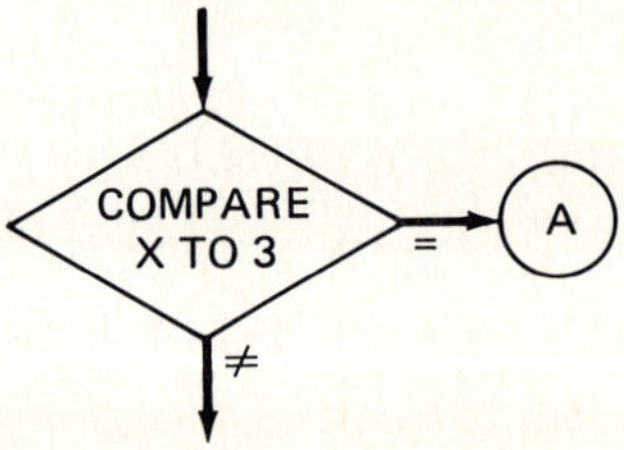

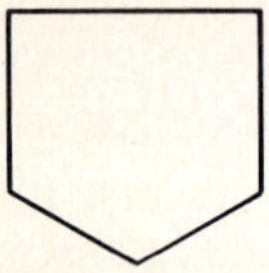

Off-Page Connector Symbol
Used to connect parts of the flowchart from one page to another.

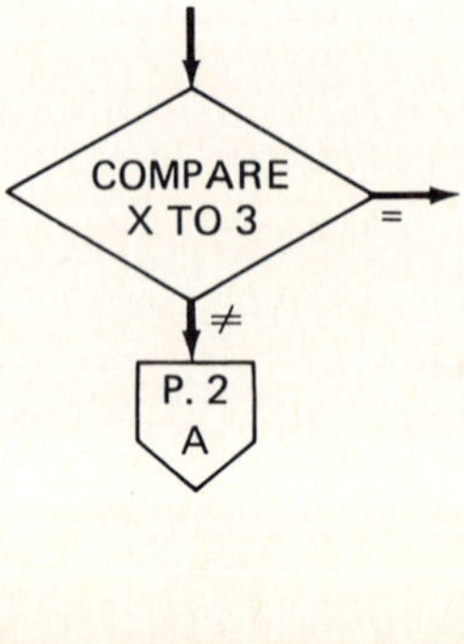

Annotation Symbol

Used to further describe or comment the flowchart.

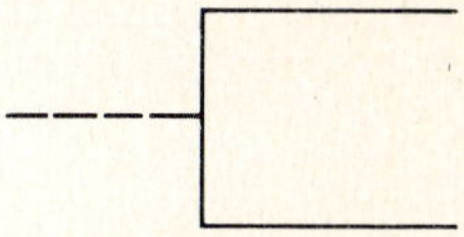

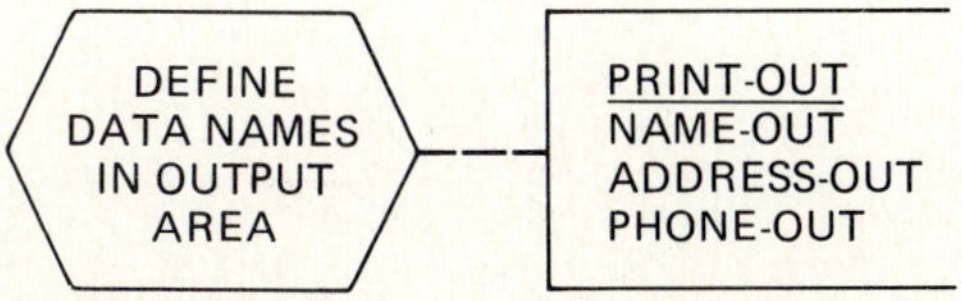

External Subroutine Symbol

Used to access ("perform" or "call") a subroutine that exists outside of the program.

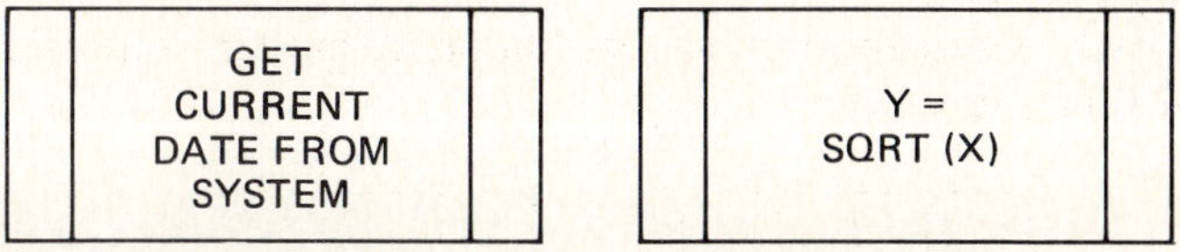

Internal Subroutine Symbol

Used to access ("perform" or "call") a subroutine that exists within the program.

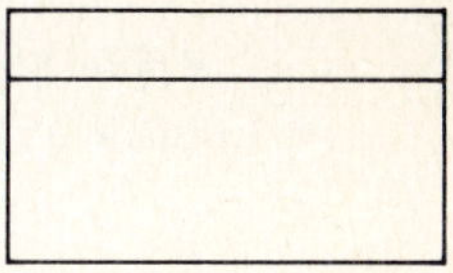

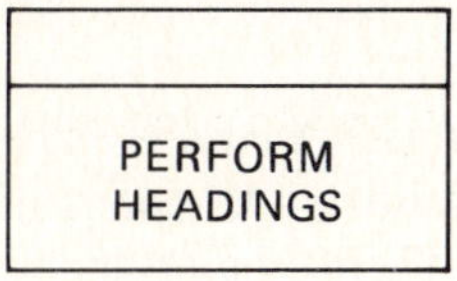

GUIDELINES FOR DRAWING FLOWCHARTS

Although there are few "hard and fast" rules for flowcharting, the following guidelines will help you construct flowcharts that are understandable and easy to read.

1. Flowcharts should be drawn from top to bottom and from left to right across the page whenever possible. In other words, draw the flowchart the way you like to read. Use arrowheads on flowlines whenever flow is not from top to bottom or from left to right.
2. Be neat! Use pencil rather than ink: it's easier to erase. Use a flowchart template to help you draw your symbols neatly. A *template* is a plastic or metal stencil sold by various manufacturers to allow you to trace symbols, much in the same way that a ruler helps you draw straight lines.
3. Avoid intersecting flowlines. Use connector symbols whenever necessary.

EXAMPLE 2-1: READ, MOVE, WRITE, INPUT AREAS, OUTPUT AREAS, AND WORK AREAS

Let's draw a flowchart to read the first record from a file, print its contents, and stop (see Figure 2-1 for the solution).

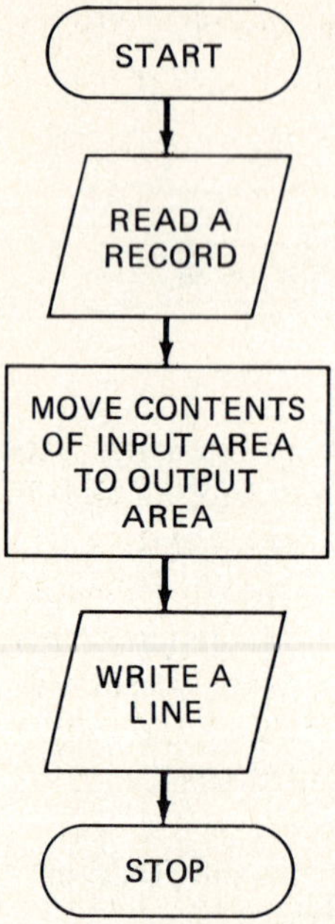

Figure 2-1
Example 2-1.

Suppose the file we want to read is a card file and the first record (card) contains the name MARY SMITH. Recall from Chapter 1 that in order to process a record, it must be in primary storage. Therefore, after beginning the program (START), the first thing that has to be done is to get the contents of the card into the memory of the computer.

To get the data into primary storage, the READ instruction is executed. READ A RECORD means take the contents of a record from secondary storage and put it in primary storage.

How does the computer know where in primary storage to put the record? When a program is executed, a certain segment of primary storage is allocated to the program for processing data. The program's area of primary storage used for processing can be thought of as being divided into three segments, called *input areas, output areas,* and *work areas.*

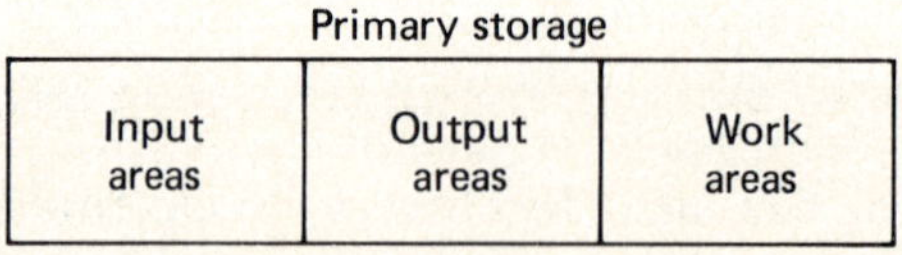

For each input file that is used in a program, one input area is assigned. For each output file (including reports) used, one output area is assigned. If, for example, a program uses three input files, one output file, and a report, it will be allocated three input areas and two output areas. For this example we will be assigned one input area and one output area. Work areas are areas that are used for neither input nor output. Examples of the use of work areas will be given later in this chapter.

When the READ instruction is executed, the contents of the record read, MARY SMITH, are put in the input area of primary storage. Whenever a record is read, it is put in the input area of primary storage assigned to its file.

Contents of Memory after READ

Input Area	Output Area	Work Area
MARY SMITH		

Before a record can be written, it must be stored in the output area assigned to its output file. To get the record from the input area to the output area, a MOVE instruction is used.* The instruction MOVE CONTENTS OF INPUT AREA TO OUTPUT AREA causes a copy of the record in the input area to be put in the output area. The record is not physically moved, however. The contents of the input area remain unchanged after the MOVE is executed. Only the contents of the output area are changed. After the MOVE instruction is executed, both the input and output areas contain the contents of the card input during the READ instruction.

Contents of Memory after MOVE

Input Area	Output Area	Work Area
MARY SMITH	MARY SMITH	

In general, the instruction MOVE AREA1 TO AREA2 does the following to the contents of storage:

Before MOVE	Contents of AREA1 = X	Contents of AREA2 = Y
After MOVE	Contents of AREA1 = X	Contents of AREA2 = X

In effect, after a MOVE instruction is executed, the contents of the sending area (AREA1) remain unchanged. The contents of the receiving area (AREA2) take on the value of the sending area.

To get the record out of the computer from primary storage, the instruction WRITE A LINE is executed. In this case, the name MARY SMITH will be printed. The STOP instruction will cause processing to terminate.

EXAMPLE 2-2: LOOPING AND CHECKING FOR END-OF-FILE (EOF)

Example 2-1 processed only one record from a file. In order to process multiple records from a file, we have to *loop* or repeat the instructions for each record input. Figure 2-2 shows the repetition of reading a record, moving the contents of the input area to the output area, and writing. There's only one error in this flowchart. Can you find it? If you found that there is no way to end the loop, you are correct. In this

*In some languages (e.g., FORTRAN and BASIC) the MOVE instruction is not necessary. In such languages, the WRITE instruction both moves the data to the output area and writes it.

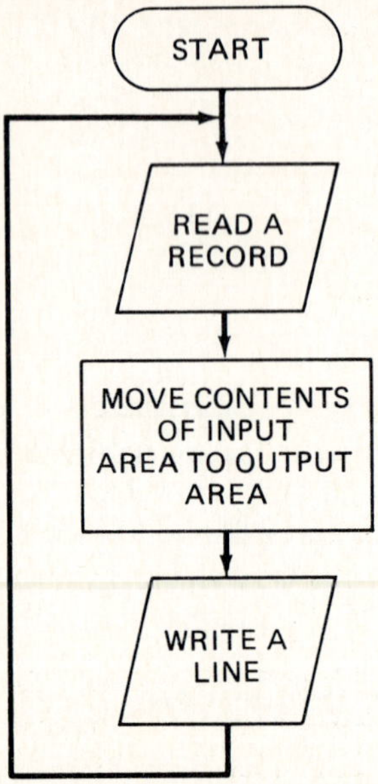

Figure 2-2
Example 2-2.

figure we have what's called an endless or an infinite loop. The main requirement when constructing a loop or using repetitive logic is that you must have a way to "get out of," or terminate, the loop. Figure 2-3 shows the corrected flowchart. In this chart, we exit the loop at *end of file (EOF).* That means we will process the entire file and then terminate. How does the computer recognize EOF, though? The computer recognizes an EOF condition by an end-of-file marker or record on the file. The end-of-file marker or record is a dummy record located at the end of the file. The EOF record does not contain data to be processed. Most programming languages provide the capability of testing for EOF as part of the READ instruction. In COBOL, the READ instruction looks like "READ RECORD AT END do something." In FORTRAN, the READ instruction may be READ(5,10,END = 99), where 5 refers to the device number, 10 refers to the format statement, and END = 99 refers to the instruction branched to at end of file.

Let's take some sample data and look at the flowchart shown in Figure 2-3.

Input File

MARY SMITH
JIM DOE
SALLY HARRIS
EOF

This file contains three data records and the end-of-file marker. We will assume that the input and output areas of storage are blank prior to starting the program.

Contents of Memory at Start of Program

Input Area	Output Area

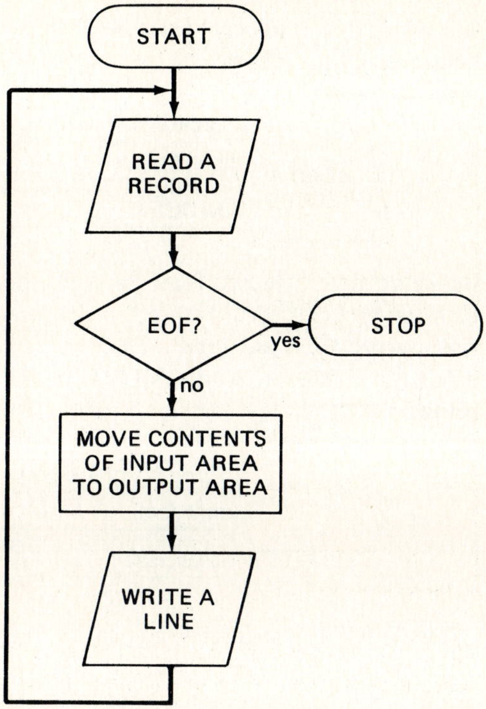

Figure 2-3
Corrected flowchart for Example 2-2.

When the READ is executed for the first time, the name MARY SMITH will be read into storage.

Contents of Memory after First READ

Input Area	Output Area
MARY SMITH	

The next instruction asks if it is EOF. The answer is "no," so the MOVE instruction is executed. After the MOVE instruction is executed, storage contains MARY SMITH in both the input and output areas.

Contents of Memory after First MOVE

Input Area	Output Area
MARY SMITH	MARY SMITH

The WRITE instruction is executed next. This will cause MARY SMITH to be printed from the output area.

Then we go back to the start of the loop to process the next record on the file. The instruction that will be executed is the READ which causes the second record on the file to be input. This record uses the same input area as the first record, because only one input area is allocated per file. The second record is placed right on top of the first record, thus erasing the first record from the input area. This is true in general.

Contents of Memory after Second READ	
Input Area	Output Area
JIM DOE	MARY SMITH

Before reading a record from an input file, you must be sure that you are finished with the previous record stored in the input area, because a READ erases the previous record from the input area.

It's not EOF yet, so the MOVE instruction is executed again, with the results being

Contents of Memory after Second MOVE	
Input Area	Output Area
JIM DOE	JIM DOE

The WRITE instruction then causes the name JIM DOE to be printed on the line after MARY SMITH. Each time a WRITE instruction is executed, a single line is printed on a report or a single record is written on a file. The records end up on the output file in the same order as they are written.

The remaining records on the input file are processed the same way as described above until the EOF marker is read. At that time, processing stops. Note that the EOF marker is not written on the output file.

Output Report

MARY SMITH
JIM DOE
SALLY HARRIS

EXAMPLES 2-3 AND 2-4: COUNTERS, WORK AREAS, AND CONNECTORS

Suppose that we don't want to print every record contained on the input file. In Example 2-3 let's assume that we want to print the contents of the first 10 records on the file and that there are more than 10 records on the file (see Figure 2-4).

Somehow we have to determine when 10 records have been processed. To do this, we need to tell the computer to count the records as they are processed. After processing 10 records, we'll have the computer STOP. Unfortunately, a computer doesn't know where to start counting unless the program tells it. The instruction COUNTER = 0 tells the computer to start at zero and puts the value zero into a field called COUNTER. (In general, writing "X = Y" is equivalent to the instruc-

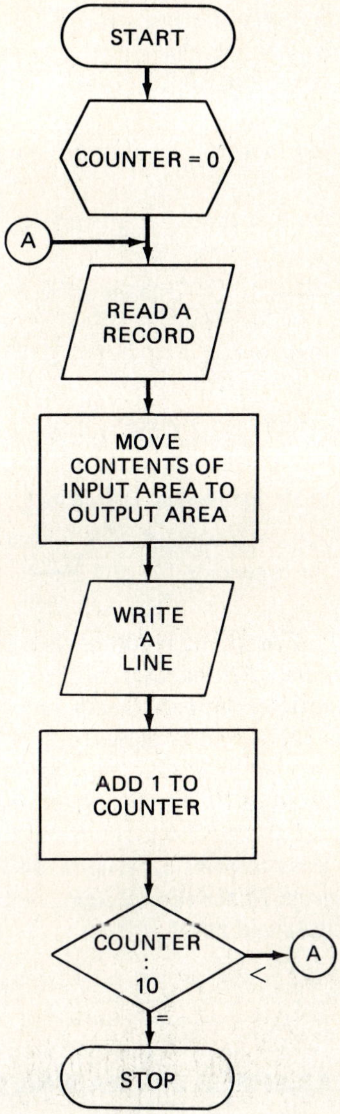

Figure 2-4
Example 2-3.

tion MOVE Y TO X.) What is COUNTER, though? COUNTER is a work area in primary storage that enables the computer to count the records that are processed. COUNTER is neither part of the input nor part of the output, so it is defined as a work area.

After initializing COUNTER to zero, the first record is read into the input area. The contents of the input area are then moved to the output area, and a line is written. We are now finished processing the first record.

The next instruction tells the computer to ADD 1 to COUNTER. So, after the first record is processed, COUNTER is equal to 1. Then we tell the computer to see if 10 records have been processed. COUNTER : 10 means "compare the contents of counter to 10." If COUNTER is equal to 10, the program stops. If COUNTER is less than 10, the program goes to (A) to read another record. Note that this is the first time that a connector symbol has been used in place of a flowline. → (A) means to look for a matching connector (A) that enters the flow of logic. In this case (A) → can be found prior to the instruction READ A RECORD. If we want to use a connector to branch (go to) another page of the flowchart, the off-page connector should be used. → P. 2 X means to look for connector (X) → on page 2 of the flowchart.

The second record is then processed, 1 is added to COUNTER (COUNTER now equals 2), and COUNTER is tested to see if it is equal to 10. The program continues to loop until the tenth record is processed. Prior to processing the tenth record, COUNTER is equal to 9. After processing the tenth record, COUNTER is incremented by 1, making it equal to 10. When COUNTER is next tested, because it is equal to 10, processing terminates.

Example 2-4 is similar to Example 2-3 in that a counter is required. This time we want to print all records on the file except for the fifth record. See Figure 2-5 on page 20 for the solution. Notice that the fifth record is never moved to the output area and never written.

EXAMPLE 2-5: NAMING FIELDS IN STORAGE

Suppose we have a file that consists of one record for each supplier of a company. Each record contains a supplier name and address. We want to produce a list of suppliers for the president of the company. Each line of the report is to show only the name. That is, we don't want to include addresses on the output. The solution is illustrated in Figure 2-6.

If this problem were handled like previous problems, we would proceed as shown at the top of the next page.

By moving contents of the input area to the output area, both the name and address will be printed when the write instruction is executed. We want to write only the name field, so we want to move only the name field to the output area. Somehow, then, we have to distinguish between the name and the address in the input area.

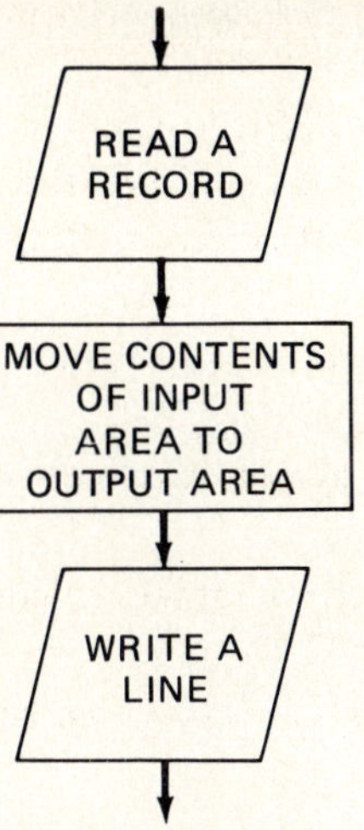

This can be done by assigning unique field names to areas in storage. We can specify that the input area contains two fields, defined as follows:

Input Area	
SUPPLIER-NAME-IN	ADDRESS-IN

When a record is read, the name is put in SUPPLIER-NAME-IN, and the address is put in ADDRESS-IN. Then instead of moving the entire input area to the output area, we will MOVE SUPPLIER-NAME-IN TO OUTPUT AREA. When the output record is written, only the name is printed.

EXAMPLE 2-6: CLEARING OUTPUT AREAS

For this example we are told to produce a phone directory listing.

Output

A list with the following format:

Line Position	*Description*	*Field Name*
1–20	Name	NAME-OUT
21–24	Blanks	
25–44	Address	ADDRESS-OUT
45–48	Blanks	
49–56	Phone number	PHONE-OUT

Printer Spacing Chart

The printer spacing chart (page 21) graphically displays the output format. Printer spacing charts are used by analysts when they design printed output and terminal displays. The columns and rows on the chart are numbered to show the spacing on

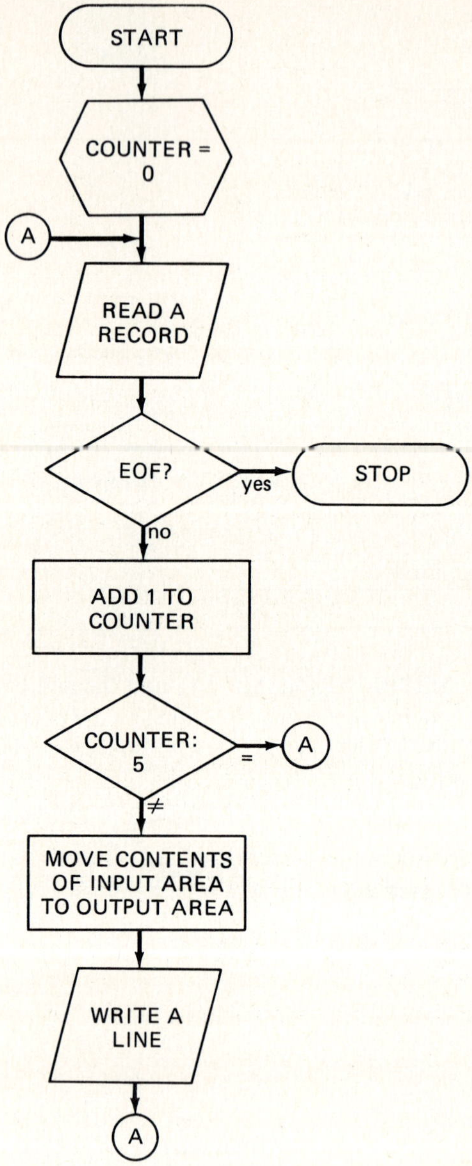

Figure 2-5
Example 2-4.

the page or display. The number of columns and rows used by the analyst depends on the paper, special form, or screen format being designed.

The following conventions will be followed on printer spacing charts in this book:

1. X's will be used to show alphanumeric and alphabetic fields.
2. 9's will be used to show numeric fields.
3. Z's in a numeric field will be used for zero suppression.
4. All literals or constants, such as heading lines, dollar signs, decimal points, etc., will be shown exactly as they are to appear on the report.

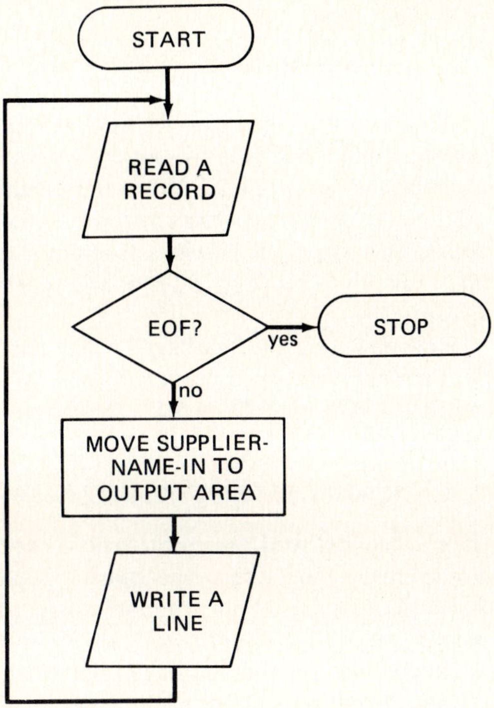

Figure 2-6
Example 2-5.

5. Items enclosed in parentheses are not to be printed. They are included for explanation only.

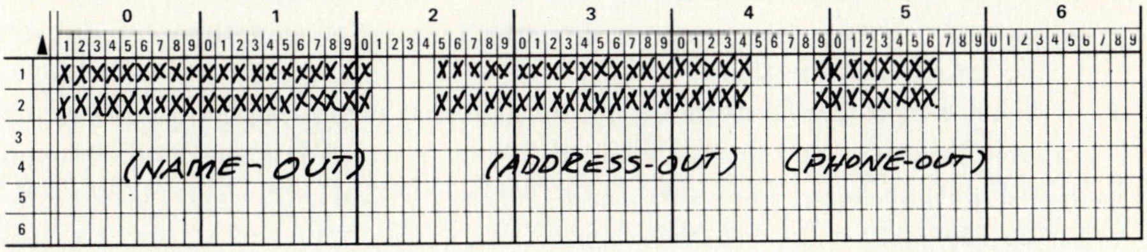

Sample Output

ANTHONY K. ALBERTSON 1821 DEE RD. 286-9865

Input

Input consists of records with the following format:

Record Position	*Description*	*Field Name*
1–20	Name	NAME-IN
21–40	Address	ADDRESS-IN
41–48	Phone number	PHONE-IN

Sample Input

ANTHONY K. ALBERTSON1821 DEE RD.   286-9865

Notice on the input that the fields are placed one right next to the other with no space between them. On the output, we want to put blanks between the fields so that the report is easier to read. When the program starts, the programmer does not know what is in the input, output, and work areas. Storage contains whatever "garbage" was left over from the previous program. You cannot realistically assume, as we have thus far, that primary storage will consist of blanks when a program begins execution.

How do we get the "garbage" out of the input area? Suppose that the first record of the input file is the record used as sample input above (ANTHONY K. ALBERTSON1821 DEE RD. 286-9865). Suppose that the contents of the input area are

CICICVGFDBSJHGUJ:LIJDEM%K)KDL%CDNHIGHIJKLM1UHXC1

prior to the first read. When the read is executed, the record read overlays the values stored in the input area, thus erasing whatever "garbage" was in the input area. After the first READ instruction is executed, the input area contains the sample record read, and the "garbage" that was previously in the input area is gone.

How do we get the "garbage" out of the output area? In past examples we've simply moved the contents of the input area to the output area. If we did that in this example, our output area would be an exact duplicate of the input area. That would get rid of the "garbage," but we don't want to print an exact duplicate of the input area. We want spaces between the fields in the output area. To get these spaces we need to do two things:

1. *Clear the output area.** Clearing the output area moves blanks to the entire output area. The blanks remain in the output area until something else is moved to the area to overlay them.
2. *Assign names* to the fields in the output area just as we assigned names to input fields in the previous example. This allows us to move data to specific locations of the output area. The instruction MOVE NAME-IN TO NAME-OUT means move the name stored in NAME-IN in the input area to the field called NAME-OUT in the output area. The remaining fields in the input and output areas are unaffected by this MOVE instruction.

Look how the contents of storage changes below while the sample input record is processed as in Figure 2-7.

Output Area after CLEAR

Field Names	NAME-OUT	ADDRESS-OUT	PHONE-OUT
Contents			

*Some languages automatically clear the output area prior to each WRITE instruction.

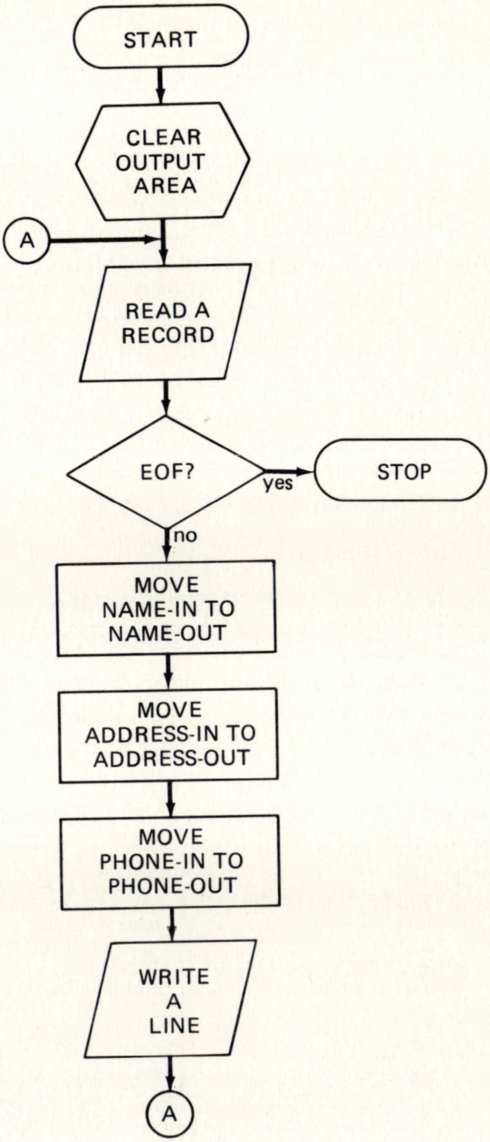

Figure 2-7
Example 2-6.

Input Area after READ

Field Names	NAME-IN	ADDRESS-IN	PHONE-IN
Contents	ANTHONY K. ALBERTSON	1821 DEE RD.	286-9865

Output Area after MOVE NAME-IN TO NAME-OUT

Field Names	NAME-OUT	ADDRESS-OUT	PHONE-OUT
Contents	ANTHONY K. ALBERTSON		

Output Area after MOVE ADDRESS-IN TO ADDRESS-OUT

Field Names	NAME-OUT	ADDRESS-OUT	PHONE-OUT
Contents	ANTHONY K. ALBERTSON	1821 DEE RD.	

Output Area after MOVE PHONE-IN TO PHONE-OUT

Field Names	NAME-OUT	ADDRESS-OUT	PHONE-OUT
Contents	ANTHONY K. ALBERTSON	1821 DEE RD.	286-9865

Note that the blanks moved to the output area between the name and address and between the address and phone number during the CLEAR are unaffected by the MOVEs. Since no data are moved to the areas between fields, we do not have to clear them again during processing, so the loop begins with the READ instruction rather than the CLEAR instruction.

EXAMPLE 2-7: IMPLIED DECIMAL POINTS, ARITHMETIC CALCULATIONS, AND EDITED OUTPUT AREAS

For this example we are told to draw a flowchart to produce a payroll report.

Output

The output is to be a report of gross pay. For each employee, the following fields are to be printed on a single line: social security number (NO-OUT), employee name (NAME-OUT), rate of pay (RATE-OUT), hours worked (HOURS-OUT), regular pay (REG-PAY-OUT), overtime pay (OVERTIME-PAY-OUT), and total gross pay (TOTAL-GROSS-OUT).

Printer Spacing Chart

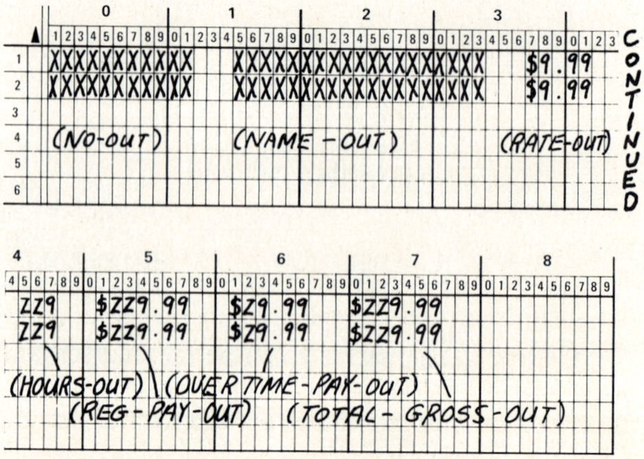

Sample Output

489-45-9890	JIM SMITH	$2.00	10	$20.00	$ 0.00	$20.00
498-34-9147	MARY JONES	$1.50	20	$30.00	$ 0.00	$30.00
102-93-6541	MARILYN DOE	$1.00	50	$40.00	$20.00	$60.00

Input

Input consists of records with the following format:

Record Position	*Description*	*Field Name*
1–11	Social security number	NO-IN
12–30	Employee name	NAME-IN
31–33	Hours worked	HOURS-IN
34–36	Rate of pay (implied decimal point between columns 34 and 35)	RATE-IN

Sample Input

```
489-45-9890 JIM SMITH        010200
498-34-9147 MARY JONES       020150
102-93-6541 MARILYN DOE      050100
```

Calculations

Regular pay = hours less than or equal to 40 * rate of pay
Overtime pay = hours greater than 40 * 2 * rate of pay
(i.e., a person earns "double-time" for all hours in excess of 40).
Total gross pay = regular pay + overtime pay

In the input description RATE-IN contains an implied decimal point. An *implied decimal point* is a space saver in a field. During processing, the computer will treat the field as if the decimal point were present even though it isn't. Implied decimal points do not affect your flowchart, but they will affect your coding. For example, in FORTRAN your FORMAT statements would have to reflect the implied decimal points, and in COBOL the PICTURE clauses in the data division would have to show the implied decimal points.

In the flowchart for this example (see Figure 2-8), first the output area is cleared. Then the loop to be processed for every record input is entered. After a record is read and checked for EOF, the social security number (NO-IN), name (NAME-IN), rate of pay (RATE-IN), and hours worked (HOURS-IN) are moved to the output area.

Before we go any further, look at the sample input and output given for this example. The input shows implied decimal points, while the output includes both decimal points and dollar signs. Users of computer reports like to have their output edited. Some things you might want to include when editing numeric output include inserting dollar signs, commas, and/or decimal points, and suppressing leading zeros in a field by replacing them with blanks. COBOL provides an easy edit capability by allowing the programmer to specify edit characters in the PICTURE clauses of output areas in the data division. When a field is moved from any area of storage to an

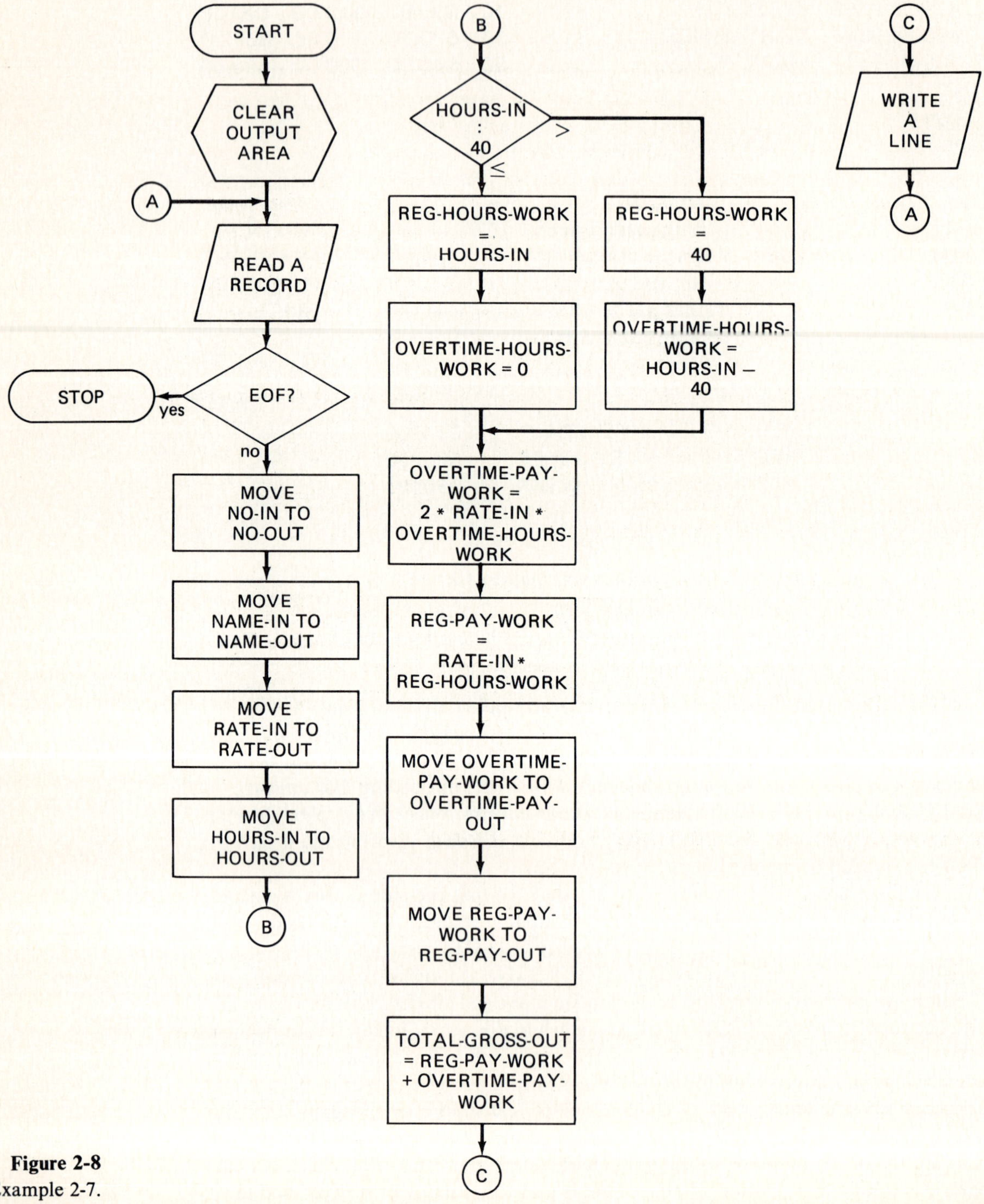

Figure 2-8
Example 2-7.

edited output area, the edit characters are automatically inserted. The process of editing does not affect your logic. However, once a field is moved to an edited output area, the output area is no longer numeric and can't be used for calculations. (Recall from Chapter 1 that numeric fields can't contain dollar signs, blanks, commas, etc., and only numeric fields can be used for calculations.) You must be careful, therefore, not to use edited output areas in calculations—use work areas instead. BASIC and FORTRAN allow for output editing by using formatted output.

Back to the flowchart. Social security number, name, hours, and rate of pay are taken from the input record. Where do regular pay, overtime pay, and total gross pay come from? Since they are not input, they must be calculated by the program. HOURS-IN is compared to 40. Based on the result of the comparison, we compute REG-HOURS-WORK and OVERTIME-HOURS-WORK. Then, for all records input, we compute OVERTIME-PAY-WORK and REG-PAY-WORK. OVERTIME-PAY-WORK and REG-PAY-WORK are then moved to output areas to allow them to be printed. Then TOTAL-GROSS-OUT is computed. The instruction TOTAL-GROSS-OUT = REG-PAY-WORK + OVERTIME-PAY-WORK means add REG-PAY-WORK and OVERTIME-PAY-WORK and move the result to TOTAL-GROSS-OUT. Notice that input and work areas rather than output areas are used in the calculation. A field called TOTAL-GROSS-WORK is not needed, however, because it is never used as part of a calculation; the result of a calculation is moved to TOTAL-GROSS-OUT. The last thing done in the loop is writing a line. Processing then returns to the beginning of the loop for the next record.

One last comment: the order in which fields are moved to the output area does not matter. The calculations could have just as easily been done first and then the input moved to the output area. The only thing that matters is that all fields must be in the output area before the WRITE instruction is executed. You can compare this to getting dressed in the morning. Whether you put your shirt or your pants on first doesn't matter. What does matter is that you are completely dressed before leaving the house.

EXAMPLE 2-8: BRANCHING AND SUBROUTINES

As you have seen in the examples so far, the flow of your program goes from one instruction to the next, top to bottom and left to right on the page unless something changes it. There are two ways to change the flow of logic in your program.

The first way to change the flow of logic is to *branch*. There are two types of branches: *unconditional branches* and *conditional branches*. An unconditional branch is a branch that occurs no matter what. An example of an unconditional branch is when a Monopoly* player picks the card that says "Go directly to jail. . . ." In Figure 2-8 an example of an unconditional branch is the branch to 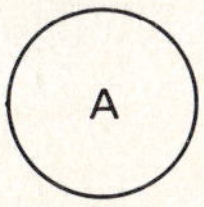

following

*Monopoly is a trademark of Parker Brothers.

WRITE A LINE. A conditional branch is a branch that occurs because a certain condition is present. In Figure 2-8, the branch to STOP if it is EOF is an example of a conditional branch.

The second way to change the flow of logic is to PERFORM (or CALL) a *subroutine*. In the illustration below, the instruction PERFORM RTN-A tells the computer to go to the subroutine named RTN-A. Upon completion of the routine, the computer goes to the instruction immediately following the PERFORM instruction.

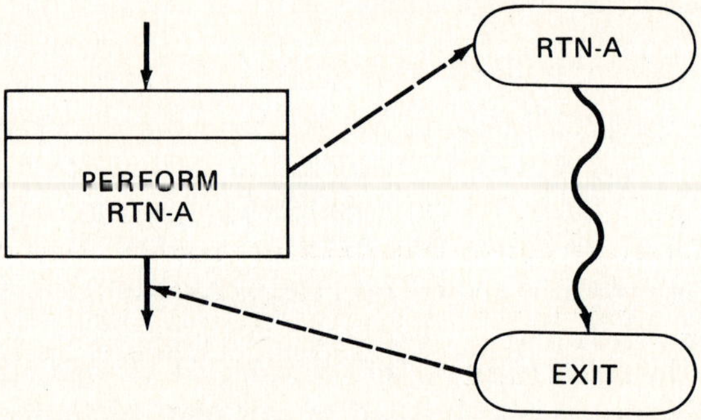

All subroutines in a flowchart start with a terminal symbol containing the name of the routine and end with a terminal symbol containing the word EXIT. Subroutines can be "nested" as shown below. Note the flow of logic as illustrated by the dotted line. The numbers in circles refer to the order in which the branches occur in the logic.

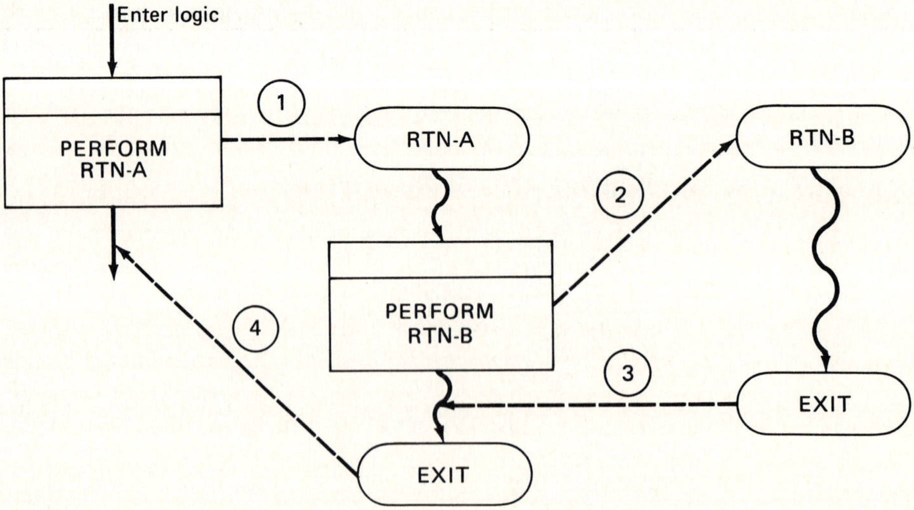

The difference between a subroutine and a branch is that after a subroutine is executed, the flow of logic returns to the calling routine at the point in the logic immediately following the PERFORM or CALL instruction. Branches are "forever," so to speak. You don't return to the instruction that caused the branch unless another branch instruction is executed to return you there.

Example 2-8 (see Figure 2-9) solves the same problem as Example 2-7. However, Example 2-8 uses a subroutine to do calculations. Note the flow of logic to the subroutine and back to the calling routine as shown by the dotted lines. (The dotted lines are not normally shown in the flowchart. In this example, they are used for illustration only.)

Subroutines can be "internal" or "external." An *internal subroutine* is a subrou-

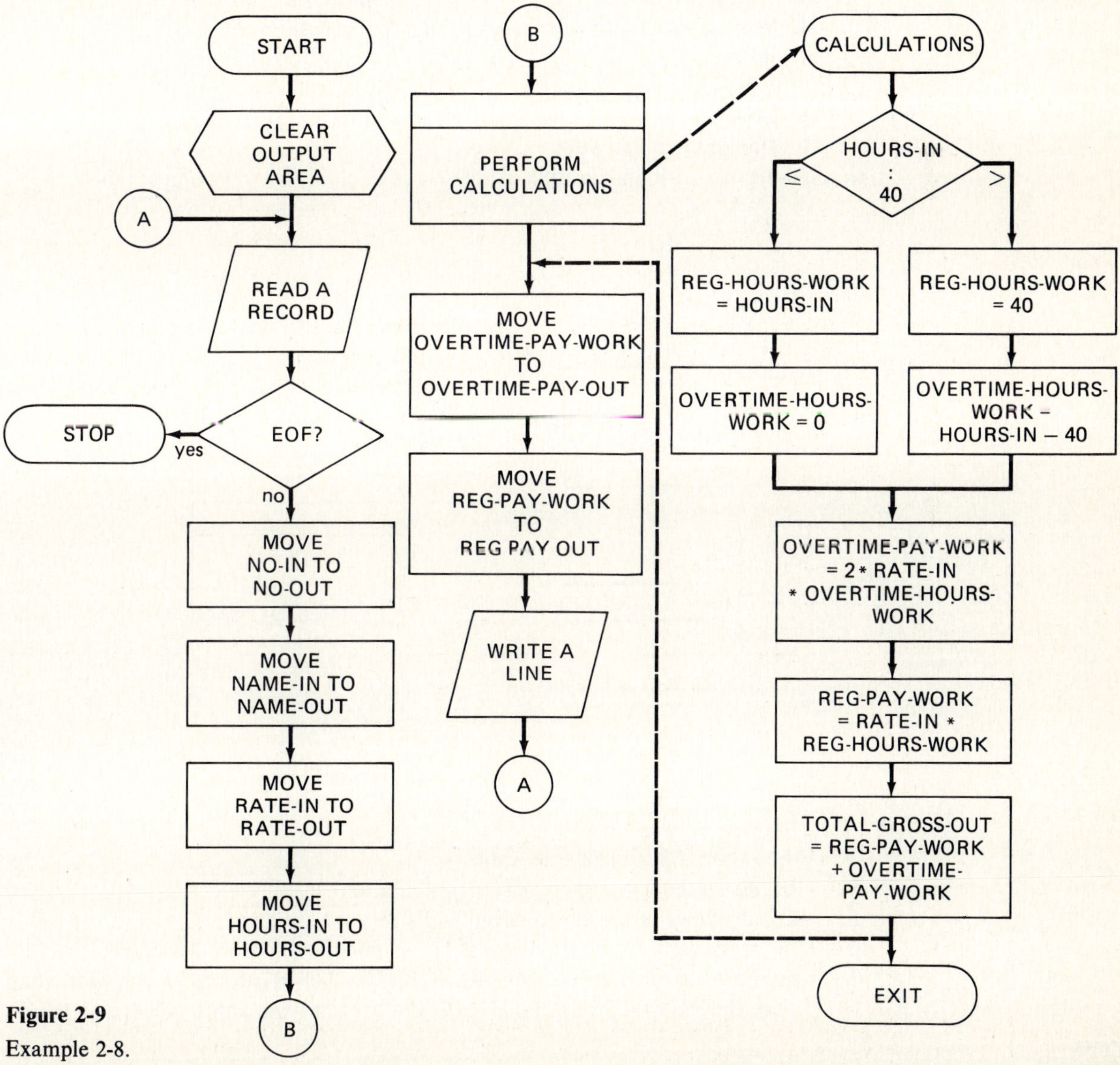

Figure 2-9
Example 2-8.

tine that is contained within your program. An *external subroutine* is contained outside of your program. Examples of external subroutines will be given in a later chapter.

QUESTIONS AND EXERCISES FOR REVIEW

1. Define the following terms:
   a. Flowchart
   b. Input area
   c. Output area
   d. Work area
   e. READ
   f. WRITE
   g. Loop
   h. Implied decimal point
   i. Conditional branch
   j. Unconditional branch
   k. Subroutine
   l. Internal subroutine
   m. External subroutine
   n. Desk checking
   o. Printer spacing chart
2. Define and give an example of the use of each of the following symbols:
   a. 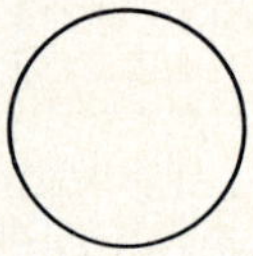
   b. 
   c. 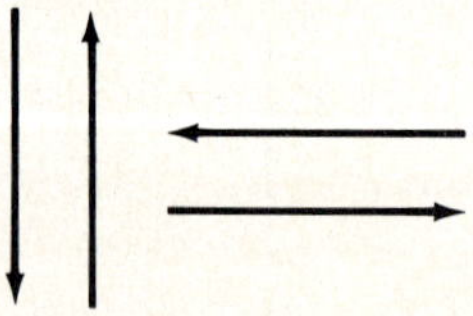
   d. 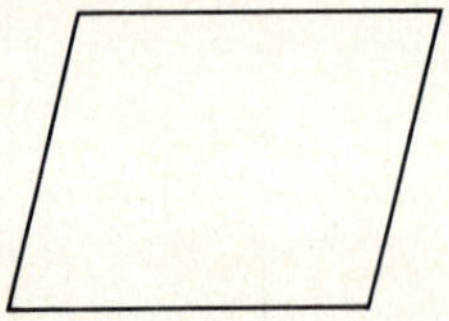
   e. 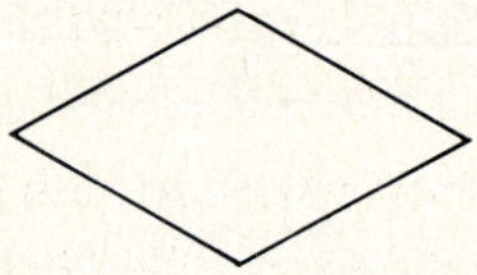
   f. 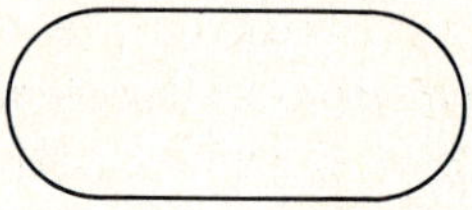
   g. 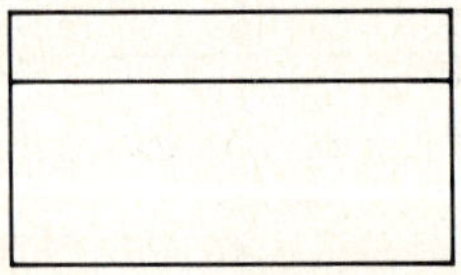
   h. 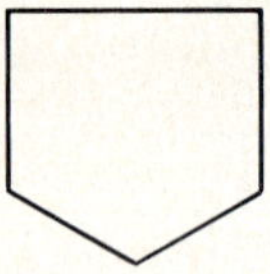
3. When should flowcharts be drawn?
4. How does a flowchart serve as documentation?
5. Why are flowcharts said to be subjective?
6. How many input and output areas is a particular program assigned?
7. Consider the instruction MOVE REC-IN TO REC-OUT. Suppose that before the MOVE instruction, REC-IN contains the value XYZ and REC-

OUT contains ABC. What are the contents of REC-IN and REC-OUT after the MOVE?

8. What causes an infinite loop?
9. Why do we assign names to fields in the input and output areas?
10. What does the instruction CLEAR OUTPUT AREA do?
11. What is the difference between a and b below?

a.

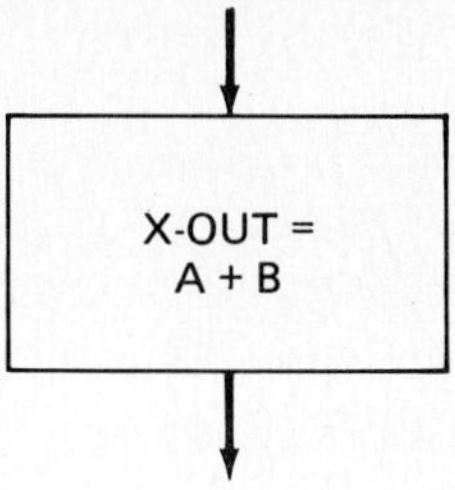

b.

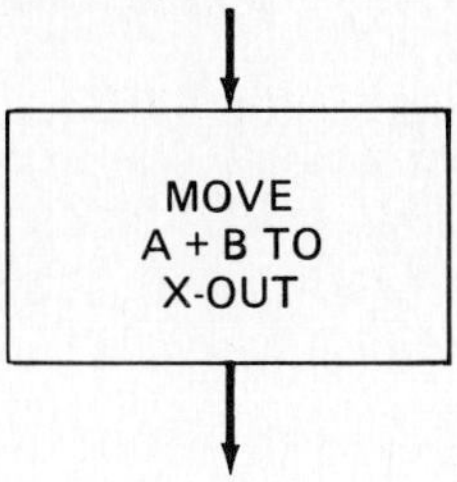

12. Why do we have to be careful when stating the following instruction?

X-OUT = FIELD-1-OUT + FIELD-2-OUT
(Assume that all fields are output areas.)

13. What is the difference between a branch and a subroutine?
14. Draw a flowchart to input records from a file, count the number of records input (COUNTER), and print the value of COUNTER at end of file.
15. Draw a flowchart to print only the third record from an input file.
16. Draw a flowchart to read student records each containing a name and a grade. As output, print the names only for those students who have a grade of A.
17. Draw a flowchart to compute sales commissions.

Output

Output consists of a report showing each salesperson's name, number, amount of sales, and commission amount.

Printer Spacing Chart

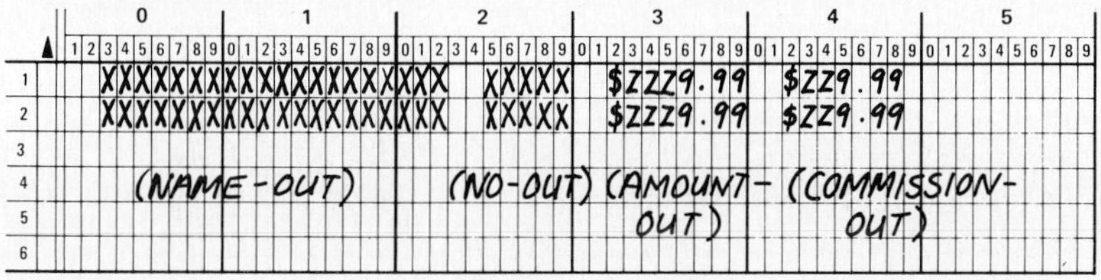

Input

Input consists of sales records containing a salesperson name, salesperson number, and amount of sale.

Record Position	*Description*	*Field Name*
1–20	Salesperson name	NAME-IN
21–25	Salesperson number	NO-IN
26–32	Amount of sale	AMOUNT-IN

Calculations

Commission amount is 1 percent of sales if sales are less than $50.00. Otherwise, commission is 2 percent of sales.

CHAPTER 3

Structured Techniques

BACKGROUND

The flowcharts in Chapter 2 are *straight-line,* or sequential (unstructured), flowcharts. This means that the logic goes from START to STOP with few, if any, subroutines. Straight-line flowcharts work fine for short programs, but if you have a long flowchart with many branches, the logic gets rather difficult to follow. In many cases, a large straight-line flowchart is so difficult to follow, it complicates rather than simplifies the logic.

A study was conducted in the mid-1960s to review concerns about complicated logic and programmer productivity. The study showed that a COBOL programmer produced an average of 10 lines of debugged code per day. That means that if a program contained 500 instructions, it would take a programmer 50 days to go through the programming process. As a result of the study, computer programmers and other professionals started to look more seriously at programming efficiency. The result of their effort is structured programming.

REASONS FOR STRUCTURING

The following are some of the advantages of using structured techniques in programming:

1. Without a standardized method for attacking a problem, a programmer may spend far more time than necessary in determining an appropriate solution and developing the program. Structured programming provides such a method.
2. Most straight-line programs contain numerous branches that continually alter the sequence of processing. This makes it difficult for anyone other than the original programmer to modify a program. (Sometimes it's even difficult for the original programmer!) Therefore, the costs and difficulties associated with program maintenance are increased. In structured programming, unconditional branches (GO TO statements) are not allowed. This encourages programmers to write *modular programs* (programs divided into functional parts by the use of subroutines), which are easier to modify than straight-line programs. Structured programming, in effect, is "GO-TO-less."
3. Because structured programs are more modular than straight-line programs, they are easier to test and debug. Modules or subroutines can be tested individually and errors found more easily.
4. It is easy to break up structured programs and assign various modules to more than one programmer to speed up the programming process.
5. In systems that use a virtual storage system, only certain segments of the program being executed are kept in main storage at any given time. This reduces the storage required to execute a program. The parts of the program not in main storage are contained in secondary storage until they are needed. Segments are then "swapped" or traded between main storage and secondary storage as needed throughout the execution of the program. In programs with many branches, the continual swapping of segments can create great inefficiencies. This is called *thrashing.* Structured programs help to minimize thrashing.

DISADVANTAGE OF STRUCTURED PROGRAMMING

Because structured programs use a lot of subroutines, they do not necessarily execute as quickly as nonstructured programs. However, since computer time has been getting cheaper and labor (programming) costs have been increasing in recent years, the extra computer cost is more than compensated for by the drastic reduction in programming costs.

RULES FOR STRUCTURING

The following rules should be adhered to when constructing a structured flowchart:

1. Only three basic structures may be used. They are the *sequence, decision* (selection), and *looping* (iteration) structures.
2. Connector symbols may not be used to allow a loop. Connectors are only allowed to continue processing from one column or page of a flowchart to another when you run out of room.
3. There may be only one entrance into and one exit out of a structure.

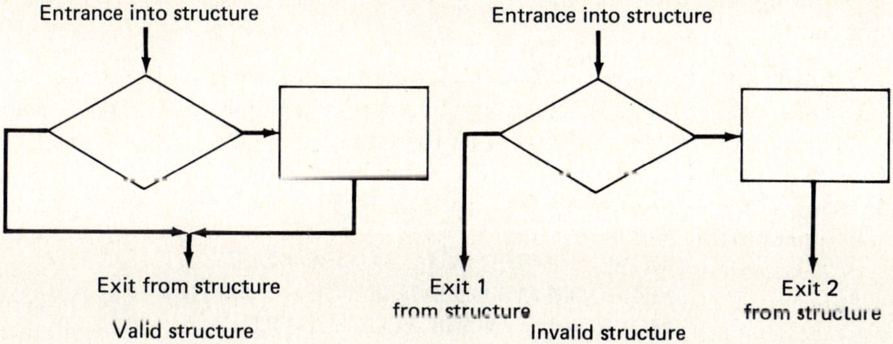

Valid structure

Invalid structure

4. Structures may be nested (i.e., one structure may be within another).
5. No GO TO statements are allowed. As noted earlier, there is another programming technique, known as *modular programming,* which is used by many organizations. In modular programming, GO TO instructions are allowed within subroutines, but a branch may not be used to get from one subroutine to another. This means that subroutines may only be entered at the start of the routine and exited at the end of the routine.
6. There can be only one STOP in a program. The STOP must be in the main routine.

SEQUENCE STRUCTURE

The sequence structure can contain any symbol except a decision symbol. In a sequence structure, the steps are executed in sequence with no instruction changing the order. For example:

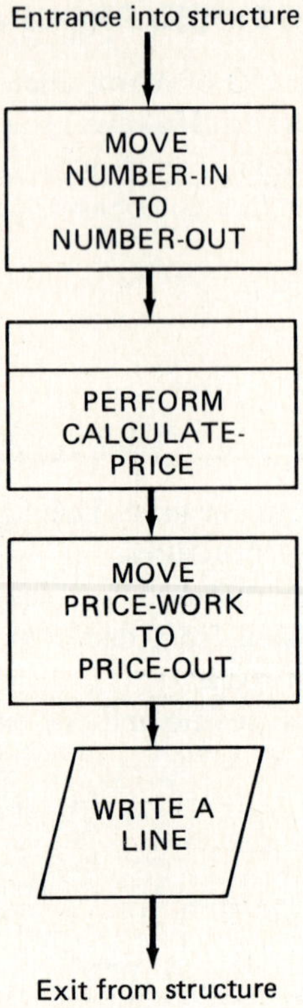

In COBOL, this would be coded as:

```
MOVE NUMBER-IN TO NUMBER-OUT.
PERFORM CALCULATE-PRICE.
MOVE PRICE-WORK TO PRICE-OUT.
WRITE LINE-OUT.
```

DECISION STRUCTURE

There are two types of decision or selection structures. The first is the *IF-THEN-ELSE structure.* It is used to show the selection of one of two logic paths based on a condition. Here are three examples:

(1)

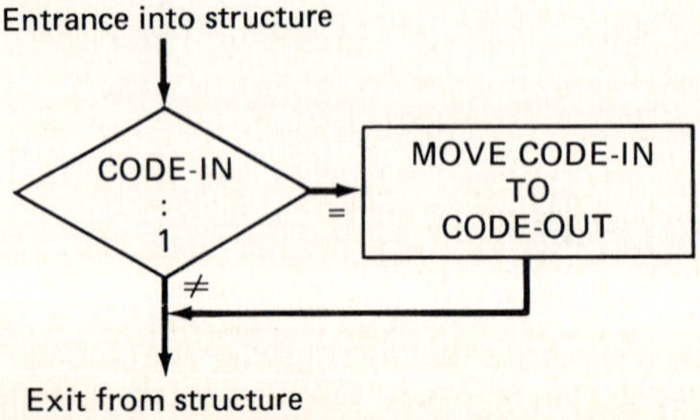

In COBOL, this would be coded as:

IF CODE-IN IS EQUAL TO 1 MOVE CODE-IN TO CODE-OUT.

(2)

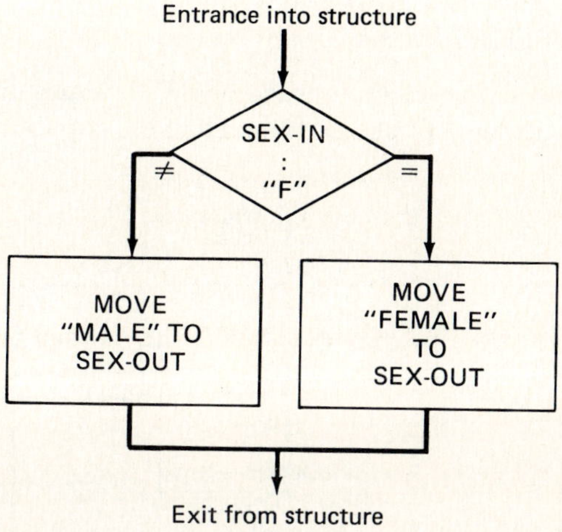

In COBOL, this would be coded as:

IF SEX-IN IS EQUAL TO "F" MOVE "FEMALE" TO SEX-OUT
ELSE MOVE "MALE" TO SEX-OUT.

(3)

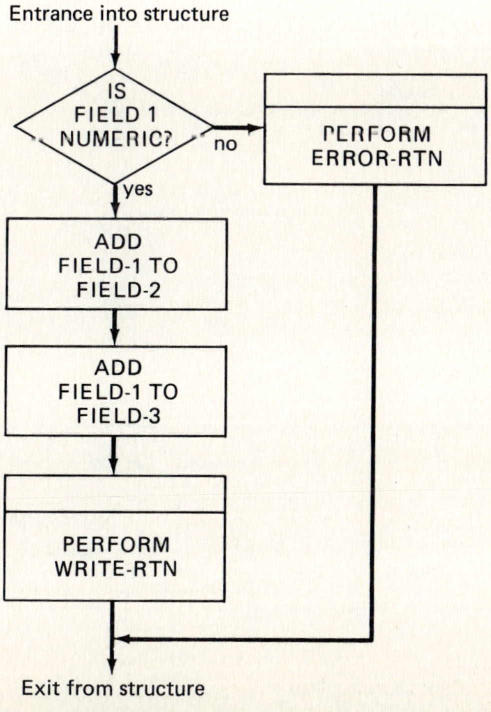

In COBOL, this would be coded as:

```
IF FIELD-1 IS NUMERIC ADD FIELD-1 TO FIELD-2
          ADD FIELD-1 TO FIELD-3
          PERFORM WRITE-RTN
ELSE PERFORM ERROR-RTN.
```

The second type of decision structure is the *CASE structure.* It is used when there are more than two logic paths to choose from. Here are two examples:

(1)

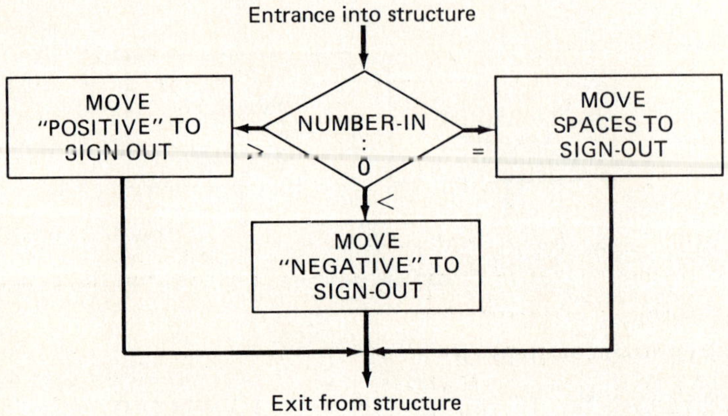

In COBOL, this would be coded as:

```
IF NUMBER-IN IS EQUAL TO ZERO MOVE SPACES TO SIGN-OUT
ELSE IF NUMBER-IN IS LESS THAN ZERO MOVE "NEGATIVE"
               TO SIGN-OUT
     ELSE MOVE "POSITIVE" TO SIGN-OUT.
```

(2)

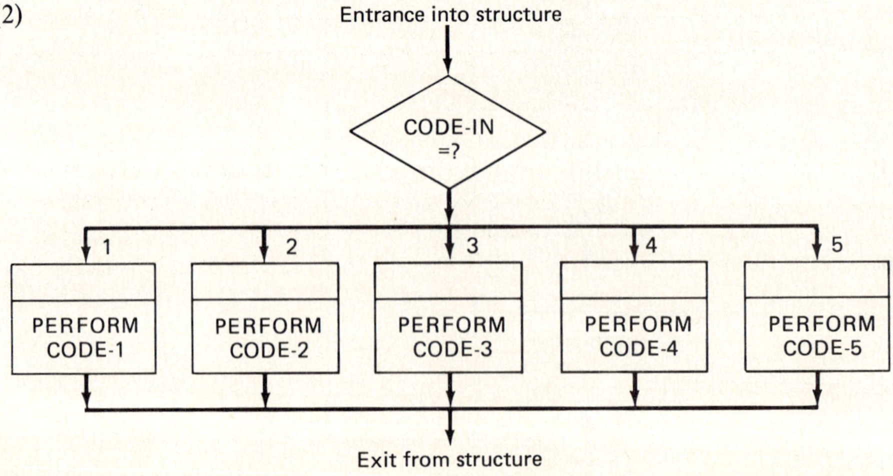

In COBOL, this would be coded as:

```
IF CODE-IN IS EQUAL TO 1 PERFORM CODE-1
ELSE IF CODE-IN IS EQUAL TO 2 PERFORM CODE-2
        ELSE IF CODE-IN IS EQUAL TO 3 PERFORM CODE-3
                ELSE IF CODE-IN IS EQUAL TO 4 PERFORM CODE-4
                        ELSE PERFORM CODE-5.
```

It is perfectly valid to "nest" structures. The illustration below shows a decision structure within a decision structure. The structures are enclosed within dotted lines.

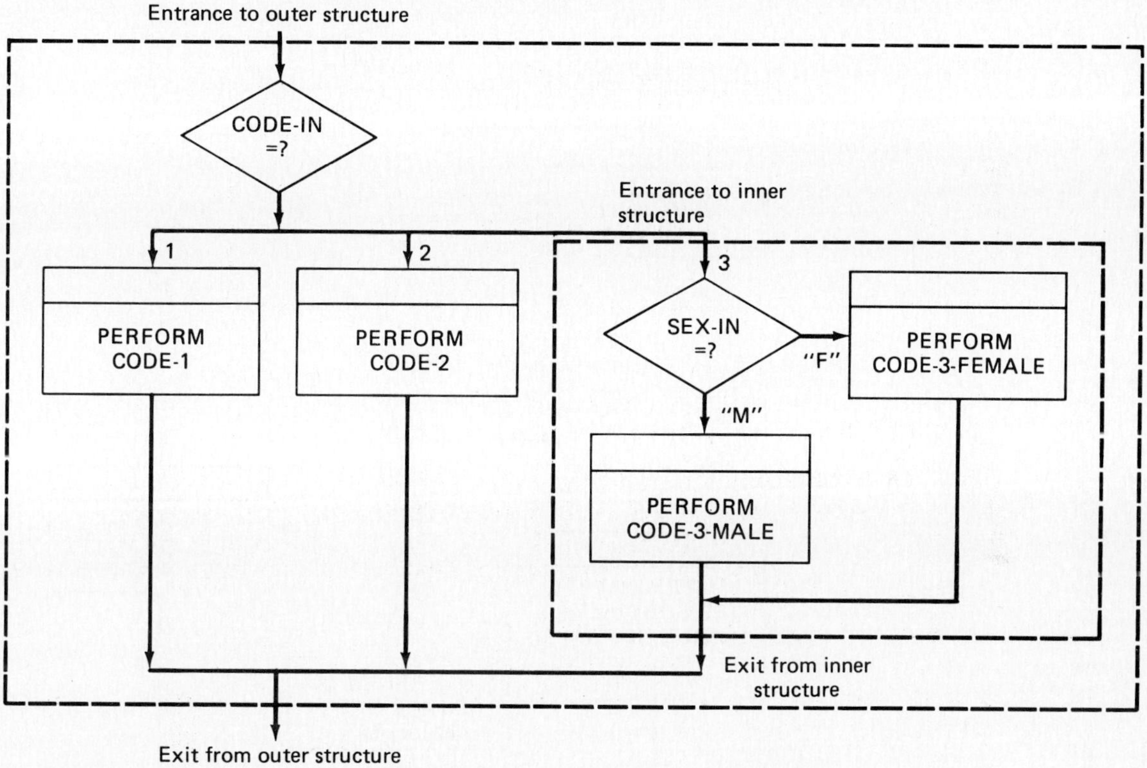

It is important when nesting structures that after an inner structure exits, it enters back into the outer structure in only one place. The following illustration shows an invalid nested decision structure. Notice that the valid decision structure requires the repetition of the PERFORM TEEN-OR-MALE-OVER-NINETEEN instruction.

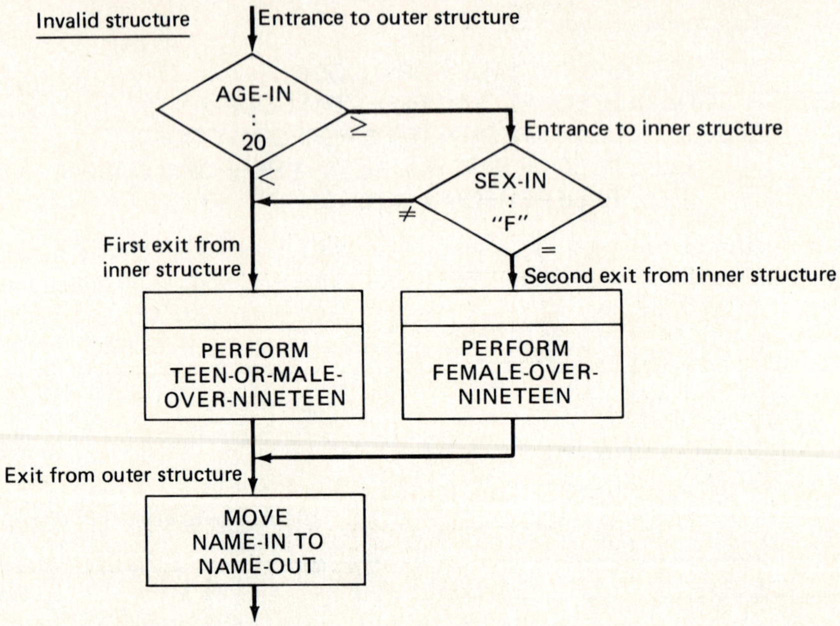

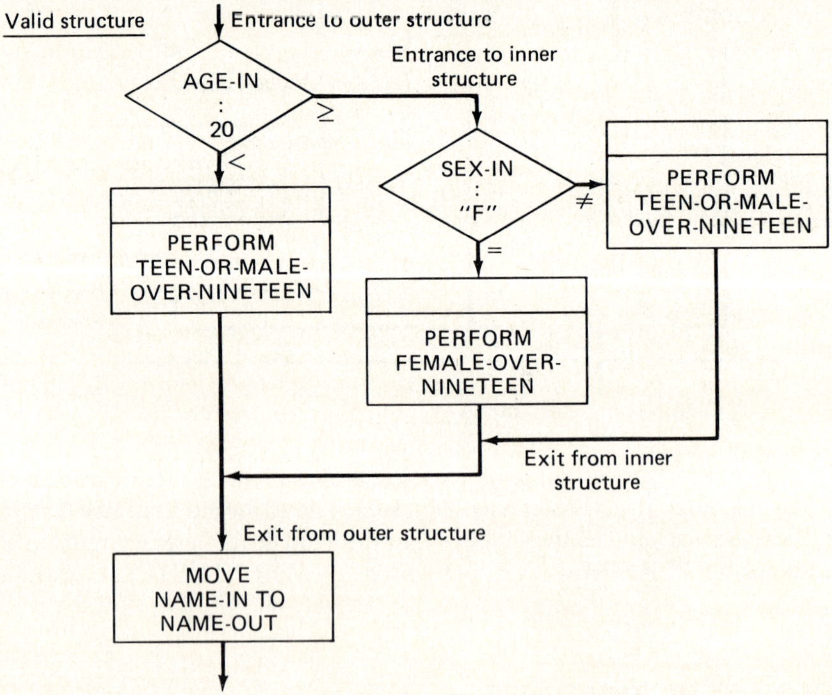

It should be noted that the CASE structure can be drawn using a series of nested IF-THEN-ELSE structures, as illustrated on the following page.

CASE structure

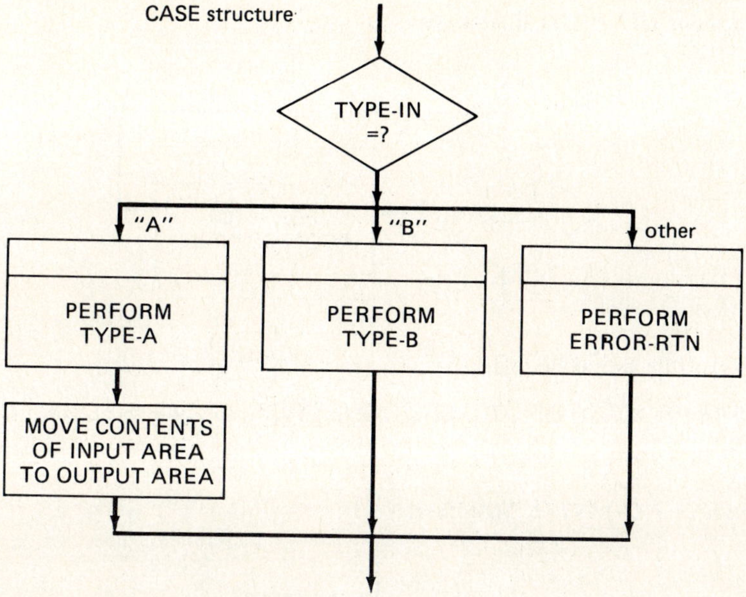

Nested IF-THEN-ELSE structure

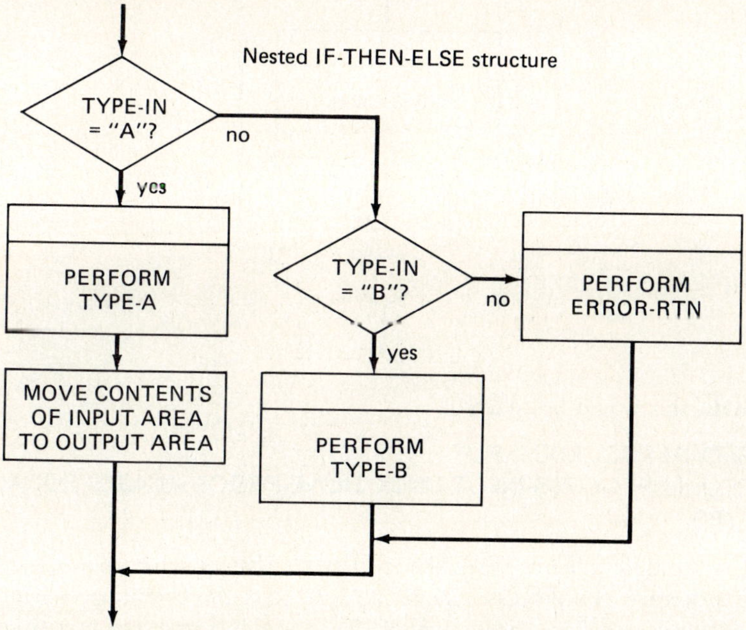

LOOPING STRUCTURE

There are two types of looping or iteration structures. They are the DO-WHILE and DO-UNTIL structures.

Example of DO-WHILE Structure

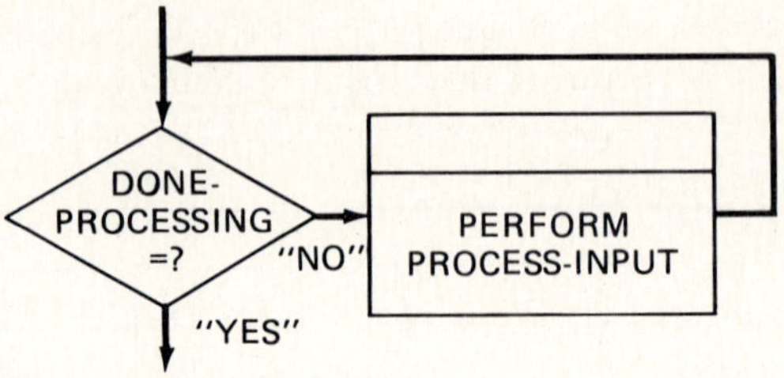

In COBOL, this would be coded as:

PERFORM PROCESS-INPUT UNTIL DONE-PROCESSING IS EQUAL TO "YES."

Example of DO-UNTIL Structure:

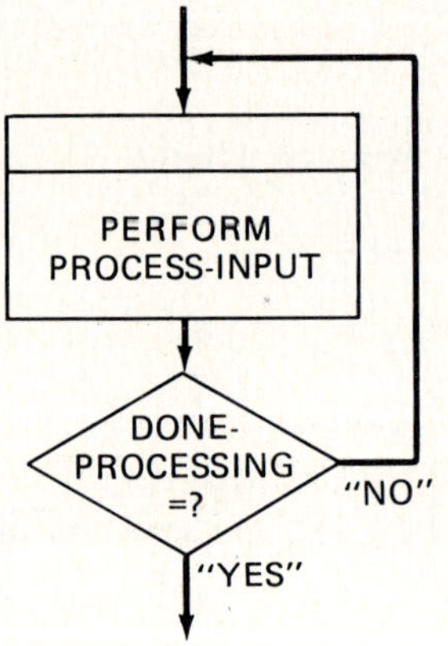

In COBOL, this would be coded as:

PERFORM PROCESS-INPUT.
PERFORM PROCESS-INPUT UNTIL DONE-PROCESSING IS EQUAL TO "YES".

What is the difference between the looping structures shown above? In the DO-WHILE structure, the process is never performed if the condition causing the exit from the loop is met. This means that if the condition is met the first time through the loop, then the process is never done. In the DO-UNTIL structure, however, the process is done before the condition is tested for the first time, and so the process will be done at least one time.

EXAMPLE 3-1: STRUCTURES, LITERALS, AND FIELD NAMES

For this example we are to draw a structured flowchart to input records from a file and print the contents of each record.

Note that this example is identical to Example 2-2 (in Chapter 2). This time, however, we want to draw a structured flowchart. The solution is shown in Figure 3-1. The reaction from most students upon seeing the solution to this example is "Why is it so complicated?" Structuring does seem to complicate this problem. In fact, forcing structured rules on a simple problem makes the solution more complicated.

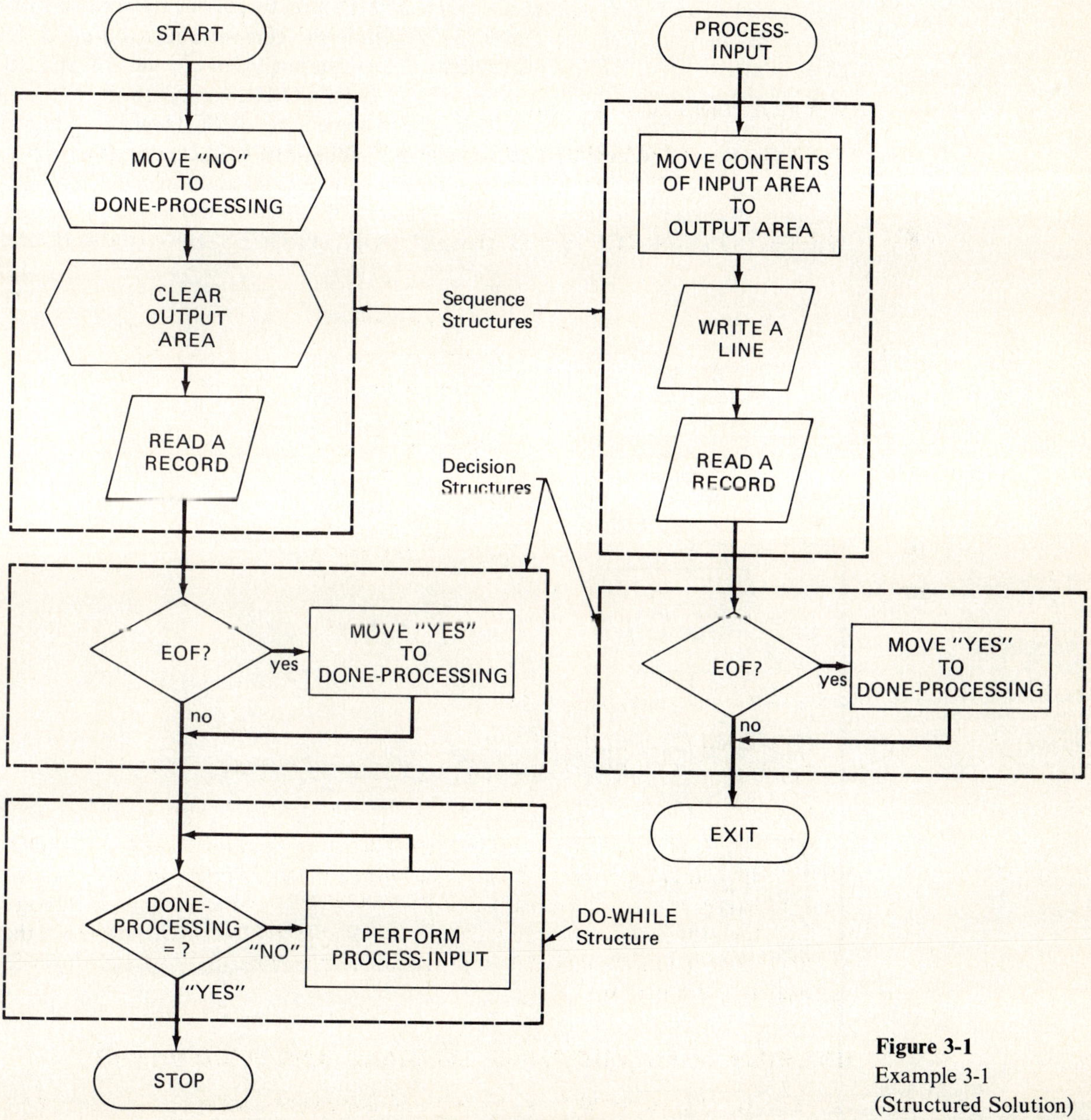

Figure 3-1
Example 3-1
(Structured Solution)

However, structuring makes a difficult problem much simpler, as you'll see in later chapters. The next question students ask is, "Can I omit any of the steps?" The answer is no, but nobody believes it until they discover it for themselves. Let's go through that discovery process.

Start with the unstructured solution to the problem, as shown in Figure 3-2. It is not structured because of the branch after WRITE A LINE that goes to READ A RECORD. When students are asked to draw this as structured, their first attempt usually looks like Figure 3-3. It does appear to be structured, but there's one thing wrong. Recall from Chapter 2 that the only time the computer lets you check for EOF is as part of a READ instruction. Follow the logic flow in the PROCESS-INPUT routine to find the flaw. After READ A RECORD, you EXIT. It isn't until you return to the main routine that the check is made for EOF. However, Chapter 2 says that the check for EOF must immediately follow the READ instruction. There cannot be an EXIT or anything else in between the READ and the check for EOF.

Figure 3-4 seems to have solved the problem discussed in the above paragraph. What is DONE-PROCESSING, though? DONE-PROCESSING is a work area

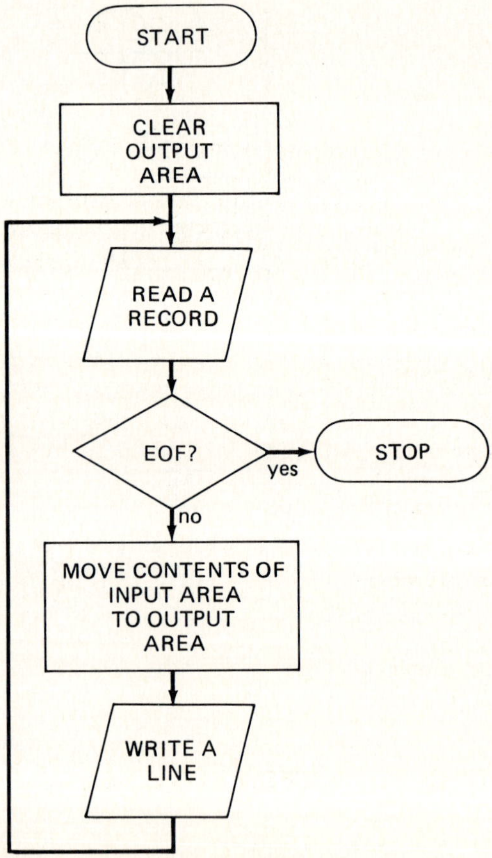

Figure 3-2
Example 3-1

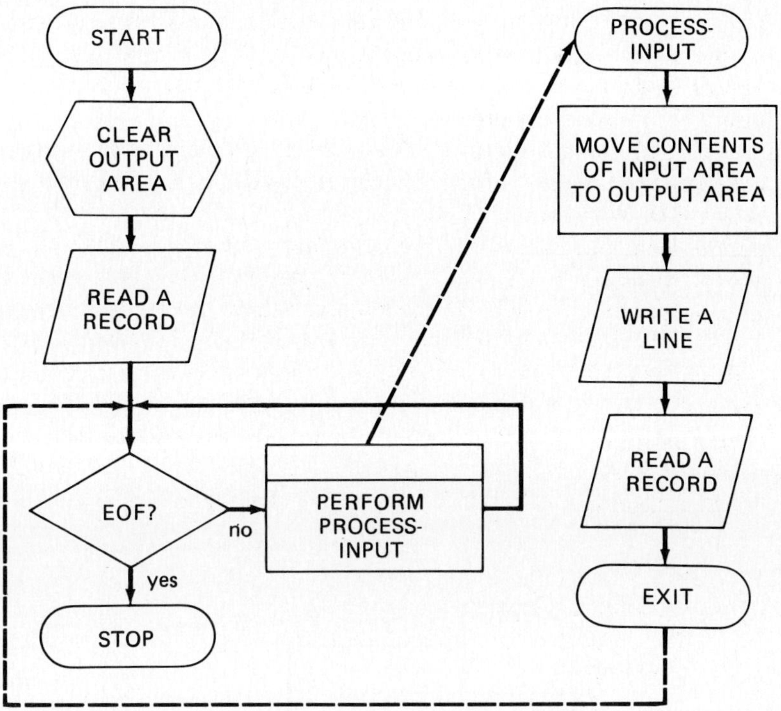

Figure 3-3
Example 3-1

that allows you to keep track of whether there are more records on the input file to be processed. What is the difference, then, between using DONE-PROCESSING and checking for EOF? Chapter 2 says that the computer only allows you to check for EOF as part of a READ instruction. There's no rule that says, however, that you can't set up a work area of your own (call it DONE-PROCESSING or anything else that you prefer) and check it anytime you want. That is exactly what is done in this example. A field called DONE-PROCESSING is initialized with the value "NO." This tells the computer that there are records on the file to be processed (i.e., we're not done processing). At the time that EOF occurs, "YES" is moved to DONE-PROCESSING to indicate that there are no more records on the file to be processed.

The flowchart in Figure 3-4 creates a new problem. The problem is illustrated below using COBOL; however, the problem occurs in all languages. The main routine would be coded as

```
        ⋮
READ RECORD AT END STOP RUN.
PERFORM PROCESS-INPUT.
PERFORM PROCESS-INPUT UNTIL DONE-PROCESSING IS EQUAL TO
   "YES".
STOP RUN.
```

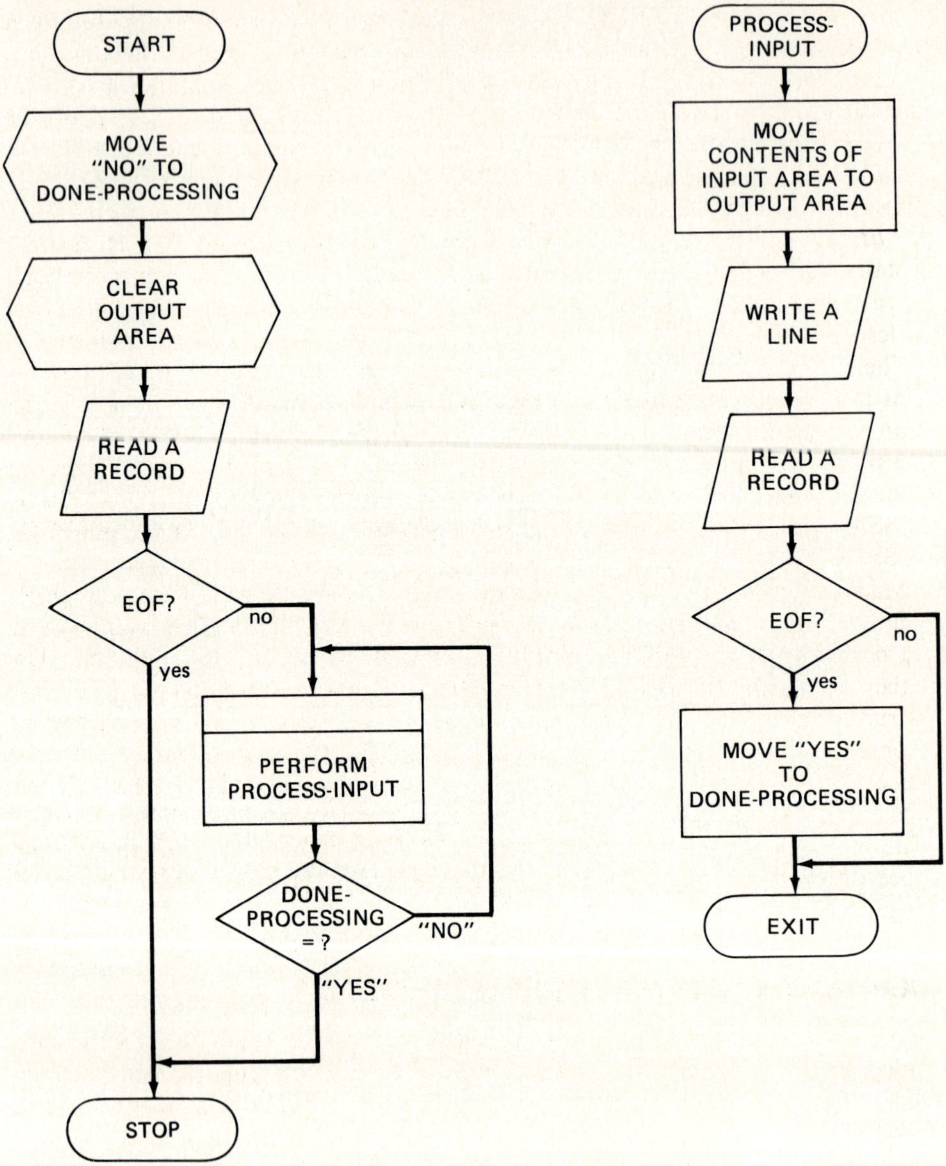

Figure 3-4
Example 3-1

This program has two STOP instructions, which is not allowed. The solution shown in Figure 3-1 solves this problem. The main routine would be coded as

```
    ⋮
READ RECORD AT END MOVE "YES" TO DONE-PROCESSING.
PERFORM PROCESS-INPUT UNTIL DONE-PROCESSING IS EQUAL TO
    "YES".
STOP RUN.
```

Two more issues need to be discussed regarding this example. The first involves the question of why the words NO and YES are enclosed in quotation marks when DONE-PROCESSING is checked. Recall from Chapter 2 that the instruction MOVE X TO Y moves the contents of field X to field Y. If field X contains the letters ABC, then after the MOVE instruction, field Y contains the letters ABC. On the other hand, the instruction MOVE "X" TO Y moves the letter X to field Y. In general, anything not in quotes refers to a field name, while anything in quotes refers to a *literal* or *constant* (a value specified directly in the instruction). The information contained between the quotation marks is treated as if it were the contents of a field. Since numbers cannot be field names, numeric literals or constants do not have to be enclosed in quotes. The instruction MOVE 3 to Y moves the number 3 to field Y.

The second issue that needs to be discussed involves the use of two READ instructions in a structured flowchart. In Figure 3-1, the first READ instruction is in the main routine. It reads only the first record on the file. The PROCESS-INPUT routine processes the record, and then it reads the next record on the file. Processing then returns to the main routine to check DONE-PROCESSING. If DONE-PROCESSING is "NO," processing returns to PROCESS-INPUT. If DONE-PROCESSING is "YES," processing stops.

Many programmers prefer to use only one READ instruction per file in a program. Figure 3-5 shows the flowchart for this problem using a single READ instruction at the beginning of the PROCESS-INPUT routine for all records on the file. The author prefers the "two-READ" method for the following reason. Since the READ instruction in the main routine is used for the first record only, it is easy to insert an error message if there were no records on the input file. It's also easy to do any special processing necessary for the first record only. In the "one-READ" method, all records are read in the PROCESS-INPUT routine, and so it would be difficult to either write an error based on the first record read being EOF or do any other special processing without using additional work areas and complicating the logic of your program.

EXAMPLE 3-2: USE OF A READ SUBROUTINE

Draw a structured flowchart to enable a college bursar to compute each student's tuition for the semester. Output is to consist of a report showing the name of each student (NAME-OUT) and the tuition due (TUITION-OUT). Tuition is calculated as follows: If a student is taking more than 10 credits, tuition is $325.00. If a student is taking 10 or fewer credits, tuition is $30.00 per credit. Each input record contains the name of the student (NAME-IN) and number of credits the student is registered for (CRD-IN).

The solution to this example is shown in Figure 3-6. Note that in the main routine ERROR is performed if there are no records on the input file. ERROR causes an error message to be printed on the report. After the message is printed, processing returns to the main routine and stops. Notice also that a separate READ routine is used in this example. Some programmers prefer the use of a separate READ routine for every file to be read. Others prefer to include the READ instruction in the routine that requires the record to be read. It is entirely up to you and the standards of the organization you work for to select which method to use.

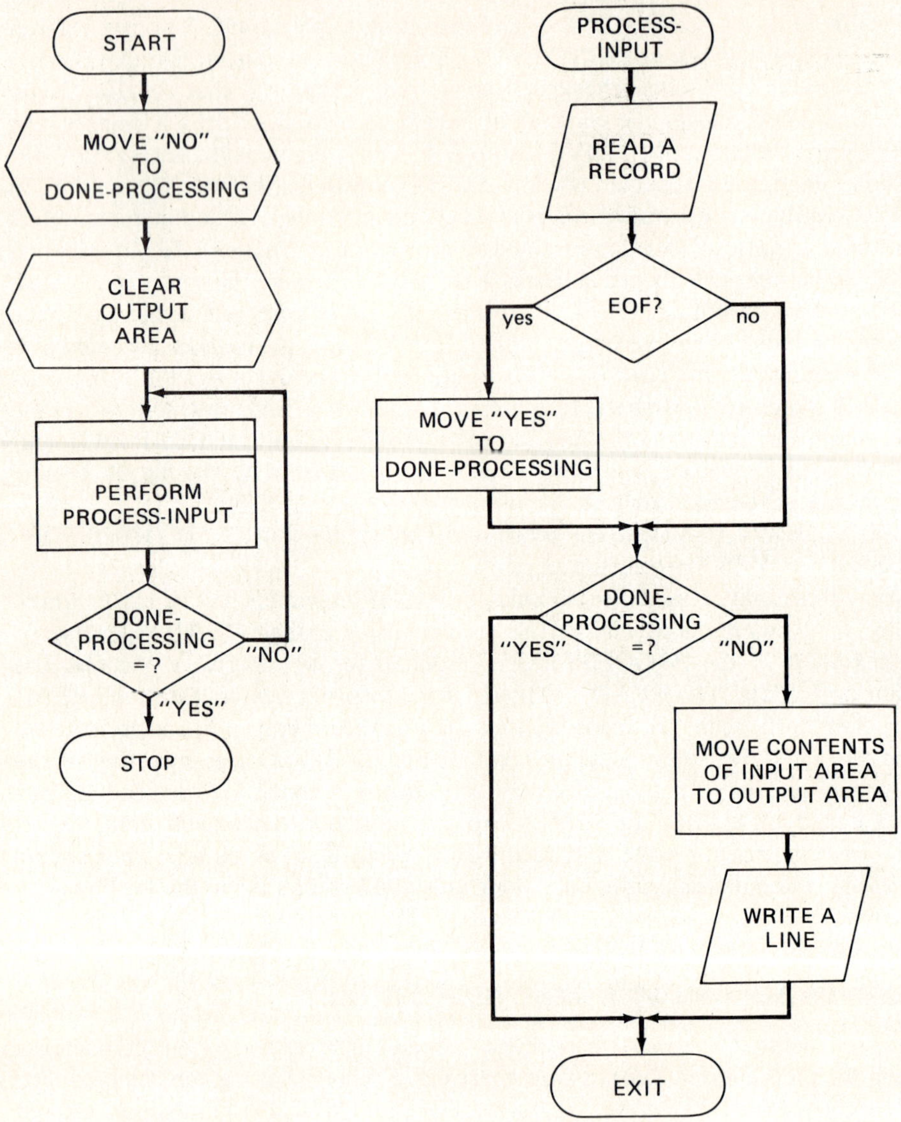

Figure 3-5
Example 3-1

PSEUDOCODE

Pseudocode is an alternative to flowcharting. Whereas flowcharts represent logic pictorially, pseudocode allows the programmer to represent his or her logic in an English-like manner. Many programmers prefer pseudocode because it is easier to change (you don't have to redraw an entire flowchart). Some programmers prefer flowcharts because they like to see a picture of the logic. Some organizations require that flowcharts be a part of the documentation; some organizations require pseudocode. Some organizations give the programmer a choice of method. So that you will

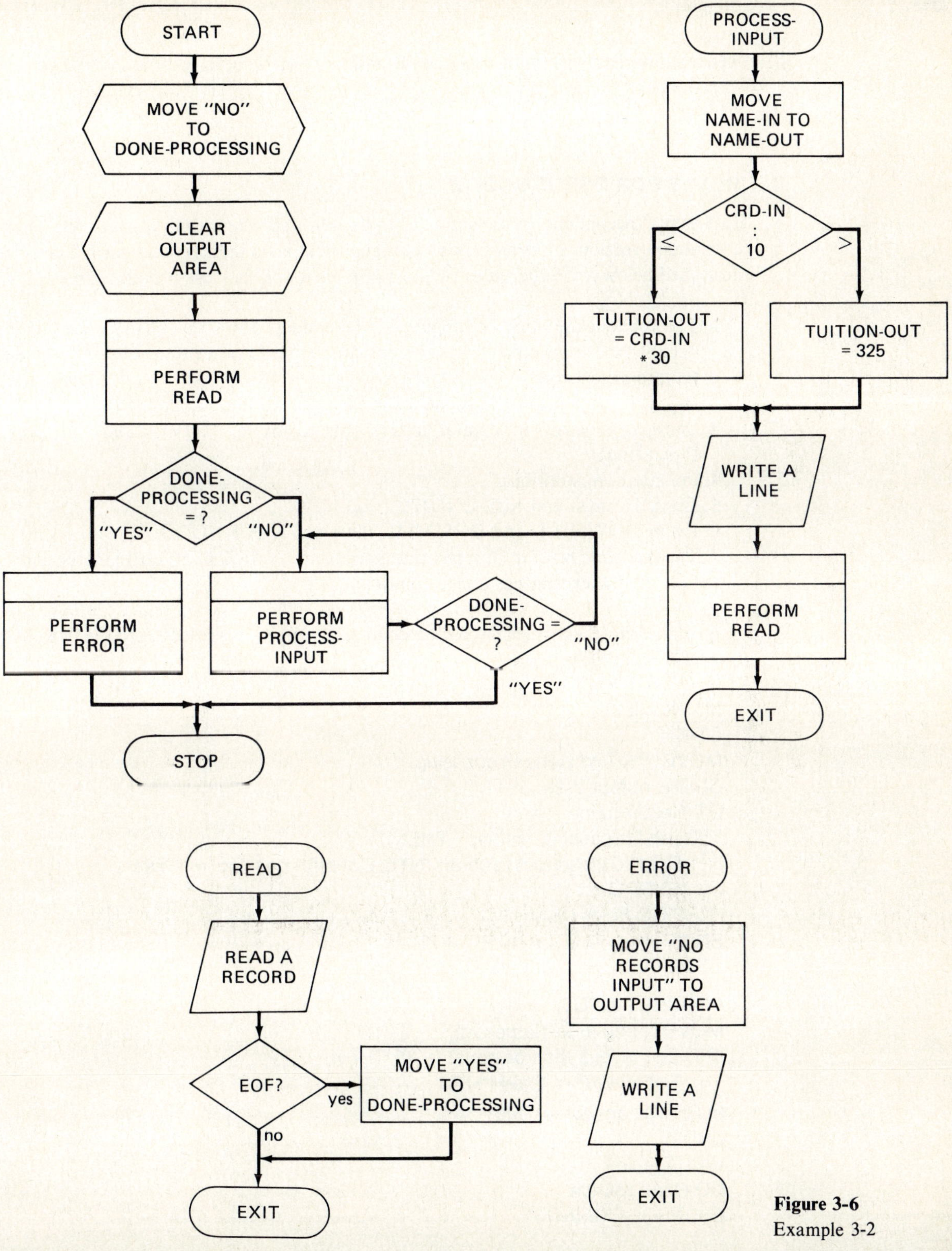

Figure 3-6
Example 3-2

become familiar with both pseudocode and flowcharts, both techniques will be used in this book.

RULES FOR PSEUDOCODE

Just as in flowcharting, there are rules to be followed when using pseudocode. However, many versions of pseudocode exist, and there is no industry standard. The rules described below are adhered to by most organizations that use pseudocode.

1. The pseudocode must be language-independent. Try to avoid the use of words peculiar to a particular programming language. In other words, try not to code the program twice.
2. Indent lines to make the pseudocode easy to read and understand.
3. Show key words in capital letters (for example, MOVE "No" to Done-Processing).
4. Punctuation is optional.
5. Every IF must end with ENDIF.
6. Every DOWHILE and DOUNTIL must end with ENDDO.
7. The *mainline routine* (the one that goes from START to STOP) is to be shown first. All other routines are to follow.

As an example, consider the pseudocode below, which corresponds to the flowchart shown in Figure 3-6.

```
MAINLINE
START
MOVE "No" to Done-Processing
CLEAR output area
DO Read routine
IF Done-Processing = "No" THEN
     DO Process-Input routine UNTIL Done-Processing = "Yes"
     ENDDO
ELSE DO Error routine
ENDIF
STOP

PROCESS-INPUT
MOVE Name-In to Name-Out
IF Crd-In is less than or equal to 10 THEN
     Tuition-Out = Crd-In * 30
ELSE Tuition-Out = 325
ENDIF
WRITE a line
DO Read routine
ENDPROCESS-INPUT
```

```
READ
READ a record
   ATEND of file MOVE "Yes" to Done-Processing
ENDREAD

ERROR
MOVE "No Records Input" to output area
WRITE a line
ENDERROR
```

HIERARCHY (STRUCTURE) CHARTS

Many times students don't know where to start when constructing a flowchart or writing pseudocode. Hierarchy charts are a useful tool to help you get started. A *hierarchy* or *structure chart* shows the routines to be used and their relationship. A sample hierarchy or structure chart is shown in Figure 3-7. The first level of the chart is the MAINLINE routine. The next level shows the routines performed by the MAINLINE (GET-READY, PROCESS-INPUT, and FINISH-UP). The next level shows the routines performed by GET-READY, PROCESS-INPUT, and FINISH-UP, and so forth, showing all routines in the program.

Notice that the READ routine has the upper right-hand corner shaded. This indicates that the READ routine is performed by more than one routine, that is, it is a *common module*.

Once the hierarchy chart is complete, the programmer can then flowchart or write pseudocode for the routines shown in the chart. Sometimes you may forget to include one or more routines that you discover you need while drawing the flowchart. If that happens, just modify your hierarchy chart and continue with the flowchart.

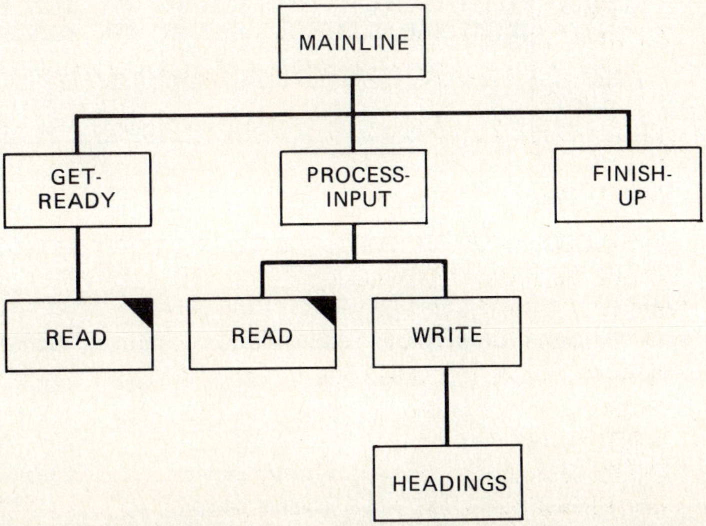

Figure 3-7

NUMBERING MODULES

Many programmers number their modules or routines by level or location in the hierarchy chart. This enables easier reference when looking for routines in the flowchart, pseudocode, or program code. When coding is done, the routines are then shown in order by their number.

The first (topmost) level of the chart is level 1000, the next level 2000, and so on. Within each level, routines are incremented by 10 to allow the insertion of additional routines. In the hierarchy chart of Figure 3-7, the second level (2000) would contain GET-READY (2010), PROCESS-INPUT (2020), and FINISH-UP (2030). Common modules use the number of the highest level in which they appear.

EXAMPLE 3-3: REVIEW

To review what has been covered in this chapter, consider the following example.

Construct a hierarchy chart, pseudocode, and flowchart for a program which will produce the following accounts receivable report.

Output

Output is to consist of the report. For each record input, the following fields are to be printed on a single line: customer number (CUST-NO-OUT), customer name (CUST-NAME-OUT), amount of purchase (AMT-OUT), the discount rate, shown with a percent (%) sign (DISC-RATE-OUT), amount of discount (DISC-AMT-OUT), and net amount (NET-AMT-OUT). All money fields are to contain dollar signs in the output.

Printer Spacing Chart

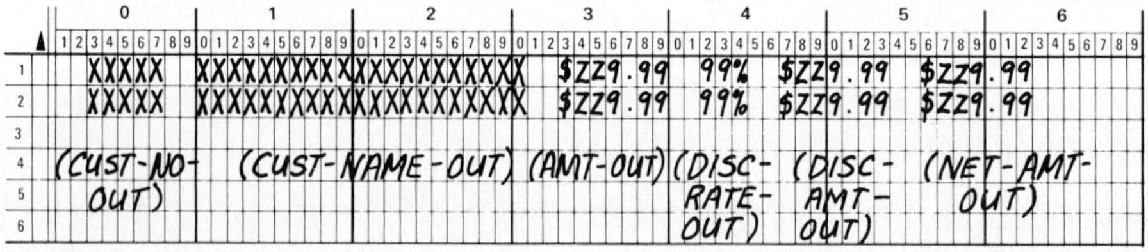

Sample Output

00001 MARY SMITH $100.00 20% $20.00 $80.00

Input

Input consists of an accounts receivable file containing records with the following format:

Record Position	*Description*	*Field Name*
1–5	Customer number	CUST-NO-IN
6–26	Customer name	CUST-NAME-IN
27–32	Amount of purchase	AMT-IN

Sample Input

00001 MARY SMITH 100.00

Calculations

For purchases less than $100.00, the discount rate is 10 percent. For purchases of $100.00 or more, the rate is 20 percent.

Amount of discount = discount rate × amount of purchase

Net amount = amount of purchase − amount of discount

Before looking at the solution, try it yourself. Remember to use work areas instead of output areas for calculations when the output area may contain nonnumeric characters such as dollar and percent signs.

The hierarchy chart for this example is:

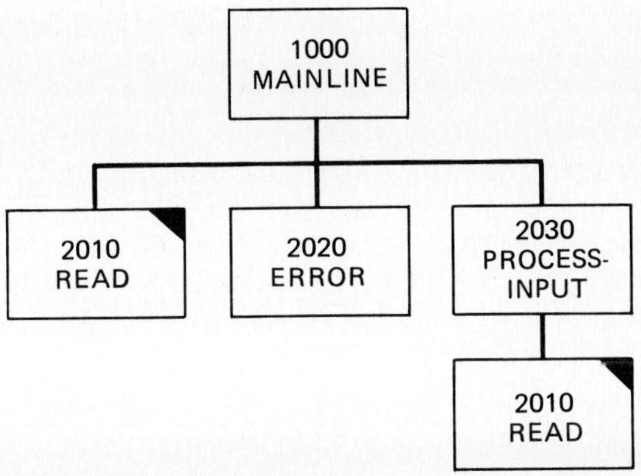

The pseudocode for this example is:

```
1000
MAINLINE
START
MOVE "No" to Done-Processing
CLEAR output area
DO Read (2010) routine
IF Done-Processing = "No" THEN
    DO Process-Input (2030) routine UNTIL Done-Processing = "Yes"
    ENDDO
ELSE DO Error (2020) routine
ENDIF
STOP

2010
READ
READ a record
    ATEND of file MOVE "Yes" to Done-Processing
ENDREAD
```

```
2020
ERROR
MOVE "No Records Input" to output area
WRITE a line
ENDERROR

2030
PROCESS-INPUT
MOVE Cust-No-In to Cust-No-Out
MOVE Cust-Name-In to Cust-Name-Out
MOVE Amt-In to Amt-Out
IF Amt-In is less than 100 THEN
     Disc-Rate-Out = 10%
     Disc-Work = .10
ELSE Disc-Rate-Out = 20%
     Disc-Work = .20
ENDIF
CALCULATE Disc-Amt-Work = Amt-In * Disc-Work
MOVE Disc-Amt-Work to Disc-Amt-Out
CALCULATE Net-Amt-Out = Amt-In − Disc-Amt-Work
WRITE a line
DO Read (2010) routine
ENDPROCESS-INPUT
```

The flowchart is shown in Figure 3-8.

ADDITIONAL TOOLS FOR LOGIC DEVELOPMENT

Although hierarchy charts, pseudocode, and flowcharts are the tools used in this book, many other tools are used for logic development. These include decision tables, HIPO, and Nassi-Schneiderman charts. A brief discussion of each follows.

Decision Tables

Decision tables are primarily used by systems analysts in communicating with users. Although many programmers find decision tables helpful when analyzing complicated decision logic, an entire flowchart cannot be replaced by decision tables.

In Example 3-3, the logic used to determine the discount rate can be illustrated using the following decision table.

Discount Rate Decision Table

Decision stub	Purchases < $100.00	T	F	Decision entry
Action stub	Rate = 10%	X		Action entry
	Rate = 20%		X	

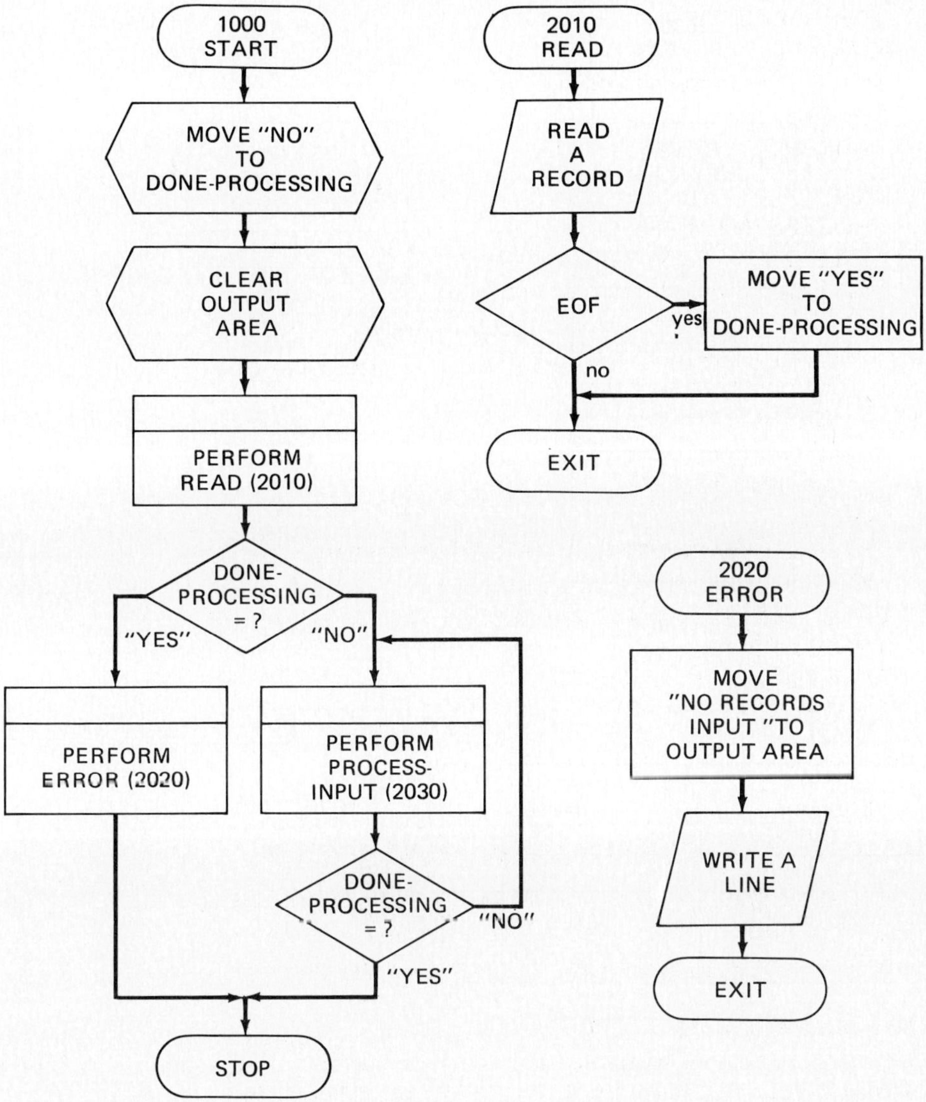

Figure 3-8
Example 3-3
(continued on next page)

Notice that the decision table is divided into four quadrants, each of which is separated by double lines. These quadrants are called the *decision stub, decision entry, action stub,* and *action entry.* The name of the table ("Discount Rate Decision Table") is shown at the top of the table.

The conditions to be tested for (decisions) are shown in the top half of the table along with their possible values (T for true, F for false). If the outcome of a decision does not affect the action, a hyphen (-) can be used in place of T or F as the decision entry.

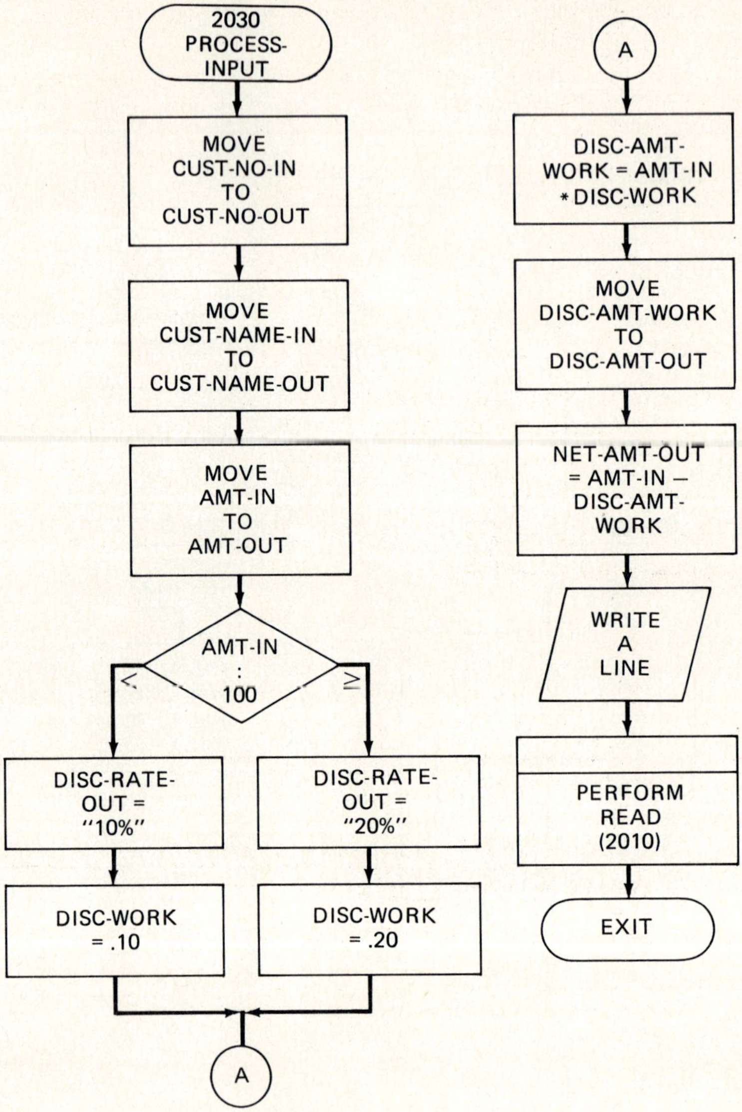

Figure 3-8
Example 3-3
(continued)

The actions to be taken based on the decision are shown in the bottom half of the table by using an X in the appropriate action entry.

As another example, consider a decision table for a company to use in determining the benefits to be paid to an employee. The following rules are to be followed:

1. Upper-management employees are to receive a company car, medical insurance, 4 weeks vacation, 20 sick days, profit sharing, and stock options.
2. Middle-management employees are to receive medical insurance, 4 weeks vacation, 15 sick days, and profit sharing.

3. Lower-management employees are to receive medical insurance, 3 weeks vacation, 10 sick days, and profit sharing.
4. Regular employees are to receive medical insurance, 10 sick days, and 2 weeks vacation if employed less than 5 years or 3 weeks vacation if employed 5 years or more.

The decision table and flowchart segment depicting the decision logic are shown in Figure 3-9.

HIPO

HIPO, which stands for hierarchy plus input-process-output, was developed by IBM. With HIPO, a hierarchy chart for the entire program and one IPO (input-process-output) diagram for each routine are constructed.

As an example, the IPO chart for the PROCESS-INPUT routine of Example 3-3 is shown in Figure 3-10. The chart shows the records and fields required as input for the routine. In the input segment of the chart, the 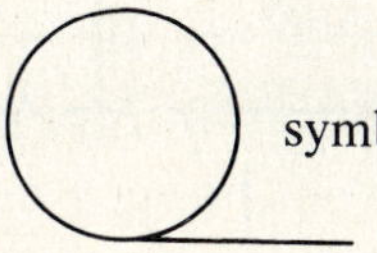 symbol indicates that the input fields are on a tape file. 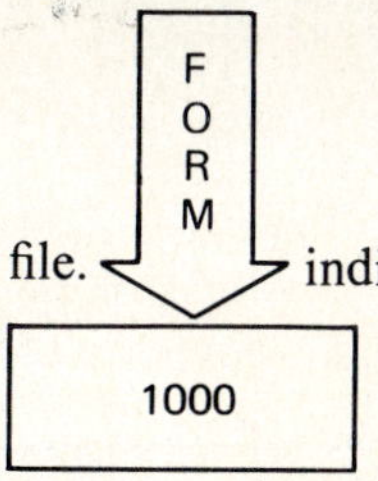

indicates the number of the routine

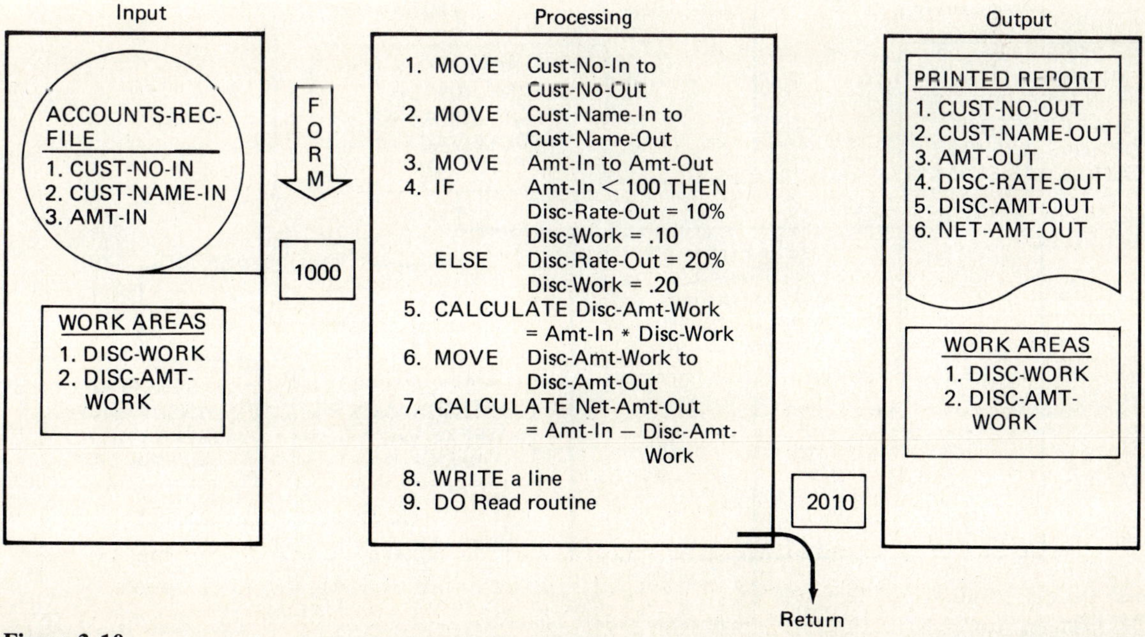

Figure 3-10

Benefits Decision Table

Upper management	T	F	F	F	F
Middle management	F	T	F	F	F
Lower management	F	F	T	F	F
Regular employee	F	F	F	T	T
Employed less than 5 years	–	–	–	T	F
Company car	X				
Medical insurance	X	X	X	X	X
Profit sharing	X	X	X		
Stock options	X				
4 weeks vacation	X	X			
3 weeks vacation			X		X
2 weeks vacation				X	
20 sick days	X				
15 sick days		X			
10 sick days			X	X	X

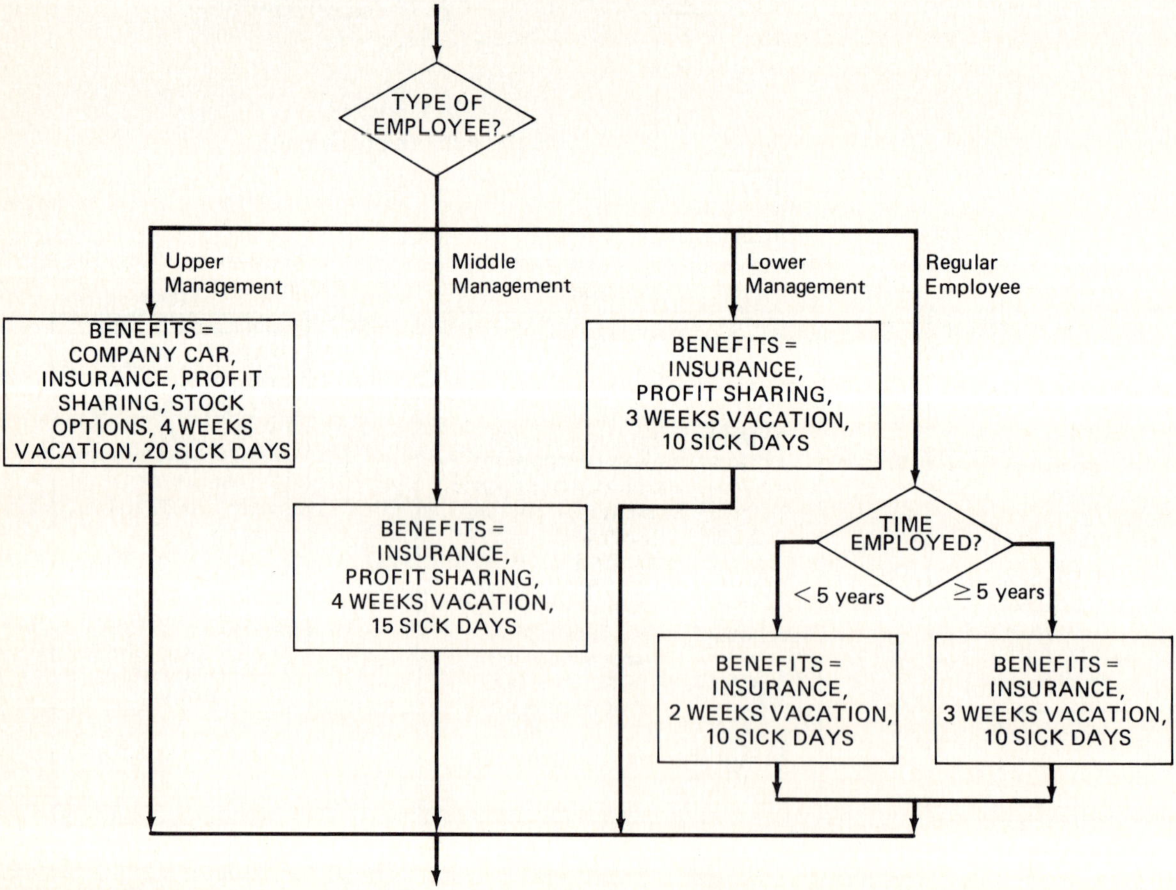

Figure 3-9

that called this routine. If the PROCESS-INPUT routine had been a common module, then numbers for all calling routines would be shown in the rectangle. In the process segment of the chart, the routine's pseudocode is shown with each step numbered. Each routine accessed by the PROCESS-INPUT routine is indicated by number in a rectangular symbol to the right of the processing segment. The output segment shows the records and fields output by the routine. The 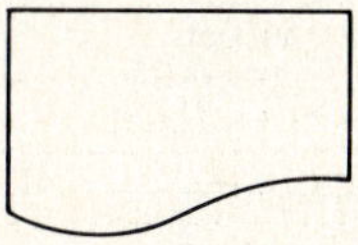 symbol indicates that the output is a printed report.

Nassi-Schneiderman Charts

Nassi-Schneiderman charts were developed by I. Nassi and Ben Schneiderman. Each routine in a Nassi-Schneiderman chart is shown using a large rectangle. A Nassi-Schneiderman chart can be used to show sequence, decision (IF-THEN-ELSE and CASE), and looping (DO-WHILE) structures. There is no way to show a GO TO or unconditional branch in a Nassi-Schneiderman chart. One Nassi-Schneiderman chart is developed for each routine in the program. The following examples show the various structures which can be used in a Nassi-Schneiderman chart.

Sequence Structure Example

Flowchart

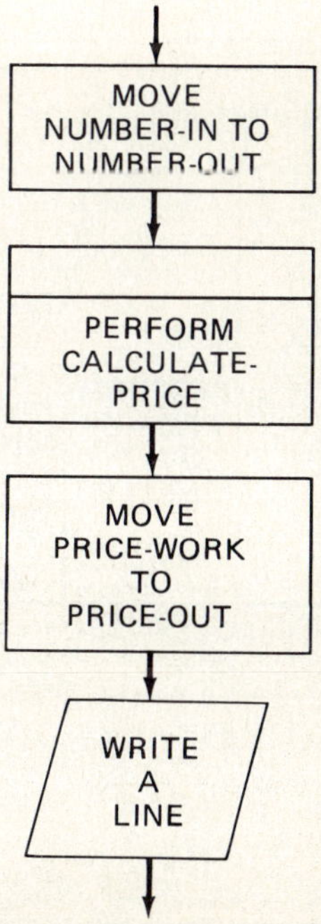

Nassi-Schneiderman chart

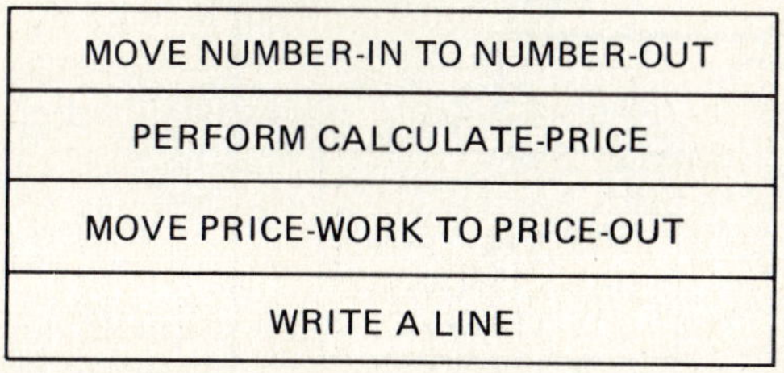

If-Then-Else Structures Examples

Flowchart

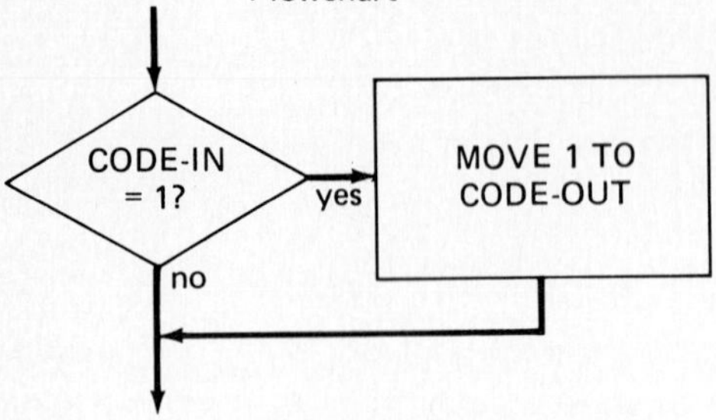

Nassi-Schneiderman chart

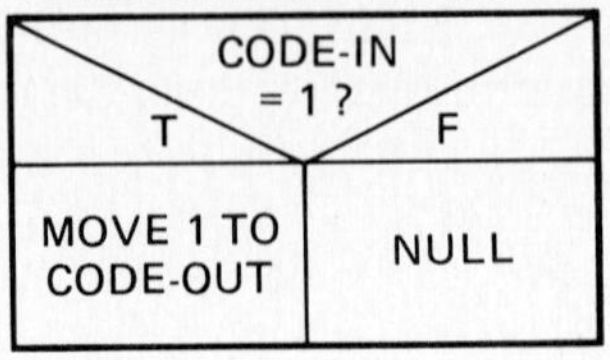

Flowchart

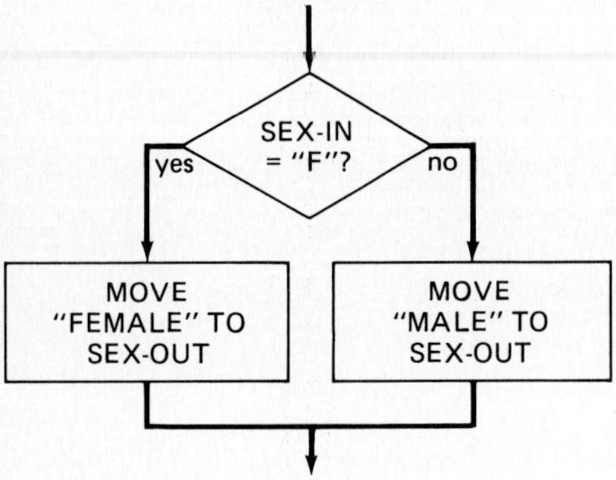

Nassi-Schneiderman chart

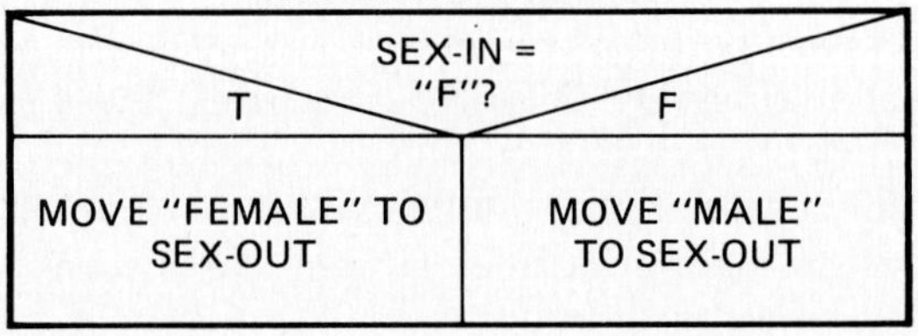

Flowchart

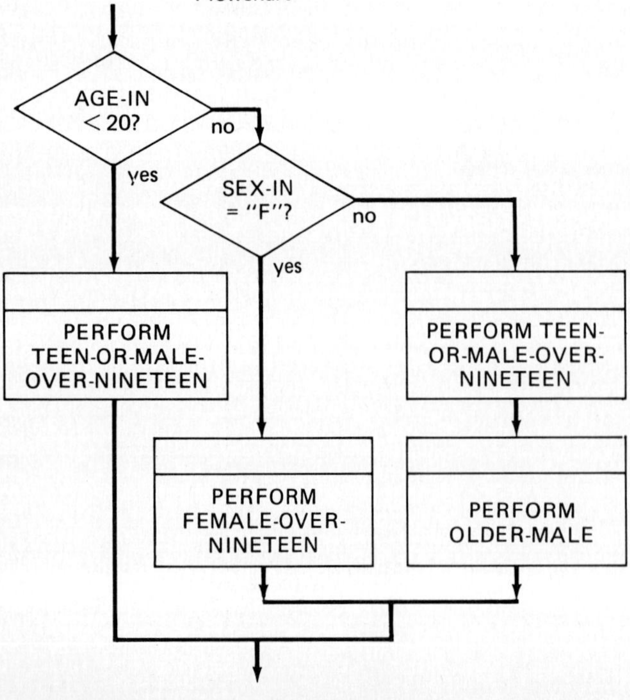

Nassi-Schneiderman chart

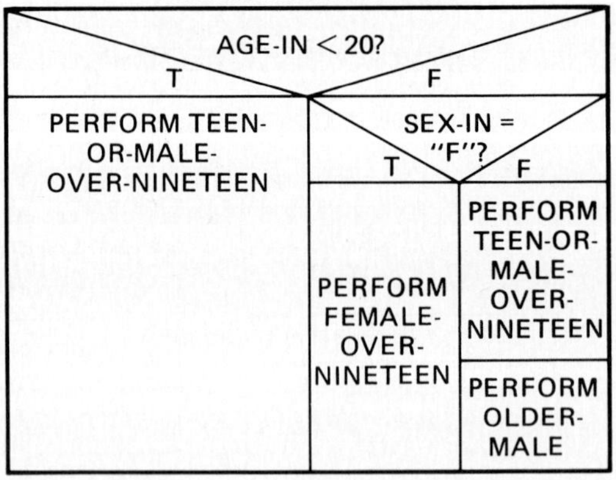

Notice in the examples that the result of a decision must be true or false rather than yes or no. If no action is to be taken based on the decision, then "Null" must be indicated on the chart.

Case-Structure Example

Flowchart

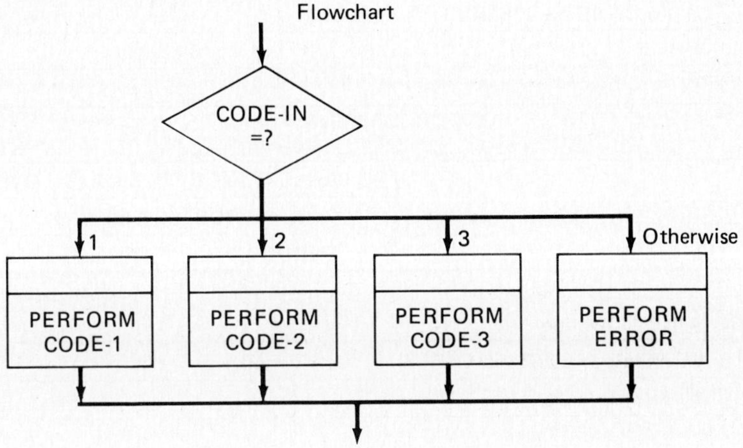

Nassi-Schneiderman chart

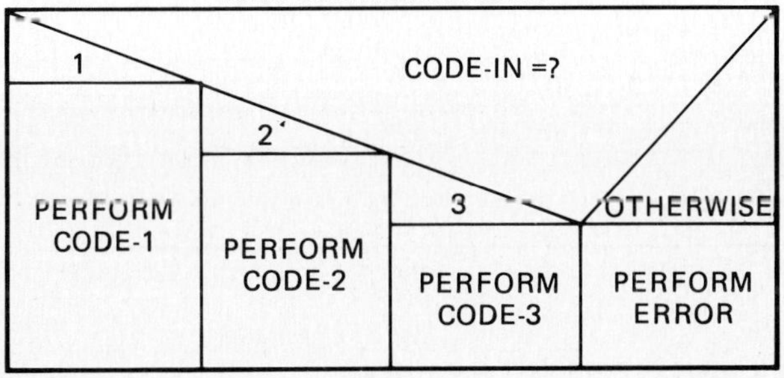

DO-WHILE Structure Example

Flowchart

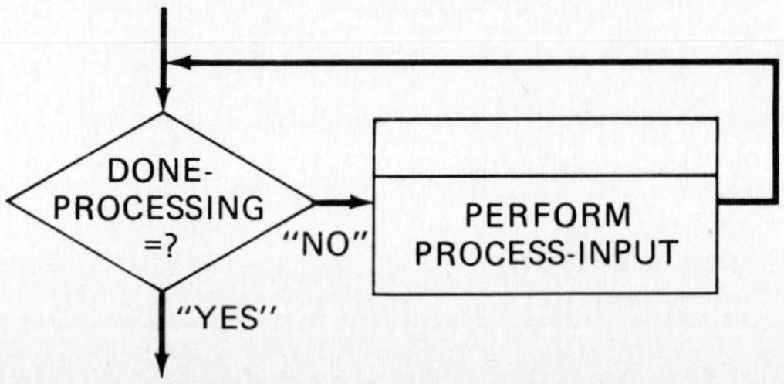

Nassi-Schneiderman chart

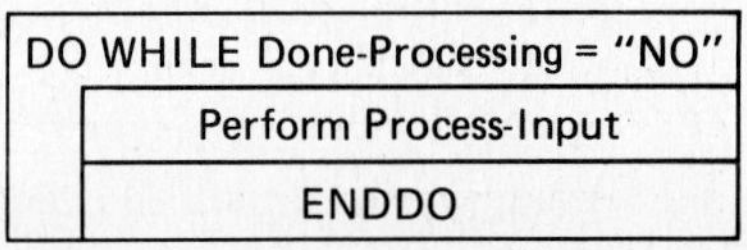

To illustrate the combination of structures in a single chart, Figure 3-11 shows the Nassi-Schneiderman charts for the MAINLINE and PROCESS-INPUT routines of Example 3-3.

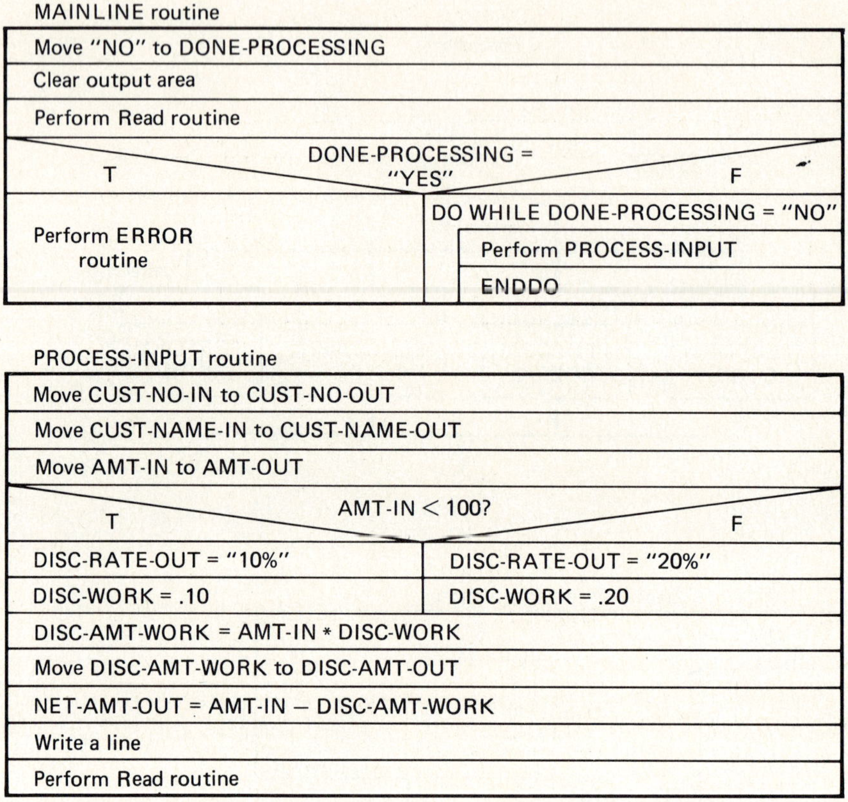

Figure 3-11

QUESTIONS AND EXERCISES FOR REVIEW

1. Define the following terms:
   a. Modular programming
   b. Nested structure
   c. Literal (constant)
   d. Pseudocode
   e. Sequence structure
   f. Decision structure
   g. Looping structure
   h. DO-WHILE structure
   i. DO-UNTIL structure
   j. IF-THEN-ELSE structure
   k. CASE structure
   l. Hierarchy (structure) chart
   m. Common module
   n. MAINLINE routine
   o. HIPO
   p. Nassi-Schneiderman chart
   q. Decision table
2. What symbol is not allowed in a sequence structure?
3. What is the difference between the IF-THEN-ELSE and CASE structures?

4. What is the difference between the DO-WHILE and DO-UNTIL structures?
5. Name the structure depicted in each of the following program segments:

a.

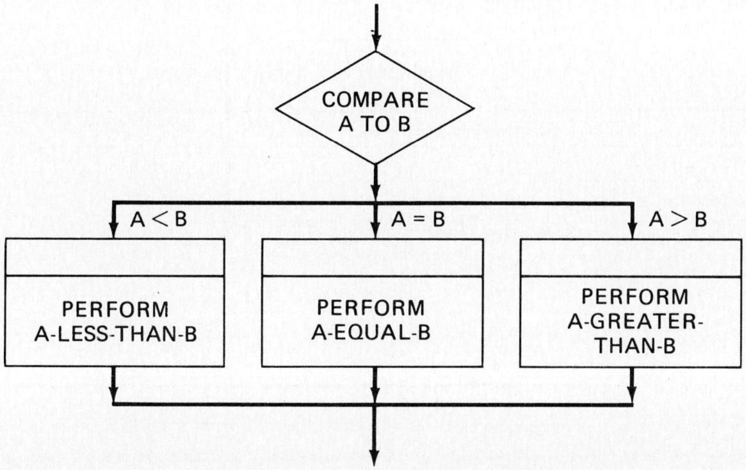

b.

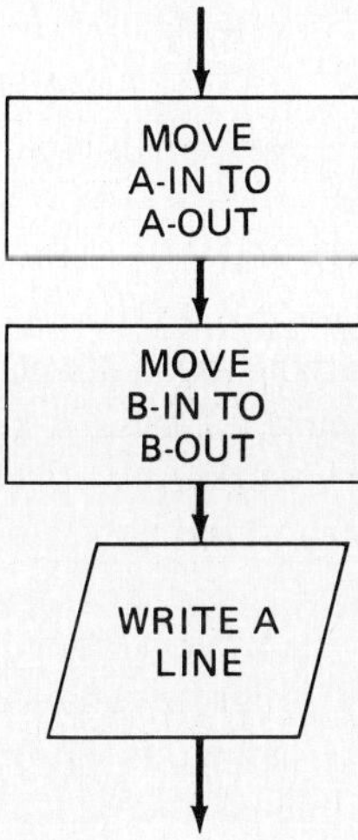

c.

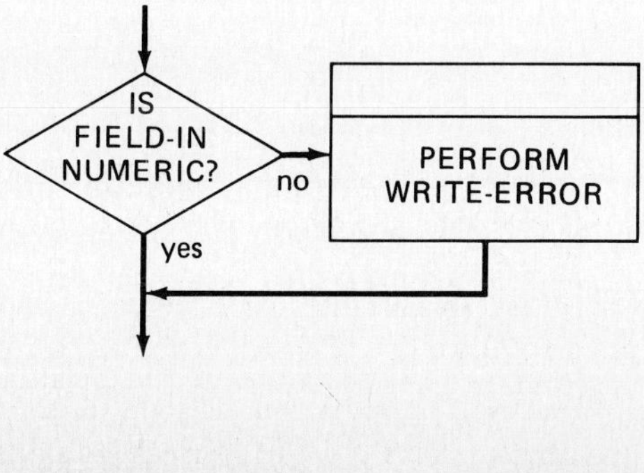

d.

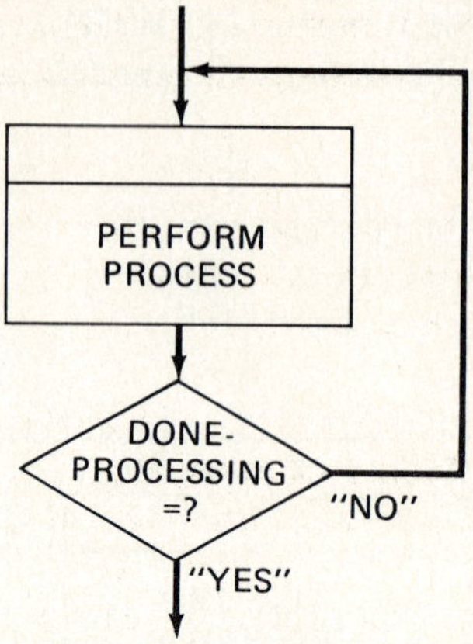

e.

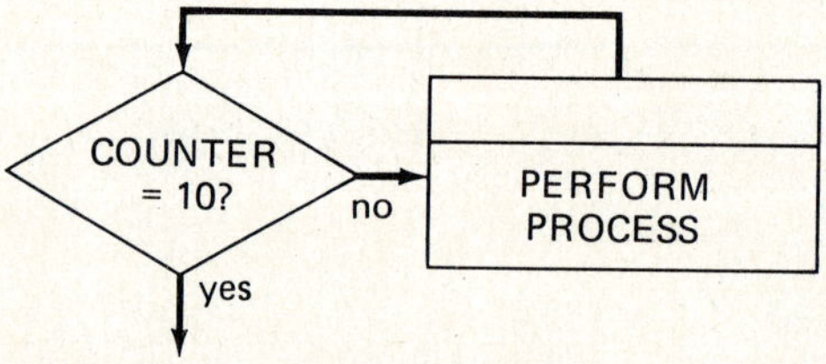

6. What does FIELDX contain after each of the following instructions?
   a. MOVE NAME TO FIELDX
   b. MOVE "NAME" to FIELDX
   c. MOVE 783 to FIELDX
7. What is the advantage of having two READ instructions (one for the first record and one for the remaining records) in a program?
8. What is the purpose of using a work area called DONE-PROCESSING?
9. Draw a hierarchy chart and structured flowchart for the sales commission problem in Exercise 17 of Chapter 2.
10. Construct the pseudocode for Exercise 9 above.
11. Draw a hierarchy chart for a program which generates a report showing the updated balance for customers' accounts. *Output* is to consist of a report with one line per customer. Each line is to contain the customer number, the previous balance, the cash received, the sales on account, interest due, and balance due. No headings are to be printed.

Printer Spacing Chart

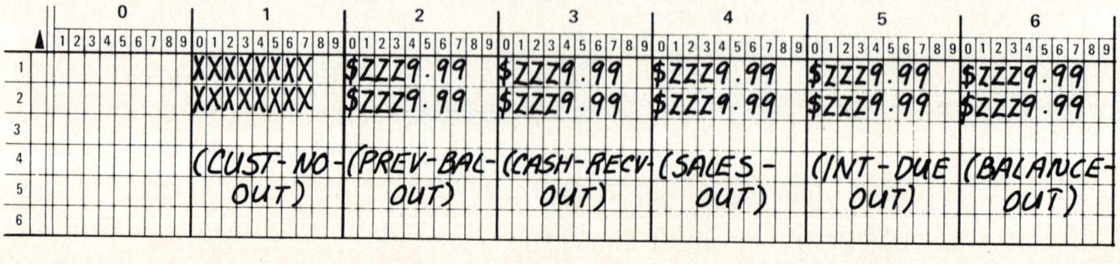

Input consists of records containing the customer's account number, his or her previous balance, the cash received this month, and the sales on account made this month.

The following rules should be adhered to when processing:

a. Interest is due on the account only if the cash received is less than the previous balance. Interest due is 5 percent of the amount by which the previous balance exceeds cash received.

$$\text{Interest due} = .05 \times (\text{previous balance} - \text{cash received})$$

If the cash received is greater than or equal to the previous balance, interest due is 0.

b. Balance due = previous balance − cash received + sales on account + interest due.

c. The output fields may not be numeric (they can contain dollar signs). Therefore, be sure to use work areas for arithmetic calculations.

12. Construct the pseudocode for Exercise 11 above.
13. Draw the flowchart for Exercise 11 above.

CHAPTER 4

Programs with One Input File

HOUSEKEEPING (GET-READY) FUNCTIONS

Housekeeping or initialization functions are the things that must be done at the beginning of the program to get ready for processing. In previous chapters we've already done some housekeeping functions when we wrote CLEAR OUTPUT AREA and DONE-PROCESSING = "NO". Unlike a processing routine which is executed for each record input, housekeeping functions are done *one* time in a program. These functions include (among other things):

1. Defining data or variable names used in input, output, and work areas.
2. Assigning initial values to fields.
3. Opening files.
4. Reading the first record of each input file.

We have not formally defined data names in storage until now. By defining the data names used in input and output areas, we are telling the computer what field names we are going to use in the program and the order the fields will appear in the records. When coding, you will have to define the fields further by stating the size of each field (i.e., how many characters it contains) and whether it is alphabetic, alphanumeric, or numeric. The coding of these definitions is handled differently (or not at all) depending on the language being used. In COBOL, the definition of all data names is done in the data division of the program. In FORTRAN and BASIC, names for input fields are defined in the READ or input instructions. Other names are defined using declaration, dimension, and assignment statements. When defining work area data names, in addition to giving names to fields, you can assign initial values. Writing DONE-PROCESSING = "NO" as part of a work area description is the same as using the instruction MOVE "NO" TO DONE-PROCESSING later in the program. It is important to remember, however, that input and output areas cannot be assigned initial values.

Students frequently ask how to do the initialization function of defining work area data names prior to flowcharting if they don't know what fields they will be using. The answer is that most people do not describe all the work areas prior to flowcharting. They include those work areas that they know will be needed and add the others as they go along.

All files to be used in a program must be opened prior to accessing them. This means that before you can read a record from a file or write a record on a file (or report), the file must be opened. You can think of an *open instruction* as making sure that the file is ready for processing. Since an OPEN must be done prior to accessing a file, the OPEN is usually done as part of the initialization routine.

The last thing to be done as part of initialization is to read the first record on each of the input files.

TERMINATION (FINISH-UP) FUNCTIONS

Termination or end-of-job functions are the things that must be done at the end of the program prior to stopping. These functions include (among other things):

1. Finishing up the processing of the last record read from the file.

2. Printing final totals.
3. Closing files.

Every file that is opened must be closed. You can think of the CLOSE as telling the computer that you are finished processing the file.

Examples of finishing up processing of the last record and printing final totals will be given later in this chapter and in the next chapter, respectively.

EXAMPLE 4-1

Suppose you are given a file with each record containing a name and address and are asked to prepare mailing labels. The hierarchy chart for this example is:

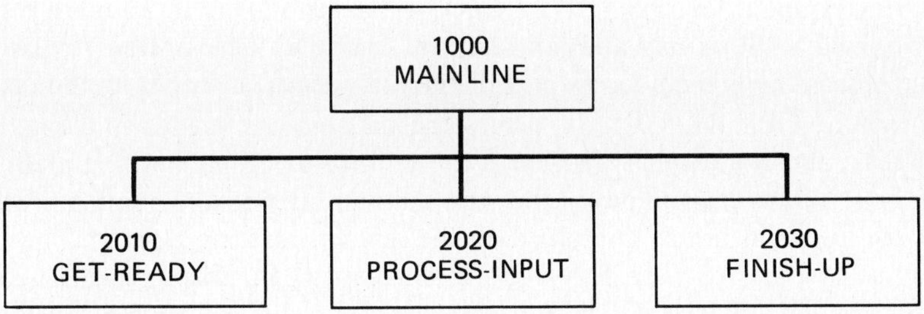

The pseudocode for this example is:

```
1000
MAINLINE
START
DO Get-Ready (2010) routine
IF Done-Processing = "No" THEN
   DO Process-Input (2020) Routine UNTIL Done-Processing = "Yes"
   ENDDO
ELSE MOVE "No Records Input" to output area
   WRITE a line
ENDIF
DO Finish-Up (2030) routine
STOP

2010
GET-READY
DEFINE data names in input, output, and work areas
OPEN files
CLEAR output area
READ a record
   ATEND of file MOVE "Yes" to Done-Processing
ENDGET-READY
```

2020
PROCESS-INPUT
MOVE contents of input area to output area
WRITE a line
READ a record
  ATEND of file MOVE "Yes" to Done-Processing
ENDPROCESS-INPUT

2030
FINISH-UP
CLOSE files
ENDFINISH-UP

Figure 4-1 shows the flowchart for the solution to this problem.

Notice that the main routine is slightly different from those of the previous chapter. In this example, the initialization functions are contained in a separate subroutine. Also, instead of having a separate error routine if there are no records input, the error processing is included as part of the main routine. Either method is valid.

Now look at GET-READY. It defines the data names used in the input areas, output areas, and work areas. The areas are defined using preparation and annotation symbols. When data names in the input area are defined, the name of the input file and the fields (in order) contained on the input record are defined. The same is done for the output area. The only work area necessary for this program is the indicator DONE-PROCESSING. When work areas are defined, initial values can be assigned to the fields, so we can assign the value "NO" to DONE-PROCESSING. Therefore, it is not necessary to include the instruction MOVE "NO" TO DONE-PROCESSING. Initial values cannot be assigned to input or output areas, so there must be a separate instruction telling the computer to CLEAR THE OUTPUT AREA.

The only other instruction that requires an explanation is the MOVE INPUT AREA FIELDS TO OUTPUT AREA instruction in PROCESS-INPUT. Instead of having a separate MOVE instruction for each field to be moved, which would result in five symbols on the flowchart, we can use one instruction and an annotation symbol to indicate the five fields to be moved.

HEADING LINES, DETAIL LINES, AND TOTAL LINES

There are three types of lines that can be written on a report. They are called heading lines, detail lines, and total lines. So far we have printed only data or detail lines, and we haven't printed any headings to indicate what the detail lines are. It is essential to include heading lines in order to produce meaningful reports.

Heading lines contain such things as the name of the report, the page number, the current date, and field descriptions for the data on the report. Heading lines should appear on each page of a report. In order to do this, the program needs to know how to get to the top of the page. *Carriage control characters* are used for this purpose. At the time that a line is written, the computer needs to be told which carriage

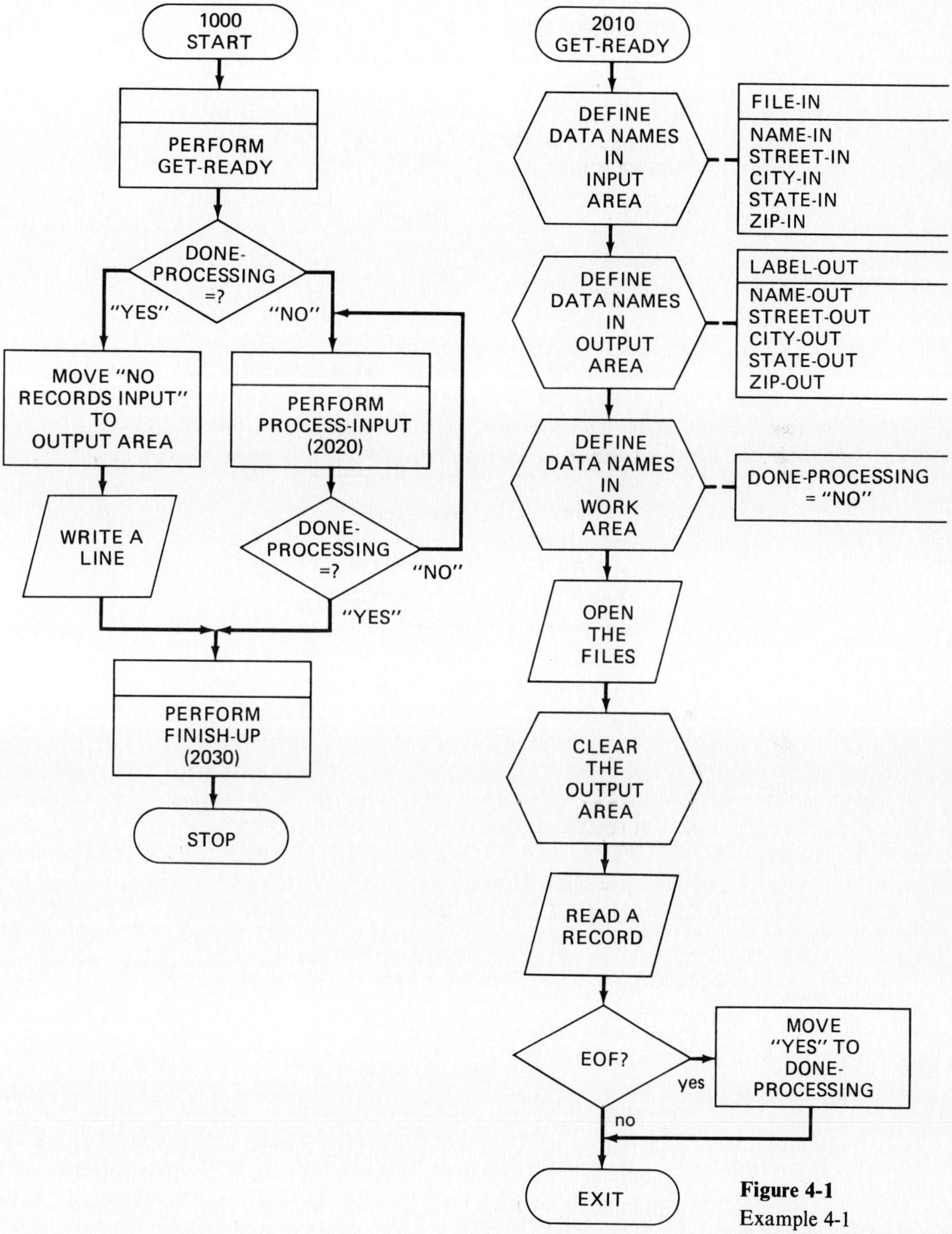

Figure 4-1
Example 4-1
(continued on next page)

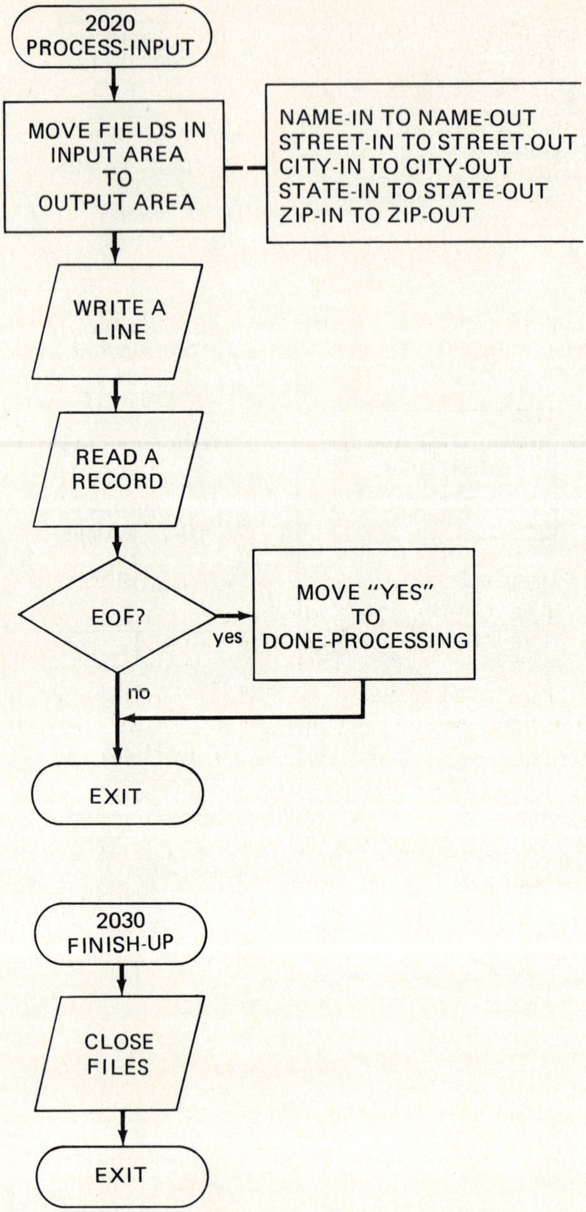

Figure 4-1
Example 4-1
(continued)

control character to use. This is accomplished in different ways depending on the programming language being used. In this book the following conventions will be used to indicate spacing:

1. WRITE A LINE AT TOP OF PAGE tells the computer to write the line at the top of the paper.

2. WRITE A LINE tells the computer to single space.
3. WRITE A LINE AFTER ADVANCING 2 LINES tells the computer to double-space (i.e., leave one blank line between printed lines). The blank line is written before the printed line, when using the term ADVANCING.
4. WRITE A BLANK LINE tells the computer to move spaces to the output area and write a blank line.

How does the computer know how many lines to put on a page? The computer will print one line at a time and keep going line after line (even over perforations in the computer paper) unless the program tells it to do otherwise. For this reason, a counter is usually included to keep track of the number of lines written on a page. Then, after the desired number of lines is written, the computer is instructed to write the next line at the top of a new page.

Total lines are used on reports to give summary information. Chapter 5 will discuss the topic of totals in more depth.

EXAMPLE 4-2: NO DATA INPUT FROM OUTSIDE OF PROGRAM, HEADING LINES, AND EXTERNAL SUBROUTINES

It usually doesn't make sense to write a program when there is no file to input, but occasionally you'll come across a program such as the one shown in this example.

We are to construct a flowchart for a program which will print the squares, the cubes, and the square roots of the integers between 1 and 500.

Output

Output consists of a report. Each line of the report is to contain the integer, the square of the integer, the cube of the integer, and the square root of the integer. Heading lines are to be included as shown below. At most 25 detail lines are to appear per page of the report.

Printer Spacing Chart

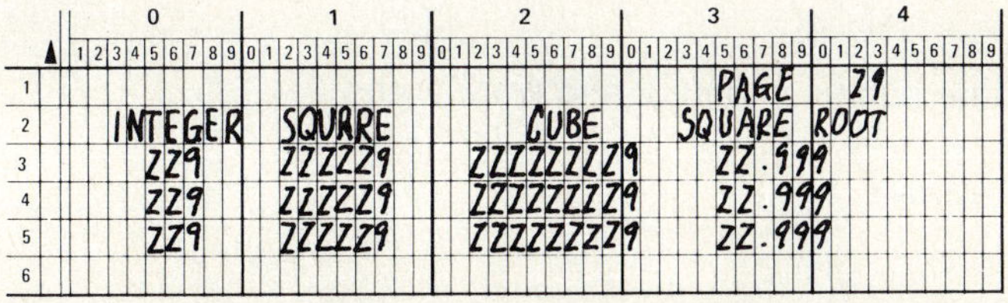

Sample Output

			PAGE 1
INTEGER	SQUARE	CUBE	SQUARE ROOT
1	1	1	1.000
2	4	8	1.414
⋮	⋮	⋮	⋮

Input

There is no input file used in this program. The hierarchy chart for this example is:

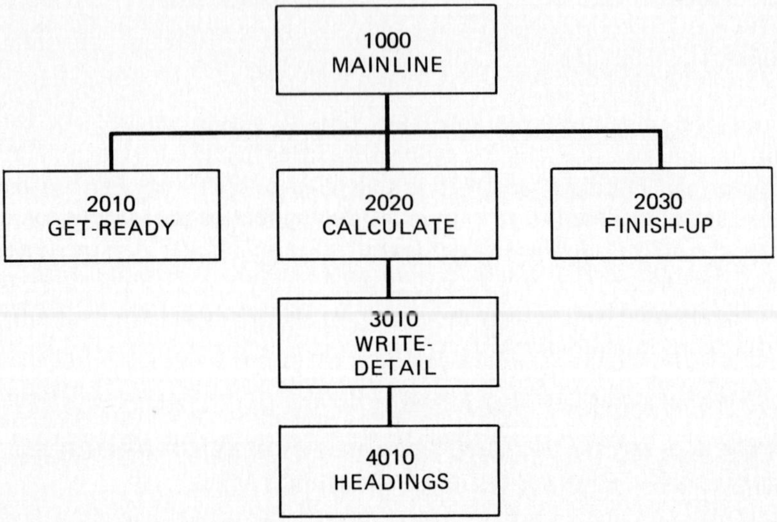

The pseudocode for this example is:

```
1000
MAINLINE
START
DO Get-Ready (2010) routine
DO Calculate (2020) routine UNTIL Integer-Counter is greater than 500
ENDDO
DO Finish-Up (2030) routine
STOP

2010
GET-READY
DEFINE data names in output and work areas
OPEN file
ENDGET-READY

2020
CALCULATE
MOVE Integer-Counter to Integer-Detail
COMPUTE Square-Detail
COMPUTE Cube-Detail
DO routine to compute Square-Root-Detail
DO Write-Detail (3010) routine
INCREMENT Integer-Counter by 1
ENDCALCULATE
```

```
2030
FINISH-UP
CLOSE files
ENDFINISH-UP

3010
WRITE-DETAIL
IF Lines-Counter = 25 THEN
   DO Headings (4010) routine
ENDIF
MOVE Detail-Line to output area
WRITE a line
INCREMENT Lines-Counter by 1
ENDWRITE-DETAIL

4010
HEADINGS
INCREMENT Page-Counter by 1
MOVE Page-Counter to Heading-Line-1
MOVE Heading-Line-1 to output area
WRITE a line at top of page
MOVE Heading-Line-2 to output area
WRITE a line
RESET Lines-Counter to 0
ENDHEADINGS
```

The flowchart is shown in Figure 4-2.

The main routine performs GET-READY, then performs CALCULATE until INTEGER-COUNTER is greater than 500. Note: INTEGER-COUNTER is a work area that is used to tell the computer the integer that is being "worked on." Finally, the FINISH-UP routine is performed.

Let's study GET-READY. There is no input area to define because there is no input file. The first thing to do, therefore, is to define the data names used in the output area. PRINT-OUT is the output line. Notice that there are no fields described for the line. In previous examples, we defined the detail line in the output area. This time we can't do that. Remember that there is only one output area that is allowed per file or report. For this program, there are three different types of output lines to be written—the first heading line, the second heading line, and the detail line. All these lines must share a single output area. To do this, each line is defined in the work area. Before a line is written, however, it must be moved to the output area.

Defining heading lines in the work area also allows the programmer to assign initial values to the lines. For example, HEADING-LINE-1 contains the literal "PAGE" and the field PAGE-NUMBER-OUT. Before the first heading line is written, the actual page number is moved to PAGE-NUMBER-OUT. Notice that when lines are defined, only the literals, the field names, and their order in the record are specified. The spacing between the fields is not indicated. This is done during coding.

In addition to report lines, three other fields are defined in the work area. The first field is called INTEGER-COUNTER and is used to control the loop in the main

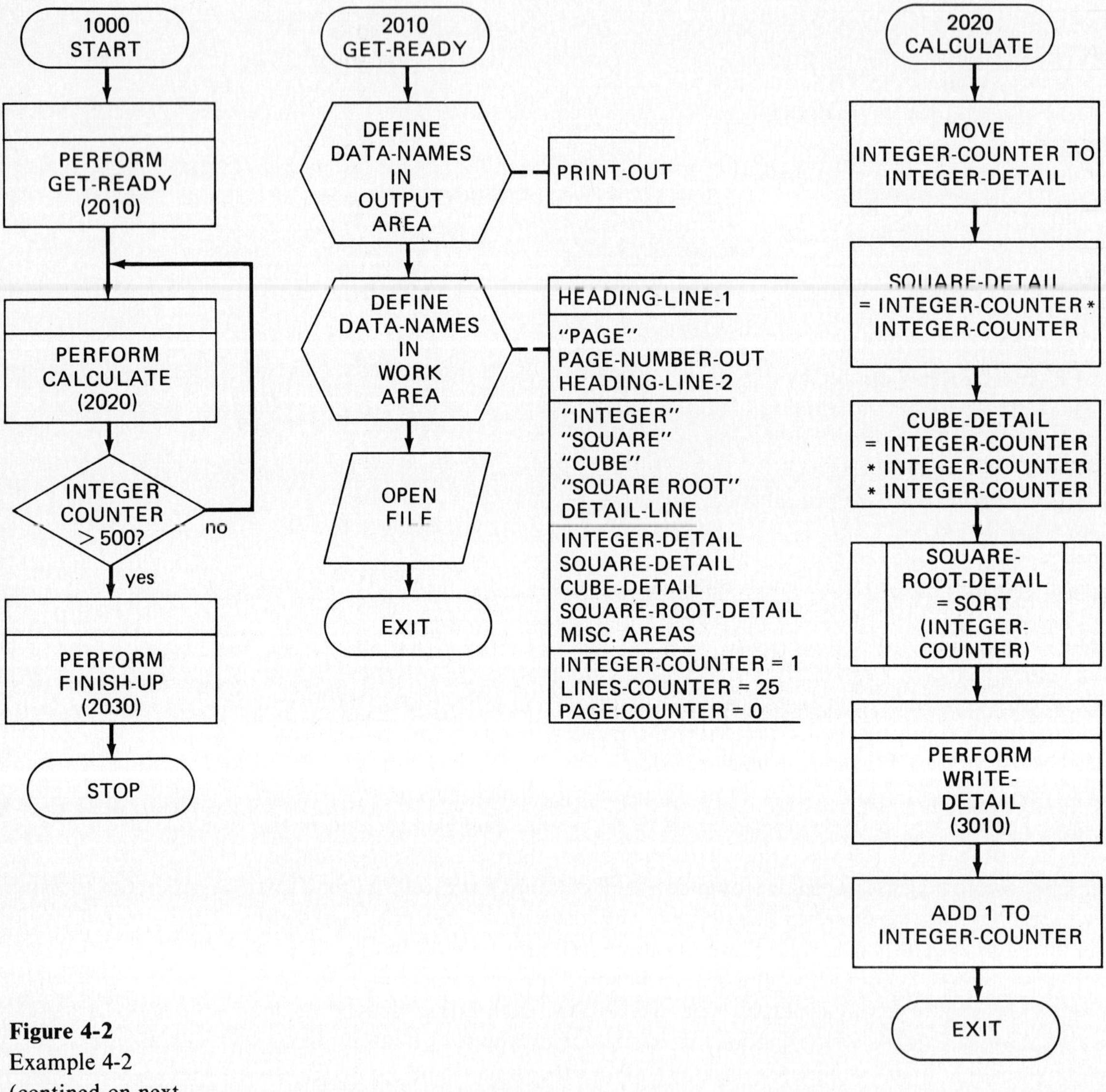

Figure 4-2
Example 4-2
(contined on next page)

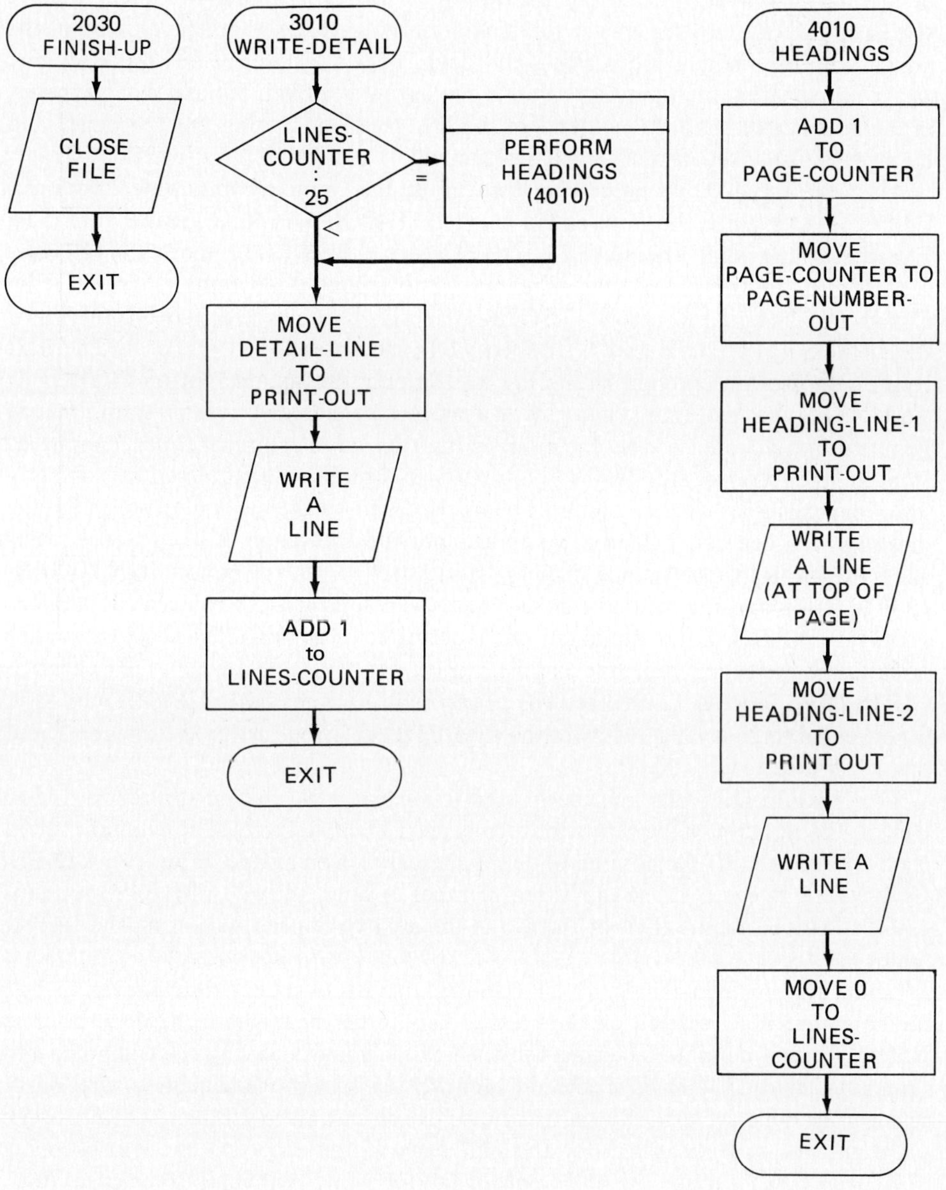

Figure 4-2
Example4-2
(continued on next page)

routine. It is given an initial value of 1 and is incremented at the end of the CALCULATE routine. The fields called LINES-COUNTER and PAGE-COUNTER will be explained later.

There is no CLEAR OUTPUT AREA instruction in this program. It has been deliberately excluded. Recall that the purpose of the CLEAR instruction is to move spaces to the output area to get rid of whatever "garbage" happened to be in the area. If, during coding, the heading and detail lines are described as the same size as the output area, then moving a line to the output area will replace the "garbage" in the output area with the contents of the line, thus eliminating the "garbage" and the need to use a separate CLEAR instruction.

After GET-READY, processing returns to the main routine which performs CALCULATE until the field called INTEGER-COUNTER is greater than 500. The first thing that the CALCULATE routine does is to move INTEGER-COUNTER to the detail line. The first time through the routine, INTEGER-COUNTER is equal to 1, so INTEGER-DETAIL becomes 1, SQUARE-DETAIL BECOMES 1 * 1, or 1, and CUBE-DETAIL becomes 1 * 1 * 1, or 1. The next instruction uses an external subroutine to compute the square root of INTEGER-COUNTER. An external subroutine is a subroutine outside of the program. It may be a routine included in the compiler, written by another programmer, purchased from another source, etc. The way an external subroutine is accessed by your program depends a lot on the computer being used and on the particular programming language. In general, however, you must provide the name of the routine being accessed (SQRT), the names of fields being used in the subroutine (INTEGER-COUNTER), and the names of fields where the results are to be placed (SQUARE-ROOT-DETAIL). After the detail line is formatted, the WRITE-DETAIL routine is called to write a detail line on the report. Finally, 1 is added to INTEGER-COUNTER. Processing then returns to the main routine. INTEGER-COUNTER is now equal to 2, so we go back to the CALCULATE routine for the integer 2, and so on, until we reach 500.

The WRITE-DETAIL routine is used to write detail lines on the report and to control the number of lines written per page. LINES-COUNTER is a work area used to keep track of the number of detail lines written on a page. Whenever LINES-COUNTER is equal to the maximum number of lines, the HEADINGS routine is called to write heading lines at the top of the next page prior to writing the current detail line.

Notice that in GET-READY, LINES-COUNTER is set equal to 25 even though no lines have been written on the report. This forces headings to be done prior to writing the first detail line on the report. In effect, you are fooling the computer into "thinking" that 25 lines have already been written on a previous page so that headings will be done even though, in reality, no detail lines have yet been written. Some programmers write headings for the first page of the report in the housekeeping (GET-READY) routine. Most do not for the following reason: In some cases (e.g., when producing an error report) there may not be any detail lines to write. If headings are done in the housekeeping routine, it is easy to end up with a report which contains heading lines and no detail lines. If heading lines are not written in the housekeeping routine, the HEADINGS routine is called for the first time when there is a detail line to be written.

After headings are written (see HEADINGS routine), 0 is moved to LINES-COUNTER. In effect, this tells the computer that no detail lines have been written on the page yet. In the WRITE-DETAIL routine, 1 is added to LINES-COUNTER after a detail line is written. Therefore, after the first detail line is written, LINES-COUNTER is equal to 1; after the second detail line is written, LINES-COUNTER is equal to 2; after the twenty-fifth detail line is written, LINES-COUNTER is equal to 25 (25 lines have been written), and headings are written prior to writing the next line.

There is one thing left to discuss regarding this program, and that is the field called PAGE-COUNTER used in the HEADINGS routine. Why use a page counter when you can simply add 1 to PAGE-NUMBER-OUT? Well, you can't just add 1 to PAGE-NUMBER-OUT, because PAGE-NUMBER-OUT may not be numeric. PAGE-NUMBER-OUT is usually defined as a field that will suppress leading zeros. This means, for example, that "PAGE 0001" will print as "PAGE   1". If you are suppressing leading zeros in PAGE-NUMBER-OUT, then you can't add to the field because it is not numeric. Therefore, we use PAGE-COUNTER, which *is* numeric. Note that PAGE-COUNTER is initialized as zero and 1 is added to it prior to printing HEADING-LINE-1.

EXAMPLE 4-3: CONTROL CODES

A control code is a value in an input field used to indicate that a certain type of processing is to be done based on the value. Sometimes the control code is used to indicate the type of record input when multiple record types can exist on the same file (as you'll see in Example 4-5). Sometimes the control code is used to indicate a particular characteristic of an input record, such as whether the record is for a freshman, sophomore, junior, or senior (as in Example 4-4).

For this example, we are asked to prepare a flowchart for the logic required to produce a payroll report showing salary before deductions (GROSS-SALARY).

Output

Output is to consist of a report. For each record input, the following fields are to be printed on a single line: salesperson name, amount of sales, regular salary, amount of commission, and gross salary. A maximum of 30 detail lines are to appear per page. Headings are to be included as shown below.

Printer Spacing Chart

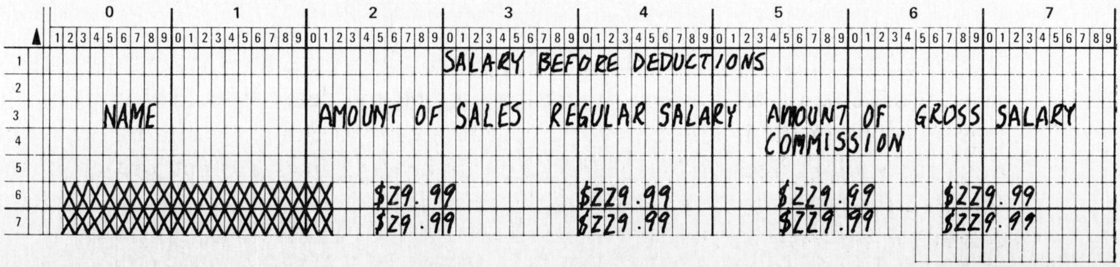

Sample Output

SALARY BEFORE DEDUCTIONS

NAME	AMOUNT OF SALES	REGULAR SALARY	AMOUNT OF COMMISSION	GROSS SALARY
BILL CART	$10.00	$100.00	$ 0.50	$100.50
CAROL DEE	$15.00	$200.00	$ 0.00	$200.00

Input

Input consists of records each containing a salesperson name, amount of regular salary, amount of sales, and a commission code. The commission code has been edited (checked) in a previous program and will contain a 1, 2, or 3.

A 1 means that the commission is to be 5 percent of all sales. A 2 means that the commission is to be 5 percent of the first $100 and 10 percent of all sales greater than $100. A code of 3 means that the salesperson earns no commission.

Sample Input

BILL CART	100.00	10.00	1
CAROL DEE	200.00	15.00	3

Calculation

Gross salary = regular salary + commission

The hierarchy chart for this example is:

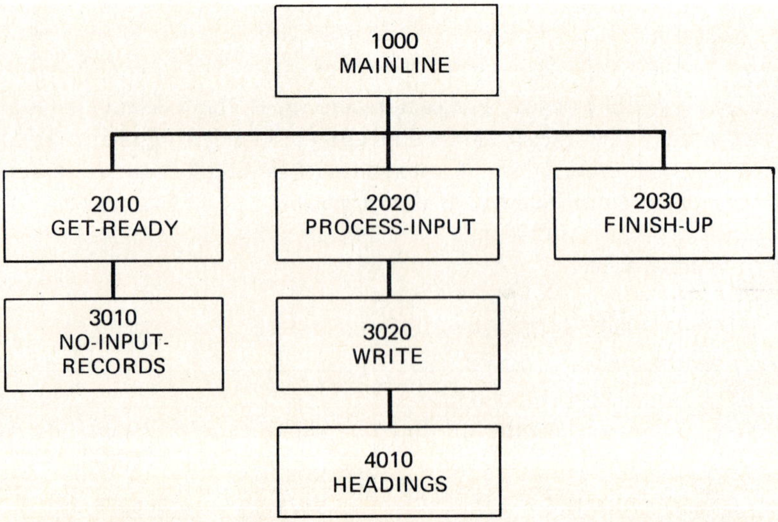

The pseudocode is left as an exercise for the reader. The flowchart for this example is shown in Figure 4-3. Notice that the control code (CODE-IN) is used in the PROCESS-INPUT routine to determine the commission (COMM-WORK).

EXAMPLE 4-4: CONTROL BREAKS

A control break occurs when a change in a control field requires special processing to be done. For example, control breaks may result in totals being printed on a report or in a change in the headings.

For this example, we are to construct a hierarchy chart, pseudocode, and a flowchart for the logic required to list the students in a school.

Output

Output is to consist of the report. Each page of the report is to contain at most 35 detail lines. A new page is to be started for each new class. Headings are to be included and are to contain the page number and class. Page numbers are to start again at 1 for each new class.

Printer Spacing Chart

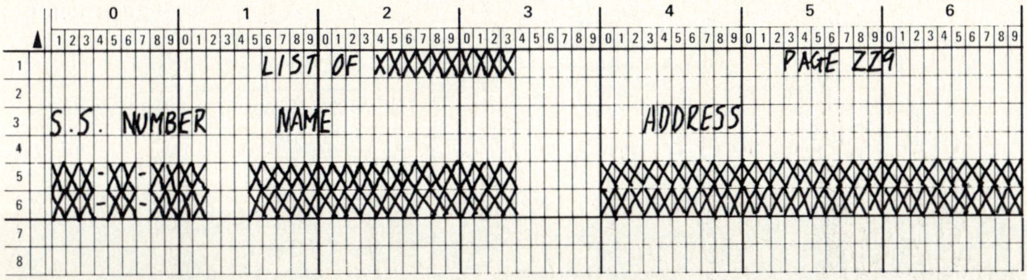

Sample Output

LIST OF FRESHMEN PAGE 1

S.S. NUMBER NAME ADDRESS

365-67-1111 FRAN SMITHY 32 RALEIGH GLENVIEW
359-34-8764 FRED KRAMER 1818 CHURCH SKOKIE

Input

Input consists of records of the following format:

Position	*Description*
1–11	Social security number
12–30	Name
31–60	Address
61	Class indicator (1 = freshman, 2 = sophomore, 3 = junior, 4 = senior)

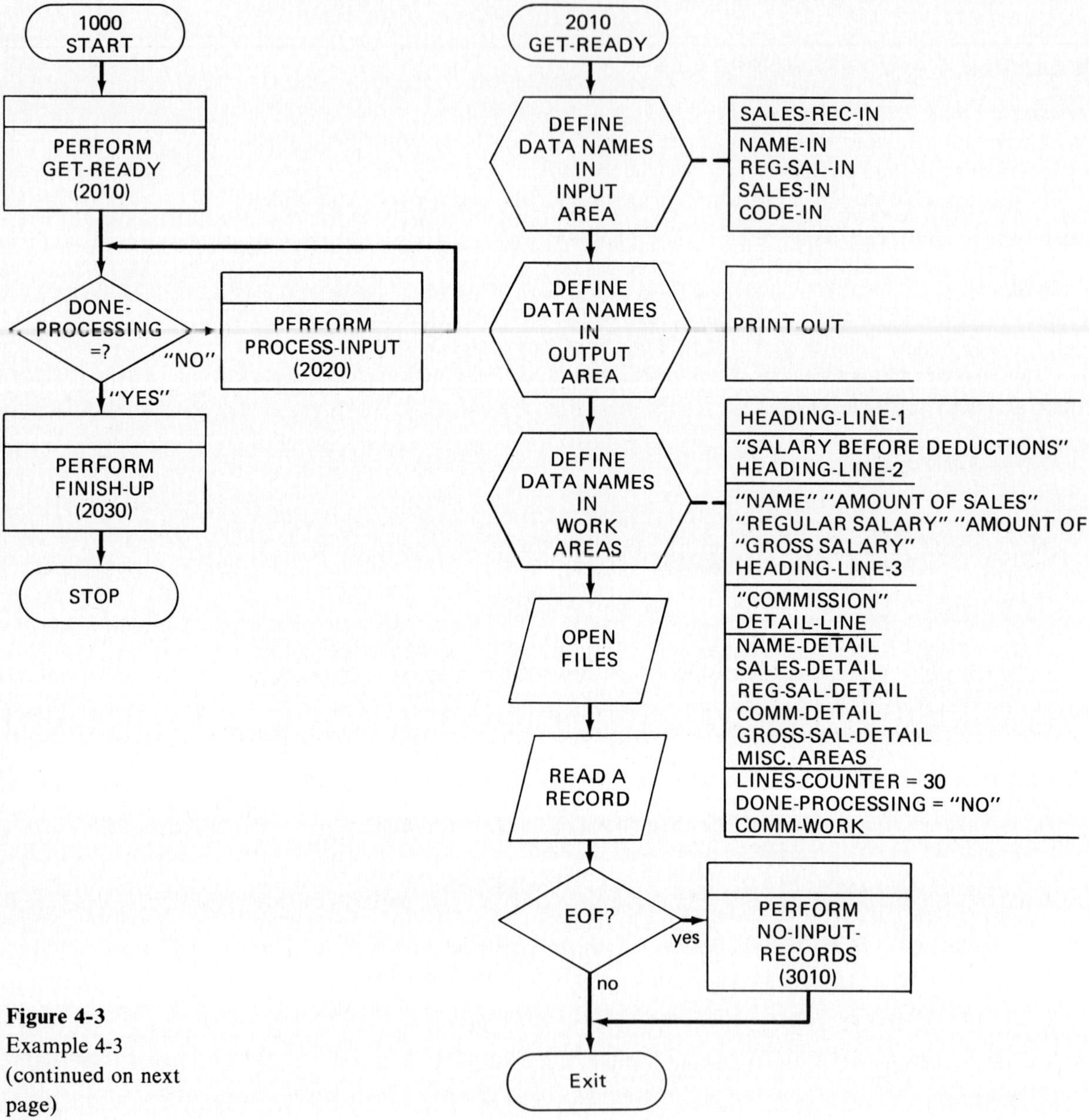

Figure 4-3
Example 4-3
(continued on next page)

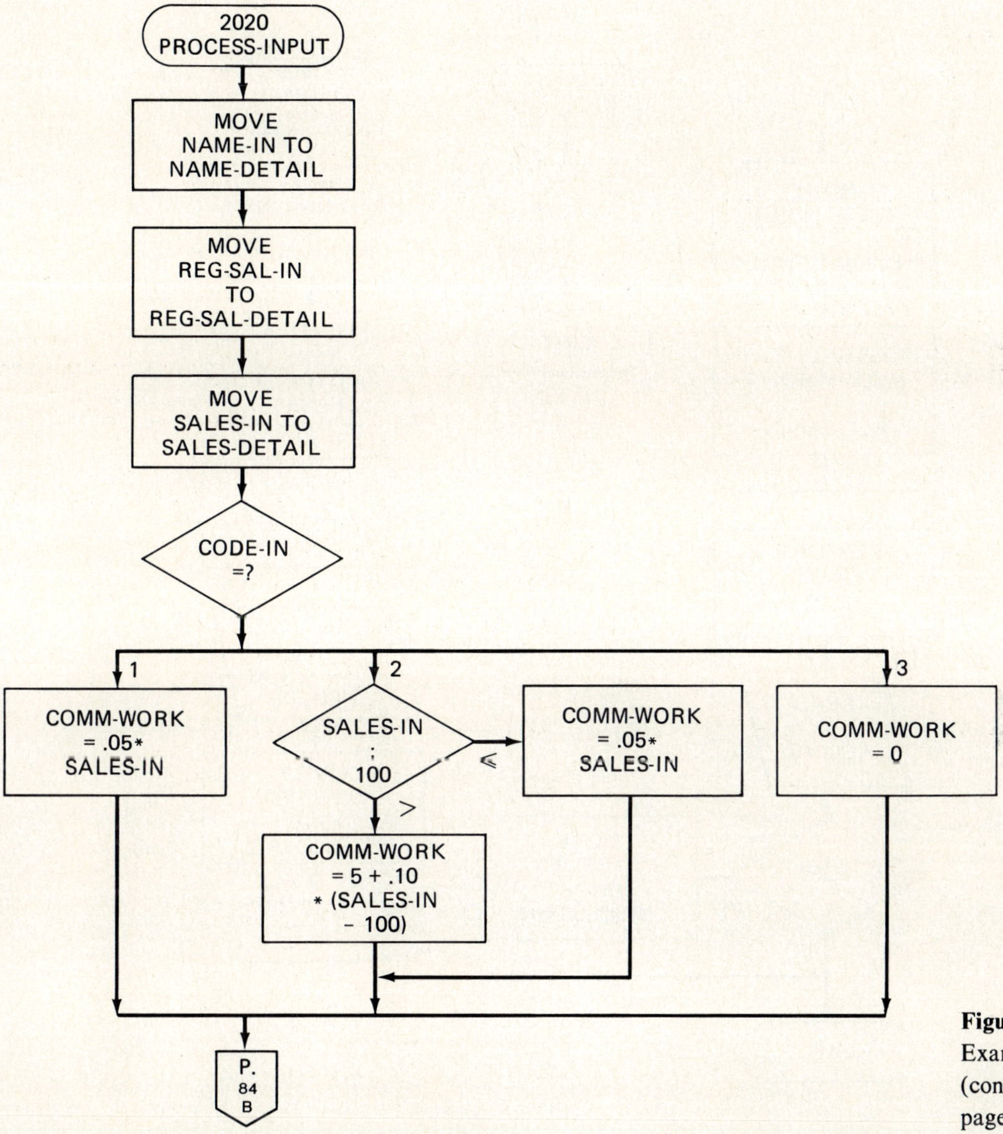

Figure 4-3
Example 4-3
(continued on next page)

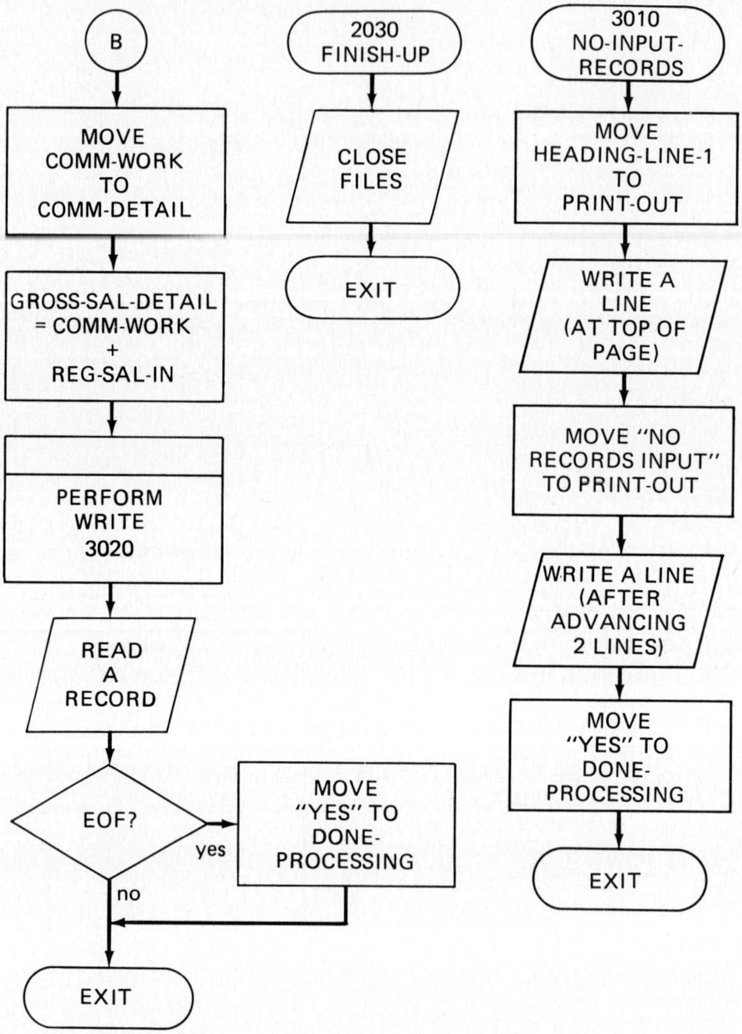

Figure 4-3
Example 4-3
(continued on next page)

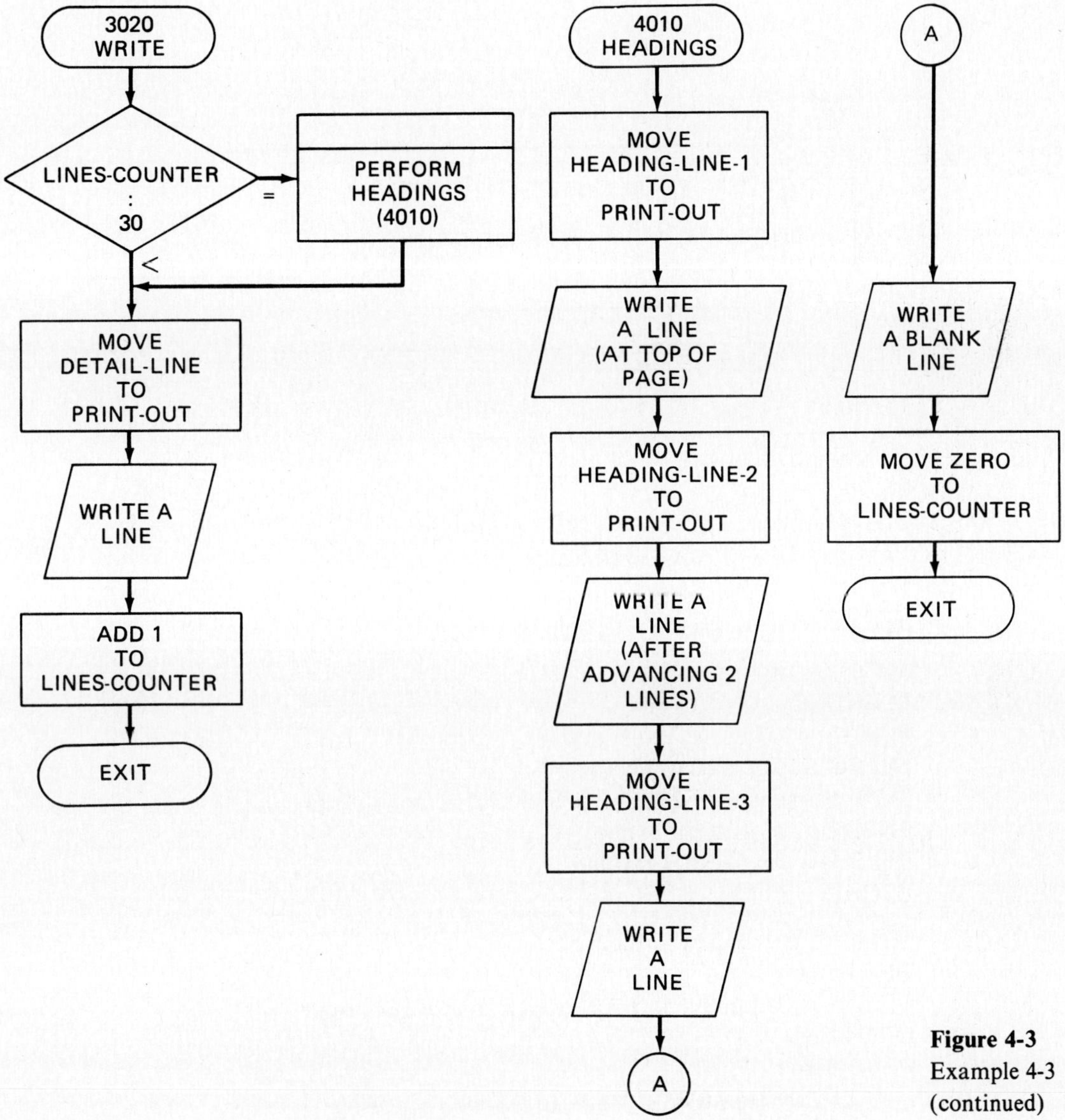

Figure 4-3
Example 4-3
(continued)

The records have been edited in a previous program to ensure a valid indicator in column 61. In addition, the records have been previously sorted by indicator (i.e., all freshmen are first, sophomores second, etc.).

The hierarchy chart for this example is:

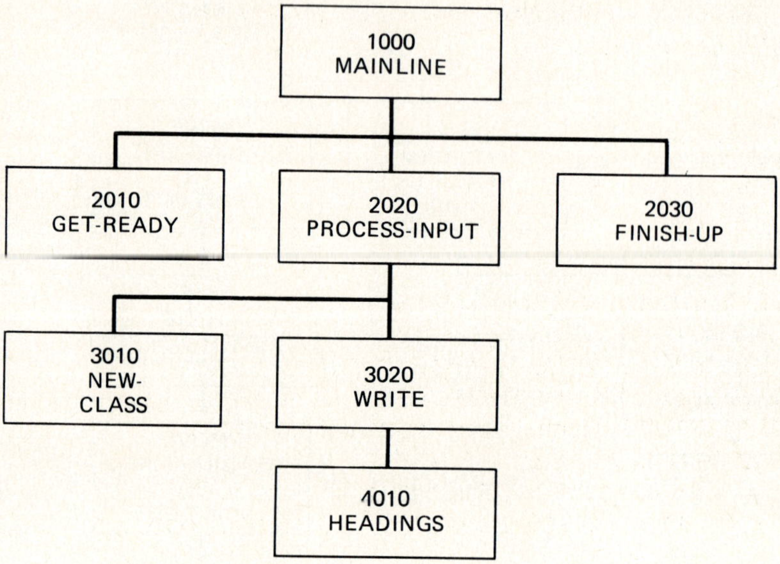

The pseudocode for this example is:

```
1000
MAINLINE
START
DO Get-Ready (2010) routine
DO Process-Input (2020) routine UNTIL Done-Processing is equal to "Yes"
ENDDO
DO Finish-Up (2030) routine
STOP

2010
GET-READY
DEFINE data names in input, output, and work areas
OPEN files
READ File-in
   ATEND of file MOVE "Yes" to Done-Processing
ENDGET-READY

2020
PROCESS-INPUT
IF Class-Ind-In is not equal to Class-Work THEN
   DO New-Class (3010) routine
```

```
ENDIF
MOVE Ssno-In to Ssno-Detail
MOVE Name-In to Name-Detail
MOVE Address-In to Address-Detail
DO Write (3020) routine
READ File-In
  ATEND of file MOVE "Yes" to Done-Processing
ENDPROCESS-INPUT

2030
FINISH-UP
CLOSE files
ENDFINISH-UP

3010
NEW-CLASS
MOVE Class-Ind-In to Class-Work
IF Class-Ind-In = 1 THEN
  MOVE "Freshmen" to Class-Heading-Out
ELSE IF Class-Ind-In = 2 THEN
          MOVE "Sophomores" to Class-Heading-Out
     ELSE IF Class-Ind-In = 3 THEN
               MOVE "Juniors" to Class-Heading-Out
          ELSE MOVE "Seniors" to Class-Heading-Out
          ENDIF
     ENDIF
ENDIF
MOVE 0 to Page-Counter
Move 35 to Lines-Counter
ENDNEW-CLASS

3020
WRITE
IF Lines-Counter = 35 THEN
  DO Headings (4010) routine
ENDIF
MOVE Detail-Line to output area
WRITE a line
ADD 1 to Lines-Counter
ENDWRITE

4010
HEADINGS
ADD 1 to Page-Counter
MOVE Page-Counter to Heading-Line-1
MOVE Heading-Line-1 to output area
WRITE a line at top of page
MOVE Heading-Line-2 to output area
```

```
WRITE a line after advancing 2 lines
WRITE a blank line
RESET Lines-Counter to 0
ENDHEADINGS
```

The flowchart for this problem is shown in Figure 4-4.

Consider the PROCESS-INPUT routine. The first decision symbol we come to asks whether CLASS-IND-IN (i.e., the 1, 2, 3, or 4 on the input record) is equal to CLASS-WORK. CLASS-WORK is the work area used to contain a class for comparison purposes. In GET-READY, CLASS-WORK is set to 0, and so for the first record input, CLASS-IND-IN is not equal to CLASS-WORK, and the NEW-CLASS routine is performed. For subsequent records on the file, NEW-CLASS is performed only at a "class break," that is, when the class code changes.

The NEW-CLASS routine saves CLASS-IND-IN in CLASS-WORK, sets up the heading line for the report, moves 0 to PAGE-COUNTER (so that the page will start again at 1), and moves 35 to LINES-COUNTER, which will force headings to be printed the next time the WRITE routine is performed.

After determining whether the NEW-CLASS routine is to be done, and performing it if necessary, the PROCESS-INPUT routine formats the detail line, writes it, and reads the next record on the file.

EXAMPLE 4-5: MULTIPLE INPUT RECORDS REQUIRED TO PRODUCE ONE OUTPUT RECORD, USING THE CURRENT DATE ON A REPORT

This example shows what to do when multiple input records from the same file are required to produce one output record or line on a report. This is a difficult program to write for beginners, so don't get discouraged!

We are asked to develop the logic to produce a weekly inventory report.

Output

Output is to consist of a weekly inventory report listing the item number and item name from the ITEM-NAME record of the input file. The date and number sold are to be printed from each NUMBER-SOLD record. Note that the item number and item name, which will be the same on each line for a particular item, are to be printed only on the first line for each item. If there are no NUMBER-SOLD records for a particular item, the message NO SALES should be printed under the NUMBER-SOLD column for that item.

A maximum of 30 detail lines are to appear per page. Heading lines are to appear as shown in the printer spacing chart below. The current date is to be included in the first heading line.

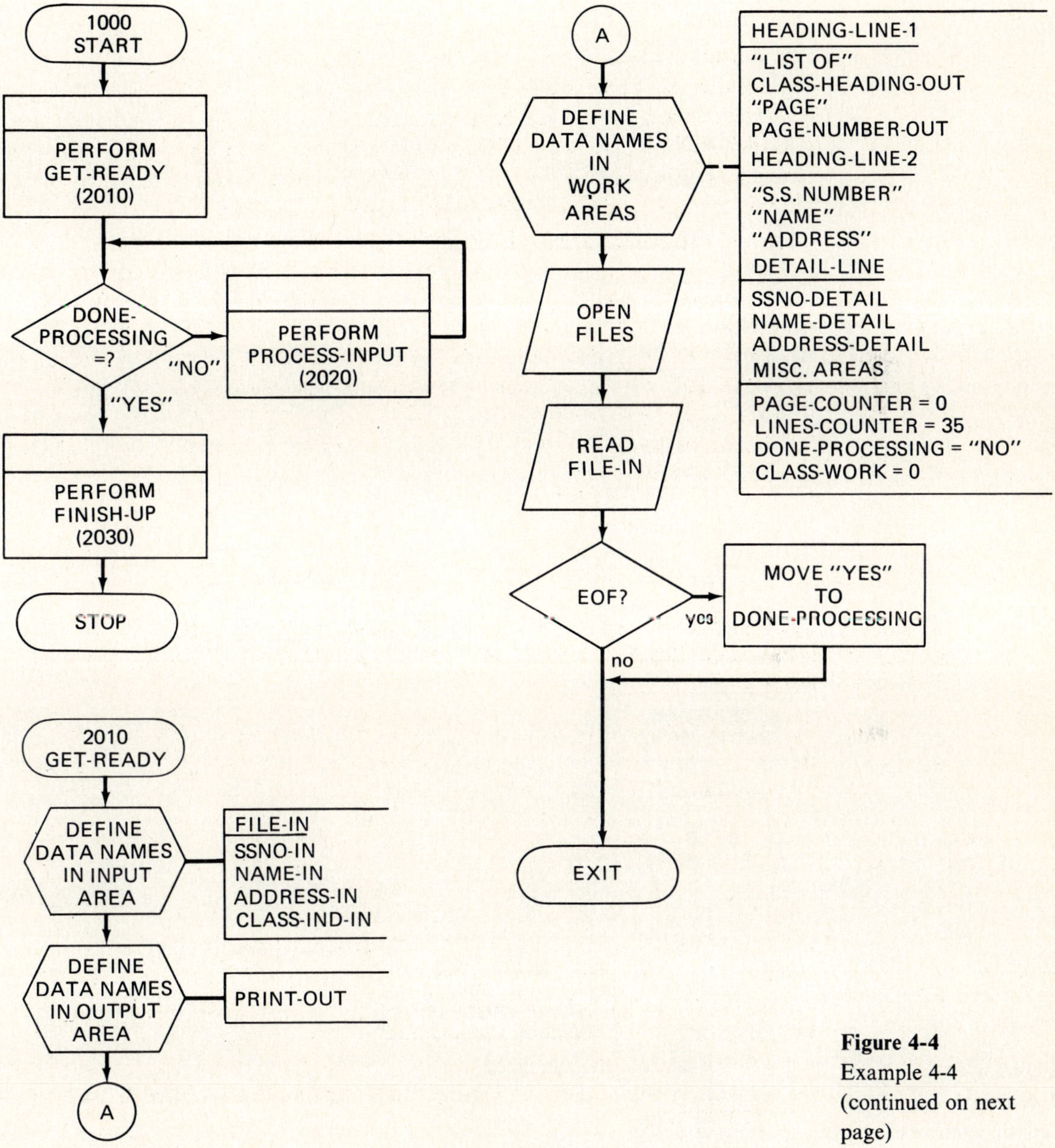

Figure 4-4
Example 4-4
(continued on next page)

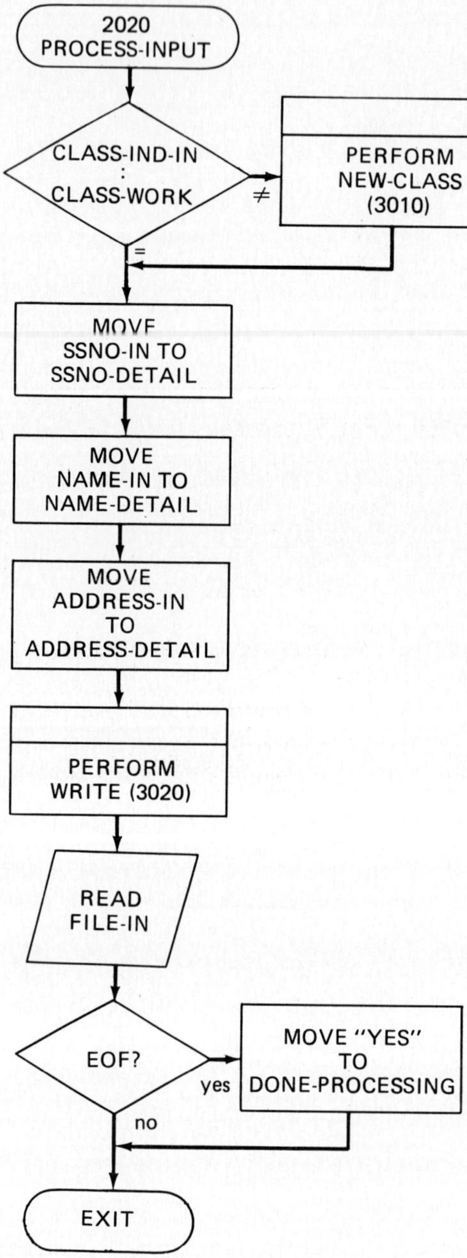

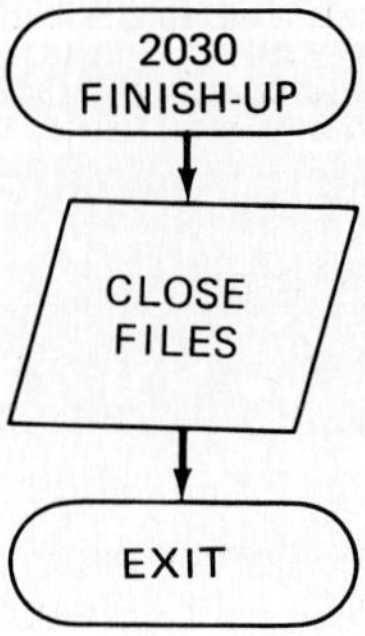

Figure 4-4
Example 4-4
(continue on next page)

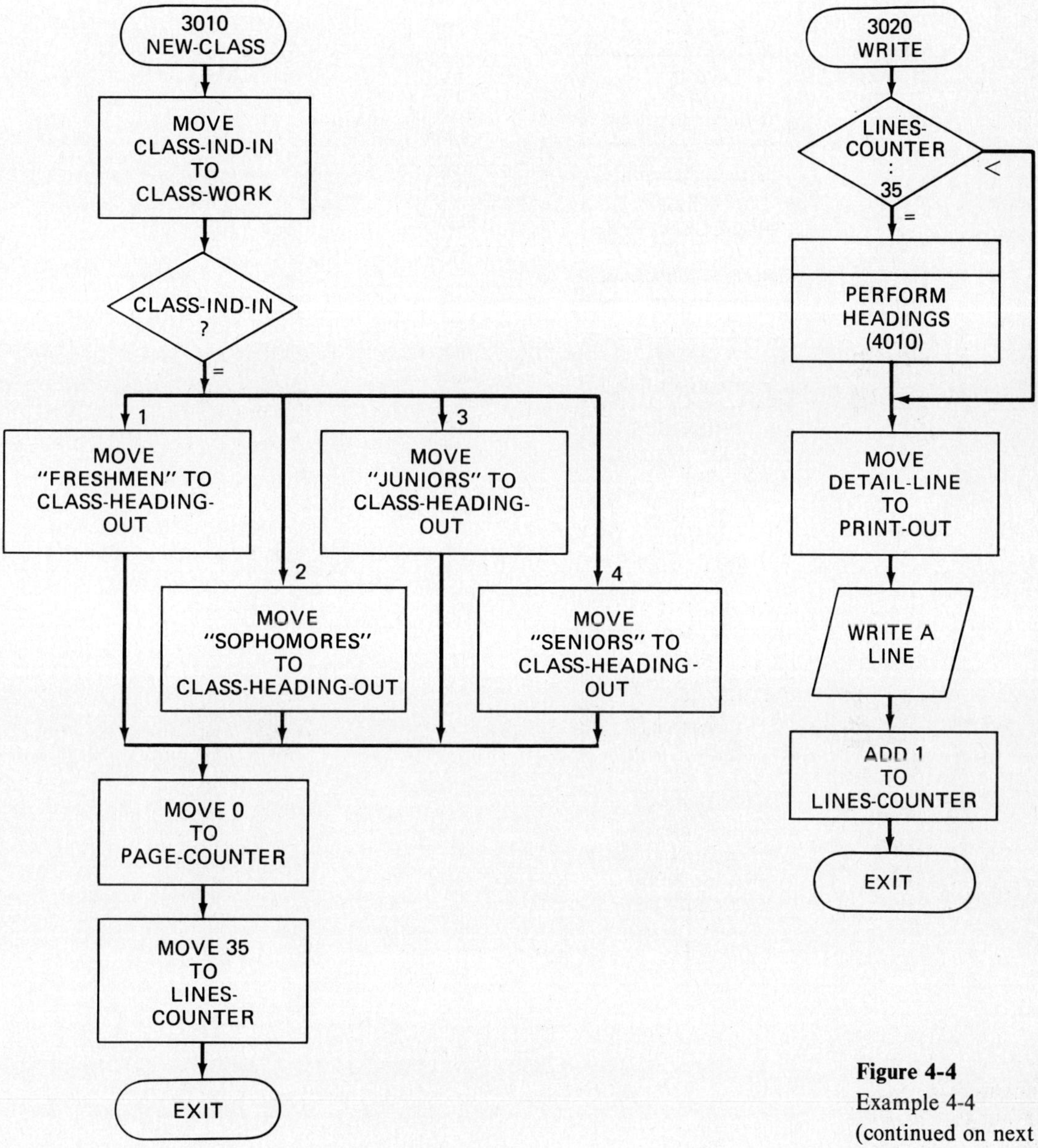

Figure 4-4
Example 4-4
(continued on next page)

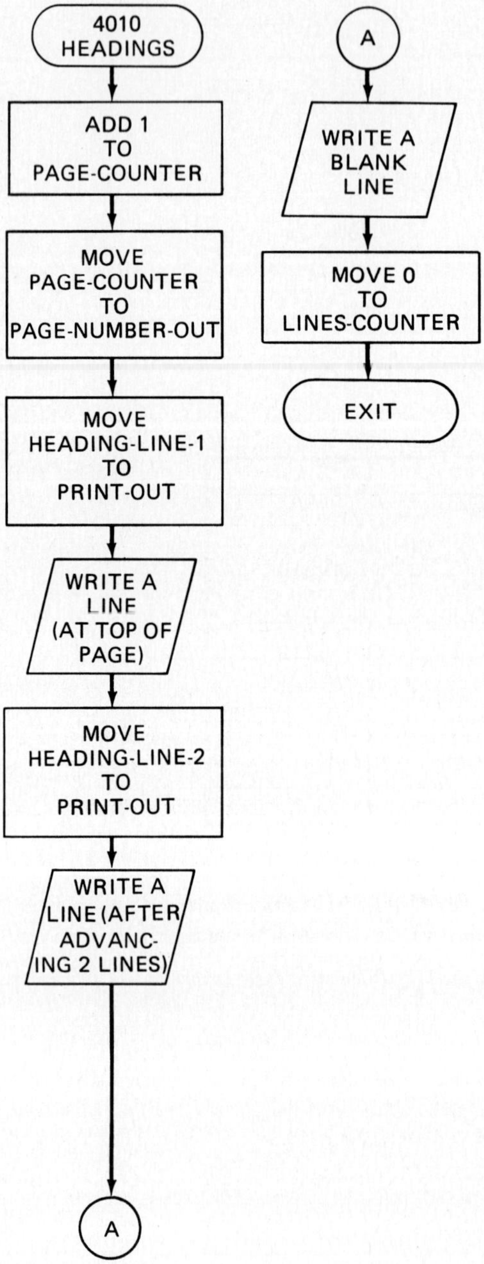

Figure 4-4
Example 4-4
(continued)

Printer Spacing Chart

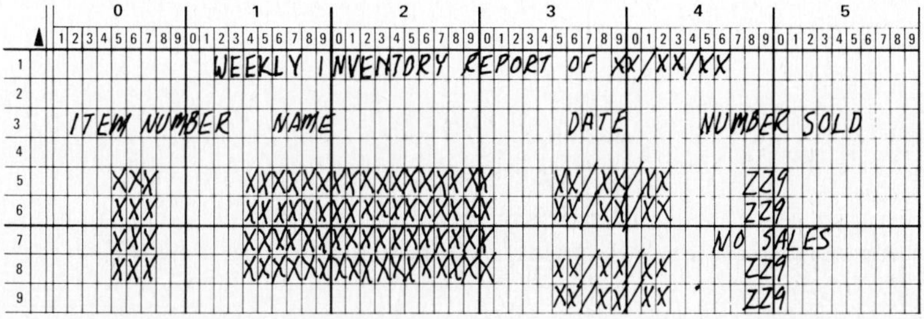

Sample Output

```
                WEEKLY INVENTORY REPORT OF 10/13/81
ITEM NUMBER      NAME                 DATE        NUMBER SOLD

    001          ITEM 1             10/12/81          100
                                    10/13/81           50
    002          ITEM 2                              NO SALES
```

Input

Input consists of two types of records for each item sold. These records are the ITEM-NAME record and the NUMBER-SOLD record. There is one ITEM-NAME record for each item stocked by the company. This record is identified by a control field of 1 in position 30. There will be zero or more NUMBER-SOLD records for each item. These records are identified by a control field of 2 in position 30. The format of the records is illustrated below.

Item Name Record		**Number Sold Record**	
Position	*Description*	*Position*	*Description*
1–3	Item number	1–3	Item number
4–20	Item name	4–9	Date (MMDDYY)
30	Code = 1	10–12	Number sold
		30	Code = 2

The input records have been sorted by a previous program by code within item number (i.e., all the NUMBER-SOLD records will follow their particular item record, and the item records are in order). In addition, the code field has been edited in a previous program to ensure that it contains a valid code.

Sample Input

```
001 ITEM 1          1
001101281100        2
```

```
001101381050        2
002ITEM 2           1
```

The hierarchy chart for this example is:

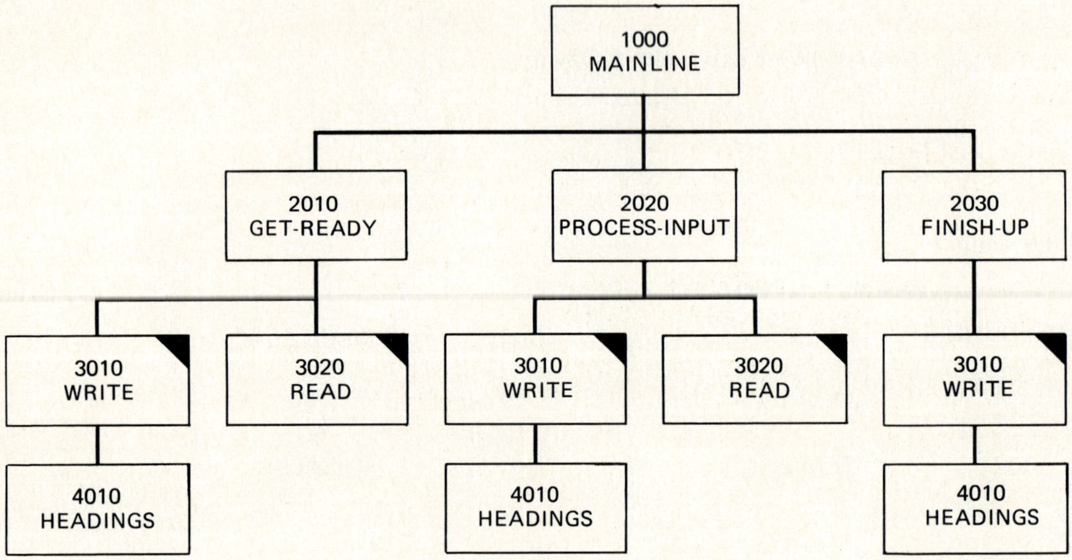

The pseudocode for this example is:

```
1000
MAINLINE
START
DO Get-Ready (2010) routine
DO Process-Input (2020) routine UNTIL Done-Processing is equal to "Yes"
ENDDO
DO Finish-Up (2030) routine
STOP

2010
GET-READY
DEFINE data names in input, output, and work areas
OPEN files
GET current date for Heading-Line-1
DO Read (3020) routine
IF Done-Processing = "Yes" THEN
   MOVE "No Records Input" to Detail-Line
   DO Write (3010) routine
ENDIF
ENDGET-READY
```

```
2020
PROCESS-INPUT
IF Code-In is not equal to 1 THEN
   MOVE MM-In to MM-Detail
   Move DD-In to DD-Detail
   MOVE YY-In to YY-Detail
   MOVE "/" to Slash-1-Detail and Slash-2-Detail
   MOVE Num-In to Num-Detail
   DO Write (3010) routine
ELSE IF Previous-Record equals 1 THEN
            MOVE "NO SALES" to No-Sales-Detail
            DO Write (3010) routine
        ENDIF
        MOVE Item-No-In to Item-No-Detail
        MOVE Item-Name-In to Item-Name-Detail
ENDIF
MOVE Code-In to Previous-Record
DO Read (3020) routine
ENDPROCESS-INPUT

2030
FINISH-UP
IF Previous-Record = 1 THEN
   MOVE "No Sales" to No-Sales-Detail
   DO Write (3010) routine
ENDIF
CLOSE files
ENDFINISH-UP

3010
WRITE
IF Lines-Counter = 30 THEN
   DO Headings (4010) routine
ENDIF
MOVE Detail-Line to output area
WRITE a line
ADD 1 to Lines-Counter
CLEAR Detail-Line
ENDWRITE

3020
READ
READ a record from File-In
   ATEND of file MOVE "Yes" to Done-Processing
ENDREAD

4010
HEADINGS
MOVE Heading-Line-1 to output area
```

WRITE a line at top of page
MOVE Heading-Line-2 to output area
WRITE a line after advancing 2 lines
WRITE a blank line
RESET Lines-Counter to 0
ENDHEADINGS

The flowchart for this example is shown in Figure 4-5.

In most computer systems, we can ask the computer to include the current date on a report or other output. The method for doing this varies from computer to computer. In the flowchart in Figure 4-5, it has simply been written as an external subroutine to get the current date. The request is included in GET-READY as a housekeeping function, because it is only necessary to get the current date one time in a program.

When the two records that can be contained on the input file are described, only one input area can be used. Remember that each file gets only one input area no matter how many records of different types the file contains. When records from the input file are read, sometimes an ITEM-NAME record will be read and sometimes a NUMBER-SOLD record will be read. The computer knows which record has been read by looking at the contents of the code field. If CODE-IN is equal to 1, then an ITEM-NAME record has been read. If CODE-IN is equal to 2, then a NUMBER-SOLD record has been read.

Whenever you get a problem like this, it is helpful to draw a diagram showing the sequence of records to be input.

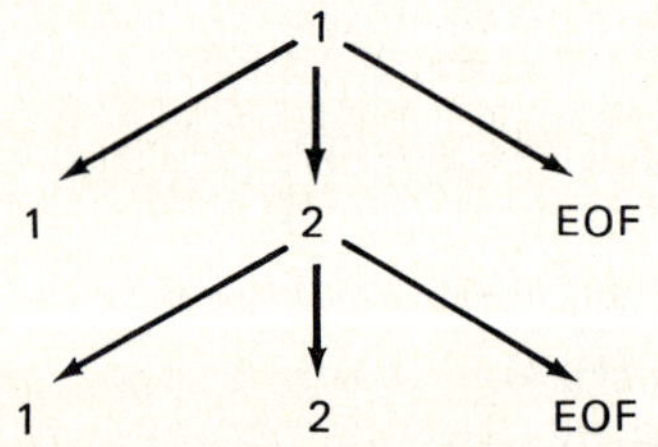

What this diagram says is that if the record we are processing has a code of 1, then the next record will be another 1, a 2, or EOF. If the record we are processing is a 2, then the next record will be a 1, another 2, or EOF. When you draw a flowchart, all these possibilities need to be taken into account.

If the code is a 1, we need to move the item number and item name to the detail line. If the code is a 2, we move the date and the number sold to the detail line. Note that on the input, the date is in the format MMDDYY, and on the output, we want to insert slashes between the month and day and between the day and year. The only way to do this is to move the month, day, and year separately, inserting the slashes as constants during PROCESS-INPUT.

The WRITE routine is normally performed only after processing a record with a code of 2. How do we determine, then, when we want to write NO SALES? Remember that a NO SALES condition results when an ITEM-NAME record (a code of

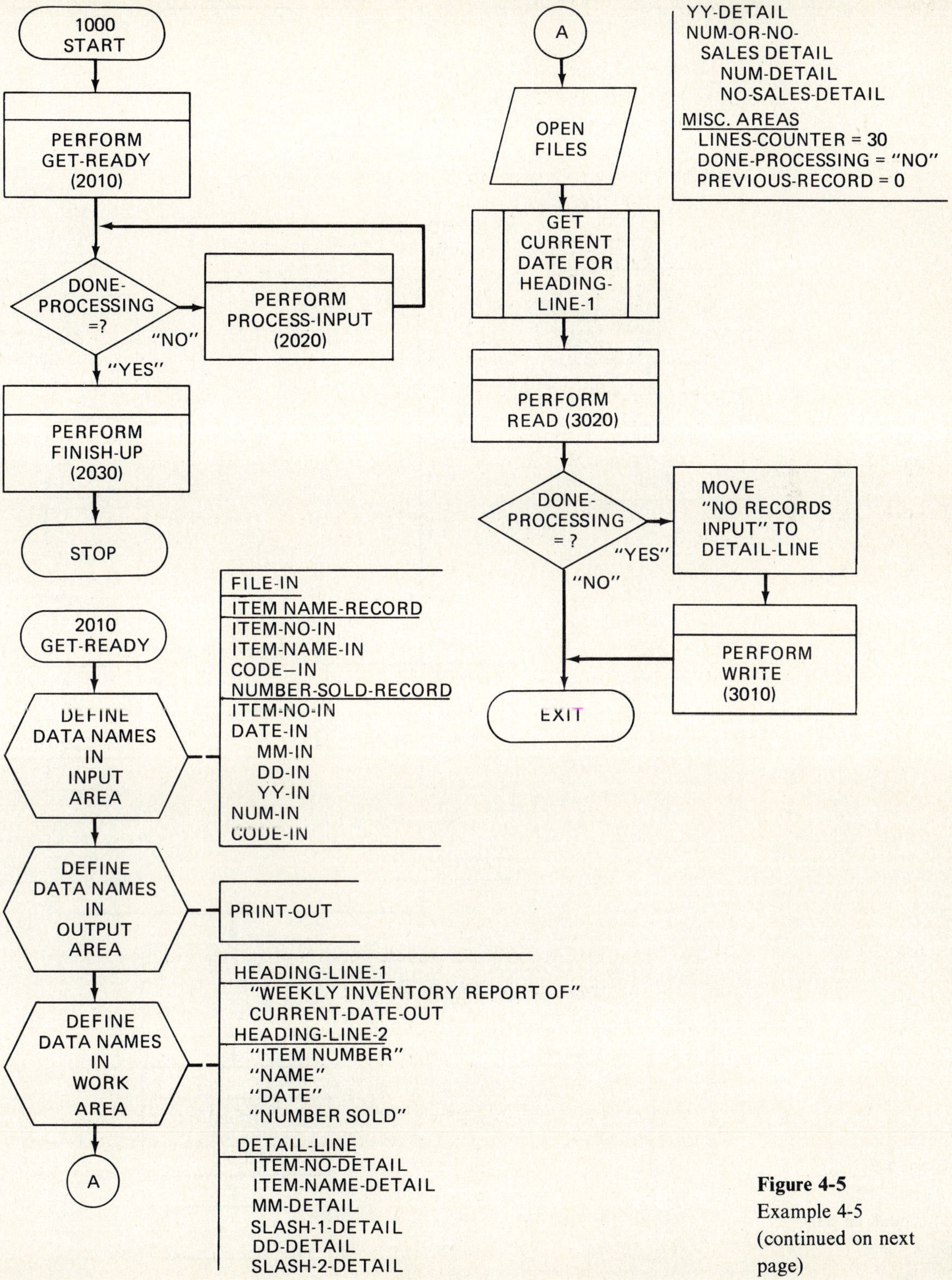

Figure 4-5
Example 4-5
(continued on next page)

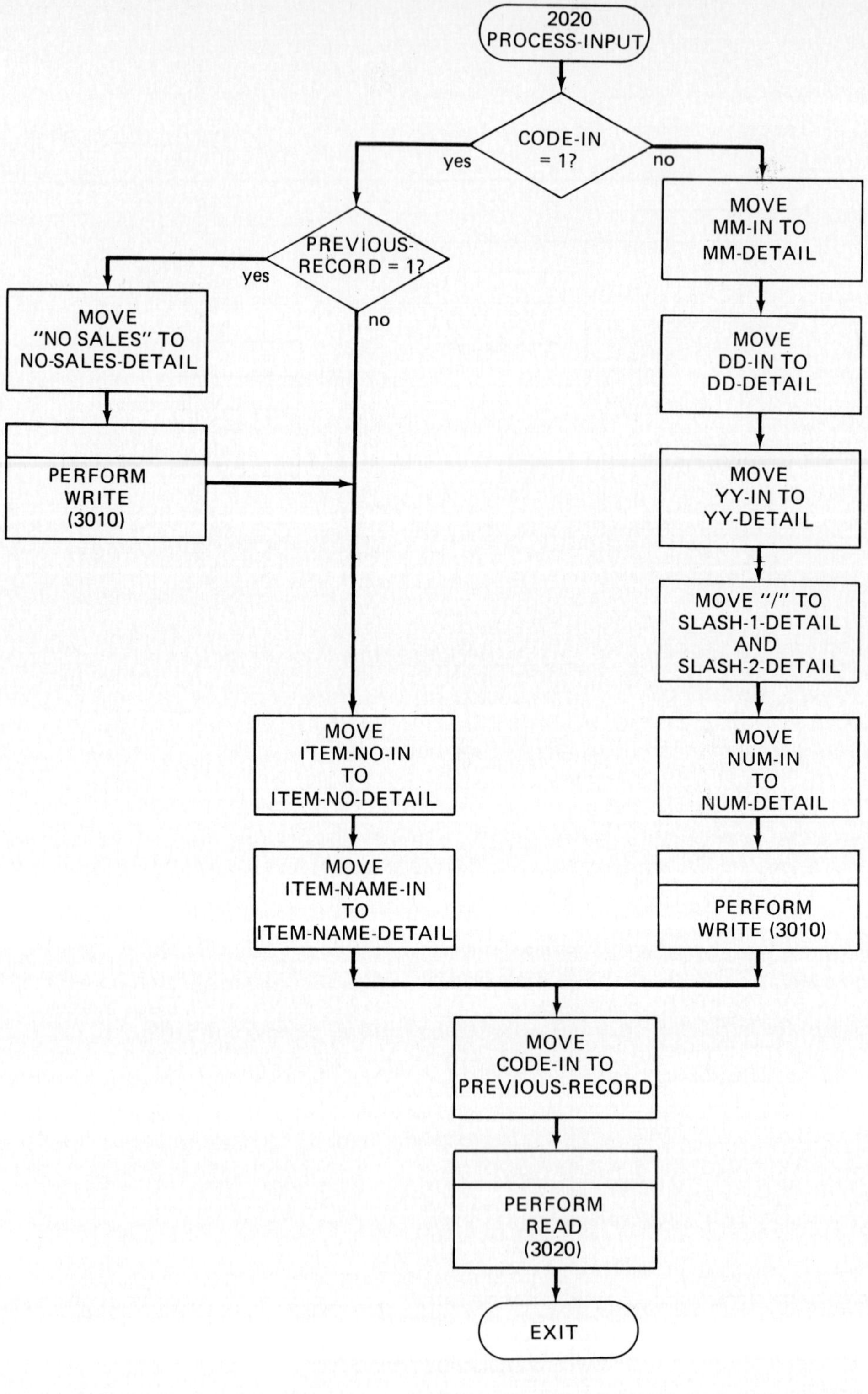

Figure 4-5
Example 4-5
(continued on next page)

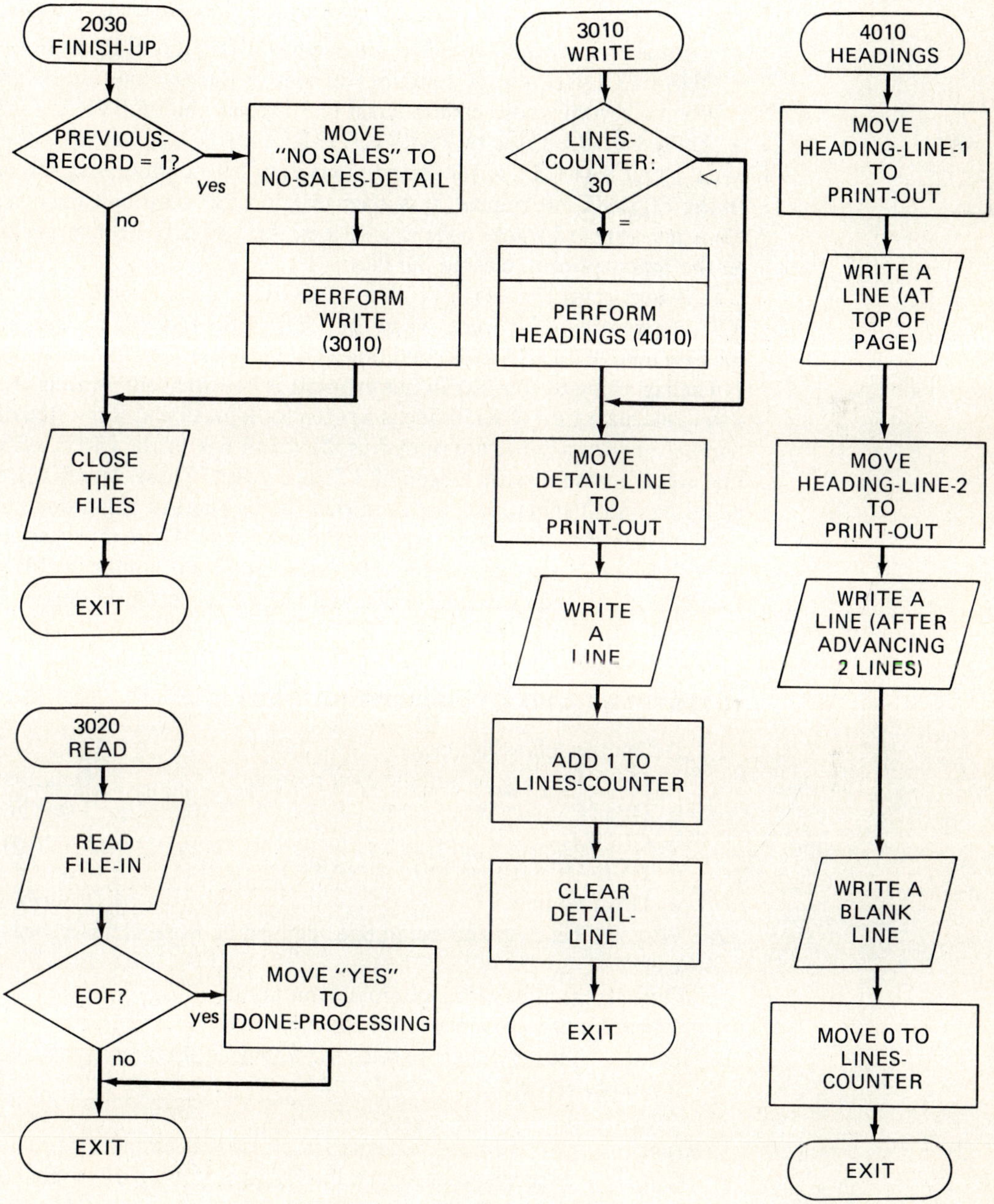

Figure 4-5
Example 4-5
(continued)

1) is not followed by a NUMBER-SOLD record (a code of 2), that is, it is followed by another ITEM-NAME record or EOF. Only one record can be in the input area at any given time, so how can we determine what the next record on the file will be? This is done by using a field in the work area called PREVIOUS-RECORD. After a record is processed, CODE-IN is moved to PREVIOUS-RECORD, and so PREVIOUS-RECORD always contains the code of the previous record processed.

When a record whose code is equal to 1 is read, the PREVIOUS-RECORD field is checked. If the value of PREVIOUS-RECORD is equal to 1, then we want to write a NO SALES line for the previous item before processing the current record. In the FINISH-UP routine, it is necessary to make sure that the last record on the file is not a record whose code is 1. If it is, the NO SALES line needs to be written on the report prior to closing the files.

It is important that PREVIOUS-RECORD not be set equal to 1 in the GET-READY routine. If it were, when the PROCESS-INPUT routine was entered for the first time, a NO SALES condition would result, which in fact would be incorrect.

The last thing to consider in this example is how to avoid printing the item number and name each time a detail line is written for a particular item. Recall that the item number and item name are moved to the detail line in the PROCESS-INPUT routine when a record with a code of 1 is processed. These values will remain in the detail line until something else is moved there. The last thing done in the WRITE routine is clearing or moving spaces to the detail line. Then, if we get multiple records with codes of 2 in sequence, the item name and item number fields will have been "wiped out" by the clear instruction and will not print on the report.

QUESTIONS AND EXERCISES FOR REVIEW

1. Define the following terms:
   a. Housekeeping or initialization routine
   b. OPEN
   c. CLOSE
   d. END-OF-JOB or TERMINATION routine
   e. Heading line
   f. Detail line
   g. Total line
   h. External subroutine
   i. Control code
   j. Control break
2. Why are heading and detail lines defined as work areas rather than as output areas?
3. Give an example of an external subroutine.
4. Construct the pseudocode for Example 4-3.
5. Draw a hierarchy chart to solve the following problem. We want to produce an inventory report.

   Output

   Output is to consist of a report. Each line of the report should contain the item number, item name, quantity at start of period, and quantity at end of period. Each page of the report is to contain at most 30 detail lines. Headings are to be included and are to contain the page number.

Printer Spacing Chart

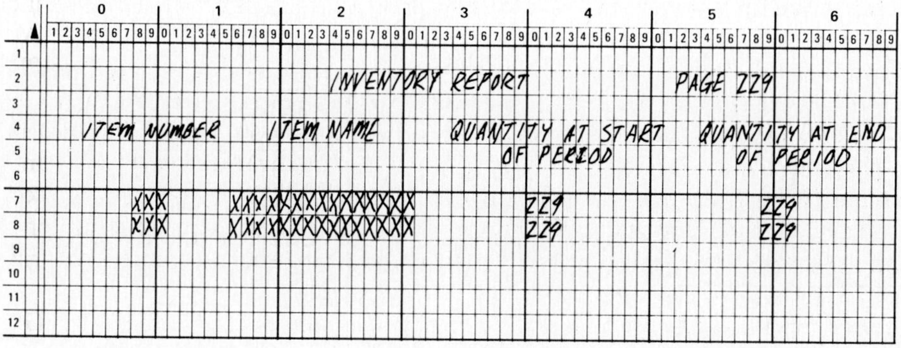

Sample Output

```
                              INVENTORY REPORT              PAGE   1

ITEM NUMBER      ITEM NAME        QUANTITYAT START    QUANTITY AT END
                                     OF PERIOD            OF PERIOD

    527       WIDGETS-TYPE-1            36                   27
    100       WIDGETS-TYPE-2           100                   48
```

Input

Input consists of records containing item number, item name, quantity at start of period, and quantity used.

Calculation

Quantity at end of period = quantity at start of period − quantity used

6. Construct the pseudocode for Exercise 5 above.
7. Draw a flowchart for Exercise 5 above.
8. Figure 4-6 shows a structured flowchart to illustrate the logic required to produce bills for a doctor. You are to make the following changes to the flowchart:
   a. Start a new page whenever a patient break (new patient number) occurs. When starting a new patient, reset the page number to 1.
   b. Include the current date on the report. The current date is to be taken from the system.
   c. Include an error to be printed on the report if upon reading the first record from the input file, you determine that there are no records on the file.

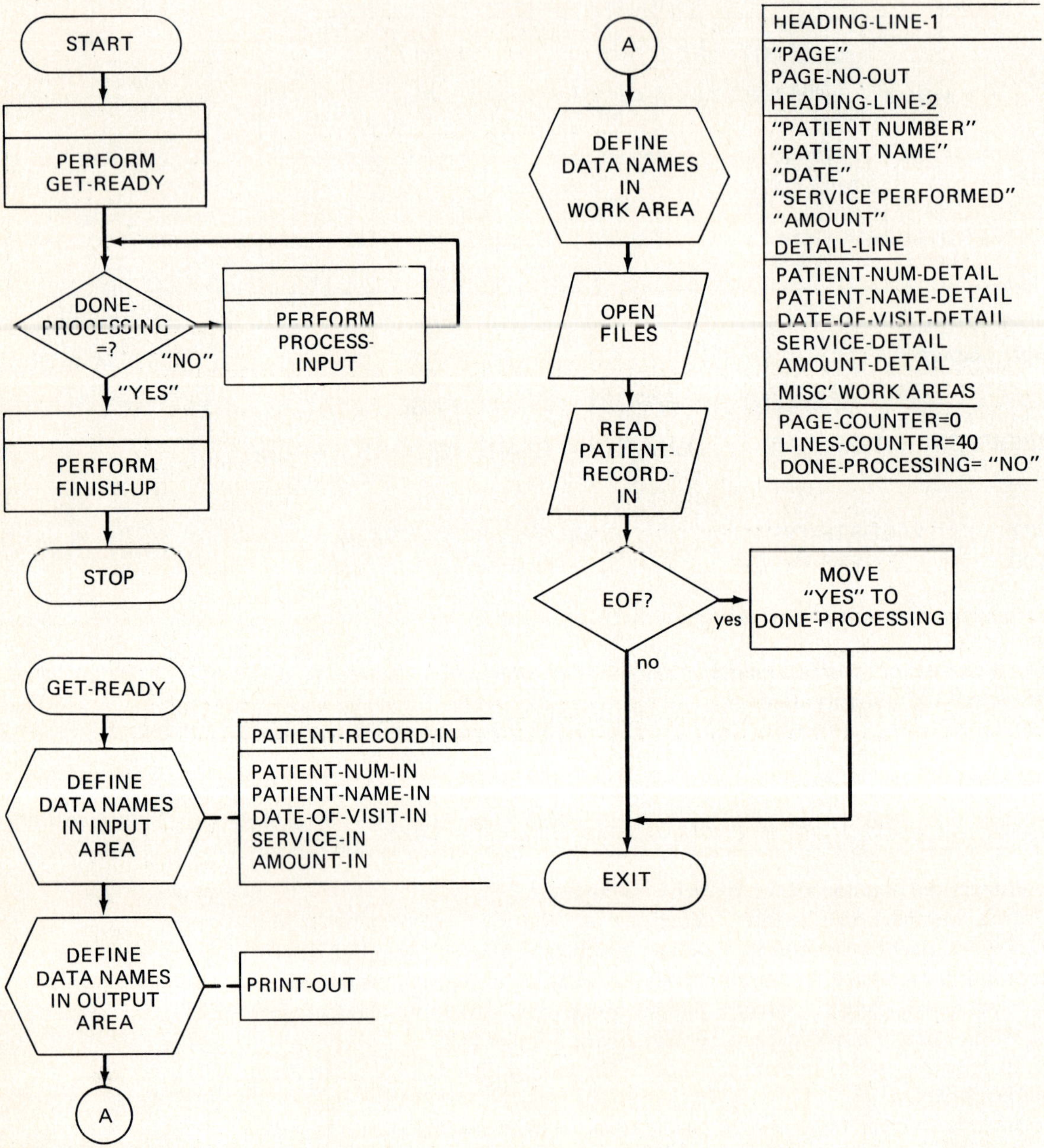

Figure 4-6
Exercise 8 (continued on next page)

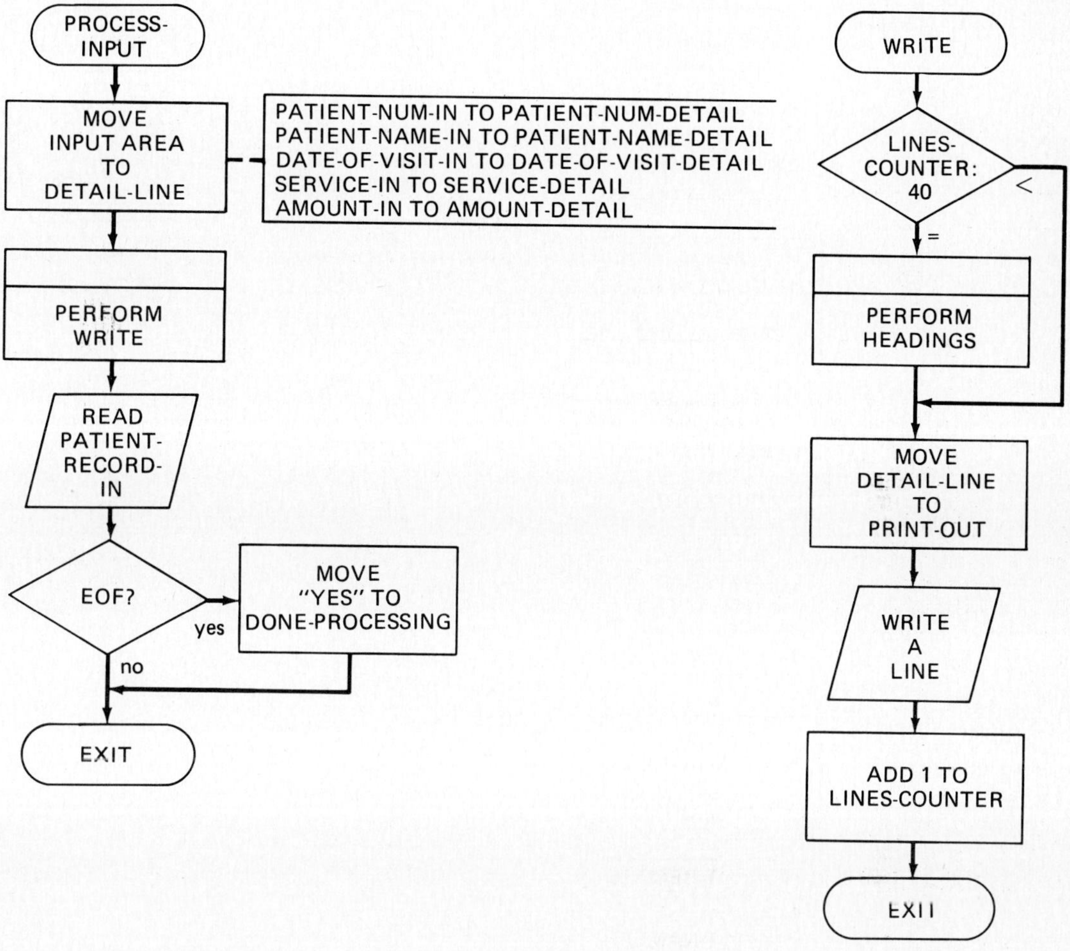

Figure 4-6
Exercise 8 (continued on next page)

d. The headings on the report are to be as shown on the printer spacing chart below:

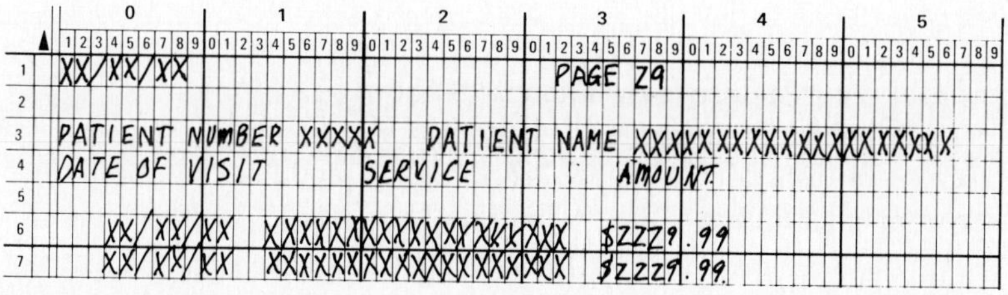

e. The detail line should show the date of visit, service, and amount.

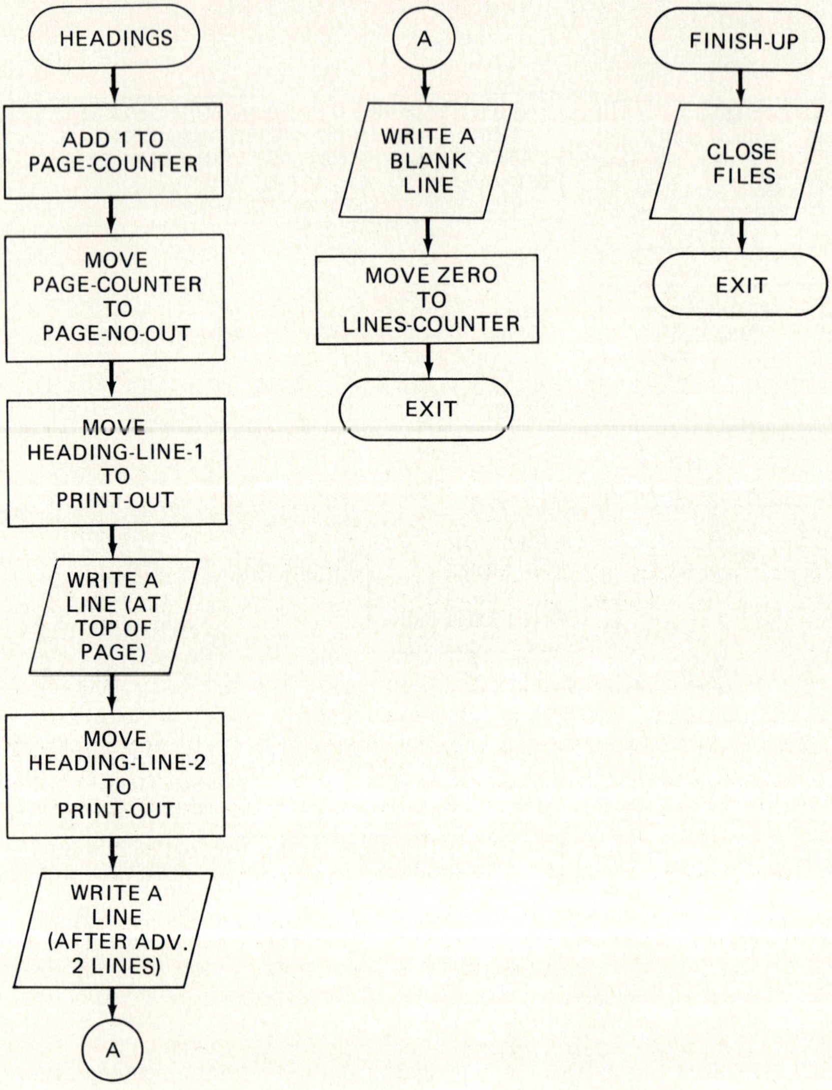

Figure 4-6
Exercise 8
(continued)

9. Construct the pseudocode for Exercise 8 above.
10. Draw a flowchart to illustrate the logic required to produce a tape file showing lab results of tests done on animals for various products that a pharmaceutical company manufactures.

Output

Output is to consist of a tape file. Each output record is to contain the product number and name from the PRODUCT record, the test number and name from the TEST record, and the animal number, date, and result from the ANI-

MAL record. If there is no ANIMAL record for a particular test, no record is to be written on the tape.

Output Format

Position	*Description*
1–4	Product number
5–26	Product name
27–29	Test number
30–51	Test name
52–55	Animal number
56–61	Date performed
62–93	Result

Input

Input is to consist of three types of records:

PRODUCT records showing the product being tested,
TEST records showing the test performed, and
ANIMAL records showing the result of the test.

There is one PRODUCT record for each product. This record is identified by having a code of 1 in position 1 of the record.

There is one TEST record for each lab test performed and at least one TEST record for each product. That means that you don't have to worry about having a PRODUCT record with no TEST records associated with it. The TEST records are identified by having a code of 2 in position 1 of the record.

There will be zero or more ANIMAL records for each test. These records are identified by having a code of 3 in position 1 of the record.

The format of the records is illustrated below. They are in correct sorted order and have been previously edited for correct codes.

Product Records

Position	*Description*
1	"1"
2–5	Product number
6–8	"000" for sorting purposes only
9–30	Product name

Test Records

Position	*Description*
1	"2"
2–5	Product number
6–8	Test number
9–30	Test name

Animal Records

Position	*Description*
1	"3"
2–5	Product number
6–8	Test number
9–12	Animal number
13–18	Date performed
19–50	Result

Sample Input

```
11010000Hyperprinium
21010001Urinalysis
21010050Blood Pressure
3101005000011101282Normal
3101005000021101282High
3101005000031101282Normal
11050000Meko Tablets
21050200White Count
```

11. Draw a hierarchy chart for Exercise 10 above.
12. Construct the pseudocode for Exercise 10 above.
13. Use the input file from Exercise 10 above. Draw a flowchart which will produce a report as output instead of a tape file.

    Each page of the report is to contain at most 40 detail lines. A new page is to be started for each new product. The product number, name, and page are to be included in the headings. Page numbers are to start again at 1 for each new product. The report is to list the test number and test name from the TEST record. The animal number, date performed, and result are to be printed for each of the ANIMAL records. If there is no ANIMAL record for a particular test, the message NO ANIMALS TESTED should be printed adjacent to the test number and name. The test number and name are printed on the first line only for a particular test.

Printer Spacing Chart

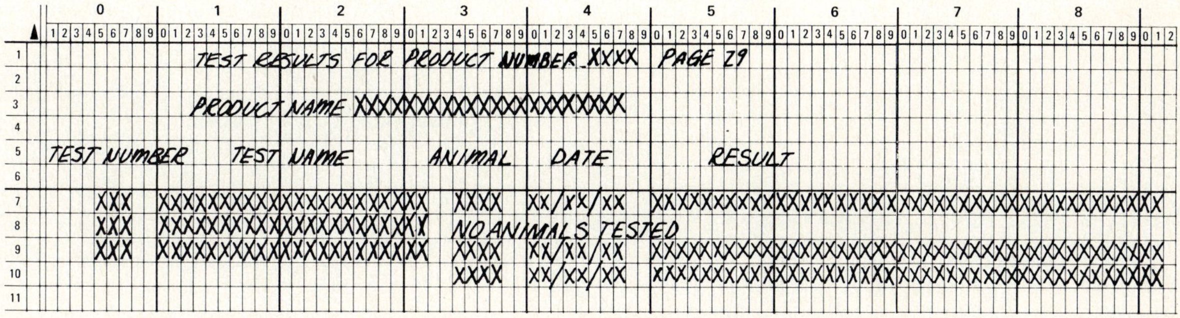

Sample Output

TEST RESULTS FOR PRODUCT NUMBER 1010 PAGE 1
PRODUCT NAME HYPERPRINIUM

TEST NUMBER	TEST NAME	ANIMAL	DATE	RESULT
001	URINALYSIS	NO ANIMALS TESTED		NORMAL
050	BLOOD PRESSURE	001	10/12/82	HIGH
		002	10/12/82	NORMAL
		003	10/12/82	

TEST RESULTS FOR PRODUCT NUMBER 1050 PAGE 1
PRODUCT NAME MEKO TABLETS

TEST NUMBER	TEST NAME	ANIMAL	DATE	RESULT
200	WHITE COUNT	NO ANIMALS TESTED		

14. Draw a hierarchy chart for Exercise 13 above.
15. Construct the pseudocode for Exercise 13 above.

CHAPTER 5

Programs that Include Totals

EXAMPLE 5-1: SINGLE-LEVEL TOTALS

In many cases it is desirable to include summary information in the form of totals on a report. Example 5-1 shows that including a final total on a report is a simple extension of what was done in the previous chapter.

We are to produce a report for the owner of a beauty salon. In this salon the operators are paid by the amount and type of work that they do. The shampoo operators receive $4.00 per customer, the hair cutters receive $5.50 per customer, the hair setters receive $6.00 per customer, the stylists receive $8.00 per customer, and the permanent-wave operators receive $10.00 per customer.

Output

Output is to consist of a report. A final total is to be shown for gross pay, where the gross pay for each operator is equal to the number of customers times pay per customer. A maximum of 50 detail lines are to appear per page. Page numbers are to be included. One blank line is to be included on the report before the total is printed.

Printer Spacing Chart

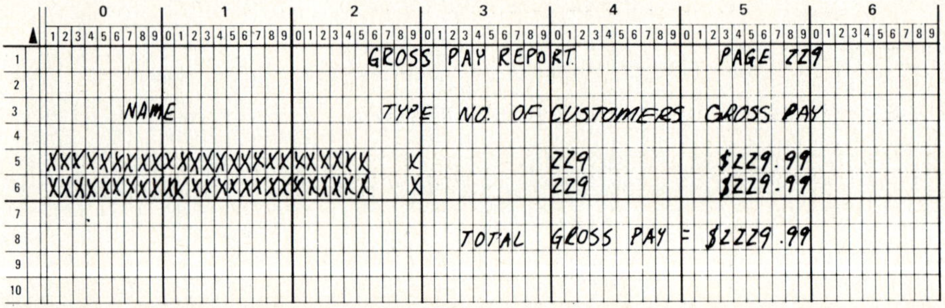

Sample Output

GROSS PAY REPORT PAGE 1

NAME	TYPE	NO. OF CUSTOMERS	GROSS PAY
SUSAN CALDWELL	1	100	$400.00
BETTY JANE CLANCY	1	120	$480.00
RUTH ANN CORBETT	1	150	$600.00
MARGARET CUSHING	2	100	$550.00

TOTAL GROSS PAY = $2030.00

Input

Input consists of records with the following format:

Position	*Description*
1–25	Name of operator
26	Type of operator (1 = shampoo, 2 = hair cutter, 3 = hair setter, 4 = stylist, 5 = permanent-wave operator)
27–29	Number of customers

The hierarchy chart for this example is:

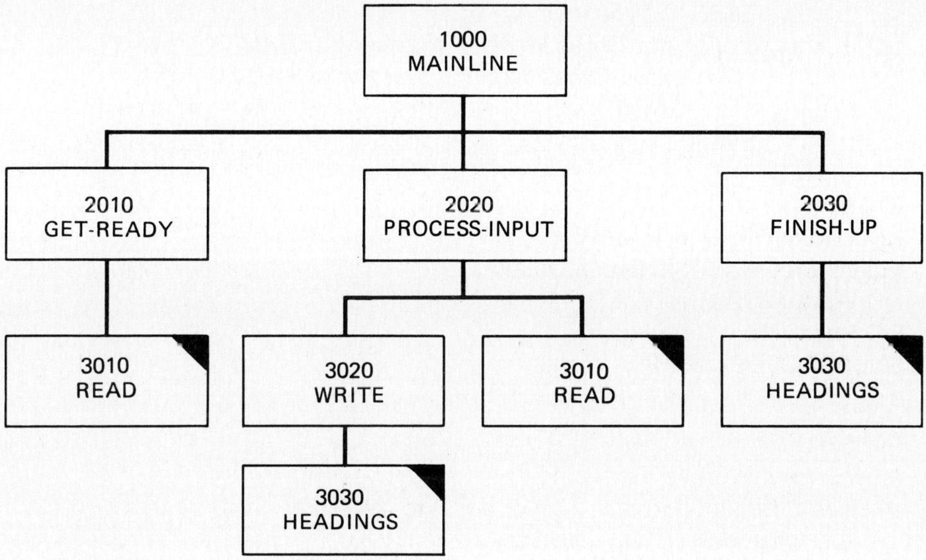

The pseudocode for this example is:

```
1000
MAINLINE
START
DO Get-Ready (2010) routine
DO Process-Input (2020) routine UNTIL Done-Processing is equal to "Yes"
ENDDO
DO Finish-Up (2030) routine
STOP
```

```
2010
GET-READY
DEFINE data names in input, output, and work areas
OPEN files
DO Read (3010) routine
ENDGET-READY

2020
PROCESS-INPUT
MOVE Name-In to Name-Detail
MOVE Type-In to Type-Detail
MOVE Number-In to Number-Detail
IF Type-In = 1 THEN
    Gross-Work = Number-In * 4.00
ELSE IF Type-In = 2 THEN
         Gross-Work = Number-In * 5.50
     ELSE IF Type-In = 3 THEN
              Gross-Work = Number-In * 6.00
          ELSE IF Type-In = 4 THEN
                   Gross-Work = Number-In * 8.00
               ELSE Gross-Work = Number-In * 10.00
               ENDIF
          ENDIF
     ENDIF
ENDIF
ADD Gross-Work to Total-Work
MOVE Gross-Work to Gross-Detail
DO Write (3020) routine
DO Read (3010) routine
ENDPROCESS-INPUT

2030
FINISH-UP
MOVE Total-Work to Total-Line
IF Lines-Counter is greater than or equal to 49 THEN
    DO Headings (3030) routine
ENDIF
MOVE Total-Line to output area
WRITE a line after advancing 2 lines
CLOSE files
ENDFINISH-UP

3010
READ
READ a record from Beauty-Salon-File-In
  AT END of file MOVE "Yes" to Done-Processing
ENDREAD
```

```
3020
WRITE
IF Lines-Counter = 50 THEN
   DO Headings (3030) routine
ENDIF
MOVE Detail-Line to output area
WRITE a line
ADD 1 to Lines-Counter
ENDWRITE

3030
HEADINGS
ADD 1 to Page-Counter
MOVE Page-Counter to Heading-Line-1
MOVE Heading-Line-1 to output area
WRITE a line at top of page
MOVE Heading-Line-2 to output area
WRITE a line after advancing 2 lines
WRITE a blank line
RESET Lines-Counter to 0
ENDHEADINGS
```

Drawing the flowchart is left as an exercise for the reader.

If totals are to be printed, a total line must be included on the report. TOTAL-LINE is defined as a work area when areas are defined in GET-READY. TOTAL-LINE is printed in the FINISH-UP routine after the entire input file is processed.

We need to accumulate the total as we process each input record. This is done by setting up a work area called TOTAL-WORK. TOTAL-WORK is given an initial value of zero. Then, as each record is processed, the gross amount calculated in the PROCESS-INPUT routine is added to TOTAL-WORK.

Note that in the FINISH-UP routine, the lines counter is checked before the total is printed. This makes it possible for the last page of the report to contain only one line—the total line. When this happens, it is usually desirable to include the total line on the previous page of the report if you are using paper that has enough room on the page to do this. This is accomplished by excluding the check of the lines counter in the FINISH-UP routine and simply writing the total line on the current page without considering the number of lines already written on the page.

EXAMPLE 5-2: SINGLE-LEVEL TOTALS WITH CONTROL BREAKS

Often it is desirable to print totals every time a control break occurs. In this example we will use the input file described in Example 5-1. The owner of the beauty salon has decided that she wants to know the total amount paid to each type of operator so that total costs and profits of the salon can be analyzed.

Assume that the input file has previously been sorted by type (i.e., all records with type 1 first, records with type 2 second, etc.). We want to modify the output of Example 5-1 to show the type in the heading line rather than in the detail line (see the printer spacing chart below). In addition, each type is to start on a new page and have its own total.

Printer Spacing Chart

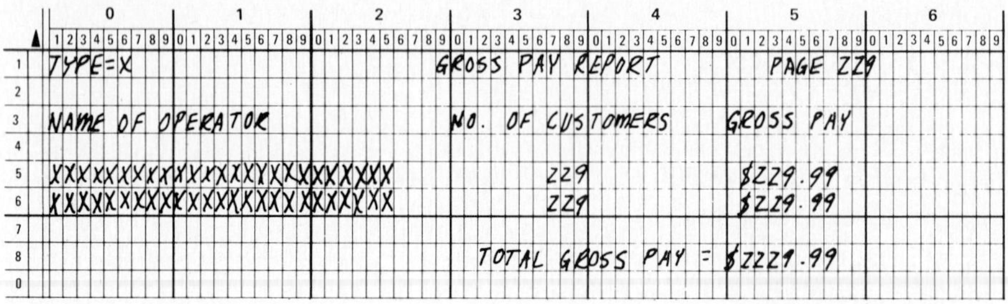

Sample Output

TYPE = 1	GROSS PAY REPORT	PAGE 1
NAME OF OPERATOR	NO. OF CUSTOMERS	GROSS PAY
SUSAN CALDWELL	100	$400.00
BETTY JANE CLANCY	120	$480.00
RUTH ANN CORBETT	150	$600.00
	TOTAL GROSS PAY =	$1480.00

When doing a program that requires totals at a control break, you have to be able to recognize when a control break occurs (review Chapter 4). When such a break occurs, you need to:

1. Print the totals for the current control field.
2. Reset the total work areas to zero so that you will start over for the new value of the control field.
3. Update the control field hold areas with the new control field value.
4. Update, if necessary, any other hold (work) areas (e.g., page number, heading lines, etc.).

When the first input record is read, the control field of the input record will not be equal to the control field hold area. Normally, this "not equal" condition would result in a control break. In Chapter 4 we performed the control break routine both when the control field changed and for the first record on the input file. In this example, however, we are printing totals at the break, and it is neither necessary nor desirable to print totals when processing the first input record.

There are two methods for handling the above "problem." The first method, as illustrated in Figure 5-1, involves updating the control field hold area with the con-

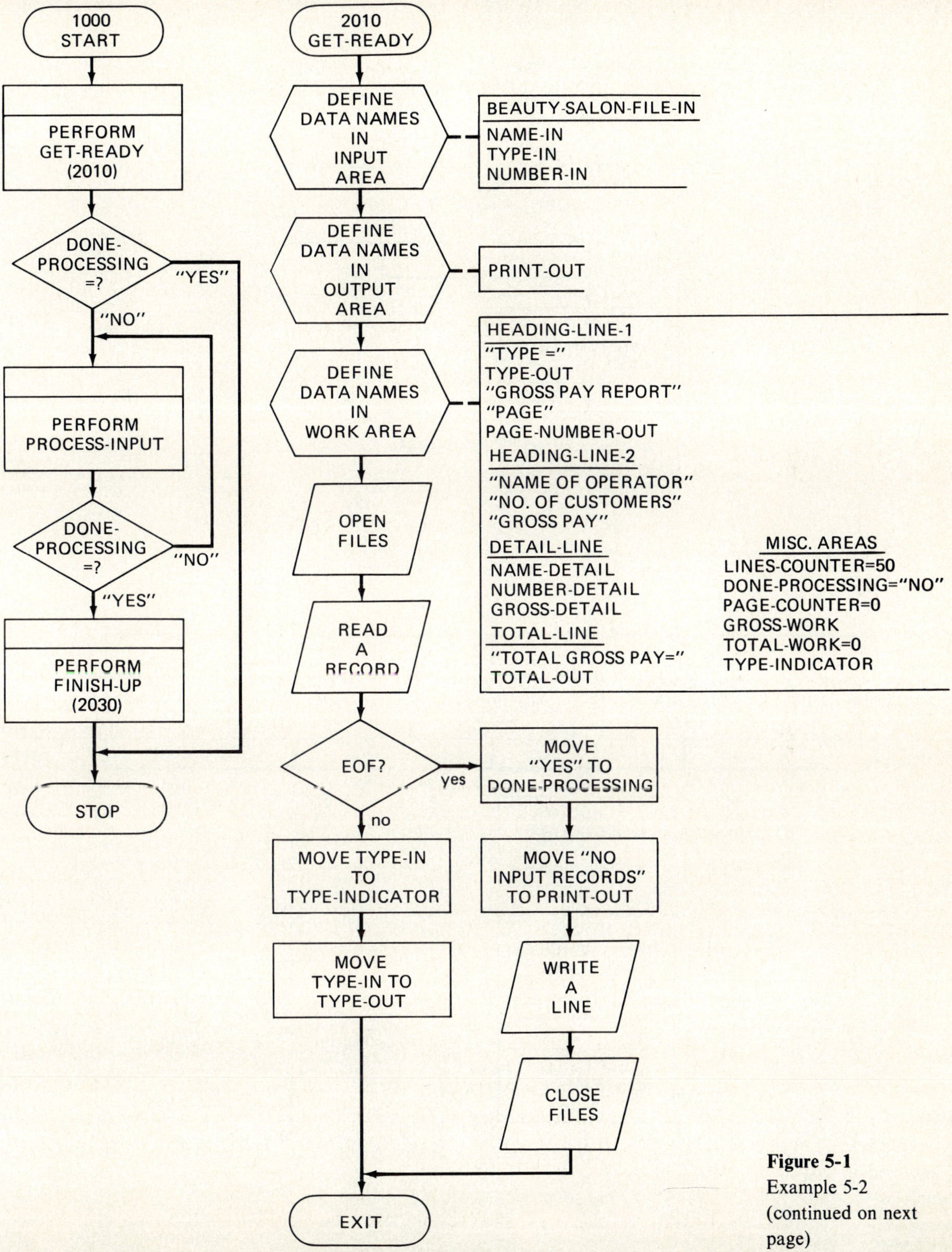

Figure 5-1
Example 5-2
(continued on next page)

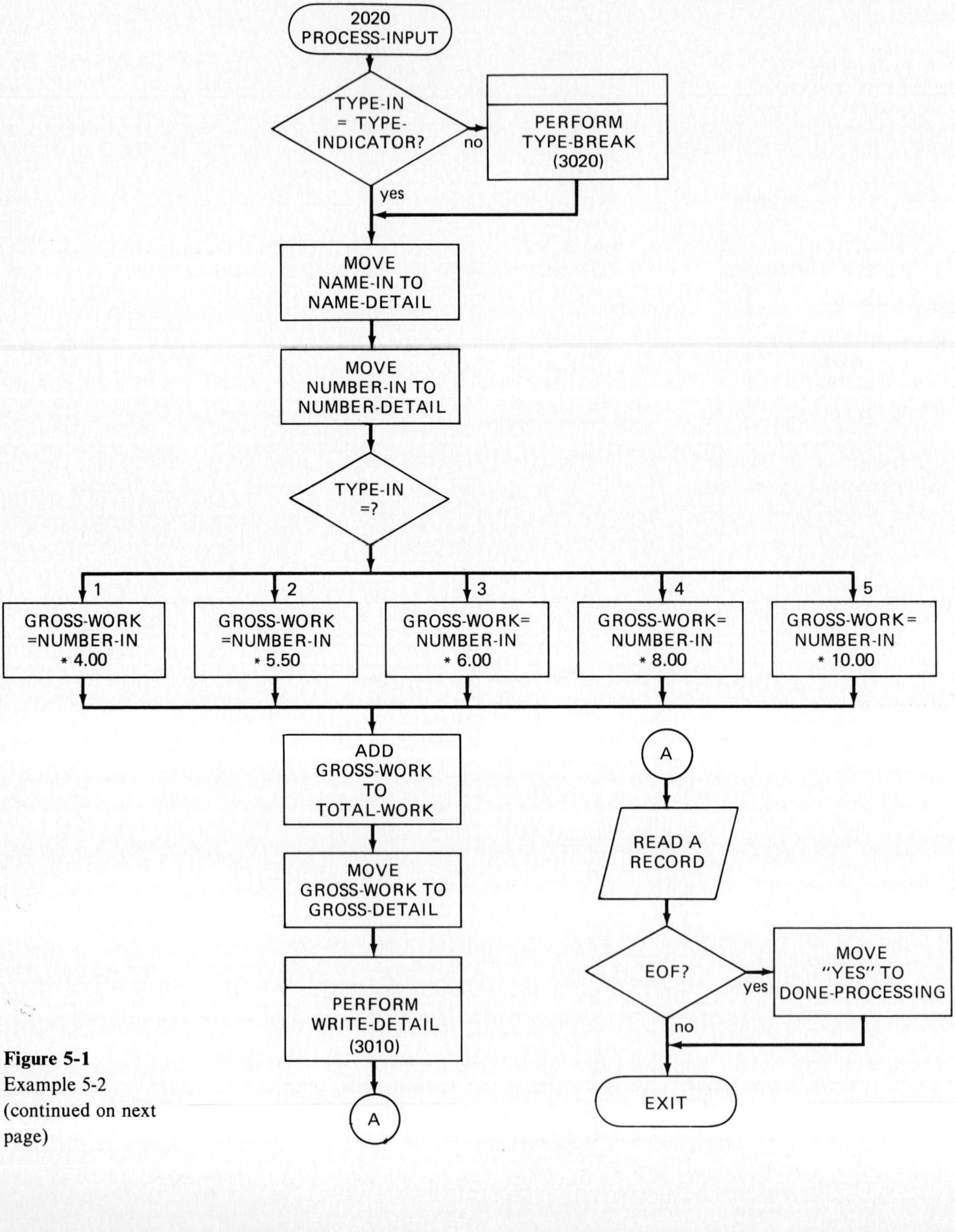

Figure 5-1
Example 5-2
(continued on next page)

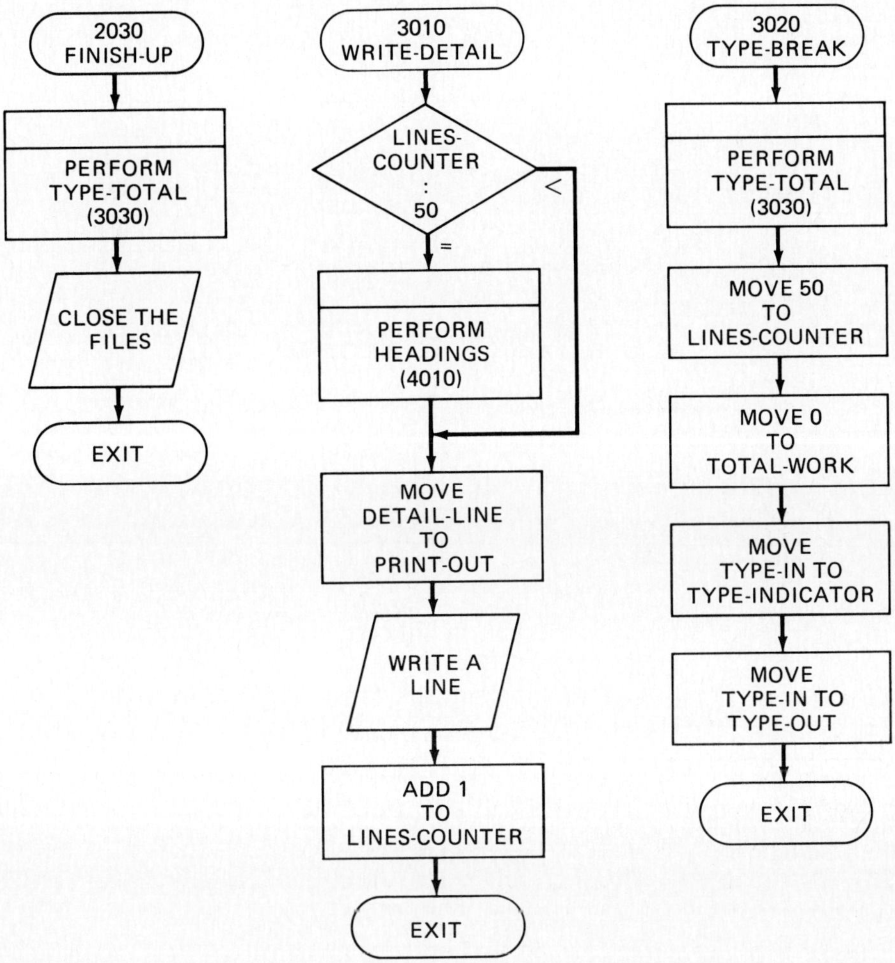

Figure 5-1
Example 5 2
(continued)

tents of the control field of the input record as part of the GET-READY routine. This will guarantee that no control break occurs when the first record of the file is processed. The second method, as shown in Figure 5-2, involves the use of a *first record indicator* or switch. When a first record indicator is used, the break occurs when the first record is processed. However, when the break routine is called, the printing of totals is bypassed.

Look at Figure 5-1. Notice that in GET-READY, after the first record is read, the type from the input record (TYPE-IN) is moved to a field called TYPE-INDICATOR. TYPE-INDICATOR is a work area used to hold the type being processed. The first thing done in the PROCESS-INPUT routine is that the type of the current record (TYPE-IN) is compared with TYPE-INDICATOR. When they are not equal, a break occurs and totals need to be printed. When the first record on the file

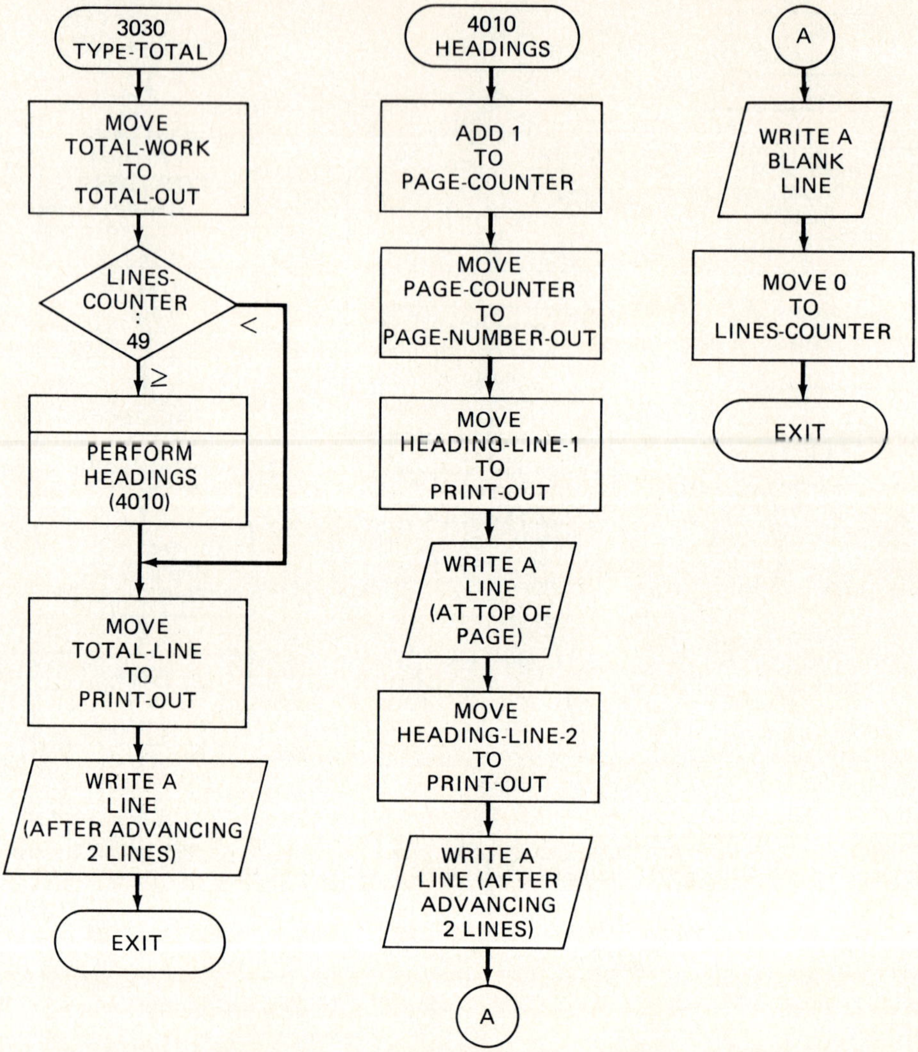

Figure 5-1
Example 5-2
(continued)

is processed, no break will occur, because an equal condition was forced in GET-READY by moving TYPE-IN to TYPE-INDICATOR. When subsequent records on the file are processed, if the file type changes, the break routine is performed before the record in the input area is processed.

Now look at the TYPE-BREAK routine. During a TYPE-BREAK, the TYPE-TOTAL routine is called to print totals. Then 50 is moved to LINES-COUNTER. This fools the computer into "thinking" that an entire page has been written, so that the next time a line is written on the report, a new page will be started. Then 0 is moved to TOTAL-WORK. If this step is inadvertently left out, then the total for

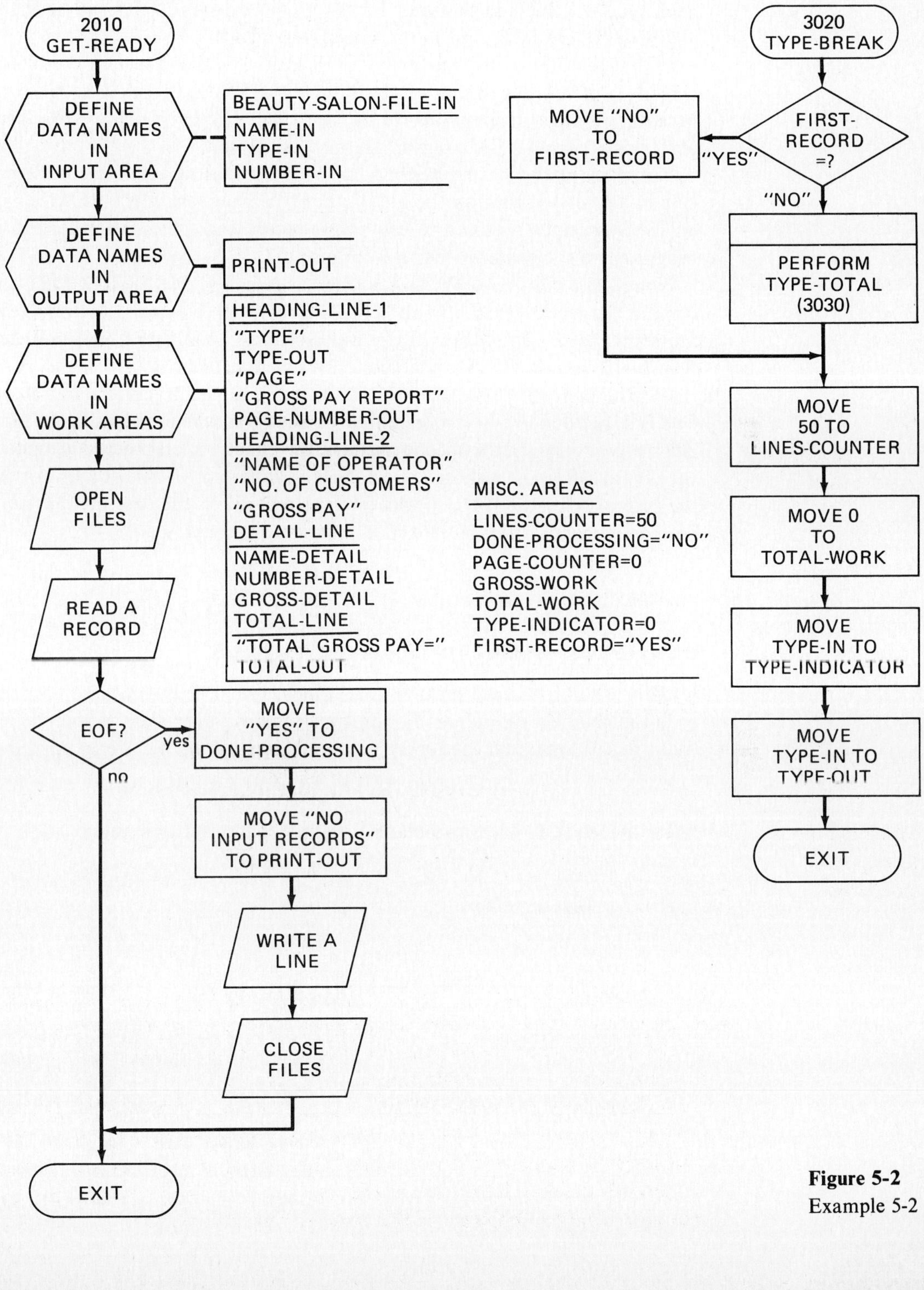

Figure 5-2
Example 5-2

each type will include the total for all previous types. TYPE-IN is then moved to TYPE-INDICATOR and to the HEADING-LINE.

EOF generates a control break. EOF indicates that the last type has been processed. It is not necessary, however, to do a TYPE-BREAK at EOF. All that is necessary is to print the totals for the last type. The FINISH-UP routine, therefore, performs TYPE-TOTAL before the files are closed.

Now look at the second method for ensuring that no totals are printed when processing the first record on the file. Figure 5-2 shows the GET-READY and TYPE-BREAK routines required to use a first record indicator. All other routines in the program are the same as shown in Figure 5-1.

Notice in GET-READY that a work area called FIRST-RECORD is set up to contain the word "YES". In the PROCESS-INPUT routine the first record on the file will cause a control break. Upon performing TYPE-BREAK, however, FIRST-RECORD equals "YES", and the totals are bypassed.

For the beginner, the second method seems easier to understand at first glance. The first method is much more efficient, however, when processing an input file that has many breaks. In the second method, the check for first record is made every time the TYPE-BREAK routine is performed. If there are 1000 breaks in the input file, the program makes 1000 checks for first record! In the first method no such comparison is made, resulting in a more efficient program.

EXAMPLE 5-3: MULTIPLE-LEVEL TOTALS

Usually when totals are printed at a control break, it is desirable to include a final or grand total on the report. For this example we are asked to include a final total (total for all types) on the report for the beauty salon. We are to print the line

GRAND TOTAL FOR ALL TYPES =

triple-spaced (i.e., leave two blank lines) after the last type total.

Printer Spacing Chart

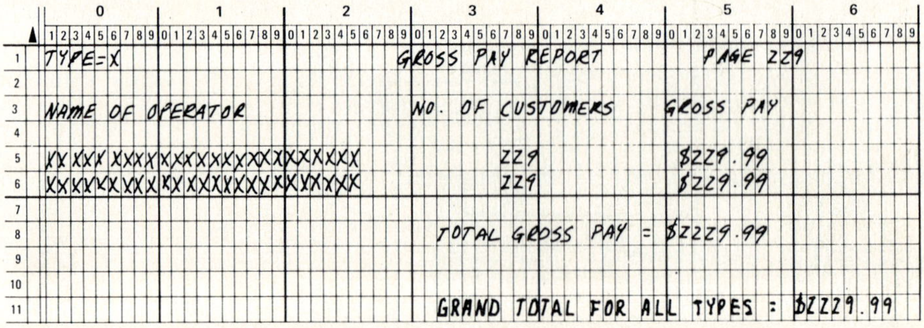

In order to accomplish this we need to:

1. Add GRAND-TOTAL-LINE when defining work areas in GET-READY:

Grand-Total-Line
"GRAND TOTAL FOR ALL TYPES ="
Grand-Total-Out

2. Define a work area called GRAND-TOTAL-WORK and initialize it to zero. This field will be used to accumulate the final total.
3. Modify the TYPE-TOTAL-ROUTINE to accumulate the final total. There are two ways to accumulate the final total.

   The first method modifies the program to add GROSS-WORK to GRAND-TOTAL-WORK in the PROCESS-INPUT routine. This results in an additional instruction being executed for each record on the input file.

   The second method is called *rolling totals*. In this method, when the type totals are printed (see TYPE-TOTAL routine in Figure 5-3), the type total (TOTAL-WORK) is added to the final total (GRAND-TOTAL-WORK). This results in an additional instruction being executed each time there is a break. This method is preferred because it is more efficient than the first method (there are normally fewer breaks than there are records on the input file).
4. Modify the FINISH-UP routine (see Figure 5-3) to print the final totals.

EXAMPLE 5-4: MULTIPLE-LEVEL TOTALS

This problem involves printing three levels of totals. It is not unusual to include three or four or even more levels of totals on a report. These totals are usually called:

1. Minor totals
2. Intermediate totals
3. Major totals
4. Grand (final) totals

For this example we are told that commissions are paid to salespeople based upon the number of units that are sold by the person. The unit commission varies with the product sold, and the total commission is based upon the number of units sold of each particular product. Commission rates and selling prices are fixed within the program as constants.

Product Number	*Commission Rate (per unit)*	*Selling Price (per unit)*
1	$0.10	$16.00
2	0.20	30.00
3	0.30	48.00
4	0.40	60.00
5	0.50	75.00

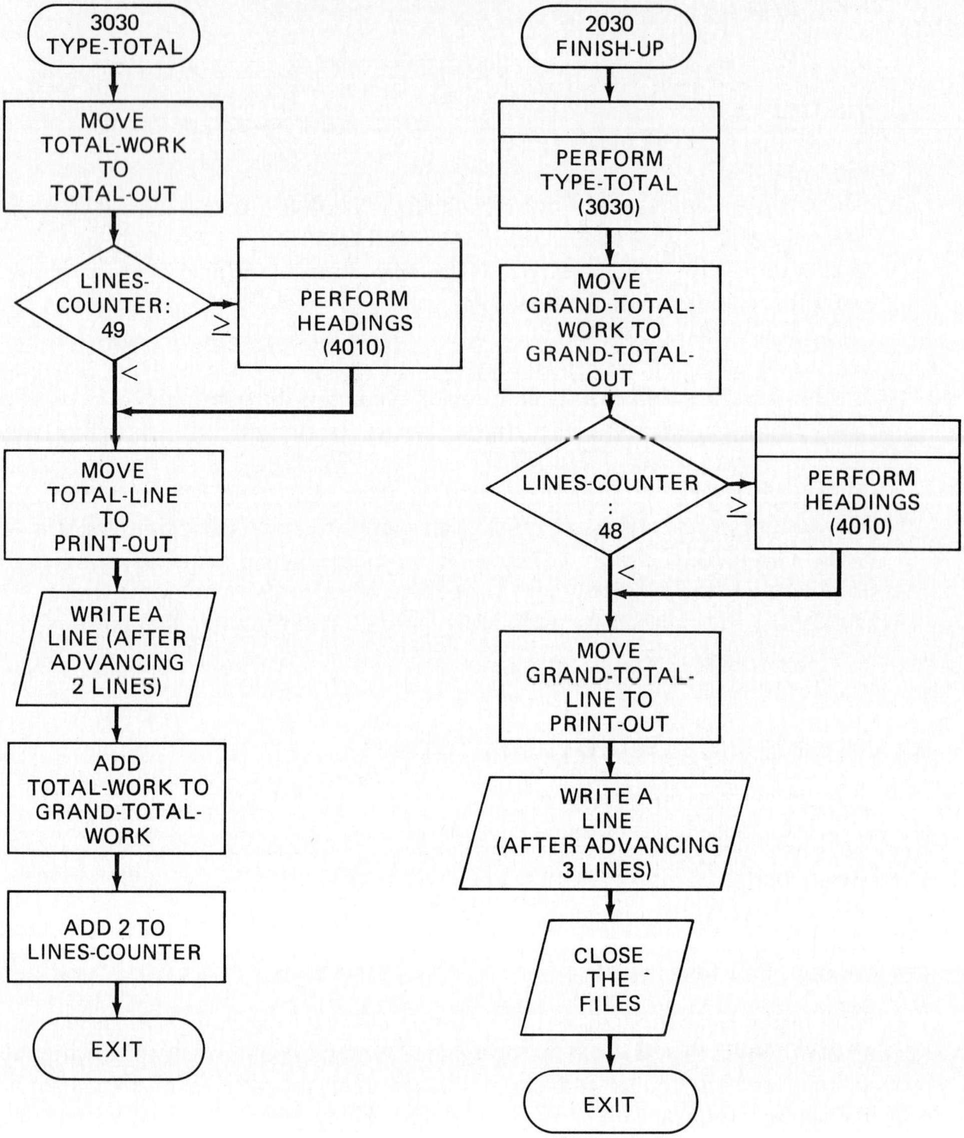

Figure 5-3
Example 5-3

Output

Output consists of a report. A maximum of 50 detail lines are to appear per page. The page number is to appear on each page. Minor totals are to be shown when the salesperson changes. Intermediate totals are to be shown when the territory changes. Grand totals are to be shown at the end of the report. The current date is to be shown in the second heading line of the report. When total lines are printed, one blank line is to precede and follow each line.

Printer Spacing Chart

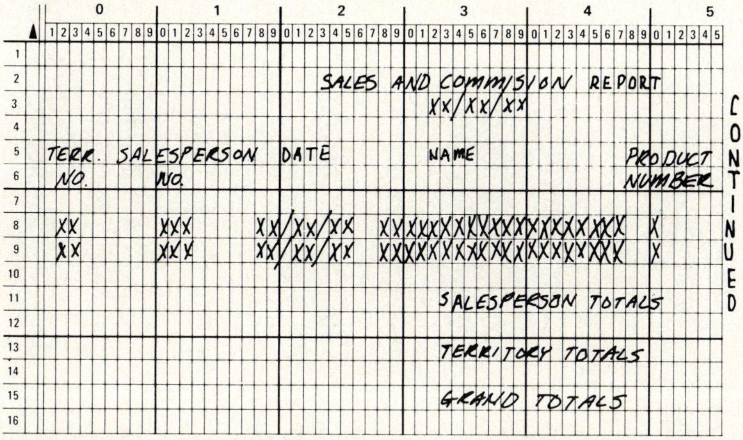

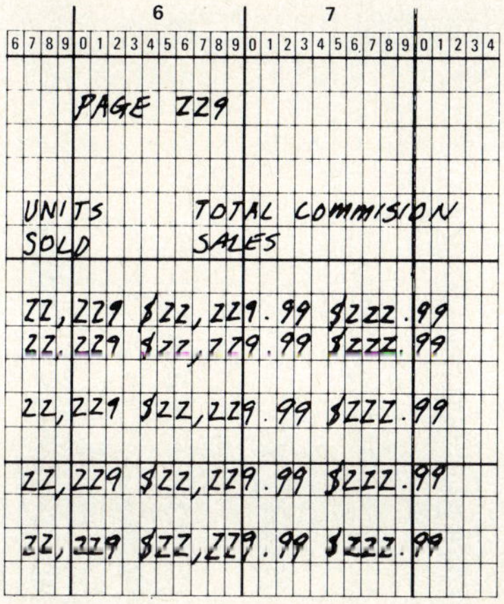

Sample Output

The sample output is on page 124.

Input

Input consists of records which have been sorted in a previous program by salesperson within territory. The records have the following format:

Position	*Description*
1–2	Territory number
3–5	Salesperson number
6–13	Date of sale
14–32	Salesperson name
33–37	Number of units sold
38	Product number

SALES AND COMMISSION REPORT PAGE 1
10/15/83

TERR. NO.	SALESPERSON NO.	DATE	NAME	PRODUCT NUMBER	UNITS SOLD	TOTAL SALES	COMMISSION
01	100	10/12/83	JIM CARYL	1	1,000	$16,000.00	$100.00
01	100	10/13/83	JIM CARYL	4	100	$ 6,000.00	$ 40.00
		SALESPERSON TOTALS			1,100	$22,000.00	$140.00
01	150	10/12/82	MARY LIMSOM	5	10	$ 750.00	$ 5.00
		SALESPERSON TOTALS			10	$ 750.00	$ 5.00
		TERRITORY TOTALS			1,110	$ 22,750.00	$145.00
02	150	10/13/83	LINDA LUCIN	3	20	$ 960.00	$ 6.00
02	150	10/12/83	LINDA LUCIN	2	800	$24,000.00	$160.00
		SALESPERSON TOTALS			820	$24,960.00	$166.00
		TERRITORY TOTALS			820	$24,960.00	$166.00
		GRAND TOTALS			1,930	$47,710.00	$311.00

Sample Input

```
0110010/12/82JIM CARYL      010001
0110010/13/82JIM CARYL      001004
0115010/12/82MARY LIMSOM    000105
0215010/13/82LINDA LUCIN    000203
0215010/12/82LINDA LUCIN    008002
EOF
```

Calculations

Total sales = units sold * selling price
Total commission = units sold * commission rate

The hierarchy chart for this example is shown in Figure 5-4. The pseudocode for this example is:

```
1000
MAINLINE
START
DO Get-Ready (2010) routine
IF Done-Processing equals "No" THEN
    DO Process-Input (2020) routine UNTIL Done-Processing is equal to
      "Yes"
    ENDDO
    DO Finish-Up (2030) routine
ENDIF
STOP

2010
GET-READY
DEFINE data names in input, output, and work areas
OPEN files
GET current date for Heading-Line-2
READ a record from Sales-In
  ATEND of file MOVE "Yes" to Done-Processing
IF Done-Processing = "Yes" THEN
  DO Headings (3010) routine
  MOVE "No Input Records" to output area
  WRITE a line
  CLOSE files
ELSE MOVE Terr-In to Terr-Compare
  MOVE Sales-No-In to Sales-No-Compare
ENDIF
ENDGET-READY

2020
PROCESS-INPUT
IF Terr-In is not equal to Terr-Compare THEN
```

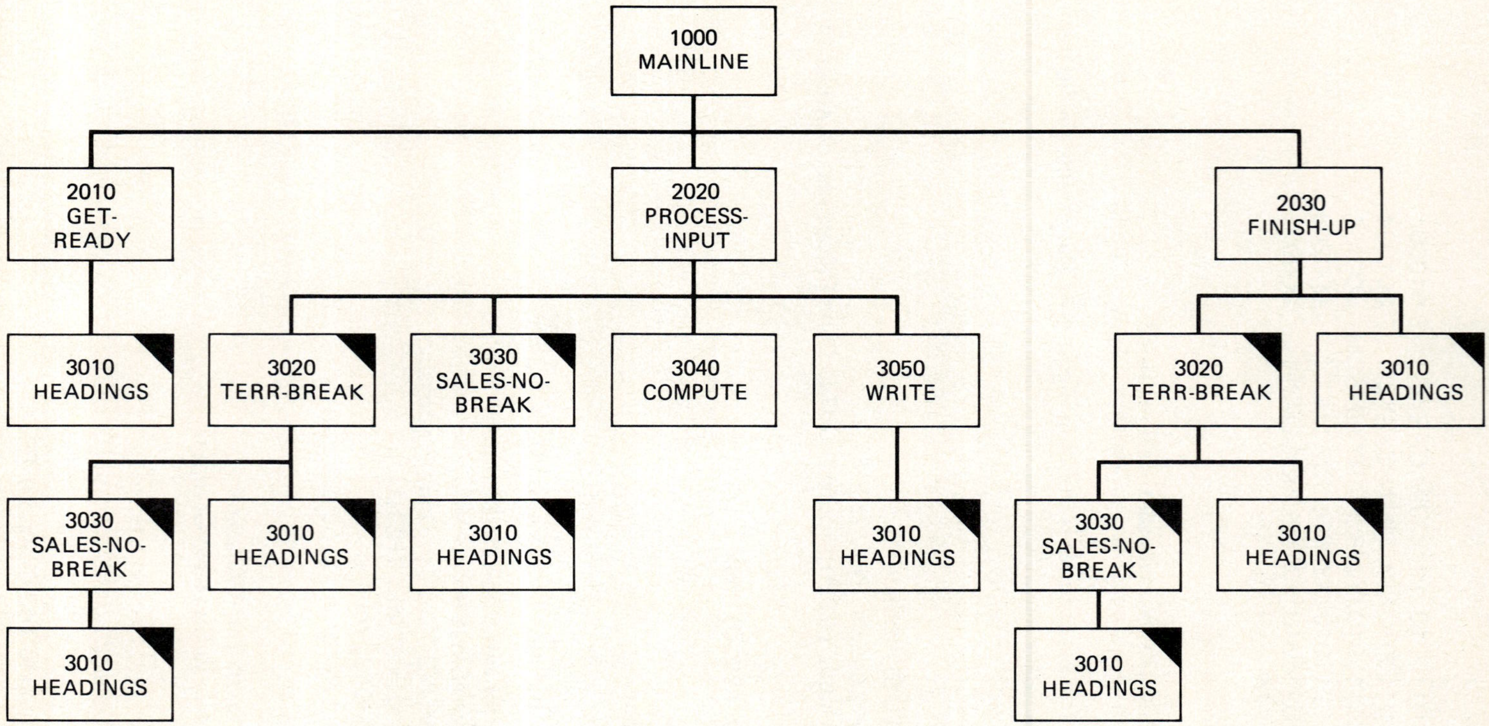

Figure 5-4
Example 5-4

```
DO Terr-Break (3020) routine
ELSE IF Sales-No-In is not equal to Sales-No-Compare THEN
          DO Sales-No-Break (3030) routine
     ENDIF
ENDIF
MOVE Terr-In, Sales-No-In, Date-In, Name-In,
  Product-In and Units-In to Detail-Line
DO Compute (3040) routine
DO Write (3050) routine
READ a record from Sales-In
  ATEND of file MOVE "Yes" to Done-Processing
ENDPROCESS-INPUT
```

2030

<u>FINISH-UP</u>

```
DO Terr-Break (3020) routine
MOVE grand totals to Grand-Totals-Line
IF Lines-Counter is greater than or equal to 50 THEN
  DO Headings (3010) routine
ENDIF
MOVE Grand-Totals-Line to output area
WRITE a line
CLOSE files
ENDFINISH-UP
```

3010

<u>HEADINGS</u>

```
ADD 1 to Page-Counter
MOVE Page-Counter to Heading-Line-1
MOVE Heading-Line-1 to output area
WRITE a line on second line of new page
MOVE Heading-Line-2 to output area
WRITE a line after advancing 1 line
MOVE Heading-Line-3 to output area
WRITE a line after advancing 2 lines
MOVE Heading-Line-4 to output area
WRITE a line
WRITE a blank line
RESET Lines-Counter to 0
ENDHEADINGS
```

3020

<u>TERR-BREAK</u>

```
DO Sales-No-Break (3030) routine
MOVE Territory Totals to Territory-Totals-Line
IF Lines-Counter is greater than or equal to 49 THEN
  DO Headings (3010) routine
```

```
ENDIF
MOVE Territory-Totals-Line to output area
WRITE a line
WRITE a blank line
ADD 2 to Lines-Counter
ADD territory totals to grand totals
MOVE 0 to territory totals
MOVE Terr-In to Terr-Compare
ENDTERR-BREAK

3030
SALES-NO-BREAK
MOVE salesperson totals to Salesperson-Totals-Line
IF Lines-Counter is greater than or equal to 48 THEN
   DO Headings (3010) routine
ENDIF
MOVE Salesperson-Totals-Line to output area
WRITE a line after advancing 2 lines
WRITE a blank line
ADD 3 to Lines-Counter
ADD salesperson totals to territory totals
MOVE 0 to salesperson totals
MOVE Sales-No-In to Sales-No-Compare
ENDSALES-NO-BREAK

3040
COMPUTE
IF Product-In = 1 THEN
     Tot-Sales = Units-In * 16.00
     Tot-Comm = Units-In * .10
ELSE IF Product-In = 2 THEN
               Tot-Sales = Units-In * 30.00
               Tot-Comm = Units-In * .20
        ELSE IF Product-In = 3 THEN
                      Tot-Sales = Units-In * 43.00
                      Tot-Comm = Units-In * .30
                ELSE IF Product-In = 4 THEN
                              Tot-Sales = Units-In * 60.00
                              Tot-Comm = Units-In * .40
                        ELSE Tot-Sales = Units-In * 75.00
                                Tot-Comm = Units-In * .50
                        ENDIF
                ENDIF
        ENDIF
ENDIF
MOVE Tot-Sales and Tot-Comm to Detail-Line
```

```
ADD Total-Units-In to Slsperson-Units-Total
ADD Tot-Sales to Slsperson-Sales-Total
ADD Tot-Comm to Slsperson-Comm-Total
ENDCOMPUTE

3050
WRITE
IF Lines-Counter = 50 THEN
  DO Headings (3010) routine
ENDIF
MOVE Detail-Line to output area
WRITE a line
ADD 1 to Lines-Counter
ENDWRITE
```

The flowchart is shown in Figure 5-5.

Within a program, the final totals are printed during the FINISH-UP routine. In addition, in the FINISH-UP routine all other levels of totals are to be printed, because EOF indicates that all levels of breaks have occurred. In the PROCESS-INPUT routine, we work backward from highest to lowest level of totals, with the second-highest level of break (i.e., the level below final totals) being tested for first. This means that if you have a file like the one in this example and you want salesperson and territory totals as well as final level totals, the first thing to be checked for in the PROCESS-INPUT routine is a change in territory. The reason for this can be illustrated by an example. Suppose the input file has territory number 1 which includes salespersons with numbers 1, 2, and 3. Further suppose that the next territory on the file is territory 2 with salespersons 3, 7, 8, and 9. If the salesperson were checked first, no change of salesperson would occur when going from territory 1 to territory 2. This is not, however, what you would want on your report! By checking territory first, we are telling the computer that when the territory changes, the salesperson will also change regardless of whether the salesperson number changes or remains the same. Therefore, at a territory break, the salesperson break should also be performed.

After checking the second-highest level, the third-highest level (in this case, salesperson) should be checked to see if a break occurred. When the salesperson changes, only salesperson totals should be printed. We continue in this way until all levels have been tested and necessary totals printed.

The following steps should be followed at any level control break:

1. Perform the level break for the next lower level. For example, the INTERMEDIATE BREAK routine should call the MINOR BREAK routine.
2. Move and print totals for the current level. For example, the INTERMEDIATE BREAK routine should print intermediate totals.
3. Accumulate (roll) the current level totals to the next level up. For example, the INTERMEDIATE BREAK routine should cause the intermediate level totals to be added to the major totals. (*continued on page 131*)

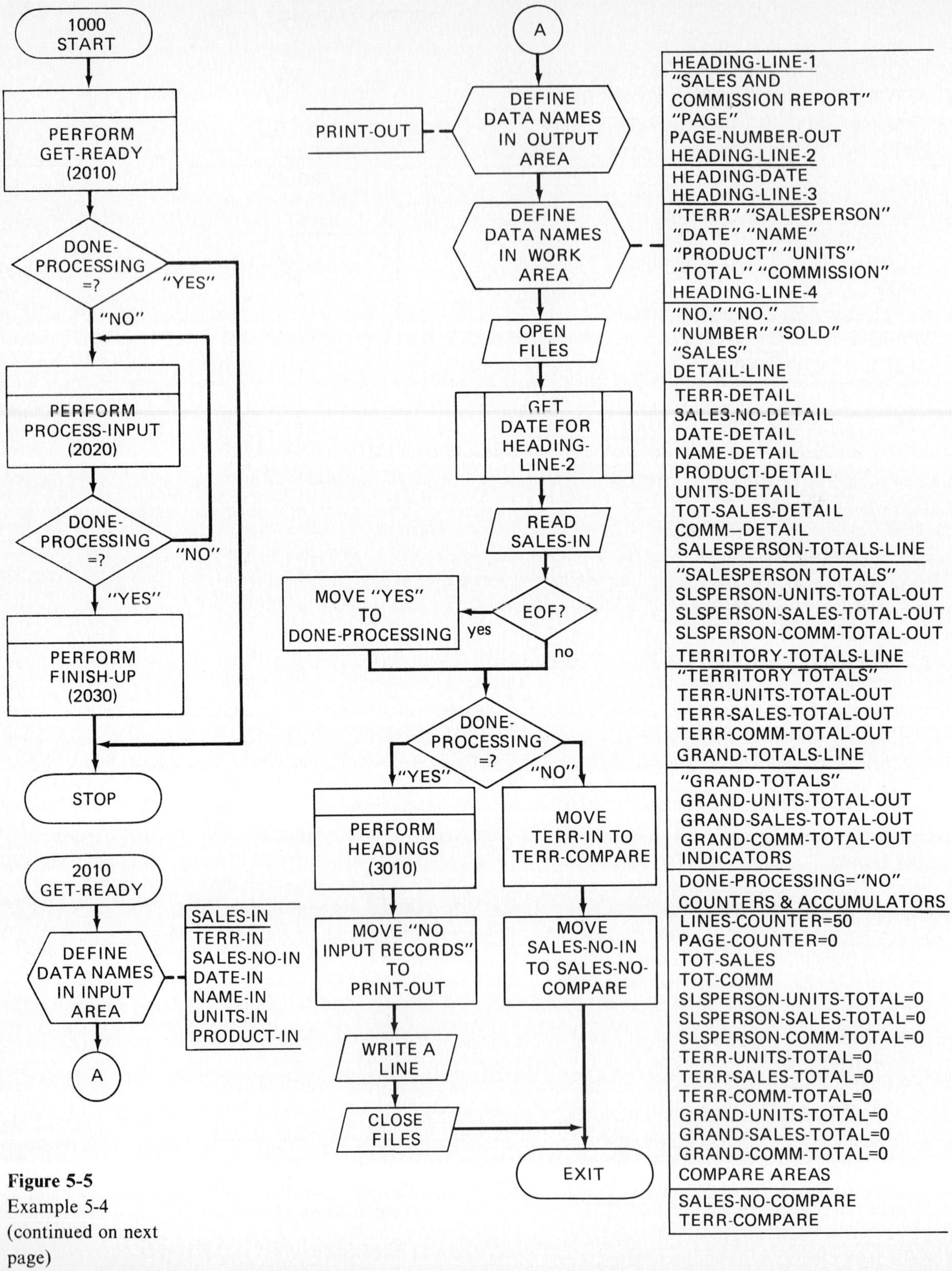

Figure 5-5
Example 5-4
(continued on next page)

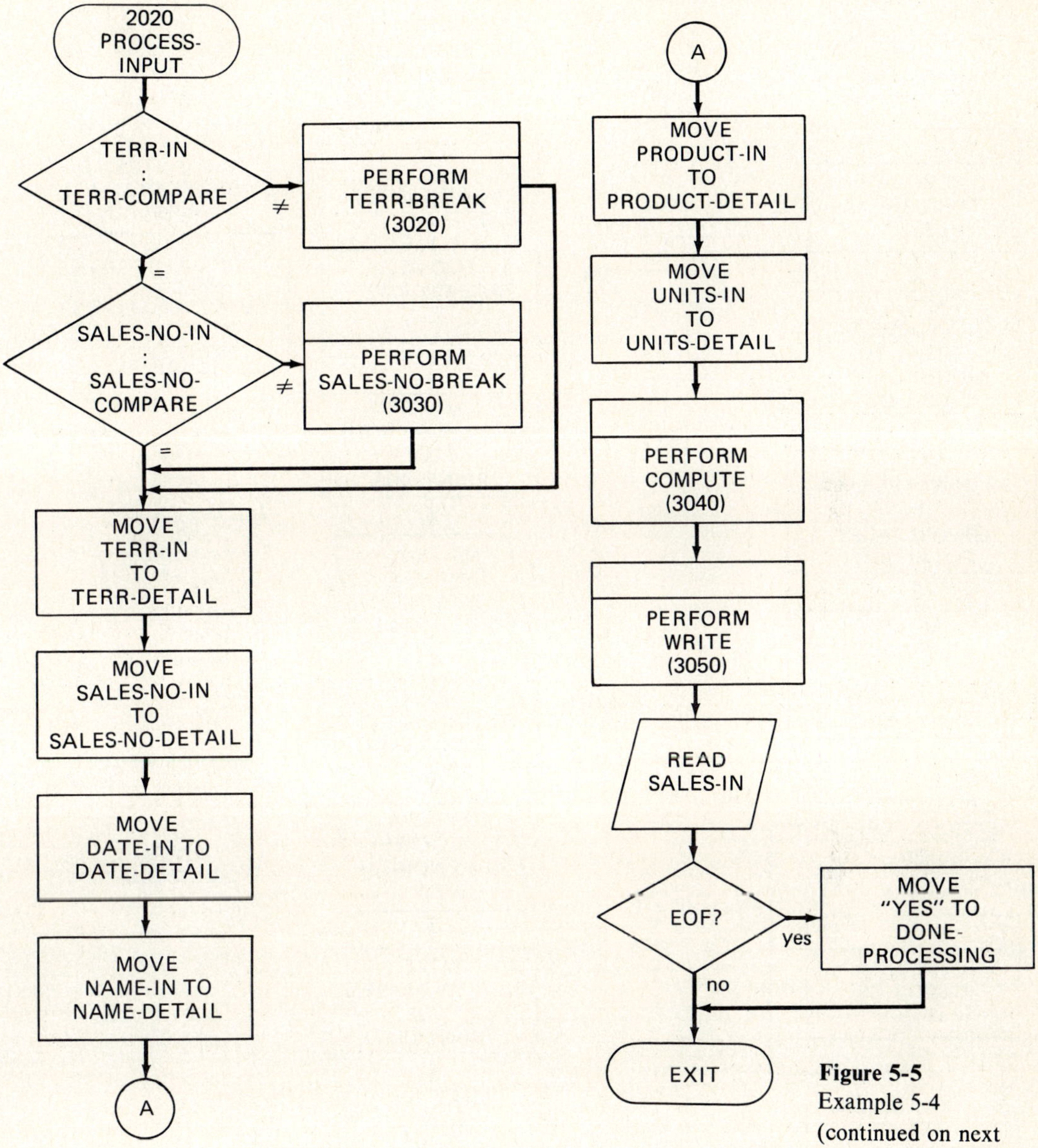

Figure 5-5
Example 5-4
(continued on next page)

4. Zero out the current level totals hold (work) areas to allow accumulation of the next set of totals. For example, the INTERMEDIATE BREAK routine should reset the intermediate total work areas to zero.
5. Update the level control break hold area to contain the value of the current record's control field.

(*continued on page 136*)

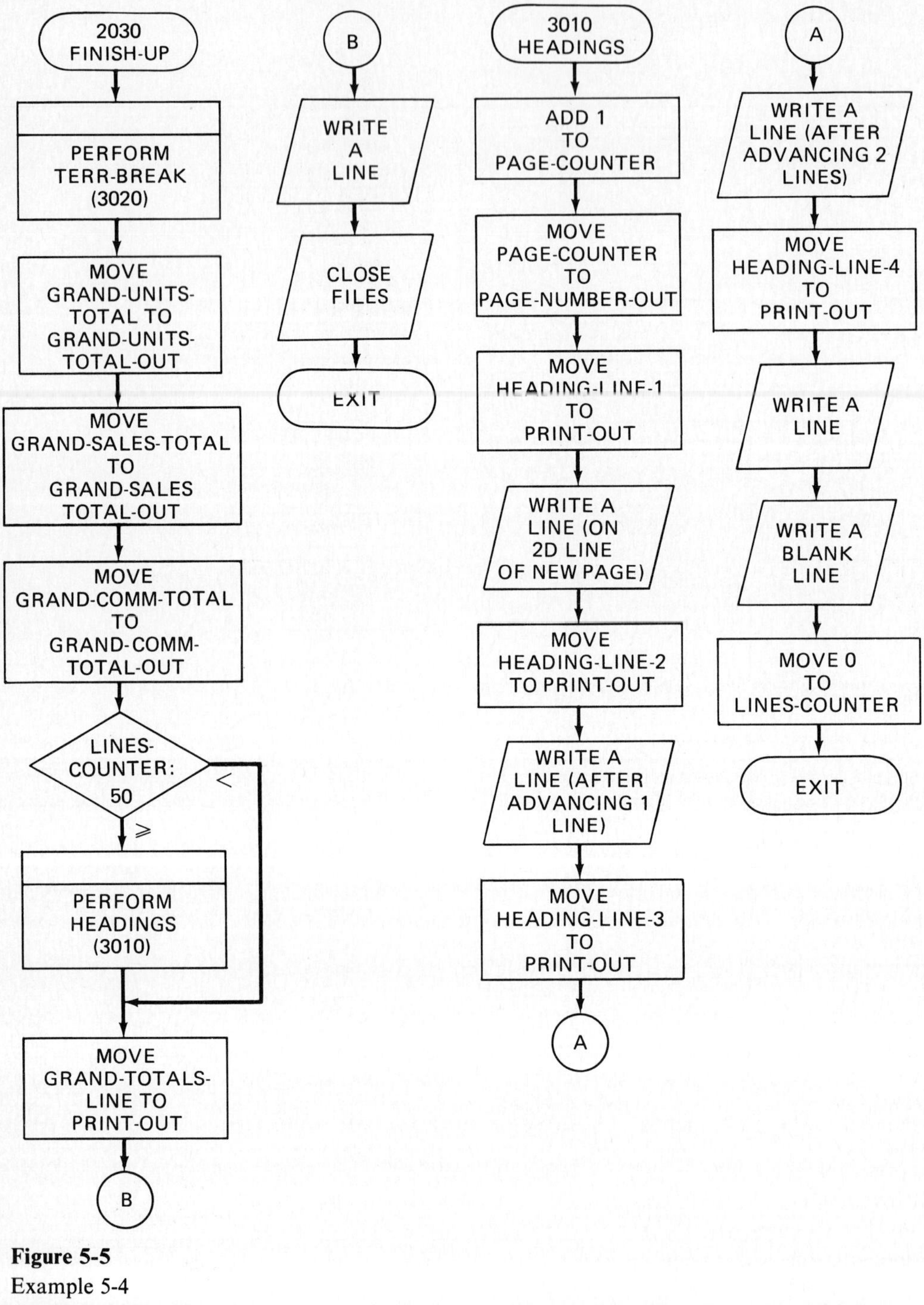

Figure 5-5
Example 5-4
(continued on next page)

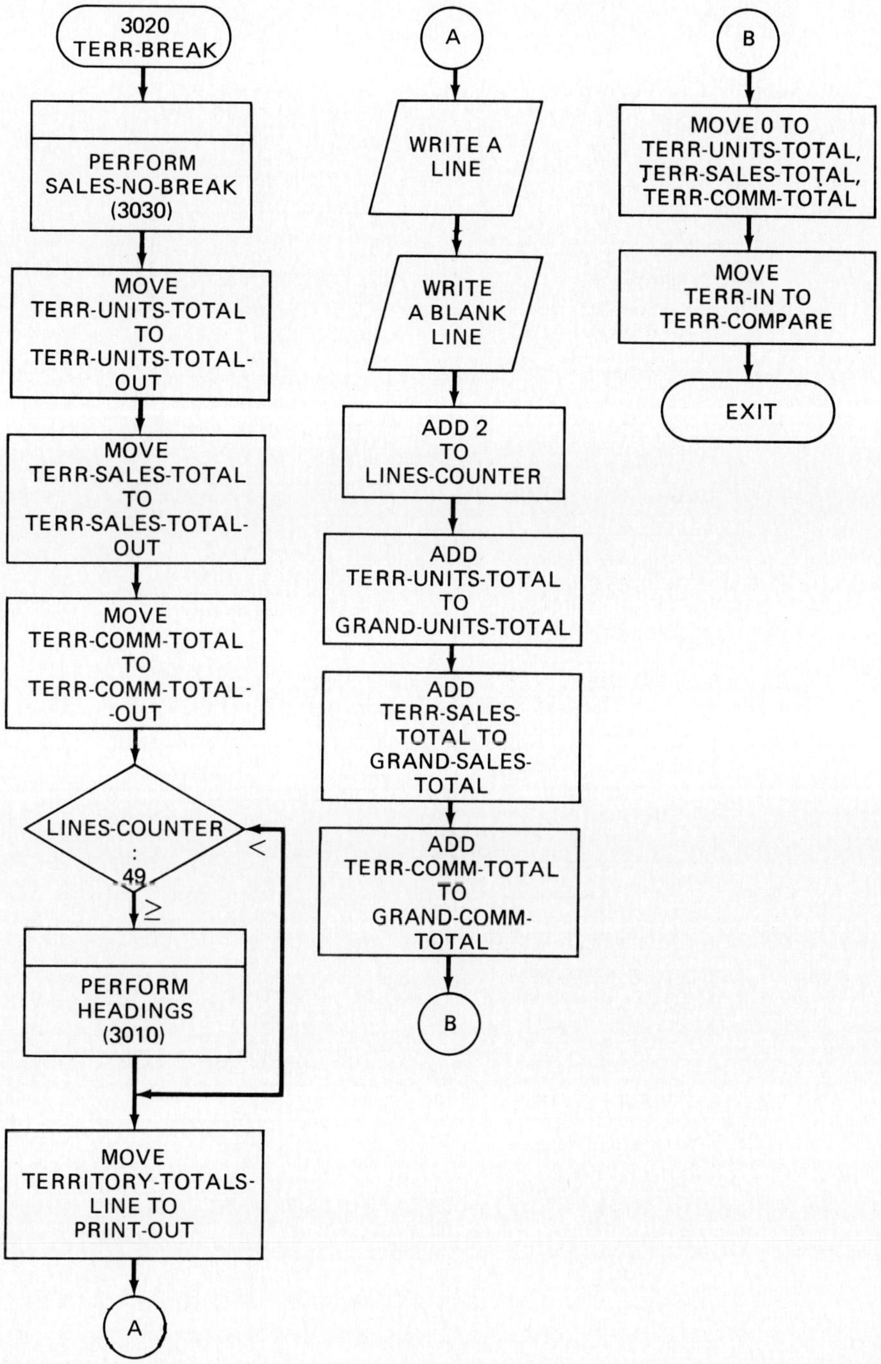

Figure 5-5
Example 5-4
(continued on next page)

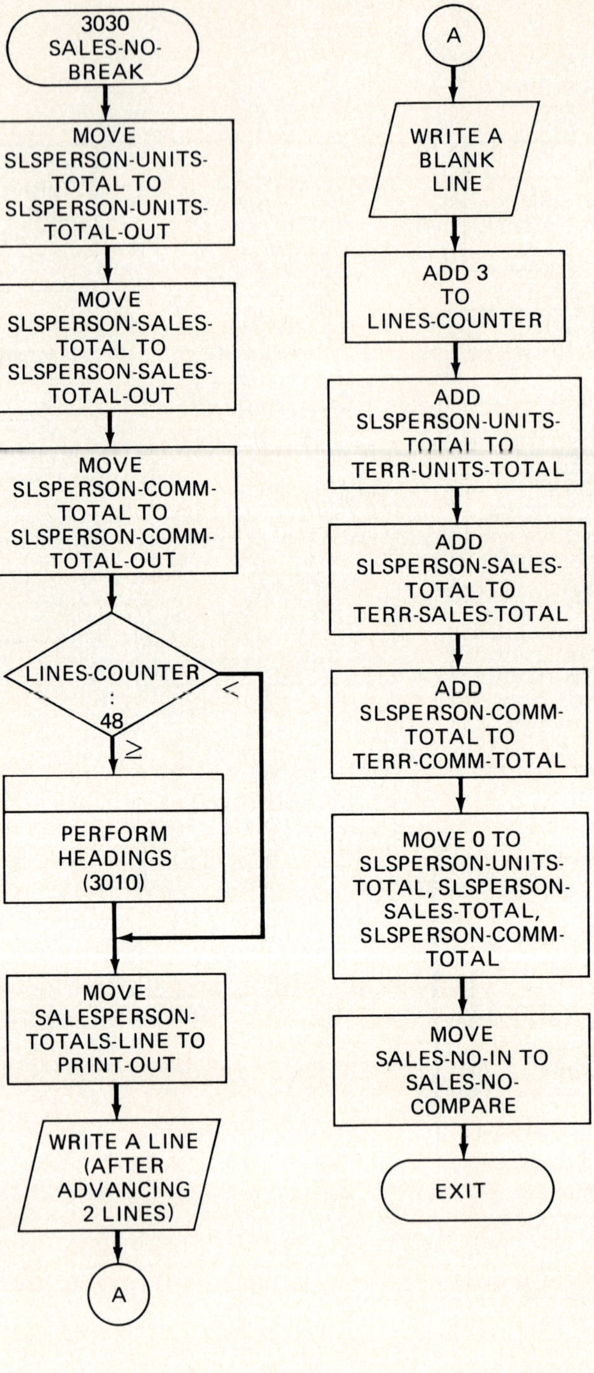

Figure 5-5
Example 5-4
(continued on next page)

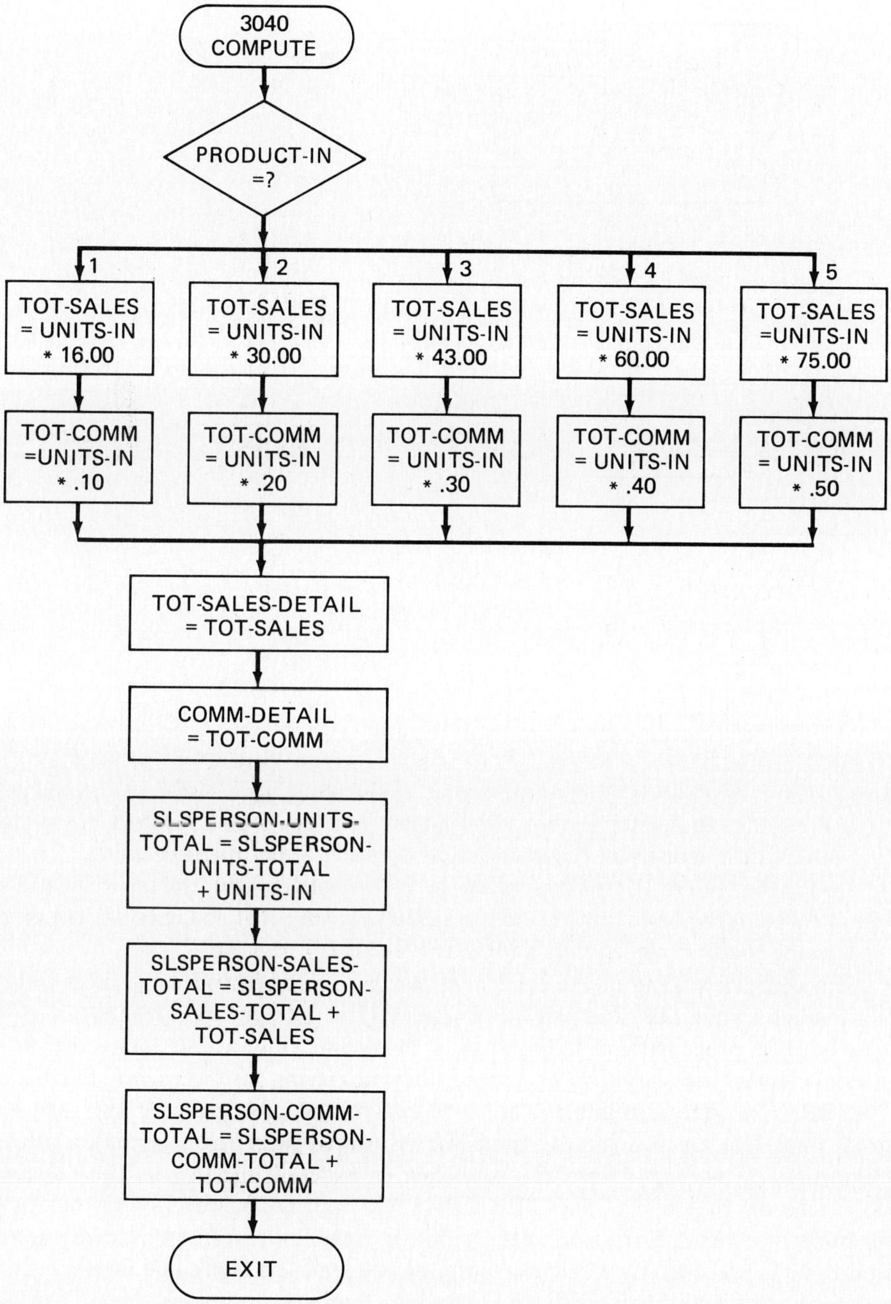

Figure 5-5
Example 5-4
(continued on next page)

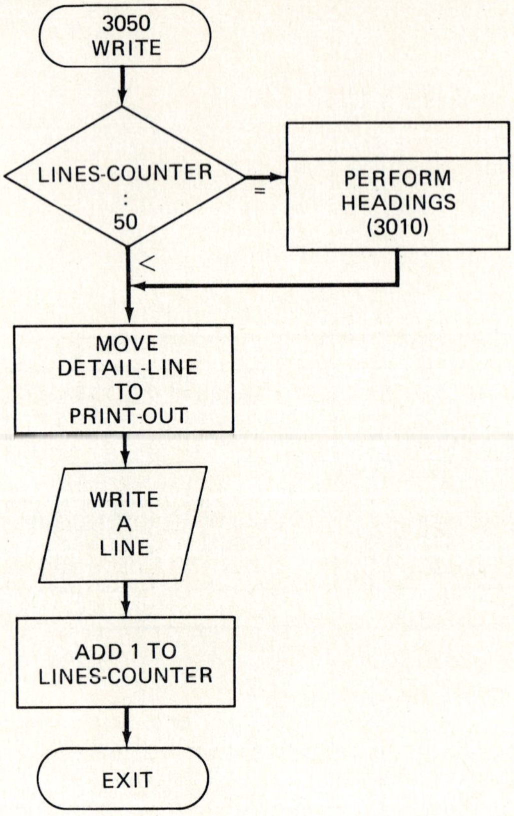

Figure 5-5
Example 5-4
(continued on next page)

It is important to do step 1 above first and to do steps 2 and 3 before doing step 4; but otherwise the order of the above steps does not affect the processing.

Notice that in GET-READY, after the first record is read, the territory and sales numbers from the first input record are saved to ensure that no break will occur when processing the first record in the PROCESS-INPUT routine.

The vertical spacing of the total lines is what seems to cause the most difficulty for students when first studying this example. The problem specifies that every total line is to be preceded and followed by a blank line. Figure 5-6 shows the possible order of lines to be printed. To ensure correct spacing on the report, the SALES-NO-BREAK routine prints a blank line before and after printing the salesperson total line. This ensures that a blank line is printed after the salesperson total line regardless of whether a territory total line or a detail line follows the salesperson total line on the report. The TERR-BREAK routine, however, does not include printing of a blank line prior to the territory total line. Notice that every territory total line is preceded by a salesperson total line, and the blank line between them is printed in the SALES-NO-BREAK routine. Similarly, no blank line is written in the FINISH-UP routine before the grand total line is printed.

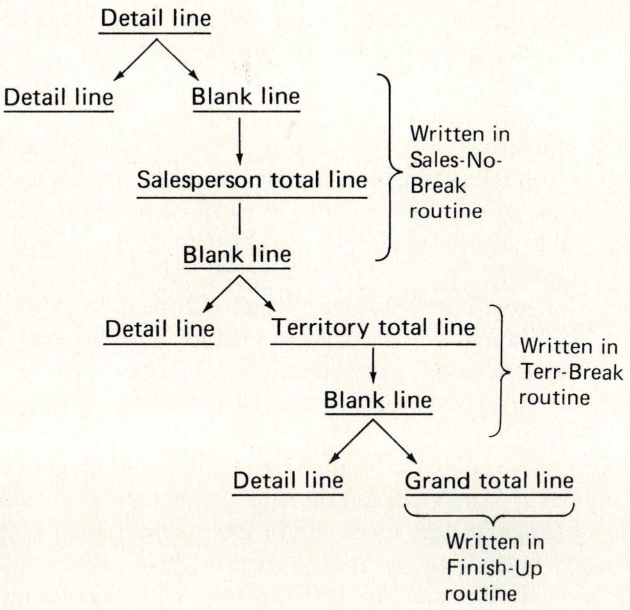

Figure 5-6

QUESTIONS AND EXERCISES FOR REVIEW

1. Define each of the following:
   a. First-record switch or indicator
   b. Single-level totals
   c. Multiple-level totals
   d. Rolling totals
2. Why is it desirable to sort the input file prior to doing a report that has multiple-level totals?
3. Why is it necessary to reset the total work areas to zero at a control break that prints totals?
4. Discuss both methods used for ensuring that totals are not printed when the first record on an input file is processed. Which method is preferable? Why?
5. Why does EOF generate a control break?
6. Why is it desirable to roll totals?
7. Why do we check for higher-level breaks before checking for lower-level breaks in a program? Give an example to illustrate.
8. What five steps should be done at any level control break (e.g., intermediate level control break)? Does the order of the five steps matter? How?
9. Draw a flowchart for Example 5-1.
10. Modify Example 5-4 to use a first-record switch. Illustrate your solution using pseudocode.
11. Modify Example 4-3 (in Chapter 4) to include final totals for amount of commission and gross salary. The total line should read "TOTALS" Total-Com-

mission-Out Total-Gross-Salary-Out. One blank line is to precede the total line. Do *not* start another page for the total line even if it means printing more than 30 detail lines on the page. Use pseudocode and a hierarchy chart to illustrate your solution.

12. Modify Exercise 8 in Chapter 4 to show an amount total for each patient. The total line is to appear double-spaced after the last detail line for the patient. Do not go to a new page to show the total. The total line should read "TOTAL AMOUNT DUE =" Total-Amount-Out. Use a flowchart to illustrate your solution.
13. Draw a hierarchy chart which will be used to solve the following problem for a bakery: You are told to produce a sales report listing the number of items and dollar amount sold of various items.

Output

Output is to consist of a sales report listing the category description, item description, number of items sold, and the sales amount. A minor total is to be shown when there is a change in item number. An intermediate total is to be shown when there is a change in category number. A final total is to be printed after all records have been processed. A maximum of 50 lines (exclusive of headings, but inclusive of total lines) are to appear per page.

Printer Spacing Chart

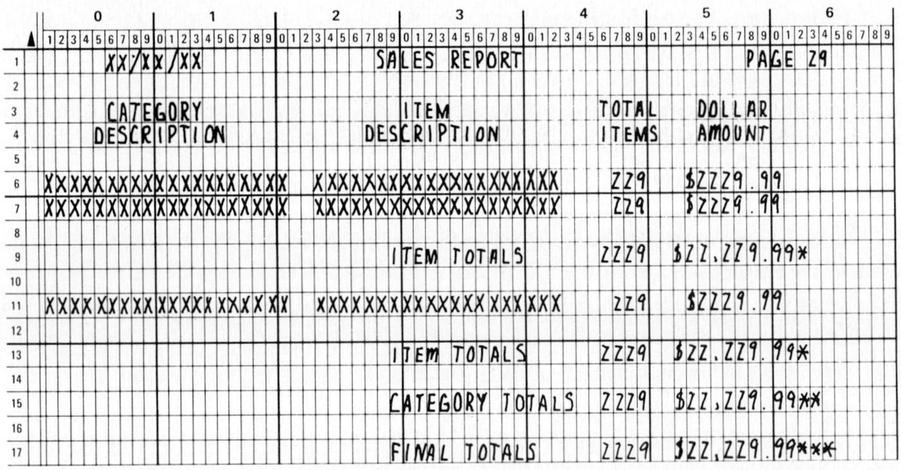

Input

Input consists of a sorted file. The sort has been done by item (i.e., chocolate chip cookies, oatmeal cookies, apple pie) within category (i.e., cookies, cakes, pies, breads). Each record contains the following information:

Position	*Description*
1–3	Item number
4–23	Description of item
24–26	Category number
27–46	Description of category
47–49	Number of items sold
50–55	Dollar amount of sale

14. Draw a flowchart for Exercise 13 above.
15. Construct the pseudocode for Exercise 13 above.

CHAPTER 6

Edit Programs and Multiple Output Files

BACKGROUND

When a computer program is run, several types of errors can occur. These include:

1. *Compilation errors due to syntax (language) errors in the code.* These errors result in messages being printed during compilation and the program not being executed. Examples include:
   a. Using a variable name that is too long. In standard BASIC, for example, variable names can be two characters in length. If you use the name A12, a compilation error will result.
   b. Branching to an instruction that doesn't exist. In COBOL, for example, the instruction "GO TO PROCESS-PARAGRAPH" if there is no PROCESS-PARAGRAPH in the program will result in an error.
2. *Errors in logic that cause a program interrupt,* that is, the program stops executing, and an error is printed. For the unfortunate programmer or analyst who happens to be responsible for a program executed during the midnight shift, program interrupts quite often result in a phone call from the computer operator in the middle of the night and an unwanted trip to work to determine and correct the problem. Examples of this type of error include:
   a. *Data exception errors,* such as attempting to do arithmetic on a field that does not contain a number or attempting to divide by zero.
   b. Accessing a nonexistent entry in a table (to be discussed in Chapter 9).
3. *Errors in logic that cause incorrect output to be produced during program execution.* Examples include:
   a. Using an ADD rather than a SUBTRACT instruction when coding.
   b. Processing data in an incorrect sequence.

Compilation errors and errors that cause a program interrupt may be unpleasant for the programmer, but usually they do not cause as much difficulty as a program that has logic errors that cause the program to run to completion and produce incorrect output that may or may not be detected!

Some of the above types of errors can be prevented by checking the input file prior to processing. A program used to check the input file for errors is called an *edit program.* Generally an error report is produced as output from an edit program. It should be noted that:

1. Many times the edit functions are done in the same program that uses the input file. In that case, a separate edit program is not necessary.
2. An edit program cannot prevent compilation errors or the type of error where the wrong instruction is used (e.g., SUBTRACT instead of MULTIPLY). Edit programs can only prevent data exception and other errors from occurring during execution if the error would have been caused by an error on the input file.

Edit programs can prevent data exception errors from occurring by checking that input fields contain the proper type of data (e.g., a field that is to be used for arithmetic contains a number). Edit programs can also do such things as range checking (e.g., ensuring that the month is in the range 1 to 12), sequence checking (e.g., seeing that the account number on the current record is greater than the number on the previous record), and checking for proper codes (e.g., ensuring that the input code field is a "1" or "2").

Keep in mind that edit programs can check whether a field is numeric, but they cannot check whether the correct number has been entered. For example, in a program that edits a payroll file, we can make sure that the pay rate is numeric, but if the rate was intended to be $5.83 and it was input as $8.35, then no error will be found by the edit program. This means that an edit program may show no errors exist on the input file, but that only means that those errors checked for by the edit program were not found. There still may be other errors on the input file.

EXAMPLE 6-1

For this example we want to edit the input file described in Example 4-5 (of Chapter 4).

Output

Output consists of a report listing the invalid records and the error messages. A maximum of 40 detail lines are to appear per page. If no errors are found during processing, print the message NO ERRORS FOUND—ALL RECORDS CORRECT.

Printer Spacing Chart

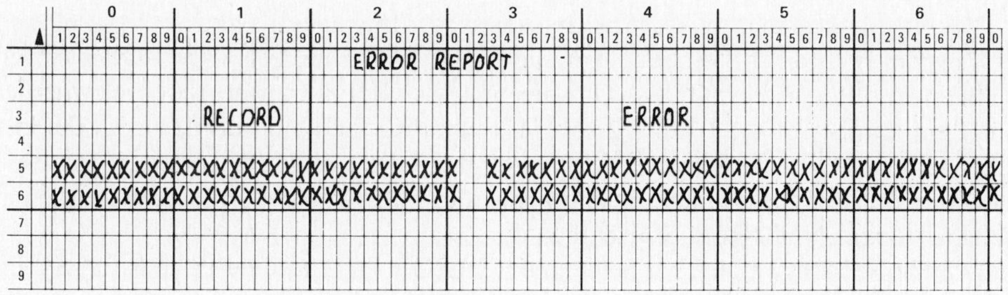

Input

The input file consists of two types of records. These are the ITEM NAME record and the NUMBER SOLD record. There is one ITEM NAME record for each item stocked by the company. This record is identified by a control field of "1" in position 30. There will be zero or more NUMBER SOLD records for each item. These records are identified by a control field of "2" in position 30. The file has been previously sorted by code within item number. This means that item number 1 will come before item number 2 on the file, and so on, and for each item, the code 1 record will come before the code 2 records.

The format of the records and editing information is shown below:

Item Name Record

Column	*Description*	*Editing Information*	*Error Message*
1–3	Item number	(no editing)	
4–20	Item name	Must not be blank	ITEM NAME BLANK
30	Code = 1	(no editing)	

Number Sold Record

Column	*Description*	*Editing Information*	*Error Message*
1–3	Item number	Must be the same as the item name record which preceded it. Note: This error will occur if an item name record is omitted from the file.	ITEM NAME RECORD MISSING FOR THIS RECORD
4–9	Date	(no editing)	
10–12	Number sold	Must be numeric	NUMBER SOLD FIELD NOT NUMERIC
30	Code = 2	(no editing)	

In addition, we need to check that the code on the input record is "1" or "2". If not, use the error message INVALID CODE.

The hierarchy chart for this example is shown on page 145.

The pseudocode solution is left as an exercise for the reader. The flowchart solution is shown in Figure 6-1. Notice that in the CODE-1 routine, ITEM-NO-IN is moved to the field called PREVIOUS-NO. Then, in the CODE-2 routine, we check whether the item number of the CODE-2 record is equal to the item number from the last CODE-1 record read. Because the records had been previously sorted, if the item numbers are not equal, then we know that the ITEM NAME record was missing for the current NUMBER SOLD record.

In FINISH-UP we check a field called ERROR-IND to determine if there were any errors on the input file. Note that ERROR-IND is initialized to "NO". At the time that an error is written on the report, and the HEADINGS routine is called, ERROR-IND is set to "YES". If, when we do FINISH-UP, ERROR-IND is still "NO", it means that no lines have been written on the error report during processing, and the NO ERROR FOUND line is written on the report.

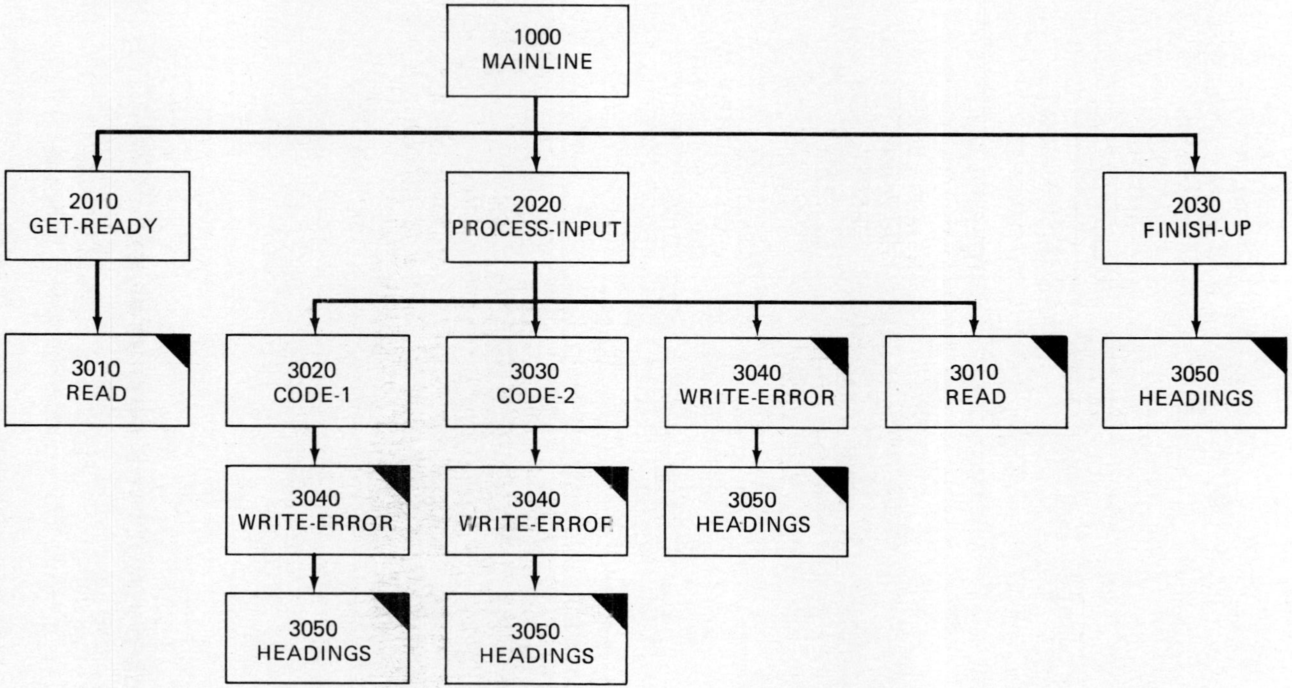
1000 MAINLINE
2010 GET-READY
2020 PROCESS-INPUT
2030 FINISH-UP
3010 READ
3020 CODE-1
3030 CODE-2
3040 WRITE-ERROR
3010 READ
3050 HEADINGS
3040 WRITE-ERROR
3040 WRITE-ERROR
3050 HEADINGS
3050 HEADINGS
3050 HEADINGS

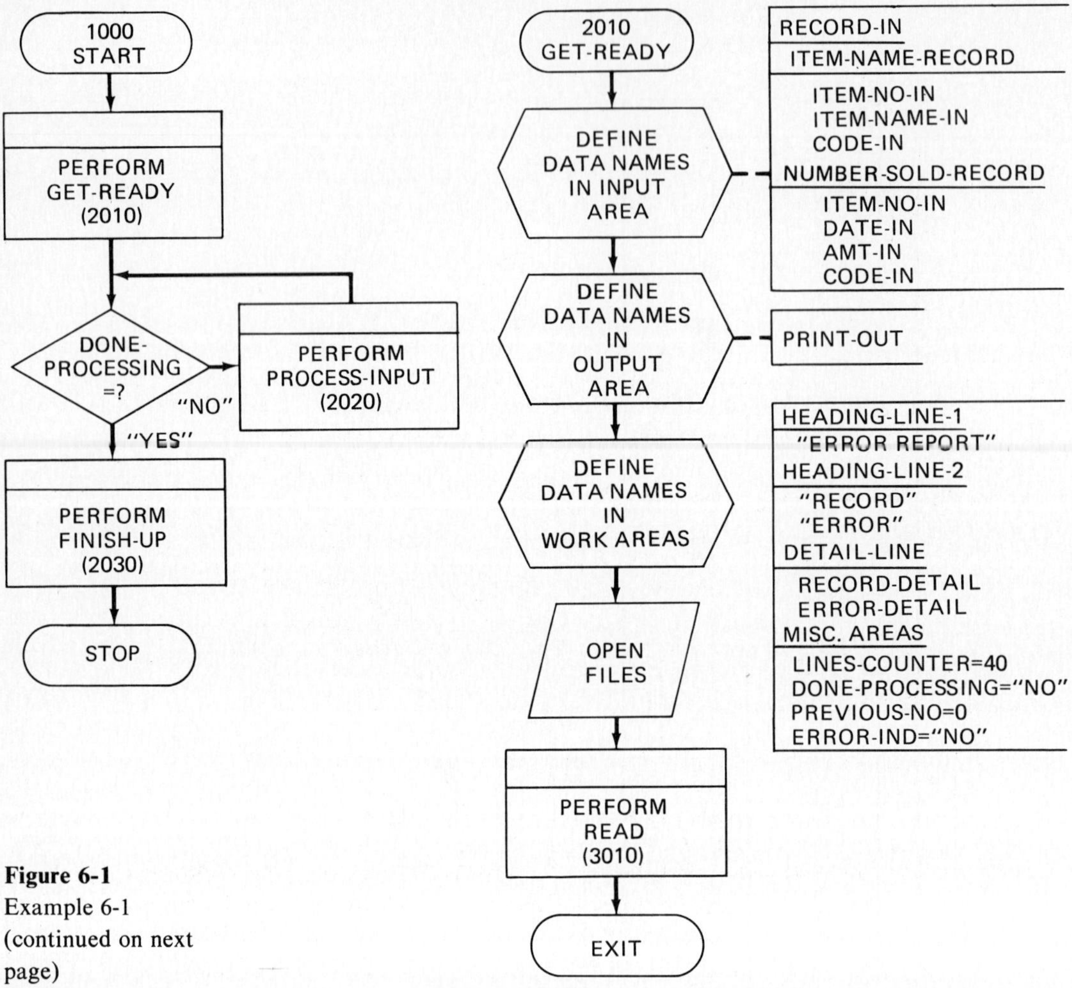

Figure 6-1
Example 6-1
(continued on next page)

EXAMPLE 6-2: MULTIPLE OUTPUT FILES

Sometimes it is desirable to produce an output file containing the valid records as well as an error report. This example shows how to do this.

In an accounts receivable system, we need to edit the input.

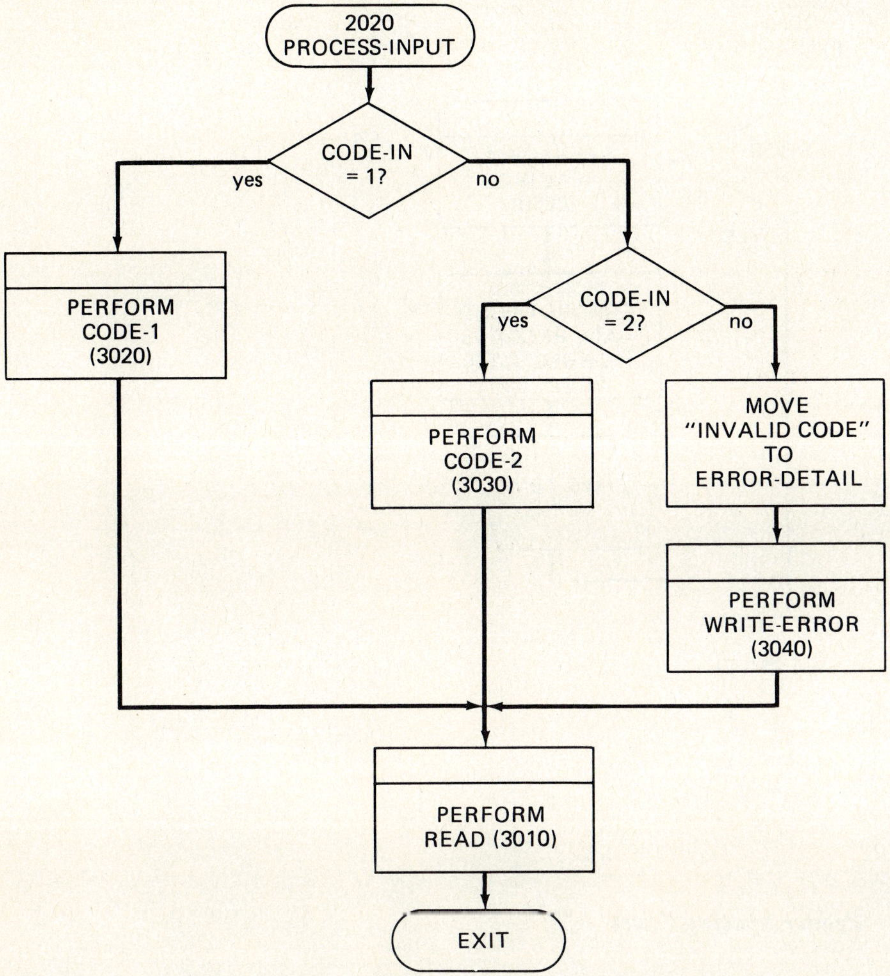

Figure 6-1
Example 6-1
(continued on next page)

Output

Output consists of a report listing the invalid records and errors as well as a file containing the valid records. The file containing the valid records is to have the same format as the input file. The report is to contain at most 30 detail lines per page. A page number is to be included. If multiple errors occur for a single input record, the record is to be listed only one time; however, all the error messages are to be shown.

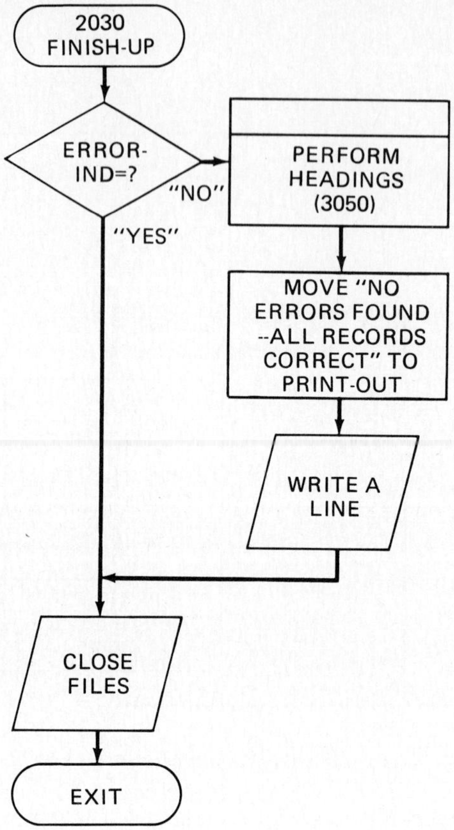

Figure 6-1
Example 6-1
(continued on next page)

Printer Spacing Chart

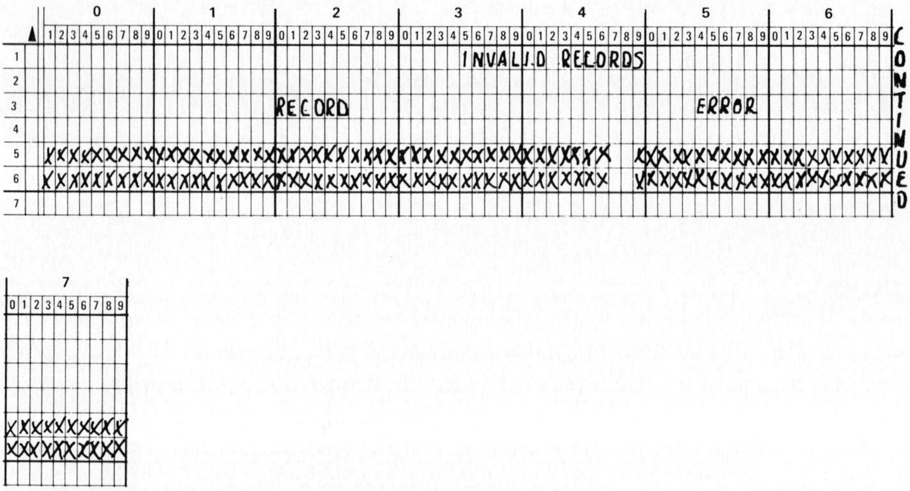

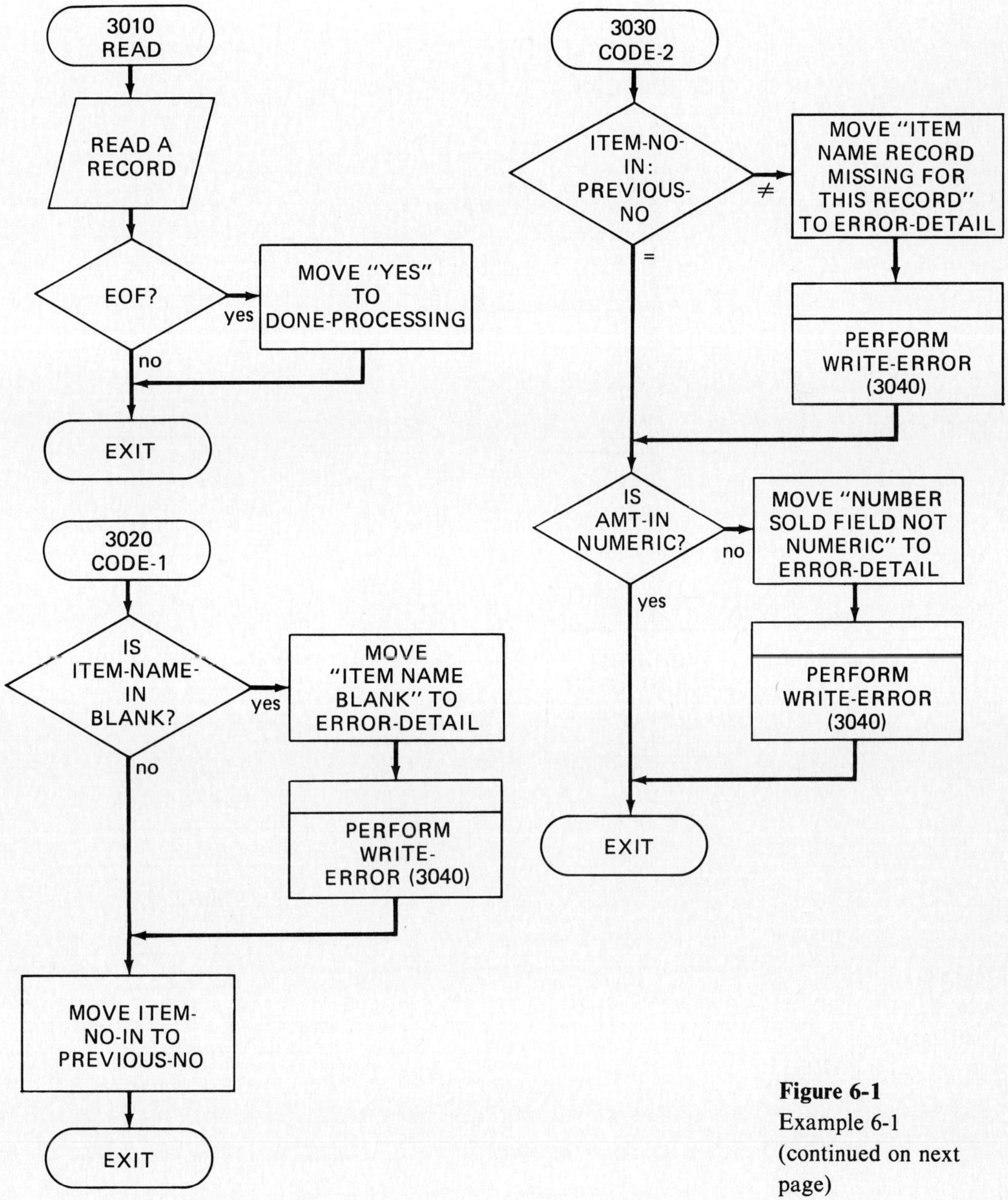

Figure 6-1
Example 6-1
(continued on next page)

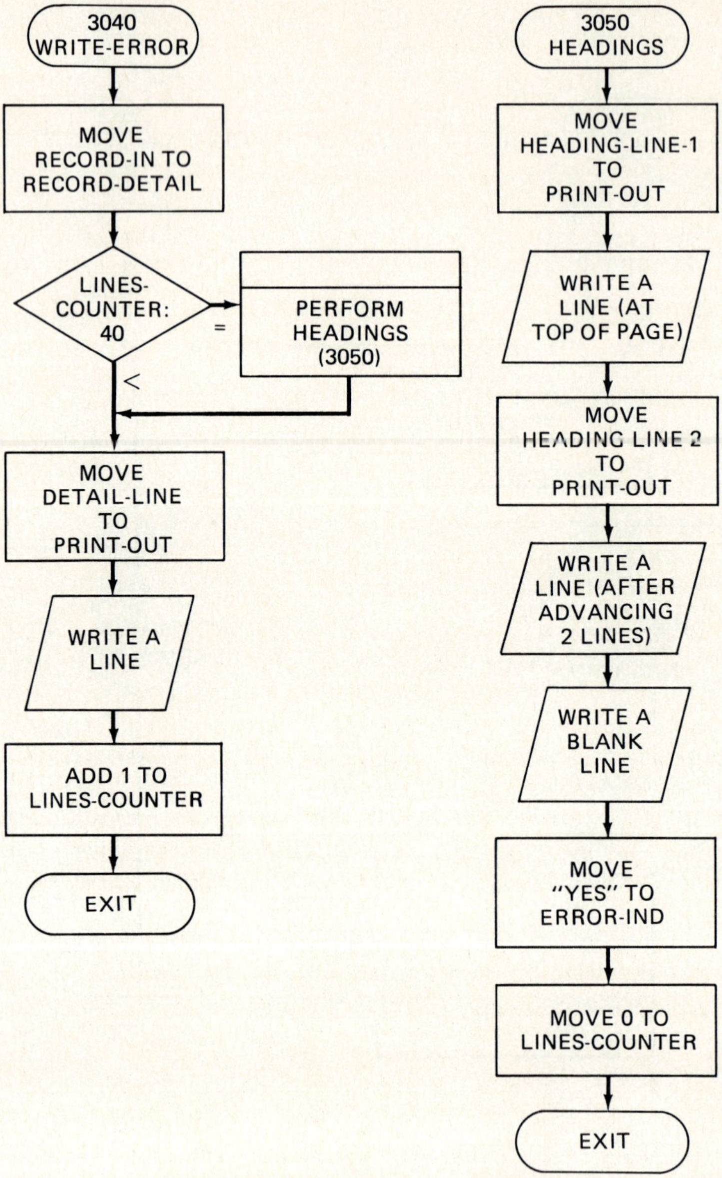

Figure 6-1
Example 6-1
(continued)

Input

Input consists of records with the following format:

Position	*Description*	*Editing Information*	*Error Message*
1–5	Customer number	Must be numeric and in increasing sequence (i.e., the number on the current record is greater than the number on the previous record)	CUSTOMER NUMBER INVALID or CUSTOMER NUMBER OUT OF SEQUENCE
6–30	Customer name	(no editing)	
31–40	Product number	Must be numeric	PRODUCT NUMBER INVALID
41–46	Quanity ordered	Must be numeric and greater than zero	QUANTITY ORDERED INVALID

Why is it necessary to check for all possible errors for each input record? Why not simply terminate the processing of a record as soon as the first error is found? In general, when correcting the invalid records listed on the report, the person making the corrections only corrects those things listed on the report. Usually no effort is made to look further at the record to be sure that no other errors have occurred. If the report indicates that the customer number is invalid and doesn't indicate that the product number is also invalid, then chances are that the person making the corrections won't even look at the product number field when correcting the customer number. Therefore, it is important to include *all* errors on the report.

The hierarchy chart for this example is shown in Figure 6-2. The pseudocode solution for this example is:

```
1000
MAINLINE
START
DO Get-Ready (2010) routine
DO Process-Input (2020) routine UNTIL Done-Processing is equal to "Yes"
ENDDO
DO Finish-Up (2030) routine
STOP

2010
GET-READY
DEFINE data names in input, output, and work areas
OPEN files
DO Read (3010) routine
ENDGET-READY
```

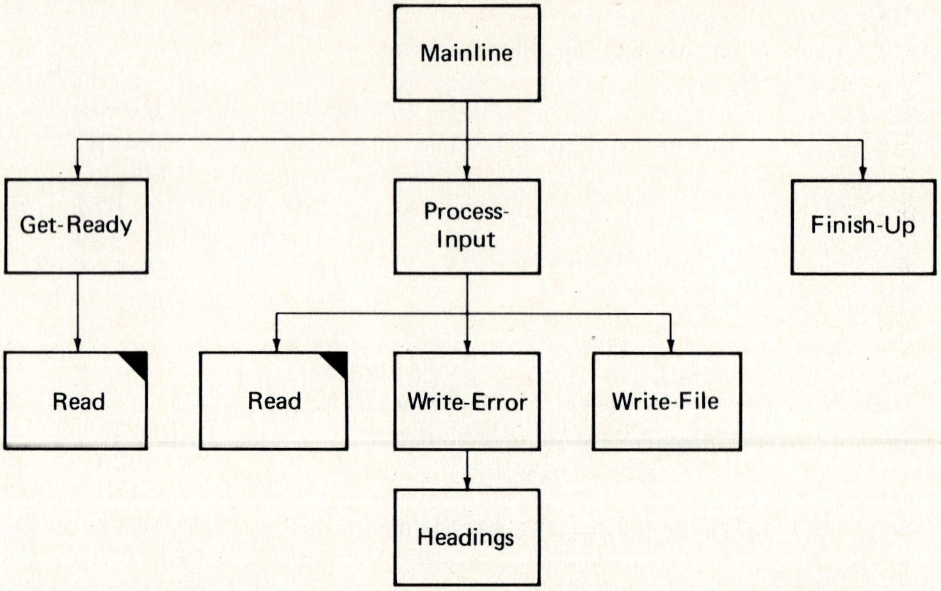

Figure 6-2

```
2020
PROCESS-INPUT
IF No-In is not numeric THEN
       MOVE "Customer Number Invalid" to Error-Detail
       DO Write-Error (3020) routine
ELSE IF No-In is not greater than Previous-Number THEN
            MOVE "Customer Number out of Sequence" to Error-Detail
            DO Write-Error (3020) routine
      ELSE MOVE No-In to Previous-Number
      ENDIF
ENDIF
IF Prod-In is not numeric THEN
      MOVE "Product Number Invalid" to Error-Detail
      DO Write-Error (3020) routine
ENDIF
IF Quant-In is not numeric THEN
       MOVE "Quantity Ordered Invalid" to Error-Detail
       DO Write-Error (3020) routine
ELSE IF Quant-In is not greater than zero THEN
             MOVE "Quantity Ordered Invalid" to Error-Detail
             DO Write-Error (3020) routine
      ENDIF
ENDIF
IF Error-Indicator is equal to "No" THEN
      DO Write-File (3030) routine
```

```
ENDIF
DO Read (3010) routine
ENDPROCESS-INPUT

2030
FINISH-UP
CLOSE Files
ENDFINISH-UP

3010
READ
READ a record from input file
        ATEND of file MOVE "Yes" to Done-Processing
IF Done-Processing is equal to "No" THEN
        MOVE "No" to Error-Indicator
ENDIF
ENDREAD

3020
WRITE-ERROR
IF Lines-Counter = 30 THEN
        DO Headings (4010) routine
ENDIF
IF Error-Indicator is equal to "Yes" THEN
        MOVE spaces to Record-Detail
ELSE MOVE Accounts-Rec-In to Record-Detail
ENDIF
MOVE Detail-Line to output area
WRITE a line
ADD 1 to Lines-Counter
MOVE "Yes" to Error-Indicator
ENDWRITE-ERROR

3030
WRITE-FILE
MOVE Accounts-Rec-In to Accounts-Rec-Out
WRITE a record
ENDWRITE-FILE

4010
HEADINGS
ADD 1 to Page-Counter
MOVE Page-Counter to Heading-Line-1
MOVE Heading-Line-1 to output area
WRITE a line at top of page
MOVE Heading-Line-2 to output area
```

WRITE a line after advancing 2 lines
WRITE a blank line
RESET Lines-Counter to 0
ENDHEADINGS

The flowchart solution is shown in Figure 6-3.

In the GET-READY routine, two output areas are specified. One area is for the report, the other is for the file containing the valid records. Before a record is written, it is necessary to move the record to its appropriate output area.

A work area called ERROR-INDICATOR is used to indicate whether an error has been written on the report for the record being processed. We need to know this information for two reasons:

1. If there are no errors for a particular record, then we want to write the record on the output file. This is done at the end of the PROCESS-INPUT routine.
2. For every record input, we want to list the contents of the record only one time on the report regardless of how many errors that record has. In the WRITE-ERROR routine, ERROR-INDICATOR is checked. If its value is "NO", we write the record on the report. If its value is "YES", we write blanks on the report where the record would be.

ERROR-INDICATOR is set to "NO" every time a new record is read. This is done in the READ routine, so that every record gets a "fresh start." When the WRITE-ERROR routine is performed to write an error message for the record, the value of the field is changed to "YES".

Look at the PROCESS-INPUT routine. It is important to note that if the number on the input record (NO-IN) is not numeric, no check is made to see if the number is greater than the previous number. Such a check wouldn't make sense. Similarly, when the quantity field (QUANT-IN) is edited, if it is not numeric, no check is made to see if it is greater than zero. Also note that the number on the input record (NO-IN) is not saved for comparison purposes in PREVIOUS-NUMBER unless it is valid. We do not want to compare the next input record with a "number" that was not numeric or otherwise invalid.

A record shown as being a sequence error on a report may not actually be the "out of sequence" record. Consider the following example. Suppose the numbers on the input records are 1, 2, 3, 4, 8, 6, 9, 10. If you trace this data through the flowchart, you will see that the record with the number 6 will be treated as out of sequence. However, suppose the numbers on the input records are 1, 2, 3, 99, 4, 5, 6, 7, 8, etc. The record out of sequence is the one with the number 99. What will appear on your report, though? The number 99 will be considered to be in sequence since it is larger than 3. Hence 99 will then be moved to PREVIOUS-NUMBER, and all the remaining records (4, 5, 6, 7, 8, etc.) will be listed as errors. It is difficult, if not impossible, to write a program that will accurately reflect which records are out of sequence. The person using the report, then, should be warned that out-of-sequence conditions *will* be listed on the report, but it may be necessary to look at the input file to determine exactly which record or records have caused the condition.

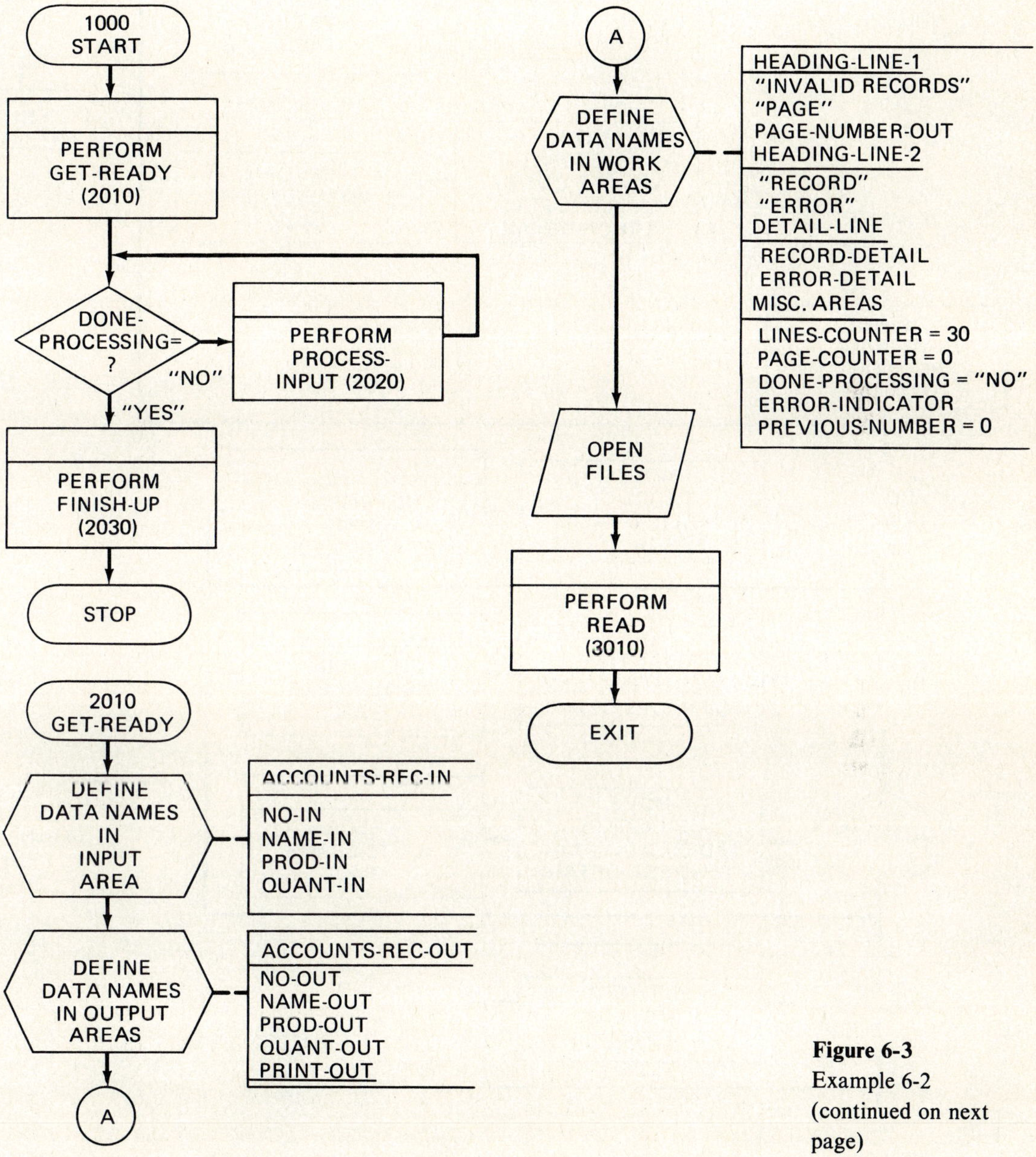

Figure 6-3
Example 6-2 (continued on next page)

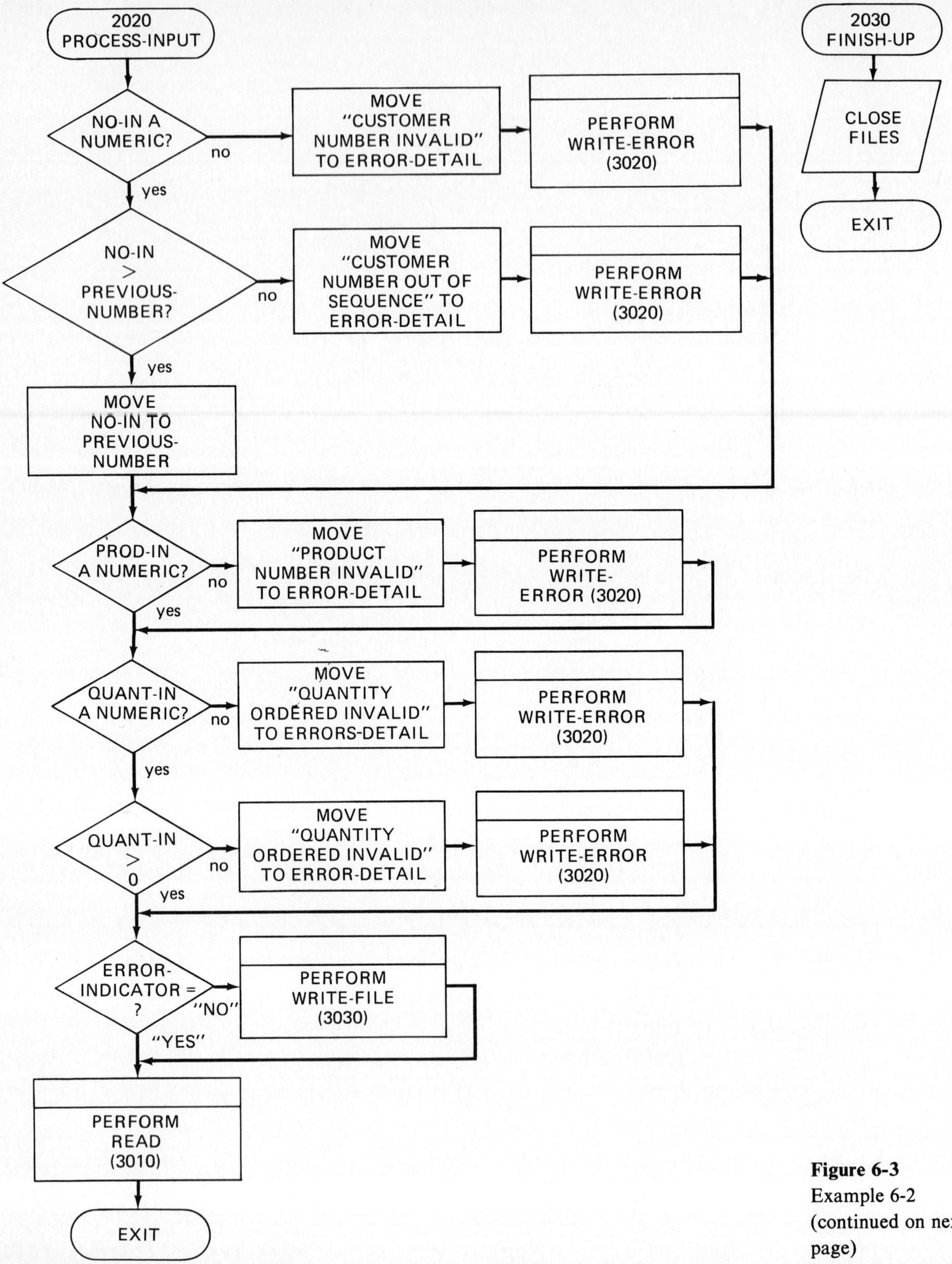

Figure 6-3
Example 6-2
(continued on next page)

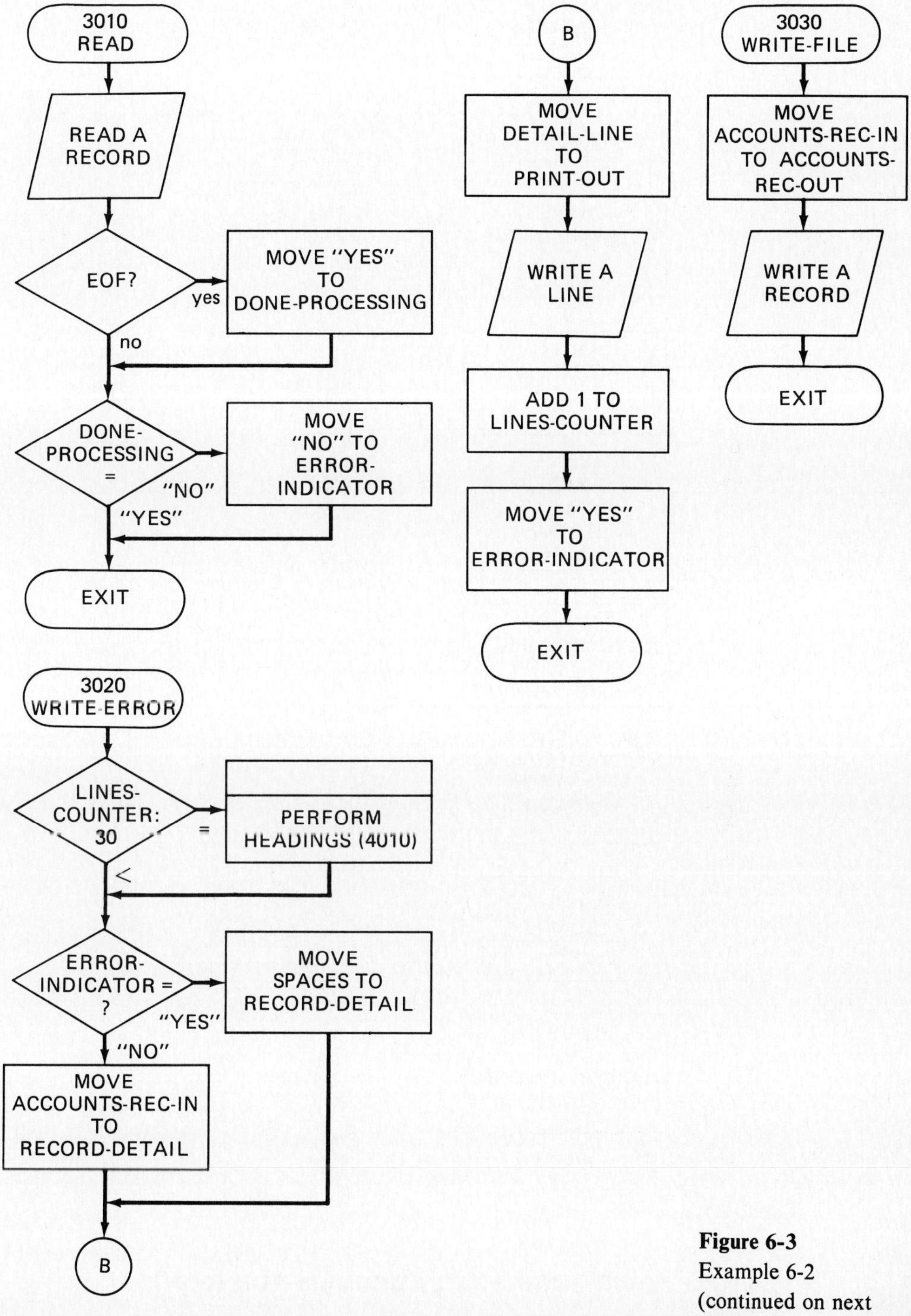

Figure 6-3
Example 6-2
(continued on next page)

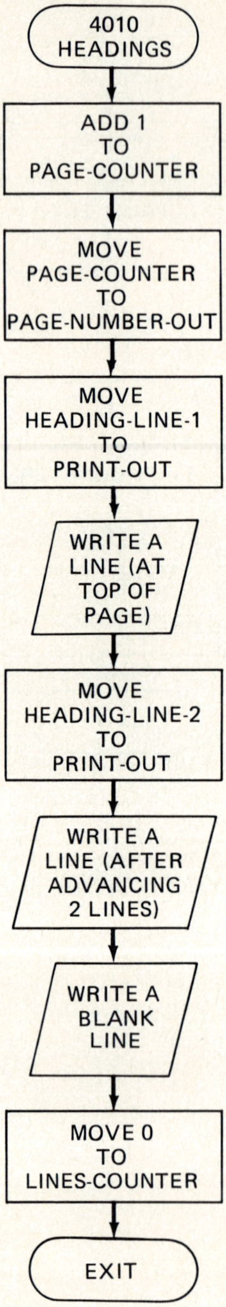

Figure 6-3
Example 6-2
(continued)

QUESTIONS AND EXERCISES FOR REVIEW

1. Define each of the following:
   a. Compilation error

b. Logic error
c. Execution error
d. Program interrupt
e. Edit program

2. Give two examples of compilation errors.
3. Give an example of a data exception error.
4. Discuss the two types of errors that can occur during program execution.
5. Give an example of an error that may occur during program execution in which no error message would be printed on the report. How is such an error detected?
6. Give three examples of input errors that can be detected using an edit program.
7. Give an example of an input error that cannot be detected using an edit program.
8. In a program using multiple output files, how many output areas are used by the program?
9. Why is it desirable to check for more errors on a particular input record after finding the first error on the record?
10. Give an example that illustrates why records listed as sequence errors on an input file might not actually be the ones that were out of sequence on the file.
11. Draw a hierarchy chart for an edit program which will check the input file of Exercise 10 in Chapter 4.

Output

Output is to consist of a report. A maximum of 40 detail lines are to appear per page. Page numbers are to be included. If no errors occur when the input file is processed, print the message NO ERRORS ON INPUT FILE on the report.

Printer Spacing Chart

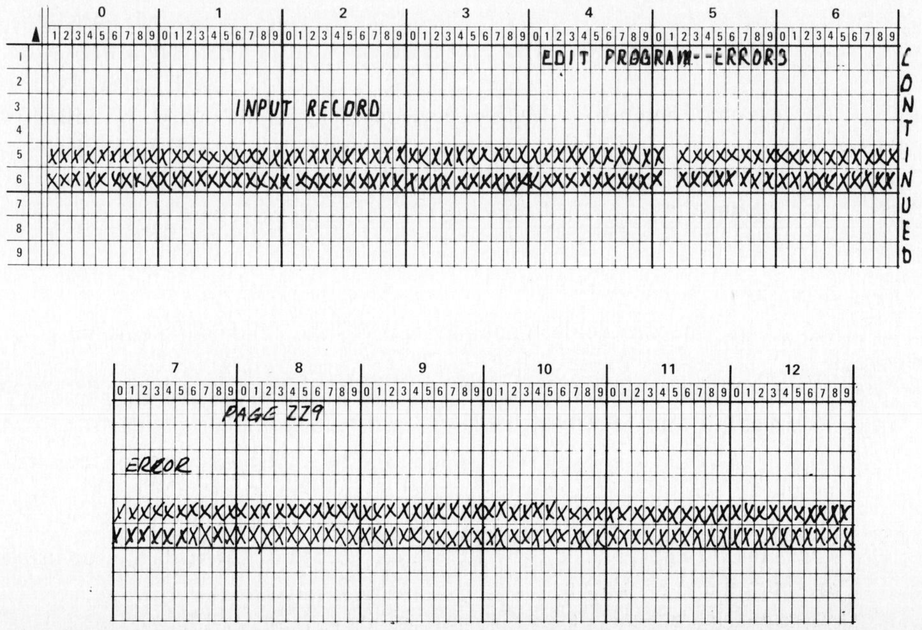

Input

Input consists of three types of records: PRODUCT records, TEST records, and ANIMAL records. The format of the records, editing information, and error messages to be included on the report are described below:

Product Records

Position	*Description*	*Editing Information*	*Error-Message*
1	Code of 1	(see editing notes below)	
2–5	Product number	Must be numeric	PRODUCT NUMBER NOT NUMERIC
6–8	"000"	(no editing)	
9–30	Product name	(no editing)	

Test Records

Position	*Description*	*Editing Information*	*Error-Message*
1	Code of 2	(see editing notes below)	
2–5	Product number	Must be numeric	PRODUCT NUMBER NOT NUMERIC
6–8	Test number	Must be numeric	TEST NUMBER NOT NUMERIC
9–30	Test name	(no editing)	

Animal Records

Position	*Description*	*Editing Information*	*Error-Message*
1	Code of 3	(see editing notes below)	
2–5	Product number	Must be numeric	PRODUCT NUMBER NOT NUMERIC
6–8	Test number	Must be numeric	TEST NUMBER NOT NUMERIC
9–12	Animal number	Must be numeric	ANIMAL NUMBER NOT NUMERIC
13–18	Date performed	(no editing)	
19–50	Result	(no editing)	

Editing Notes

In addition to the specific fields mentioned above, the following fields must be checked:

a. The code field (position 1) must be 1, 2, or 3. If not, use the error message INVALID CODE FIELD.
b. Every PRODUCT record must be followed by a TEST record for the same product. The TEST record must immediately follow the PRODUCT record. If it doesn't, the error message NO TEST RECORD FOR THIS PRODUCT should appear. Use the PRODUCT record as the record to be listed on the report.

c. Every TEST record must be for the same product as the PRODUCT record which preceded it. There may be multiple TEST records for a particular product. If the TEST record is for the wrong product, use the error message INCORRECT PRODUCT ON TEST RECORD—DOES NOT MATCH PRODUCT RECORD.

d. Every ANIMAL record must be for the same product and test as the TEST record which preceded it. There may be 0 or more ANIMAL records for a particular test. If the ANIMAL record is for the wrong product or test, use the error message INCORRECT PRODUCT OR TEST NUMBER ON ANIMAL RECORD—DOES NOT MATCH TEST RECORD.

12. Draw a flowchart for Exercise 11 above.
13. Construct the pseudocode for Exercise 11 above.
14. Draw a hierarchy chart and flowchart or pseudocode for a program which will edit the input file described below.

Output

Output consists of a report of the invalid records and a file containing the valid records. The valid record file is to use the same record format as the input file. If no errors occur during processing, the message NO ERRORS is to be written on the report. A maximum of 50 detail lines are to appear per page. If multiple errors occur for a particular record, the record is to be listed only once. Page numbers are to be included.

Printer Spacing Chart

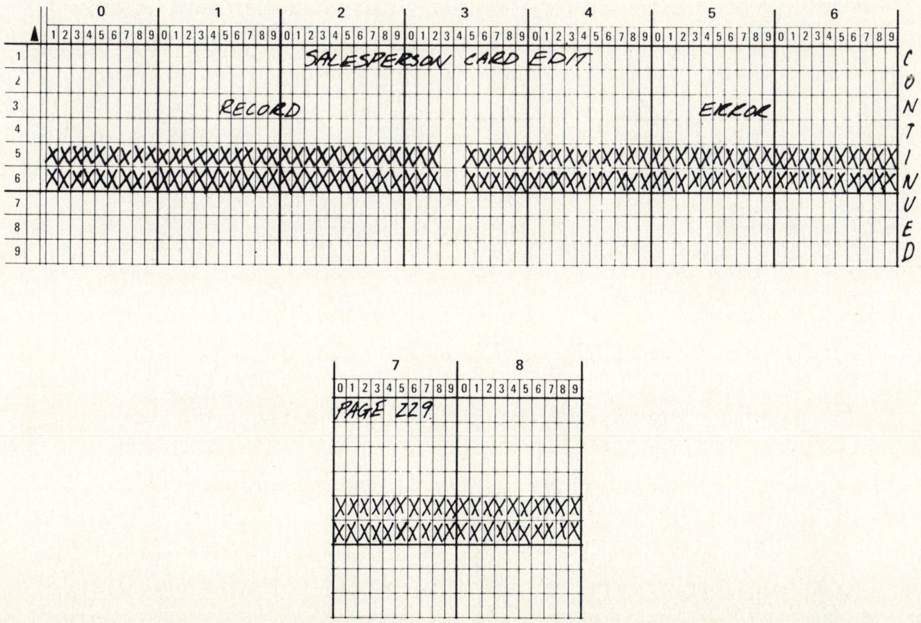

Input

Input consists of records of the following format:

Position	*Description*	*Editing Information*
1–3	Salesperson number	Must be numeric
4–25	Salesperson name	Must be alphabetic
26–30	Number of units sold this month	Must be numeric and greater than or equal to zero
31–32	Month	Must be numeric and in the range 1 to 12

Processing

a. All fields must be checked according to the editing information above.
b. In addition, check the salesperson number to be sure that it is in increasing sequence (i.e., the number on the second record is greater than the first, etc.).
c. The following error messages are to be used:
(1) SALESPERSON NUMBER NOT NUMERIC
(2) SALESPERSON NUMBER OUT OF SEQUENCE
(3) SALESPERSON NAME NOT ALPHABETIC
(4) NUMBER OF UNITS SOLD NOT NUMERIC
(5) NUMBER OF UNITS SOLD NOT GREATER THAN OR EQUAL TO 0
(6) MONTH NOT NUMERIC
(7) MONTH NOT IN THE RANGE 1 to 12
Note: Check for the errors in the above order. All errors are to be checked for with the following exceptions: If error 1 occurs, do not check for error 2; if error 4 occurs, do not check for error 5; if error 6 occurs, do not check for error 7.

CHAPTER 7

Extract Programs and Sorts

BACKGROUND

Until now, every record on the input file has been used to create the output file(s). Sometimes it is desirable to use only some of the records from the input file to create the output file(s). A program that selects certain records from a file to create a new file (or report) containing only the selected records is called an *extract program.*

EXAMPLE 7-1: SELECTION BASED ON ONE CRITERIA

For this example the administration of a school wants a list of students who reside in Skokie for purposes of arranging a carpool.

Output

Output is to consist of a report containing the names and addresses of students residing in Skokie. A maximum of 50 detail lines are to appear per page. Page numbers are to be included on the report.

Printer Spacing Chart

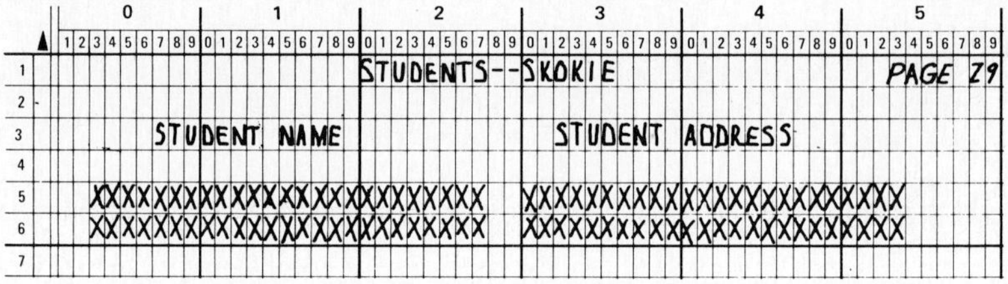

Input

Input consists of a tape file. Each record of the file has the following format:

Position	*Description*
1–25	Student name
26	Category of student (D = day; E = evening)
27–50	Street address
51–65	City

This is a fairly straightforward problem. For every record input, it is necessary to check the CITY field. If the city is Skokie, then the record is included on the report. If the city is not Skokie, the record is bypassed and the next record is read into the input area.

The hierarchy chart for this example is shown on the next page.

The pseudocode solution for this problem is:

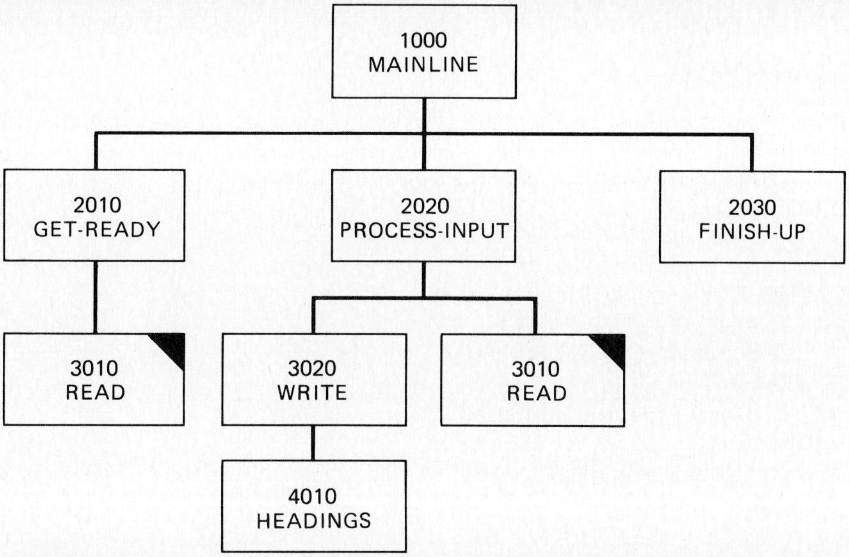


```
1000
MAINLINE
START
DO Get-Ready (2010) routine
DO Process-Input (2020) routine UNTIL Done-Processing is equal to "Yes"
ENDDO
DO Finish-Up (2030) routine
STOP

2010
GET-READY
DEFINE data names in input, output, and work areas
OPEN files
DO Read (3010) routine
ENDGET-READY

2020
PROCESS-INPUT
IF City-In is equal to "Skokie" THEN
   MOVE Name-In to Name-Detail
   MOVE Address-In to Address-Detail
   DO Write (3020) routine
ENDIF
DO READ (3010) routine
ENDPROCESS-INPUT

2030
FINISH-UP
CLOSE files
ENDFINISH-UP
```

```
3010
READ
READ a record from input file
   ATEND of file MOVE "Yes" to Done-Processing
ENDREAD

3020
WRITE
IF Lines-Counter = 50 THEN
   DO Headings (4010) routine
ENDIF
MOVE Detail-Line to output area
WRITE a line
ADD 1 to Lines-Counter
ENDWRITE

4010
HEADINGS
ADD 1 to Page-Counter
MOVE Page-Counter to Heading-Line-1
MOVE Heading-Line-1 to output area
WRITE a line at top of page
MOVE Heading-Line-2 to output area
WRITE a line after advancing 2 lines
WRITE a blank line
RESET Lines-Counter to 0
ENDHEADINGS
```

Drawing the flowchart is left as an exercise for the reader.

EXAMPLE 7-2: SELECTION BASED ON MULTIPLE CRITERIA (AND COMPARISONS)

Most extract programs look for records that will meet multiple criteria. When multiple criteria are tested for, the order in which the criteria are tested will affect the efficiency of the program. In this chapter some guidelines will be given to help in writing efficient programs. However, when multiple criteria are to be tested for in the most efficient manner, some knowledge of statistics is necessary. Since this is not a course in mathematics, a relatively unsophisticated explanation will be given.

In this example we are to use the same input file as was used in Example 7-1. This time, however, we are to extract the records for the day students who live in Skokie and prepare a tape containing the selected records. The format of the tape file is identical to that of the input file.

In order for a record to be selected, two conditions must be true. The value of the CATEGORY field on the input record must be "D" *and* the value of the CITY field must be "Skokie". Therefore two decisions must be included in the PROCESS-INPUT routine:

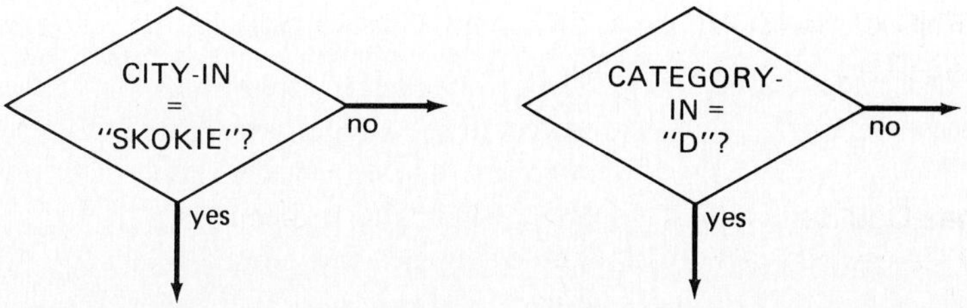

Which decision should be first? Assume that the analyst has told us that 50 percent of the input file consists of records for day students and that 20 percent of the input file consists of records for residents of Skokie. For those of you who have some knowledge of statistics and sampling theory, we can assume that the conditions are *independent*. That is, we can assume that the probability of one condition occurring (living in Skokie) does not depend on the other condition occurring (being a day student). This means that we can assume that 20 percent of the day students live in Skokie and 50 percent of the Skokie residents are day students. If that is not true, then the following argument for the order of testing the conditions will not work.

Suppose that there are 100 records on the input file. Further suppose that we check the CITY field first. Of the 100 records, 20 percent, or 20 records, will be Skokie

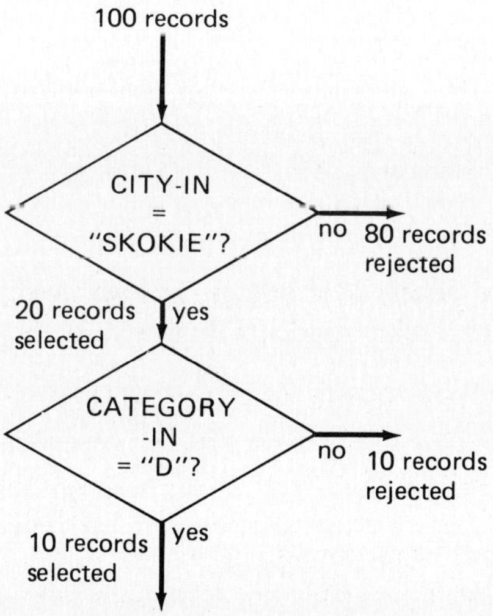

residents and will be selected; 80 percent, or 80 records, will not be for Skokie residents and will be rejected. Since both conditions must be true to select a record, we do not have to do any further comparisons for anyone who does not live in Skokie. Next we check the CATEGORY field. Of the 20 Skokie residents, 50 percent, or 10, will be day students. This means we will end up selecting 10 records from the input file. After processing the input file, the computer will have done

100 + 20 = 120 comparisons

- 100: Comparisons made to test for city.
- 20: Skokie residents that are tested to see if they are day students. These are the records which have been selected in the first comparisons.

If we had checked the CATEGORY field first, we would compare 100 records to see if they were day students and select 50 percent of these, or 50 records. Those 50

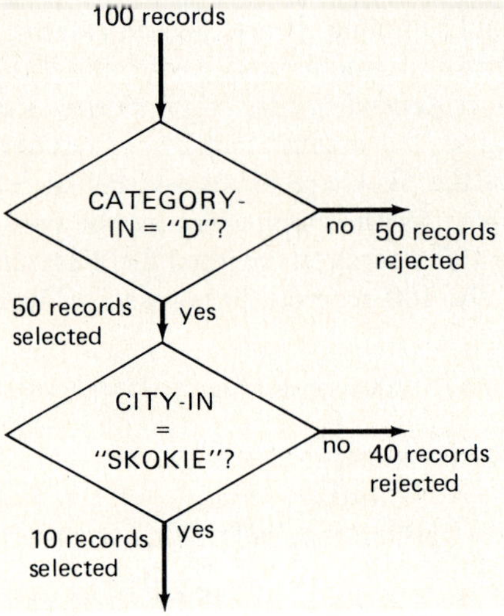

records would have to be checked for village, and we would select 20 percent of 50, or 10 records, as being for Skokie residents. In this case, the computer will have done

100 + 50 = 150 comparisons

- 100: Comparisons made to test for category.
- 50: Day students who are tested to see if they are Skokie residents.

Therefore, the most efficient method checks for CITY first.

It can be generalized that in an "and" comparison in which the conditions are independent, checking for the condition with the *smallest* probability of occurrence (lowest percentage) first is the most efficient. This will result in the elimination of the greatest number of records from subsequent comparisons.

The flowchart solution is shown in Figure 7-1.

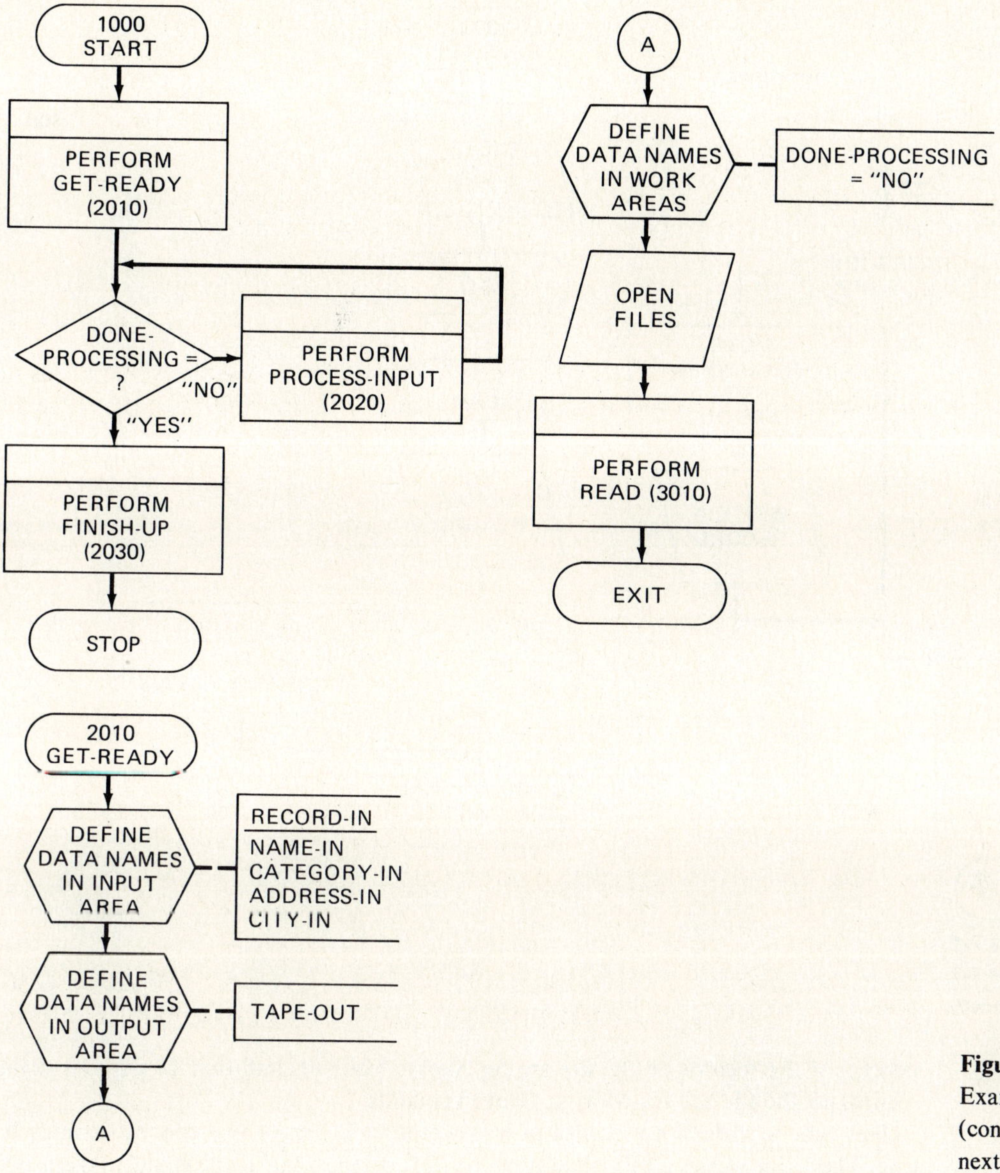

Figure 7-1
Example 7-2
(continued on next page)

EXAMPLE 7-3: SELECTION BASED ON MULTIPLE CRITERIA (OR COMPARISONS)

In this example, we again want to use the input file used in Example 7-1. This time we want to extract the records for students who live in Morton Grove *or* Skokie regardless of the student's category. Assume that the analyst has told us that 20

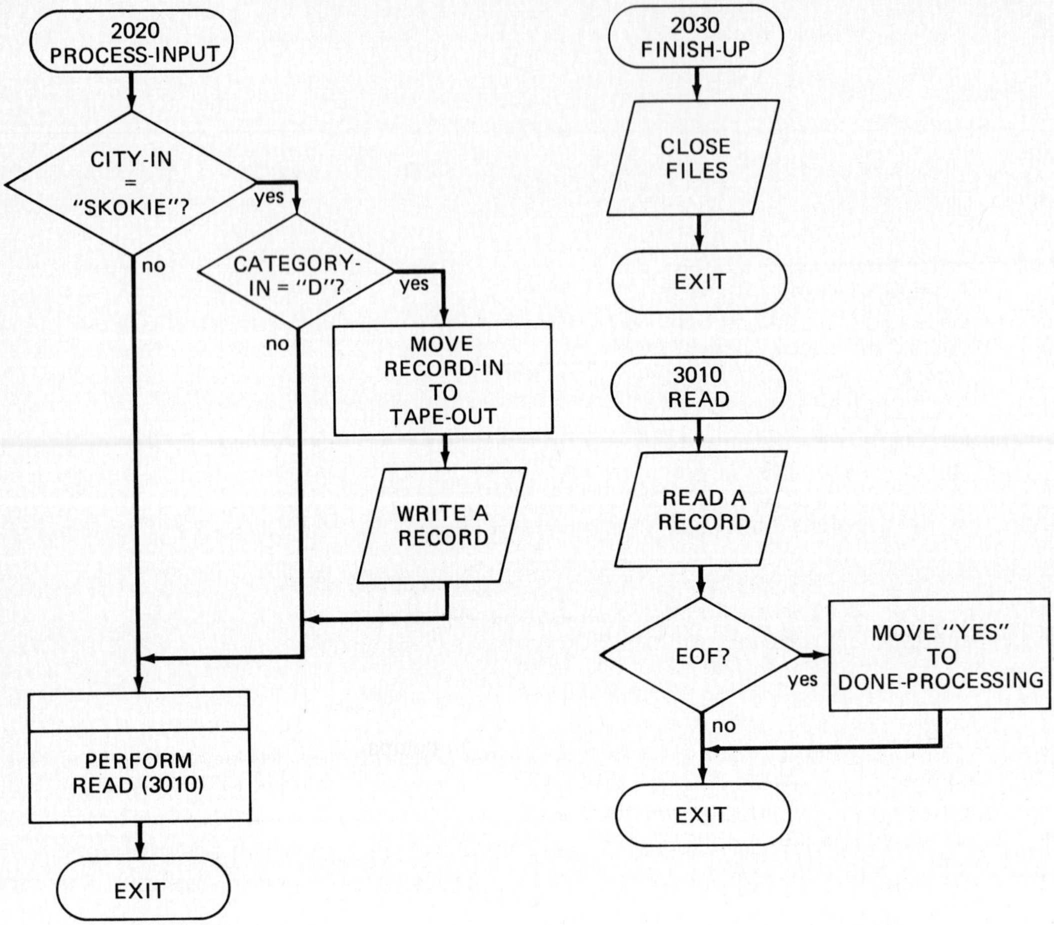

Figure 7-1
Example 7-2
(continued)

percent of the records on the file are for Skokie residents and that 10 percent of the records on the file are for Morton Grove residents.

This time in order for a record to be selected, only one of two conditions must be true. The value of the CITY field must be "Morton Grove" *or* "Skokie". Again two decisions must be included in the PROCESS-INPUT routine.

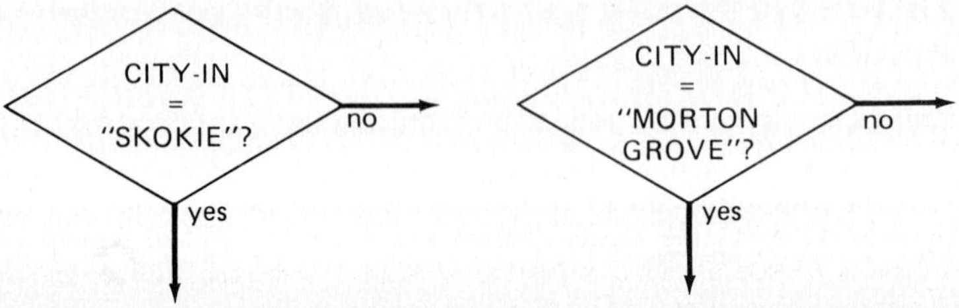

We must now decide which decision should be first. Suppose that there are 100 records on the input file. Suppose also that we check for "Morton Grove" first:

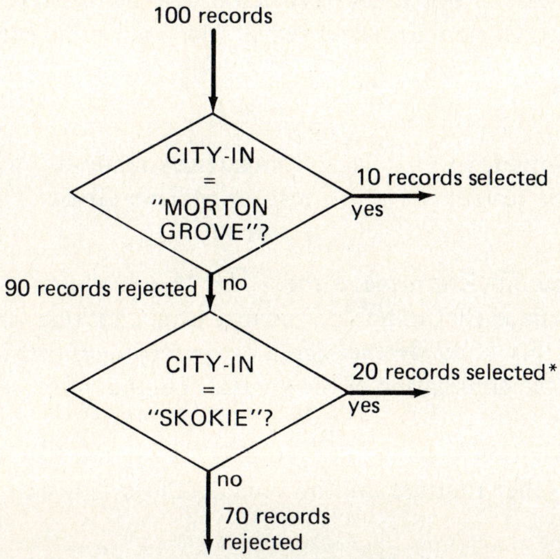

Of the 100 records, 10 percent of the file, or 10 records, will be selected; 90 percent of the file, or 90 records, will not be selected. Of the 90 records not selected, we must check to see if any of them are for Skokie residents. This means that the computer will do

100 (Comparisons made to test for Morton Grove residents.) + 90 (Comparisons made to test for Skokie residents.) = 190 comparisons

If we had checked for "Skokie" first, we would compare 100 records and select 20

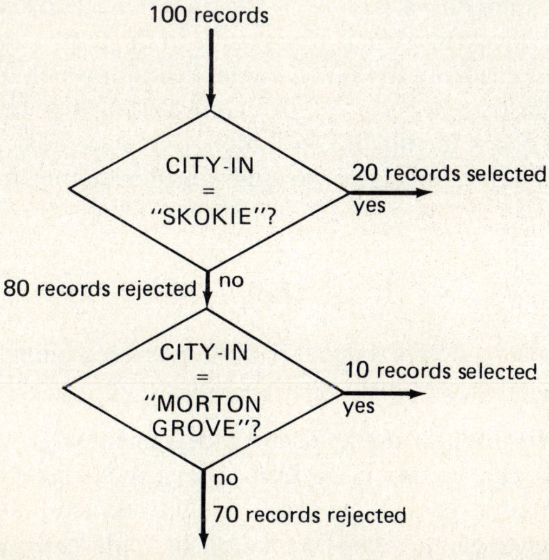

*Since the conditions are *mutually exclusive,* i.e., the occurrence of one condition prevents occurrence of the other, 20 percent of the original file will be Skokie residents.

percent, or 20 records; 80 would not be selected. We then would check the 80 records to see if any are for Morton Grove residents. This means the computer will do

100	+	80	= 180 comparisons
Comparisons made to test for Skokie residents.		Comparisons made to test for Morton Grove residents.	

Therefore, the most efficient method checks for "Skokie" first.

It can be generalized that in an "or" comparison, checking for the condition with the *largest* probability of occurrence (greatest percentage) first is the most efficient. This will result in the elimination of the greatest number of records from subsequent comparions.

The flowchart solution is shown in Figure 7-2. Only the PROCESS-INPUT routine is shown. All other routines are the same as those shown in Figure 7-1.

EXAMPLE 7-4: SELECTION BASED ON MULTIPLE CRITERIA (AND AND OR COMPARISONS)

The above examples show how to handle multiple decisions if the criteria are all "and" conditions or all "or" conditions. This example shows how to handle comparisons that mix "and" and "or" criteria.

This time we want to select those records which are for day students living in Morton Grove or Skokie. Figure 7-3 shows the possible order of the decisions and the number of comparisons the computer will have to make, assuming that we start with an input file containing 100 records. From studying Figure 7-3, you can see that the most efficient method for comparing is to check for the value in the CATEGORY-IN field first, then check CITY-IN for Skokie residents, and finally check CITY-IN for Morton Grove residents. This results in the fewest number of comparisons. In general, when checking for "and" comparisons in which one or more of the fields can contain more than one value ("or" condition), check the fields with only one choice first. Then check the field(s) with more than one choice, checking for the possibility with the highest percentage (greatest likelihood of occurrence) first.

SUMMARY

In conclusion, the following points should serve as review regarding the order of comparisons in an extract program:

1. In an "and" comparison, if the fields are independent (e.g., the percent of day students does not change as you go from village to village), then checking the field with the smallest percentage (least likely to occur) first is most efficient. Continue comparing going from the smallest to the largest percent.

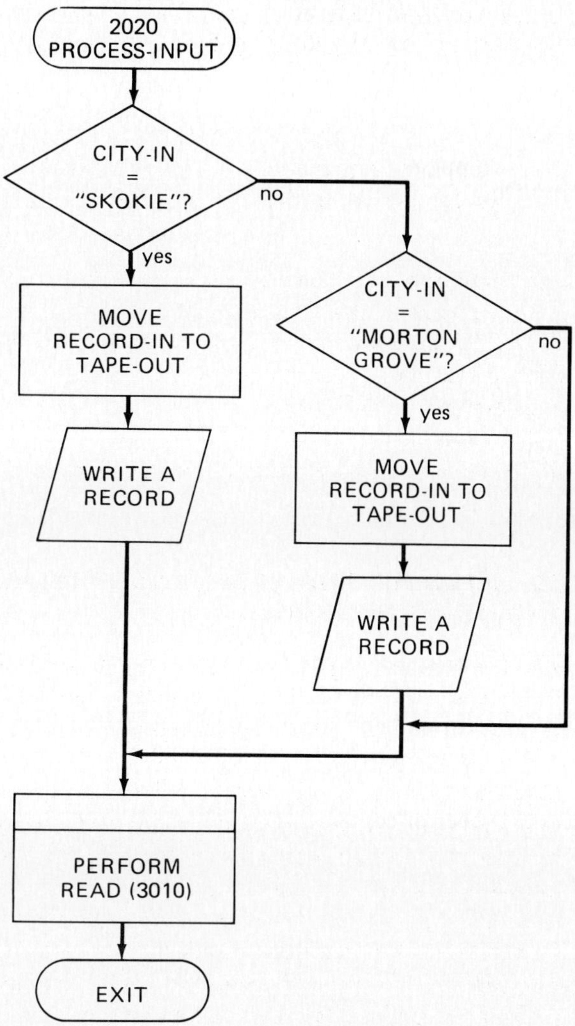

Figure 7-2
Example 7-3

2. In an "or" comparison, if the fields are mutually exclusive (the occurrence of one condition prevents the occurrence of the other condition—e.g., a person cannot live in both Skokie and Morton Grove), then check the largest percentage (most likely to occur) first. Continue comparing going from the largest to the smallest percent.
3. When combining "and" and "or" conditions, determine the most efficient method by determining how many comparisons the computer will have to make during execution of the program and minimize the number of comparisons. If some fields have more than one possible value which may be selected, check the fields with only one possible value first.

(*a*) 100 records input

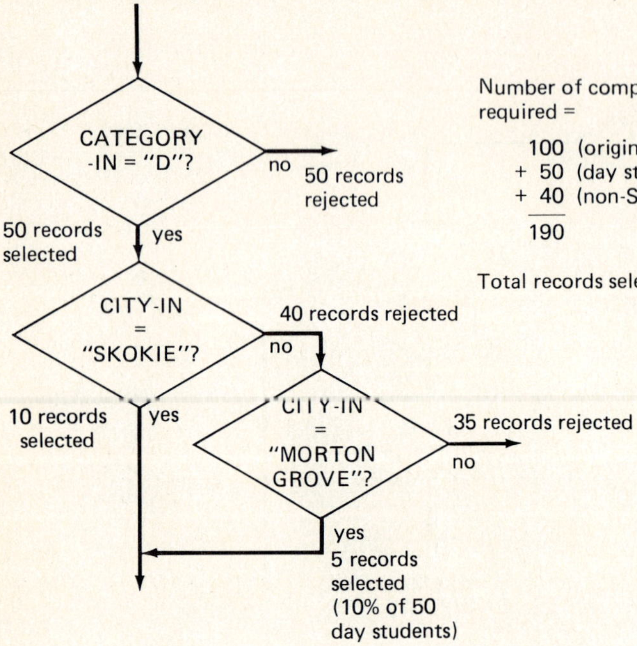

Number of comparisons required =

```
  100  (original records)
+  50  (day students selected to be tested for city)
+  40  (non-Skokie residents to be tested for Morton Grove)
  ---
  190
```

Total records selected = 15

(*b*) 100 records input

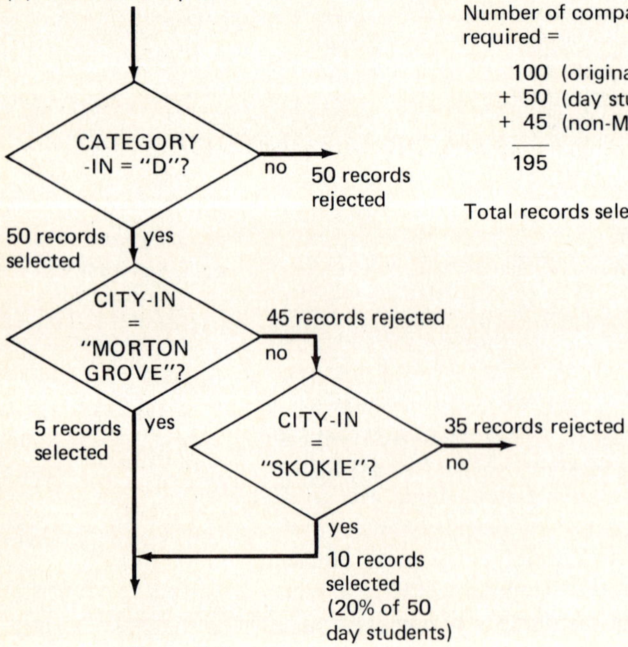

Number of comparisons required =

```
  100  (original records)
+  50  (day students selected to be tested for city)
+  45  (non-Morton Grove residents to be tested for Skokie)
  ---
  195
```

Total records selected = 15

Figure 7-3
Example 7-4
(continued on next page)

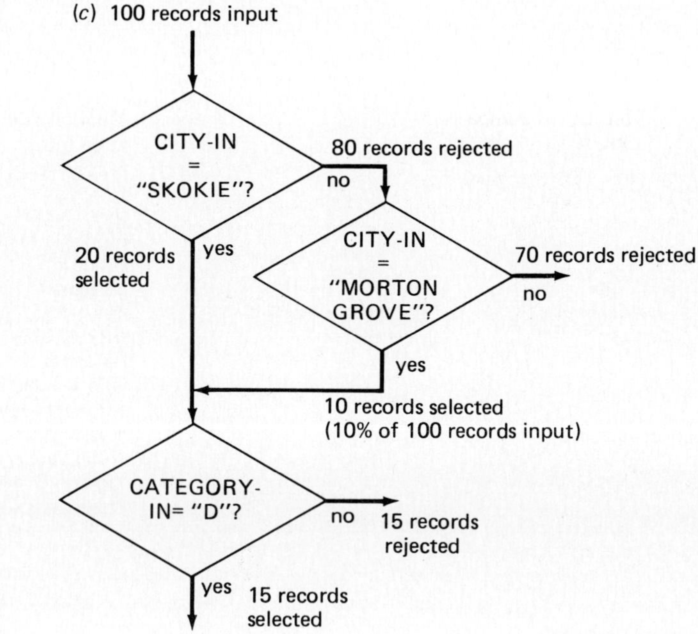

Number of comparisons required=

100 (original records)

\+ 20 (Skokie residents to be tested for category)

\+ 80 (non-Skokie residents to be tested to see if they are Morton Grove residents)

\+ 10 (Morton Grove residents to be tested for category)

210

Total records selected = 15

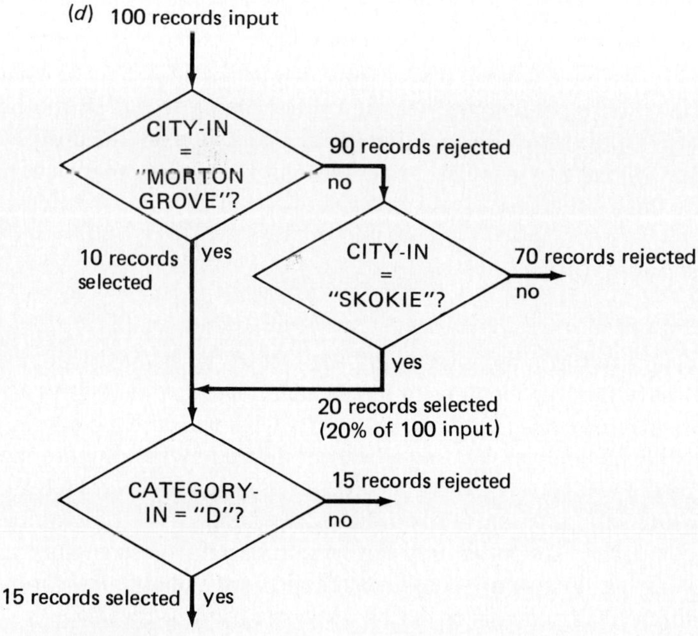

Number of comparisons required =

100 (original records)

\+ 10 (Morton Grove residents to be tested for category)

\+ 90 (non-Morton Grove residents to be tested to see if they are Skokie residents)

\+ 20 (Skokie residents to be tested for category)

220

Total records selected = 15

Figure 7-3
Example 7-4
(continued on next page)

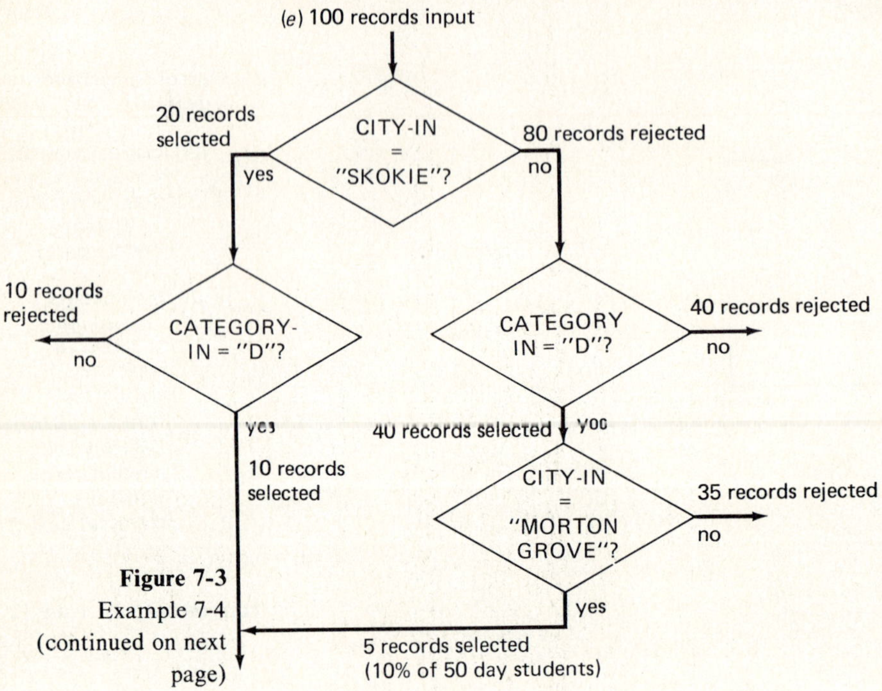

Figure 7-3
Example 7-4
(continued on next page)

Number of comparisons required =

100 (original records)

\+ 20 (Skokie residents to be tested for category)

\+ 80 (non-Skokie residents to be tested for category)

\+ 40 (non-Skokie residents who are day students to be tested to see if they are Morton Grove residents)

240

Total records selected = 15

In the examples we have done in this chapter, it was assumed that we knew something about the relative percentages for the criteria being tested on the input file. That's not always true. If such information is not available from the analyst or user, the programmer will have to make his or her best guess as to the relative percentages and, therefore, which condition to test for first.

SORTS

Often it is desirable to sort a file, that is, put the records in the file in an order based on a field or fields within the file prior to processing. Some computer languages, such as COBOL, provide for *embedded (internal) sorts.* This means that a sort instruction is part of the language and can be used whenever desired by the programmer. Some languages, such as FORTRAN, do not provide internal sorts. When such a language is used, a separate sort program needs to be used whenever the programmer needs to sort a file. Sometimes sort programs can be purchased from computer manufacturers when operating systems are bought. Such sorts are called *utility sorts.* In some cases a programmer will code his or her own sort program or routine.

Regardless of the method used for sorting, a sort program or instruction takes a lot of time to execute. By using an extract program to cut down the number of rec-

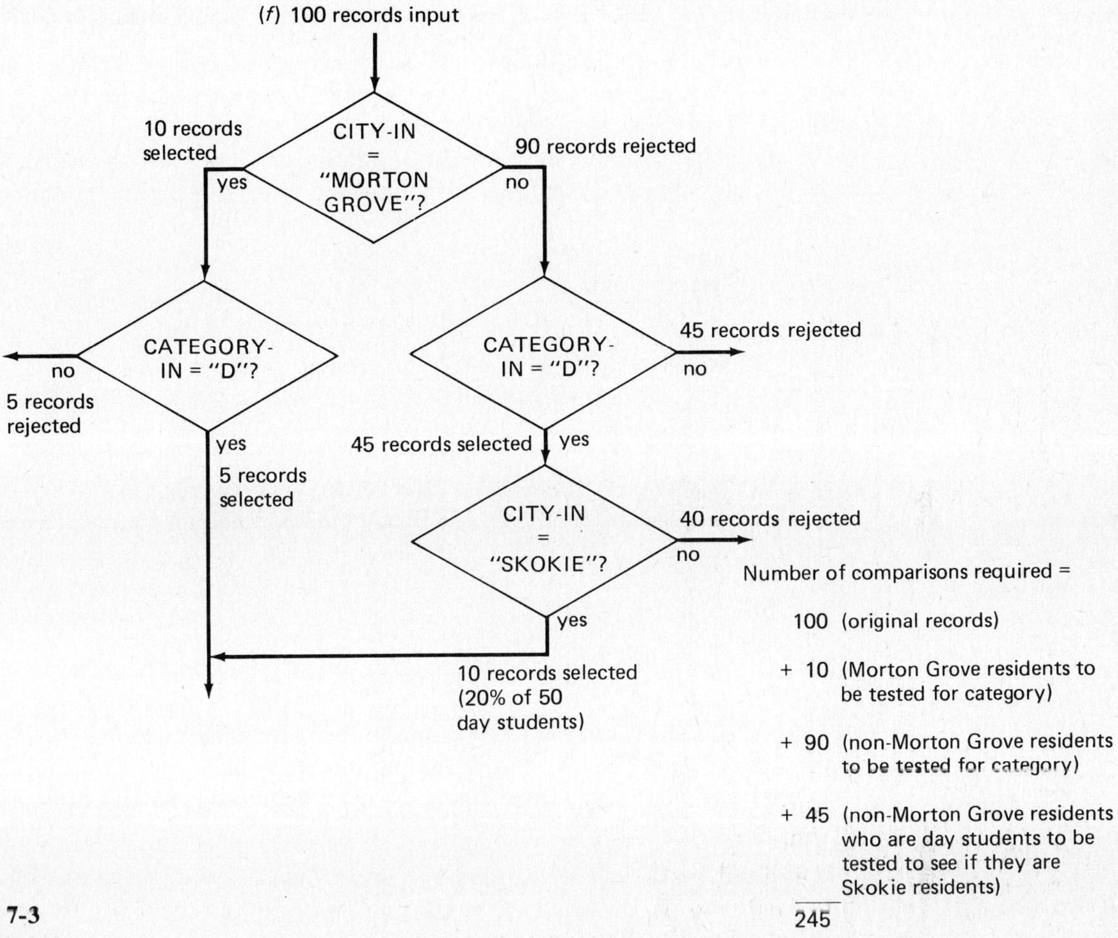

Figure 7-3
Example 7-4
(continued)

ords that need to be sorted, you will speed up the program considerably. Suppose, for example, that your input file is a school file containing one record for each student in the school. Further suppose that you want to list the freshmen students in alphabetical order. You could sort the entire file and then extract the freshmen. This would involve sorting every record on the file. On the other hand, you could extract the freshmen first and then sort only the selected records. This involves sorting only a portion of the file and is, therefore, more efficient.

If you were to use a separate sort program to generate the list of freshmen in alphabetical order, you would need to use three programs. The first program would extract the freshmen. The second program would sort the selected records. The third program would then list the sorted records.

EXAMPLE 7-5: EXTRACT PROGRAM WITH AN EMBEDDED SORT

This example uses an embedded sort. We will extract the desired records from a file (SORT-IN routine), sort the records using a sort instruction, and list the sorted records (SORT-OUT routine) all in one program.

We are to modify Example 7-2 to sort the records alphabetically by name. Instead of producing a tape as output, we are to produce a report using the printer spacing chart below:

Printer Spacing Chart

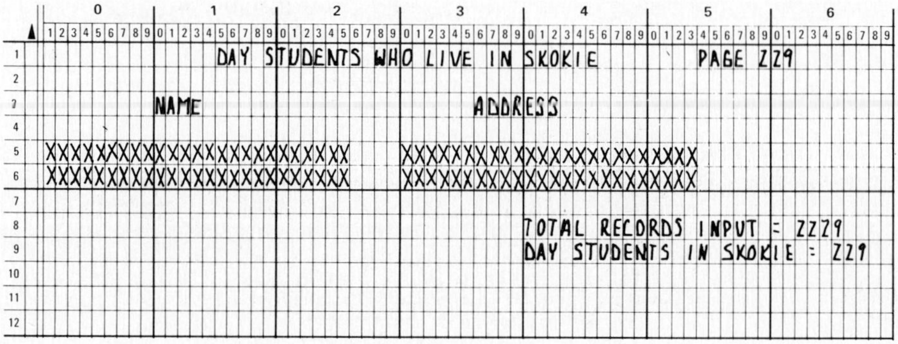

A maximum of 50 detail lines are to appear per page. Total lines are to appear at the end of the report as shown in the output format.

A hierarchy chart is shown in Figure 7-4. The pseudocode for this example is:

```
1000
MAINLINE
START
DO Get-Ready (2010) routine
IF Done-Processing-Input is equal to "Yes" THEN
   DO Headings (2050) routine
   MOVE "No Input Records" to output area
   WRITE a line
   CLOSE files
ELSE DO Sort-In (2020) routine
   SORT file in alphabetical order on name field
   DO Sort-Out (2030) routine
   DO Finish-Up (2040) routine
ENDIF
STOP

2010
GET-READY
DEFINE data names in input, output, sort, and work areas
OPEN files
```

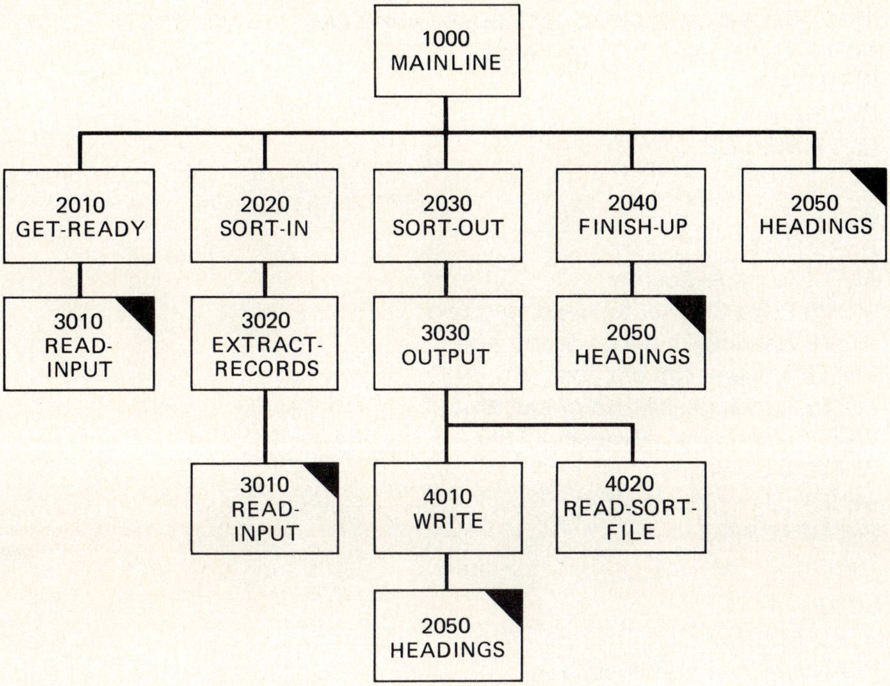

Figure 7-4
Example 7-5

DO Read-Input (3010) routine
ENDGET-READY

2020
SORT-IN
DO Extract-Records (3020) routine UNTIL Done-Processing-Input = "Yes"
ENDDO
ENDSORT-IN

2030
SORT-OUT
DO Output (3030) routine UNTIL Done-Processing-Sort-File = "Yes"
ENDDO
ENDSORT-OUT

2040
FINISH-UP
IF Lines-Counter is greater than or equal to 48 THEN
  DO Headings (2050) routine
ENDIF
MOVE Total-Records-Input to Total-Records-Input-Out
MOVE Total-Line-1 to output area
WRITE a line after advancing 2 lines

```
MOVE Total-Day-Skokie to Total-Day-Skokie-Out
MOVE Total-Line-2 to output area
WRITE a line
CLOSE files
ENDFINISH-UP

2050
HEADINGS
ADD 1 to Page-Counter
MOVE Page-Counter to Heading-Line-1
MOVE Heading-Line-1 to output area
WRITE a line at top of page
MOVE Heading-Line-2 to output area
WRITE a line after advancing 2 lines
WRITE a blank line
RESET Lines-Counter to 0
ENDHEADINGS

3010
READ-INPUT
READ a record from Input File
  ATEND of file MOVE "Yes" to Done-Processing-Input
ENDREAD-INPUT

3020
EXTRACT-RECORDS
ADD 1 to Total-Records-Input
IF City-In = "Skokie" and Category-In = "D" THEN
  MOVE Record-In to Sort-Record
  WRITE Sort-Record on Sort File
  ADD 1 to Total-Day-Skokie
ENDIF
DO Read-Input (3010) routine
ENDEXTRACT-RECORDS

3030
OUTPUT
DO Read-Sort-File (4020) routine
IF Done-Processing-Sort-File is equal to "No" THEN
  MOVE Name-Sort to Name-Detail
  MOVE Address-Sort to Address-Detail
  DO Write (4010) routine
ENDIF
ENDOUTPUT
```

```
4010
WRITE
IF Lines-Counter = 50 THEN
  DO Headings (2050) routine
ENDIF
MOVE Detail-Line to output area
WRITE a line
ADD 1 to Lines-Counter
ENDWRITE

4020
READ-SORT-FILE
READ a record from Sort File
  ATEND of file MOVE "Yes" to Done-Processing-Sort-File
ENDREAD-SORT-FILE
```

The flowchart solution is shown in Figure 7-5.

The main routine first performs GET-READY. If there are no records on the input file, an error message is printed and processing stops. If there are records on the input file, the SORT-IN routine is performed to extract the records to be sorted. After the records are extracted, they are sorted in alphabetical order based on the name field. The sorted records are then listed by performing the SORT-OUT routine. FINISH-UP is then performed to print the totals and close the files.

The sort instruction requires that a temporary sort file (usually a disk file) be set up by the program. This file does not need to be specified when the input and output areas to be used by the program are defined. It also does not need to be opened or closed in the program. The specifying, opening, and closing of the file are done by using the sort instruction. The programmer does, however, need to define a *sort area* in the GET-READY routine. Every time an embedded sort instruction is used, a sort area must be defined in main memory.

The SORT-IN routine is performed for each record on the input file. The sole purpose of SORT-IN is to control the loop which calls the EXTRACT-RECORDS routine. The EXTRACT-RECORDS routine increments the counter which keeps track of the total number of records input. Then the routine determines if the record is to be extracted. If the record is extracted, it is written on a temporary file used by the sort instruction. Just as a detail line needs to be moved to the output area prior to printing, a record to be sorted must be moved to the sort work area prior to being written on the sort file. Finally, the routine adds 1 to the counter which keeps track of the total number of day students who live in Skokie.

EXTRACT-RECORDS is performed until DONE-PROCESSING-INPUT has a value of "yes". At that time, all the selected records have been written on the sort file and the file is sorted. The sorted records are then read from the sort work file and listed on the report. Each record read is put into the sort work area. Before a line on the report is written, the record must be moved first to the detail line and then to the output area used by the report.

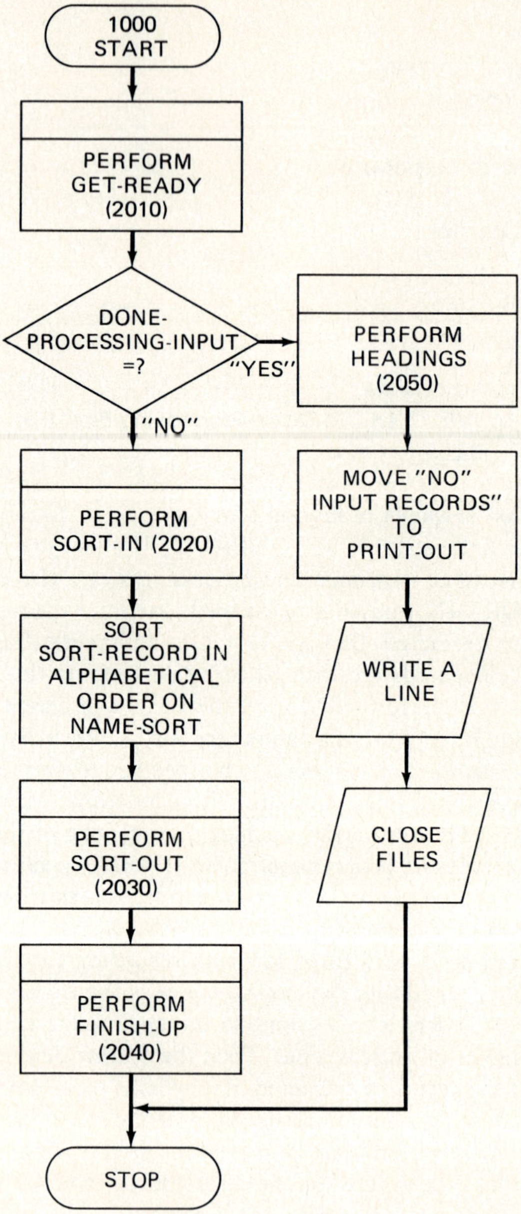

Figure 7-5
Example 7-5
(continued on next page)

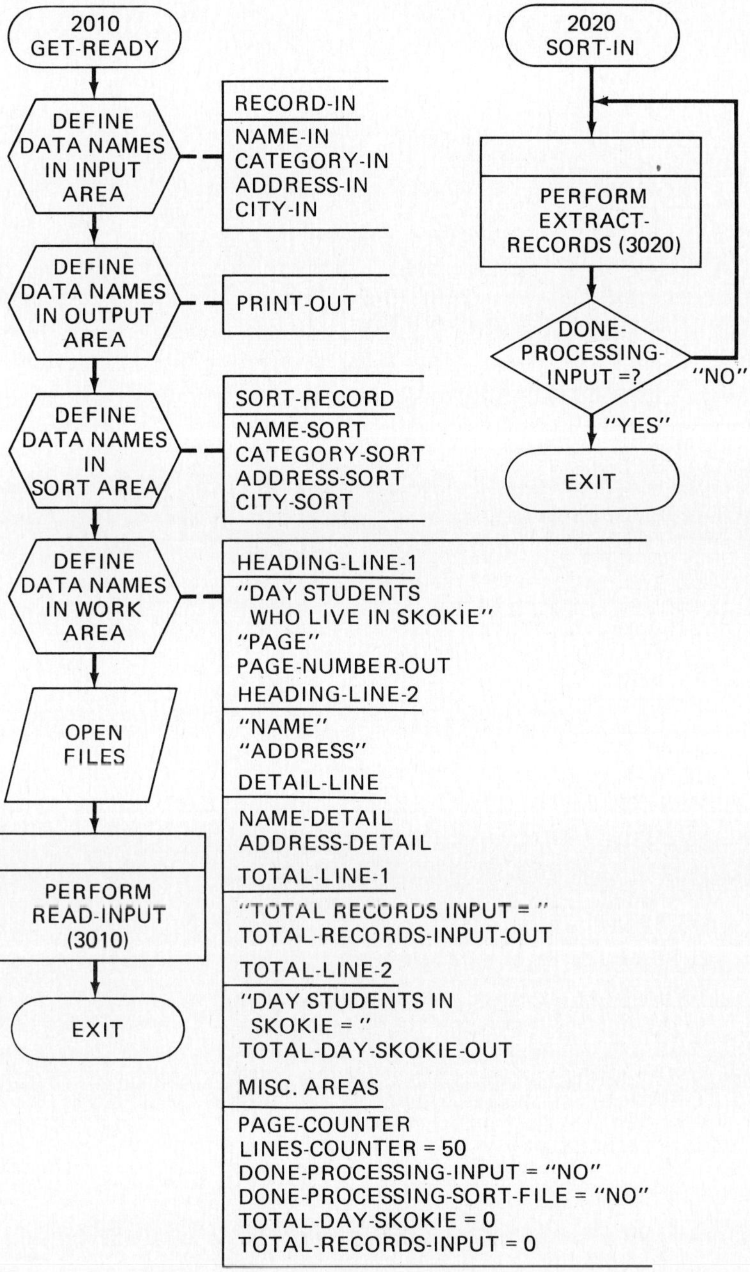

Figure 7-5
Example 7-5
(continued on next page)

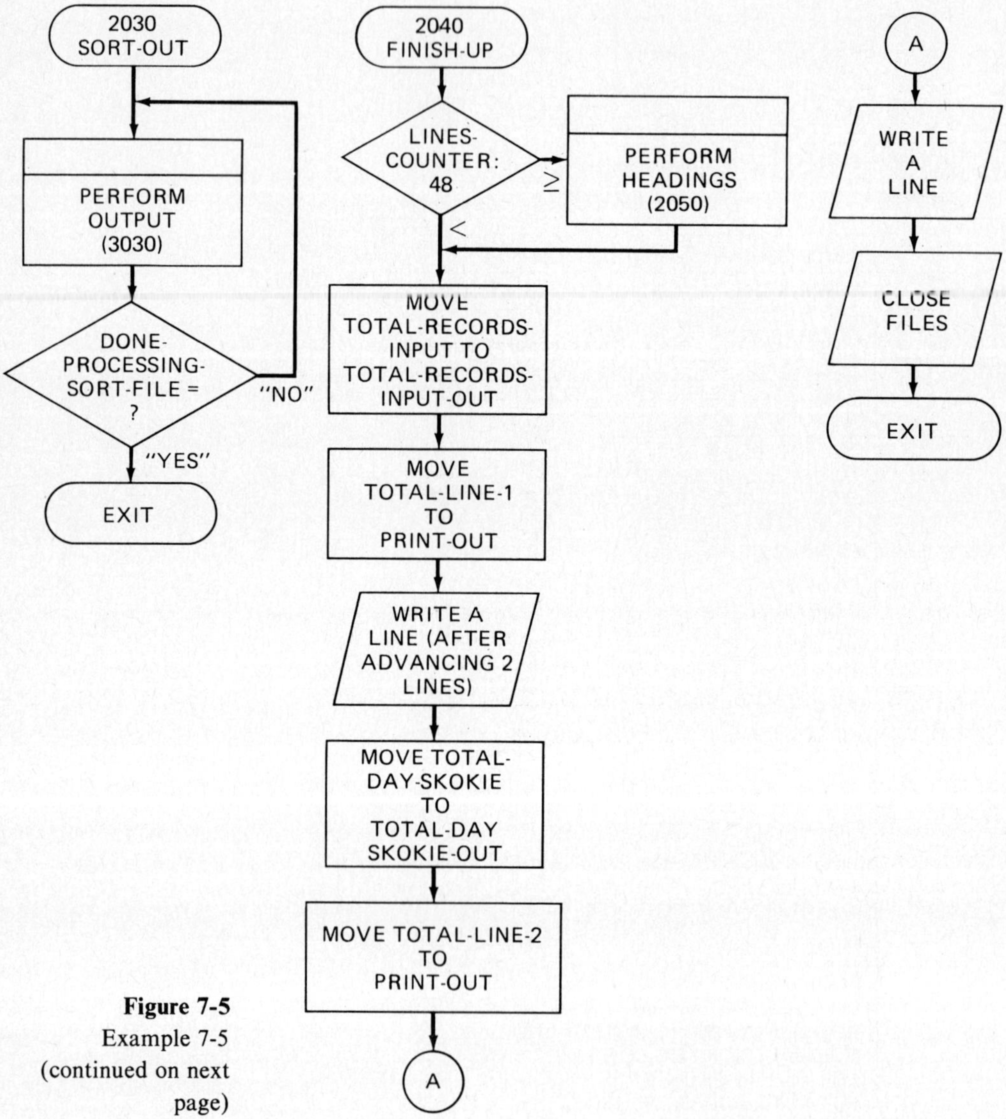

Figure 7-5
Example 7-5
(continued on next page)

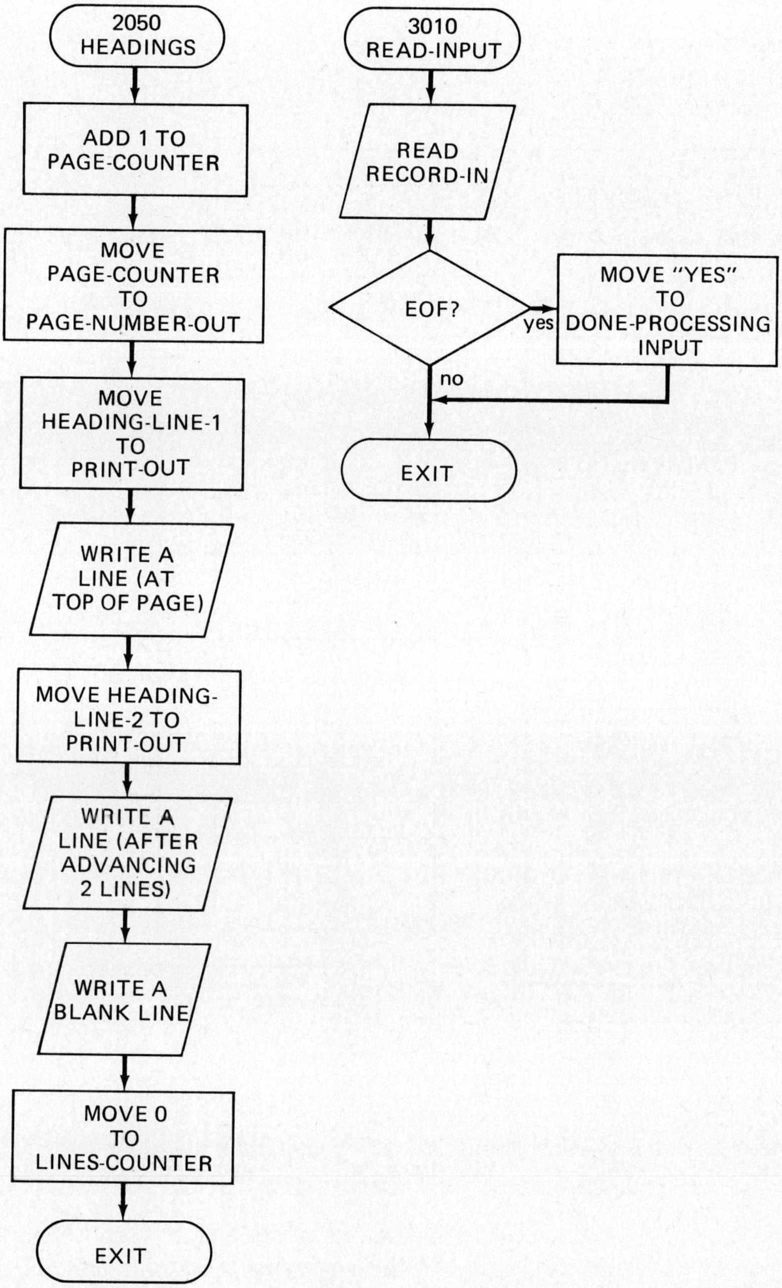

Figure 7-5
Example 7-5
(continued on next page)

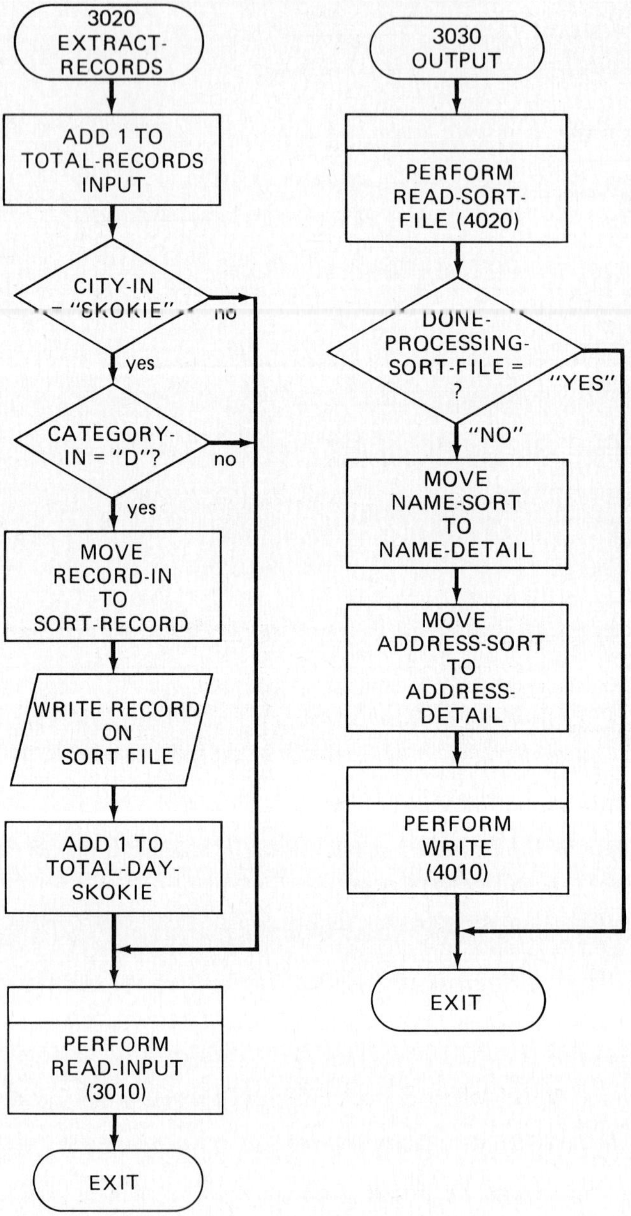

Figure 7-5
Example 7-5
(continued on next page)

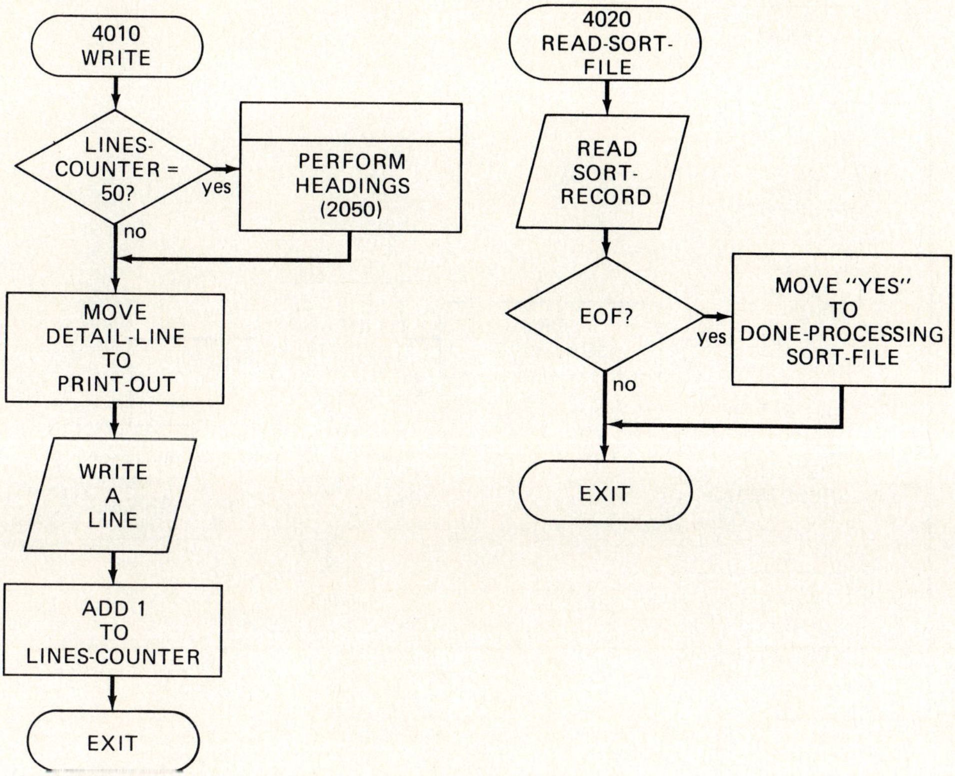

Figure 7-5
Example 7-5
(continued)

To aid in understanding the logic of this example, Figure 7-6 shows a simplified nonstructured flowchart of the path of the records from start to finish. Headings, totals, etc., are not shown in this figure.

QUESTIONS AND EXERCISES FOR REVIEW

1. Define the following terms:
   a. Extract program
   b. Embedded sort
   c. Utility sort
   d. Sort work area
2. How does the order of testing for particular conditions affect the efficiency of an extract program?
3. What does a sort program do?
4. Why do sort instructions and programs usually have an extract program associated with them?
5. If the language you are using does not have a sort instruction and you must use a utility sort, why is it necessary to have three programs to extract, sort, and list the records to be extracted?

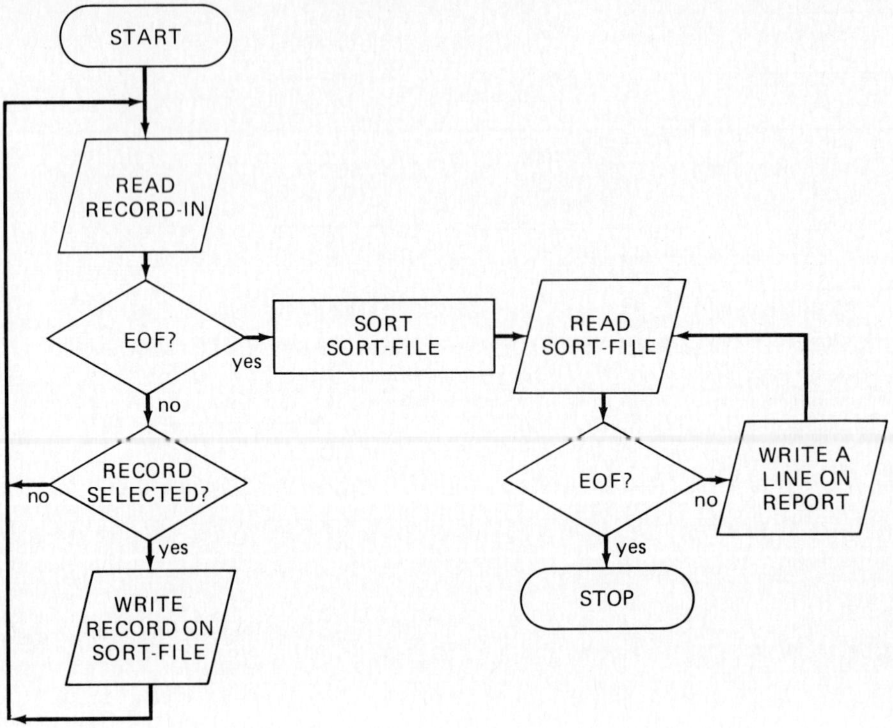

Figure 7-6
Example 7-5

6. In each of the following cases, in what order should the conditions be tested? Why?
   a. Input consists of a student file. You are to select the freshmen who are over 21 years old. Assume that 25 percent of the file represents freshmen, that 10 percent of the file represents students who are over 21 years old, and the conditions are independent.
   b. Input consists of a file for realtors. You are to select the houses that have three or four bedrooms. Assume that 80 percent of the input file is for three-bedroom houses and 10 percent of the input file is for four-bedroom houses.
   c. Input consists of a personnel file. You are to select the employees who are computer programmers or systems analysts and have had 10 or more years of experience. Assume that 5 percent of the input file is for employees with 10 or more years of experience, that 20 percent of the input file is for programmers, and that 5 percent of the input file is for systems analysts. Assume independence and mutual exclusivity.
7. A dairy company is trying to determine which of its customers buy more than 3 gallons of milk a week so that the company can include them in a special promotion. You are to draw a hierarchy chart for the program to list the selected customers.

Output

Output consists of a report listing the names and addresses of the customers selected. A maximum of 30 detail lines are to be included per page.

Printer Spacing Chart

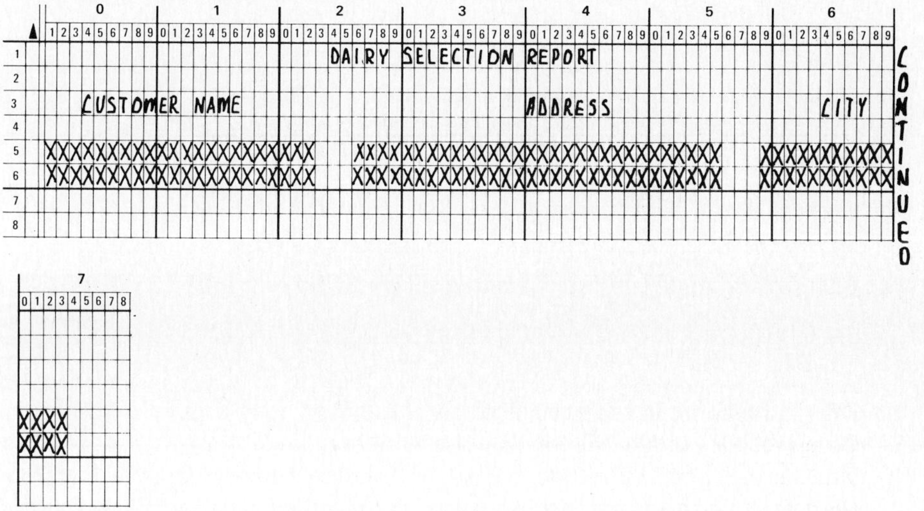

Input

Input consists of a file containing a record for each customer. The format of each record is as follows:

Position	*Description*
1–3	Customer number
4–25	Customer name
26–55	Street address
56–70	City
71–72	Gallons of milk per week
73–74	Cartons of cottage cheese per week

8. Draw a program flowchart for exercise 7 above.
9. Construct the pseudocode for Exercise 7 above.
10. Use the input file and report format of Exercise 7 above. This time include an embedded sort which sorts the records in alphabetical order by name after they have been extracted. Draw a hierarchy chart and flowchart or pseudocode to show your solution.
11. Use the same input file as described in Exercise 7 above. Draw a hierarchy chart for a program which will select records for customers who live in Niles and buy more than two cartons of cottage cheese per week. Assume that 10 percent of the input file represents Niles residents and that 5 percent of the

input file represents customers who buy more than two cartons of cottage cheese per week.

Output

Output consists of a report listing the names and addresses of the customers to be selected. A maximum of 50 detail lines are to be included per page.

Printer Spacing Chart

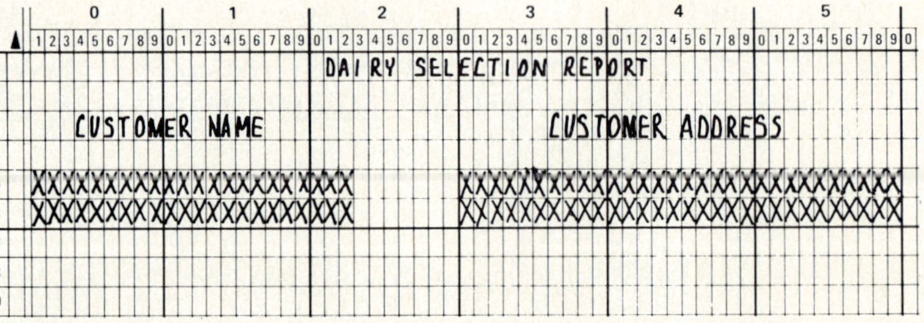

12. Draw a program flowchart for Exercise 11 above.
13. Construct the pseudocode for Exercise 11 above.
14. Use the input file and report format of Exercise 7 above. Draw a hierarchy chart for a program which will select those records for customers who live in Niles or Park Ridge and buy less than 2 gallons of milk and more than 2 cartons of cottage cheese per week. Assume that 10 percent of the input file represent Niles residents, that 12 percent of the input file represent Park Ridge residents, that 90 percent of the customers on the input file buy less than 2 gallons of milk per week, and that 5 percent of the input file represents customers who buy more than 2 cartons of cottage cheese per week.

    Totals are to be included on the report. One blank line is to be printed on the report before the totals are printed. The total lines are to read:

    TOTAL RECORDS ON INPUT FILE = XXXX
    TOTAL RECORDS SELECTED = XXXX

15. Draw a flowchart for Exercise 14 above.
16. Construct the pseudocode for Exercise 14 above.
17. Modify Exercise 14 above so that the output is sorted in alphabetical order by name. Use an embedded sort.
18. Draw a flowchart for Exercise 17 above.
19. Construct the pseudocode for Exercise 17 above.

CHAPTER 8

Date Records, Parameter Records, and Interactive Programs

DATE RECORDS

Some computer systems do not provide the capability of obtaining the current date from the system. In some cases, even when the current date can be obtained from the system, the date needed on a report or file is not the current date. For example, in a payroll system, the program that produces paychecks may be run on Thursday, though checks are distributed on Friday. Friday's date would be the desired date on the checks. In cases such as this, the "system date" cannot be used, and it is necessary to input the desired date using a date record. The date record can either be the first record on the input file or be found on a file by itself.

EXAMPLE 8-1: DATE RECORD INCLUDED AS FIRST RECORD OF INPUT FILE

For this example, we are to print a list of patients in a hospital.

Output

Output is to consist of a report. The date input from the date record should be used in the heading line. If no date record is input (i.e., if the first record on the input file is not the date record), then print the error message NO DATE RECORD INPUT and terminate processing. A maximum of 50 detail lines are to appear per page.

Printer Spacing Chart

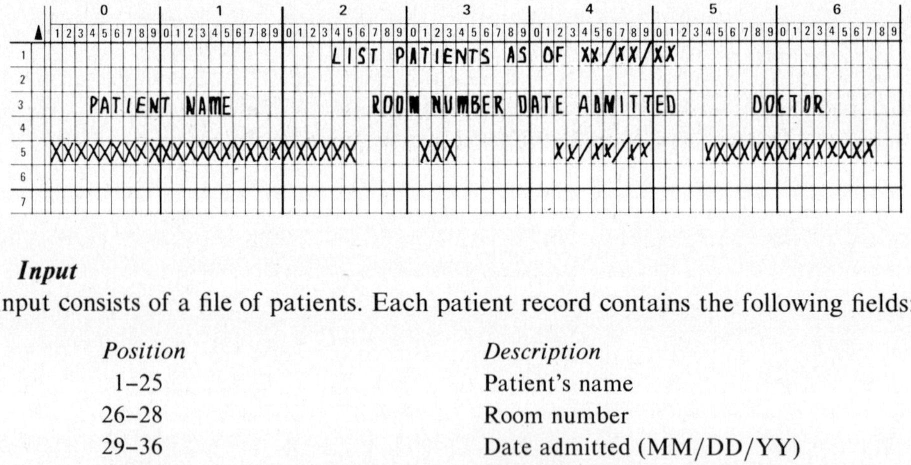

Input

Input consists of a file of patients. Each patient record contains the following fields:

Position	*Description*
1–25	Patient's name
26–28	Room number
29–36	Date admitted (MM/DD/YY)
37–50	Doctor's name
51–58	Blanks or current date

The first record on the input file contains the current date in the format MM/DD/YY (that is, month, day, and year). The date is in columns 51 to 58 of the record. In the date record, positions 1 to 50 are blank.

The hierarchy chart and pseudocode construction are left as an exercise for the reader.

The flowchart solution is shown in Figure 8-1. After input, output, and work areas

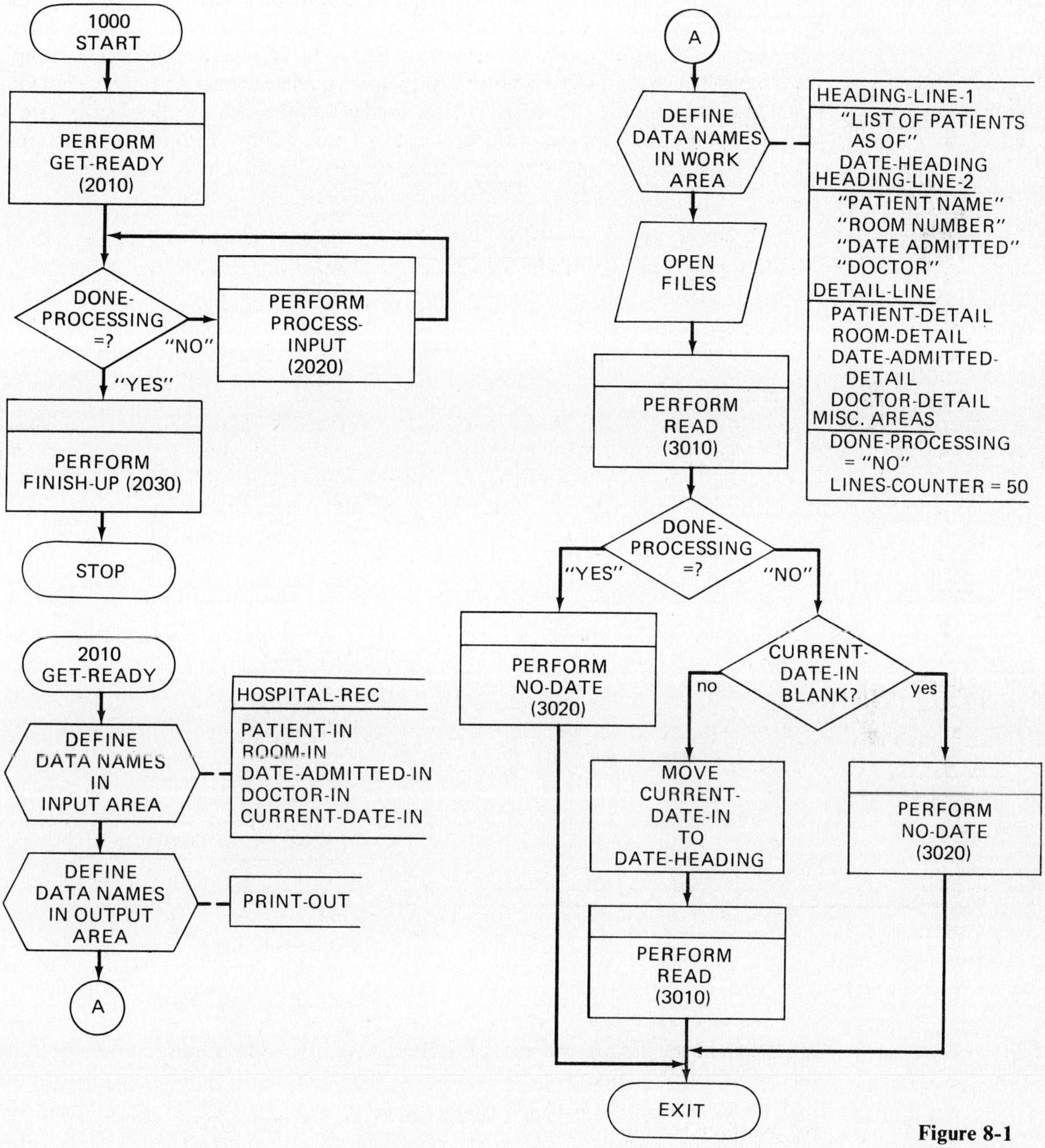

Figure 8-1
Example 8-1
(continued on next page)

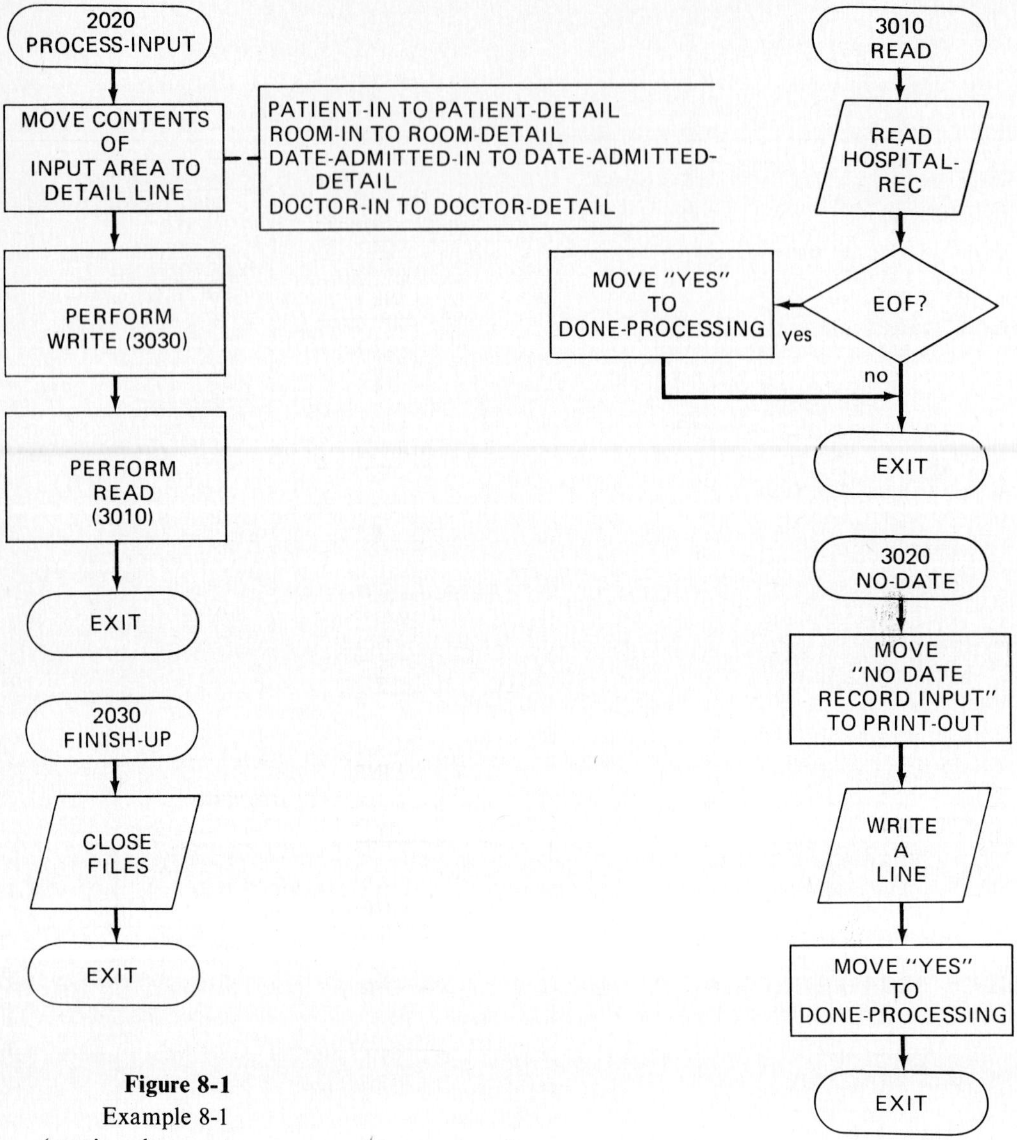

Figure 8-1
Example 8-1
(continued on next page)

are defined and files are opened in GET-READY, the date is moved to the heading line as follows: The first record is read from the input file. If EOF is obtained on the first read, then the NO-DATE routine is performed. If EOF is not obtained, the CURRENT-DATE-IN field is check for blanks. If CURRENT-DATE-IN is blank, there is no date record input and the NO-DATE routine is performed. If CURRENT-DATE-IN is not blank, the date is moved to the heading line and the second record (first patient record) is read from the input file.

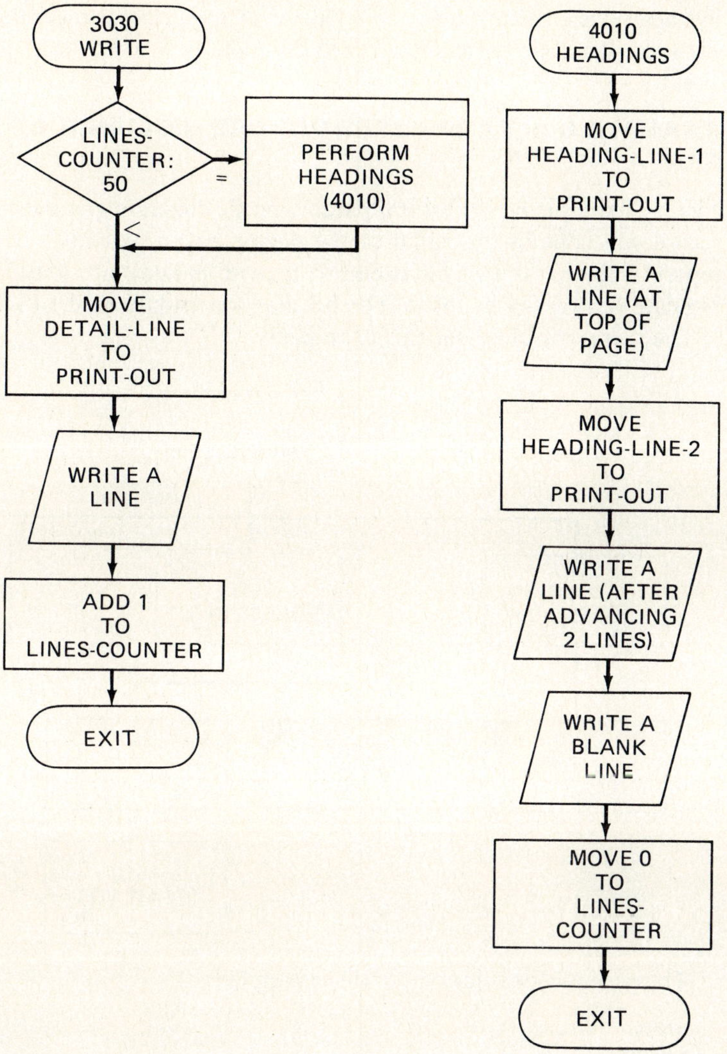

Figure 8-1
Example 8-1
(continued on next page)

PARAMETER RECORDS

Parameter records are used to describe special processing that is to be done on a file. They can be used with extract programs to indicate which records are to be selected from a file. Instead of a user writing a program in which the records to be selected are specified in the program and can only be changed by modifying the program and recompiling it, the selection criteria are specified as parameter records. Then, if the user wants to change the selection criteria, he or she can simply change the parameter records without having to change the program. Just as with date records, parameter records can either be the first records(s) on the input file or be found on a file by themselves. Example 8-2 below is for one parameter record, but a program can use more than one parameter record as input.

EXAMPLE 8-2: PARAMETER RECORD INCLUDED AS A SEPARATE FILE

Modify Example 8-1 to input a parameter file containing one record. The parameter record will contain the name of the doctor whose patients are to be listed on the report. If the parameter file is empty, then all patients are to be listed on the report. No date record will be input. The heading line should read LIST OF PATIENTS.

The hierarchy chart for this example is:

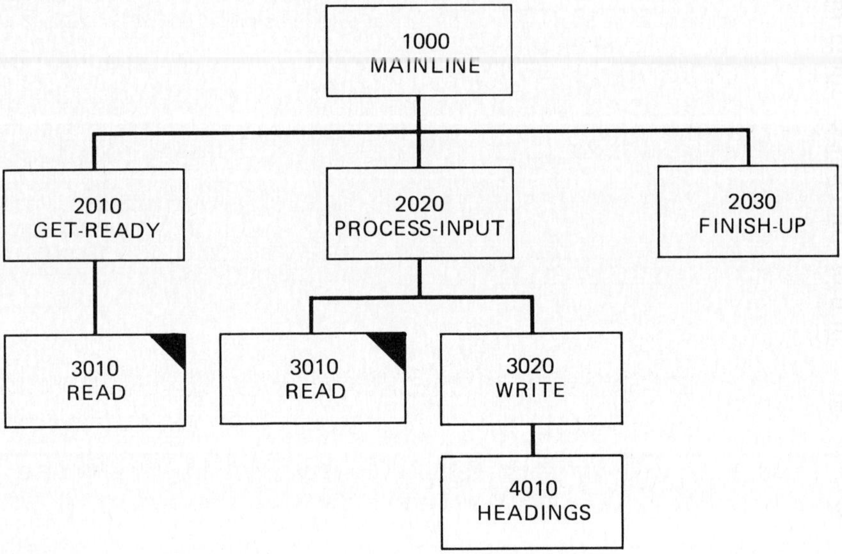

The pseudocode solution for this example is:

1000
<u>MAINLINE</u>
START
DO Get-Ready (2010) routine
DO Process-Input (2020) routine UNTIL Done-Processing = "Yes"
ENDDO
DO Finish-Up (2030) routine
STOP

2010
<u>GET-READY</u>
DEFINE data names in input, output, and work areas
OPEN Files
READ Parameter-File record
   ATEND of file MOVE spaces to Doctor-Param

```
DO Read (3010) routine
ENDGET-READY

2020
PROCESS-INPUT
IF Doctor-Param = spaces THEN
   MOVE input area fields to Detail-Line fields
   DO Write (2020) routine
ELSE IF Doctor-Param = Doctor-In THEN
           MOVE input area fields to Detail-Line fields
           DO Write (3020) routine
      ENDIF
ENDIF
DO Read (3010) routine
ENDPROCESS-INPUT

2030
FINISH-UP
CLOSE files
ENDFINISH-UP

3010
READ
READ a record from Hospital File
   ATEND of file MOVE "Yes" to Done-Processing
ENDREAD

3020
WRITE
IF Lines-Counter = 50 THEN
   DO Headings (4010) routine
ENDIF
MOVE Detail-Line to output area
WRITE a line
ADD 1 to Lines-Counter
ENDWRITE

4010
HEADINGS
MOVE Heading-Line-1 to output area
WRITE a line at top of page
MOVE Heading-Line-2 to output area
WRITE a line after advancing 2 lines
WRITE a blank line
RESET Lines-Counter to 0
ENDHEADINGS
```

Drawing the flowchart is left as an exercise for the reader.

In the GET-READY routine, a separate parameter file must be defined when the input areas are defined. After the files are opened, the parameter file is read. If there are no records on the file, then spaces are moved to the DOCTOR-PARAM field in the parameter record input area. In PROCESS-INPUT, if DOCTOR-PARAM is blank, then the record is automatically listed on the report.

INTERACTIVE PROCESSING

Sometimes the information required for processing is input via a terminal. A computer program that asks questions which are answered by a user at a terminal is called an *interactive program.* One use of an interactive program is the creation of a parameter file as shown in example 8-3 below.

EXAMPLE 8-3: USE OF AN INTERACTIVE PROGRAM TO CREATE A PARAMETER FILE

This example is for an interactive program used to create a parameter file. The parameter file will be used in a program (not shown in this example) to select records from the hospital file, as described in Example 8-1.

The user of the program will be requested to enter a maximum of five doctor's names. Figure 8-2 shows the lines to be written at the terminal, the possible

PARAMETER FILE CREATE

DO YOU WISH TO LIST PATIENTS FOR ALL DOCTORS (Y OR N)?

Response can be Y or N.

If response is Y, write a parameter record in which the NAME field contains all zeros. Terminate processing.

If response is N, continue with the next line to be written to the terminal.

If response is neither Y nor N, write the line ERROR—RESPONSE MUST BE Y OR N, and repeat the line DO YOU WISH TO LIST . . .

YOU MAY ENTER A MAXIMUM OF 5 NAMES

ENTER DOCTOR'S NAME OR END TO TERMINATE

Response can be END or a name for a doctor.

If response is END, terminate processing.

If response is a name, write a parameter record containing the name. Repeat the line ENTER DOCTOR'S NAME . . . A maximum of five names may be entered. After processing the fifth name, write the line YOU HAVE ENTERED 5 NAMES. NO MORE NAMES MAY BE ENTERED. Terminate processing.

Figure 8-2
Example 8-3

responses, and the programming paths to be followed based on the responses. (Note: All lines to be written at the terminal are underlined in the figure for ease of reading.)

The hierarchy chart and pseudocode construction are left as an exercise. The flowchart solution is shown in Figure 8-3. In the WRITE-LINE-2 routine, it is important to note that both responses (Y and N) are checked for. Never assume a response in interactive programs. If, for example, "Y" was not the response entered, do not assume that the user responded with "N"; because if the user happened to enter "X" as a response, it would be treated as "N." The program loops until the response entered for LINE-2 is "Y" or "N."

QUESTIONS AND EXERCISES FOR REVIEW

1. Define each of the following terms:
   a. Parameter record
   b. Interactive program
2. Give two examples in which a date record should be used instead of the "system date."
3. Why is it necessary in interactive programs to check all possible responses to a terminal query?
4. Modify Example 8-2 to have the parameter record be the first record on the input file, rather than being a file by itself. Draw a hierarchy chart and a flowchart.

   Input: The input record consists of 65 positions. Positions 1 to 50 are the same as described in Example 8-1. Positions 51 to 65 are used for the parameter information. On patient records, positions 51 to 65 are blank. On the parameter record, positions 1 to 50 are blank.
5. Draw a hierarchy chart for a program that lists specific patients from the input file described in Example 8-1. In addition to the patient file, the parameter file created in Example 8-3 is to be used as input. The report format described in Example 8-1 is to be used as output. List the patients for those doctors specified in the parameter file.
6. Draw a flowchart for Exercise 5 above.
7. Construct the pseudocode for Exercise 5 above.
8. Draw a hierarchy chart for an interactive program which will create an order file. The lines to be written at the terminal, the possible responses, and the programming paths to be followed are described below. All lines to be written at the terminal are underlined for ease of reading. The underlines are not to appear on the terminal.

   <u>ORDER FILE CREATE</u>
   <u>ENTER CUSTOMER NUMBER OR STOP TO END</u>
      Responses can be STOP or a customer number.
      If the response is STOP, terminate processing.

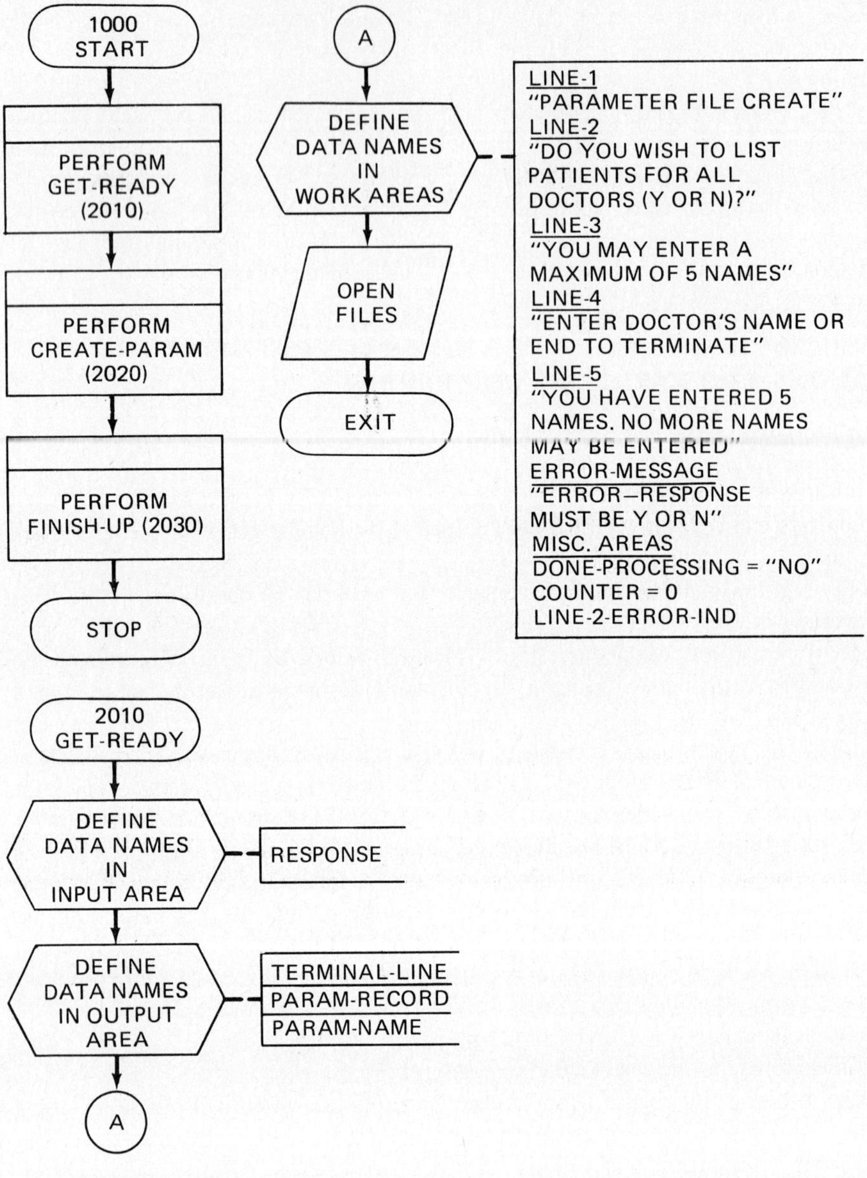

Figure 8-3
Example 8-3
(continued on next page)

If the response is a customer number, move the customer number to the customer number field of the order record, and continue with the next query.

ENTER PRODUCT NUMBER OR STOP

Response can be STOP or a product number.

If the response is STOP, return to the "enter customer number" query.

(*continued on p. 204*)

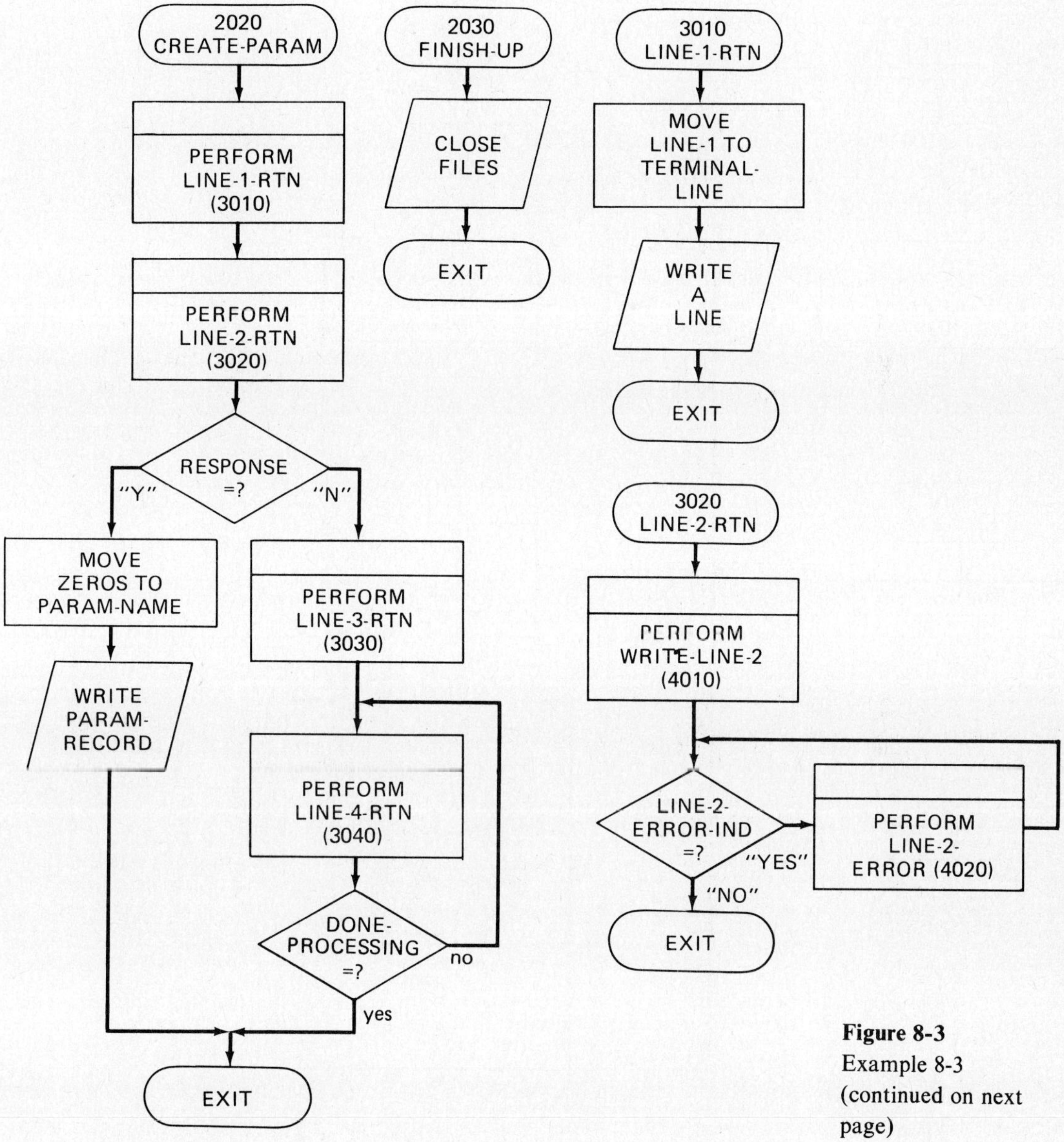

Figure 8-3
Example 8-3
(continued on next page)

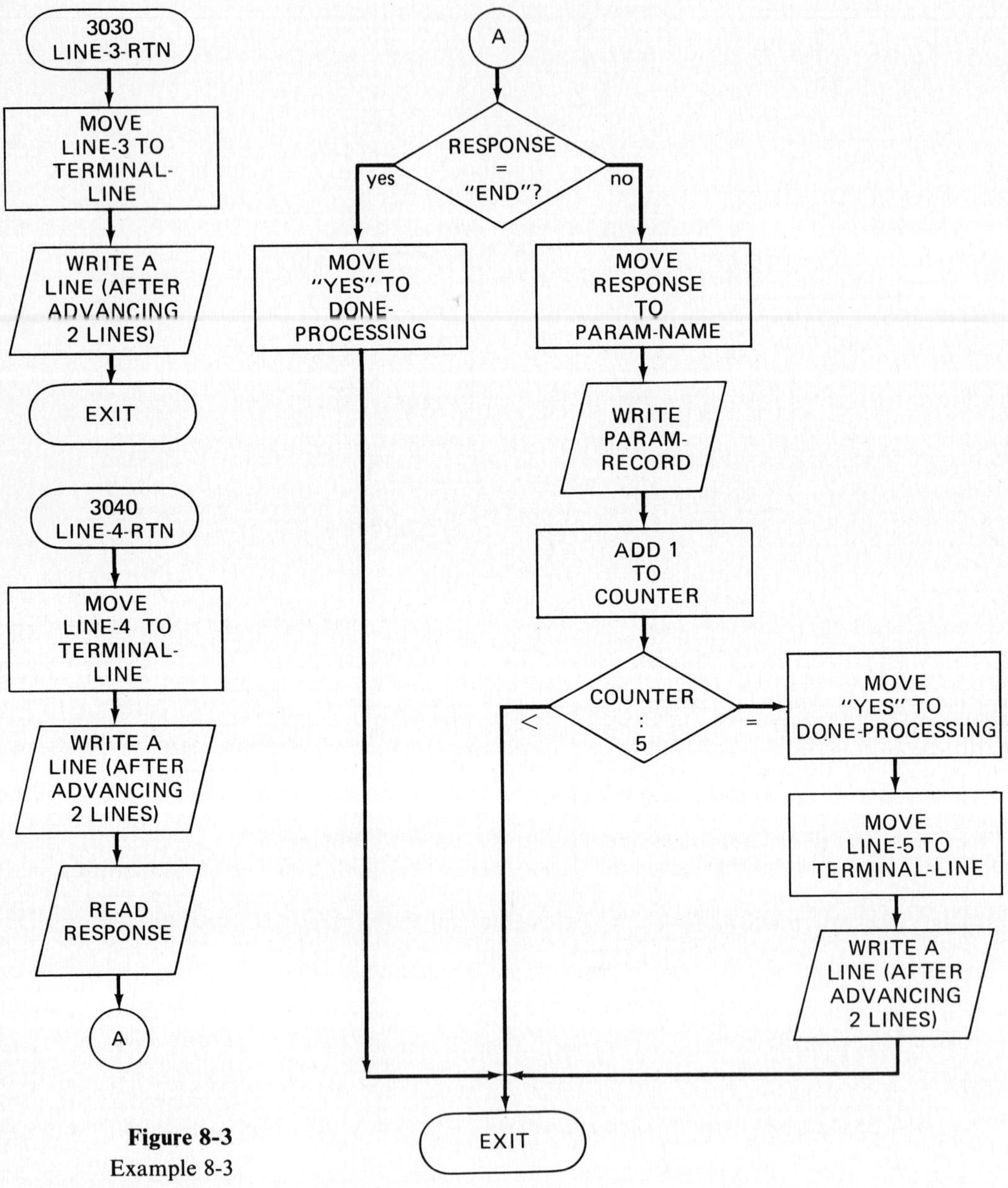

Figure 8-3
Example 8-3
(continued on next page)

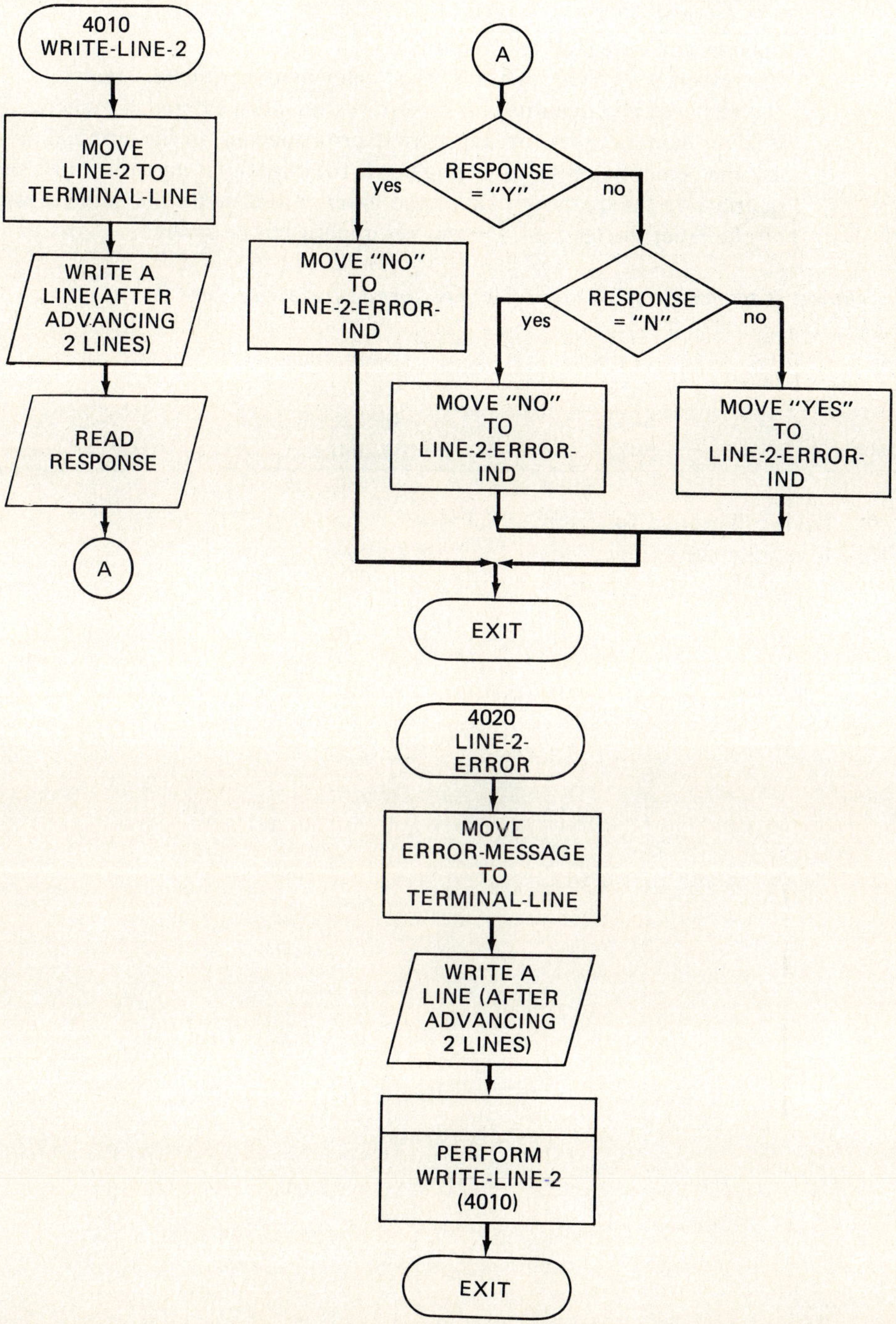

Figure 8-3
Example 8-3
(continued)

If the response is a product number, move the product number to the product number field of the order record, and continue with the next query.

ENTER QUANTITY OR STOP

Responses can be STOP or a quantity.

If the response is STOP, return to the "enter product number" query.

If the response is a quantity, make sure the quantity entered is numeric. If it is not numeric, write an appropriate error message to the terminal, and ask the "enter quantity" query again. If the quantity is numeric, move the quantity to the quantity field of the order record, write the order record on the order file, and ask for another quantity to be entered.

Output is to consist of an order file. The format for each record is:

Position	*Description*
1–5	Customer number
6–8	Product number
9–12	Quantity

9. Draw a flowchart for Exercise 8 above.
10. Construct the pseudocode for Exercise 8 above.

CHAPTER 9

Using Tables

BACKGROUND

Tables are used quite often both in your life and in business data processing. For example, tax tables are used to determine the income tax a person owes, metric conversion tables are used to equate gallons and liters, and mathematical tables are used to find the square root of a number. Other names for tables which you may encounter include matrices, lists, and arrays.

In data processing, tables are used to organize data in a program so that both a decrease in the number of field names required and a simplification of the program's logic are possible by making it simple to use loops to replace the program's multiple decisions.

EXAMPLE 9-1: TABLE VS. NONTABLE PROCESSING

Suppose that a report of test results is to be prepared.

Output

Output is to consist of a report showing, in student number order, the total points accumulated for each student. Total points are calculated by adding the points on each record for a particular student.

Printer Spacing Chart

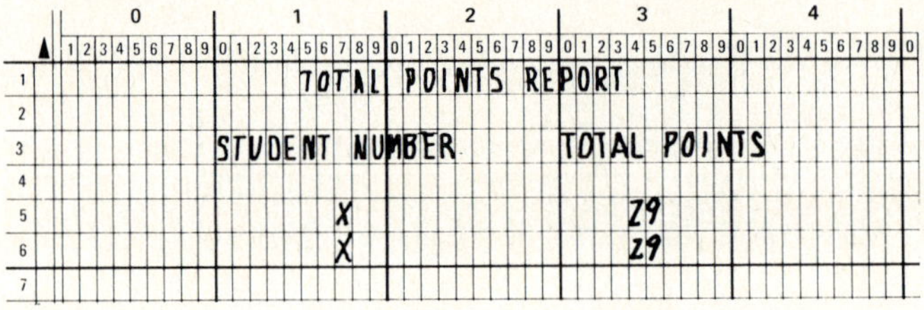

Input

Input consists of unsorted records as follows:

Position	*Description*
1–3	Student number (an integer between 1 and 5)
4–6	Points

It is not known how many records are entered per student. The input has been edited in a previous program to ensure that both input fields are numeric and the student number is in the range of 1 to 5.

Construction of the hierarchy chart and pseudocode is left as an exercise. The flowchart solution is shown in Figure 9-1. If the input records had been sorted, this would be a simple control break problem. Since the records are not sorted, each record needs to be read and the points for each student need to be accumulated in a separate work area. The PROCESS-INPUT routine must determine which work area to use based on the student number contained in the input record. After all the records have been read, the FINISH-UP routine is called to write the report.

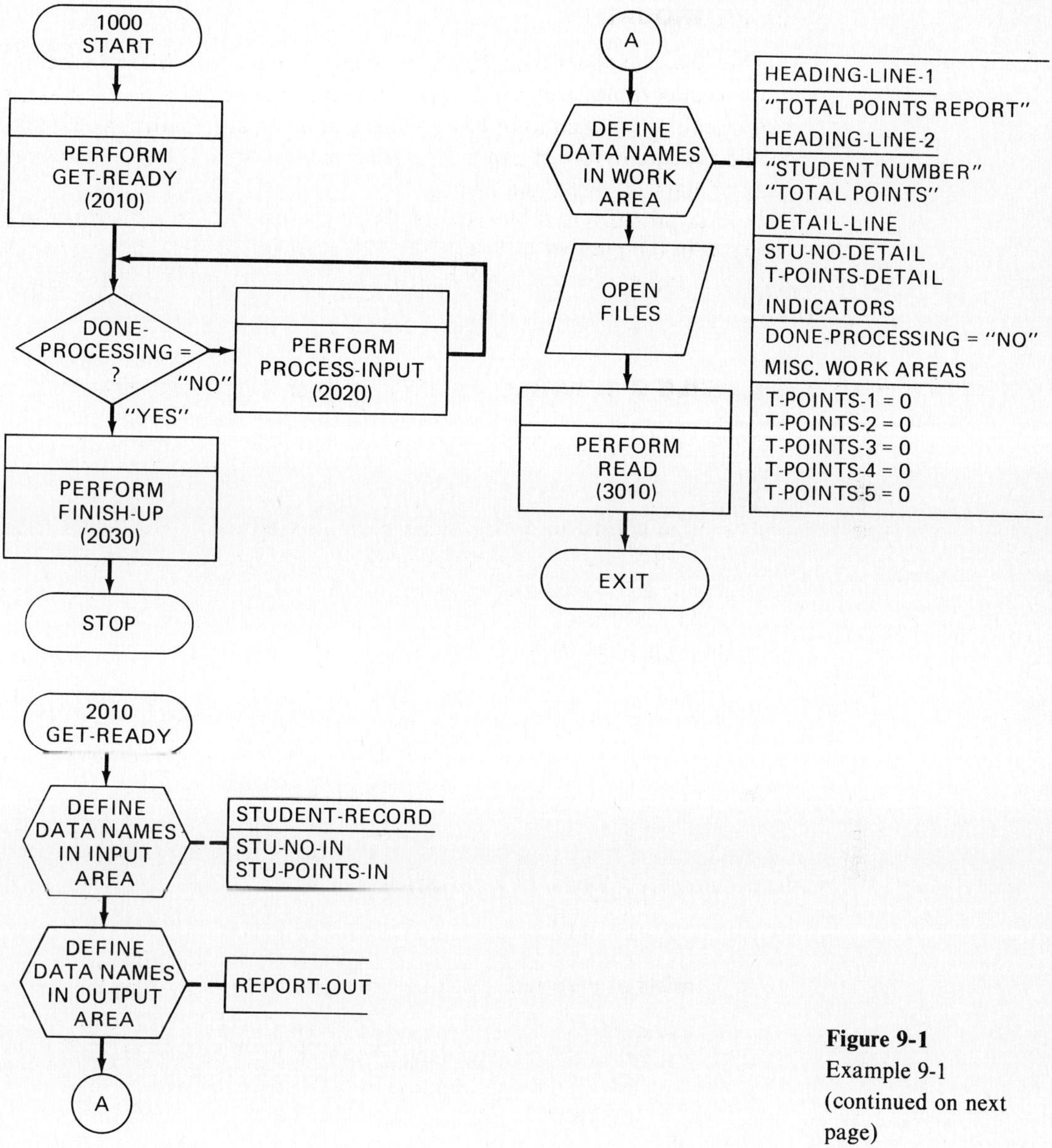

Figure 9-1
Example 9-1
(continued on next page)

Suppose that instead of five students, there were 30 students to be processed. Instead of five variable names, we would need 30 variable names. Instead of five comparisons in the PROCESS-INPUT routine, we would need 30 comparisons. Instead of five lines of output, we would need to write 30 lines of output. Just imagine for a minute how long the PROCESS-INPUT and FINISH-UP routines would be! This is a case where it would be helpful to use a table.

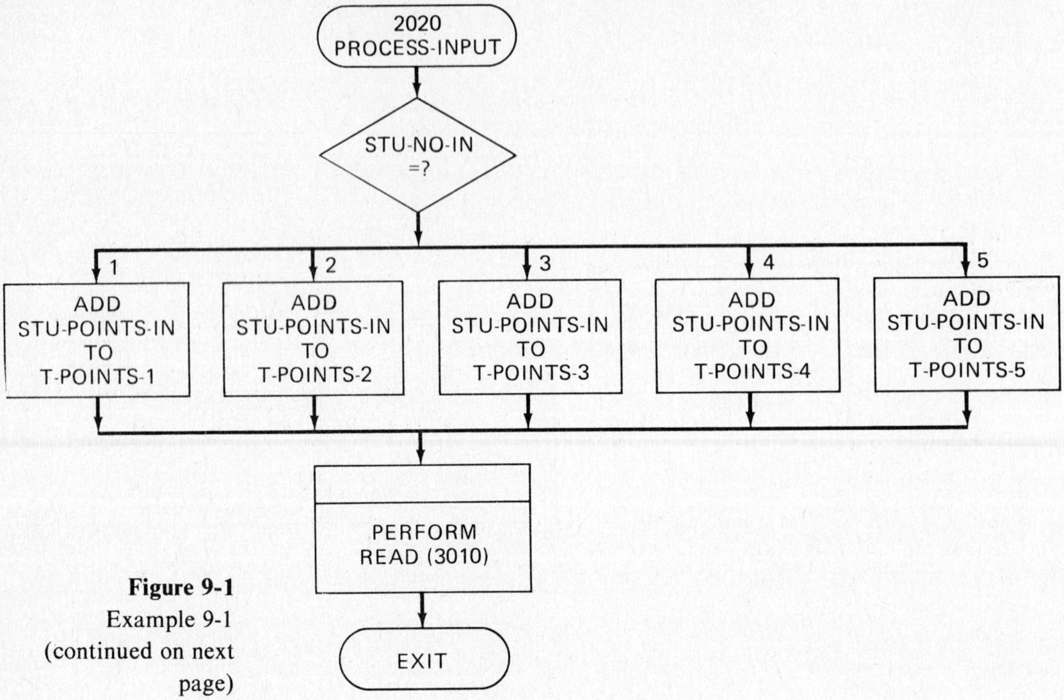

Figure 9-1
Example 9-1
(continued on next page)

Let's create a table that contains 30 entries, or locations. Each entry will contain the accumulated points for a particular student.

ENTRY 1	POINTS FOR STUDENT 1
ENTRY 2	POINTS FOR STUDENT 2
ENTRY 3	POINTS FOR STUDENT 3
ENTRY 4	POINTS FOR STUDENT 4
ENTRY 5	POINTS FOR STUDENT 5
ENTRY 6	POINTS FOR STUDENT 6
ENTRY 7	POINTS FOR STUDENT 7
	.
	.
	.
ENTRY 25	POINTS FOR STUDENT 25
ENTRY 26	POINTS FOR STUDENT 26
ENTRY 27	POINTS FOR STUDENT 27
ENTRY 28	POINTS FOR STUDENT 28
ENTRY 29	POINTS FOR STUDENT 29
ENTRY 30	POINTS FOR STUDENT 30

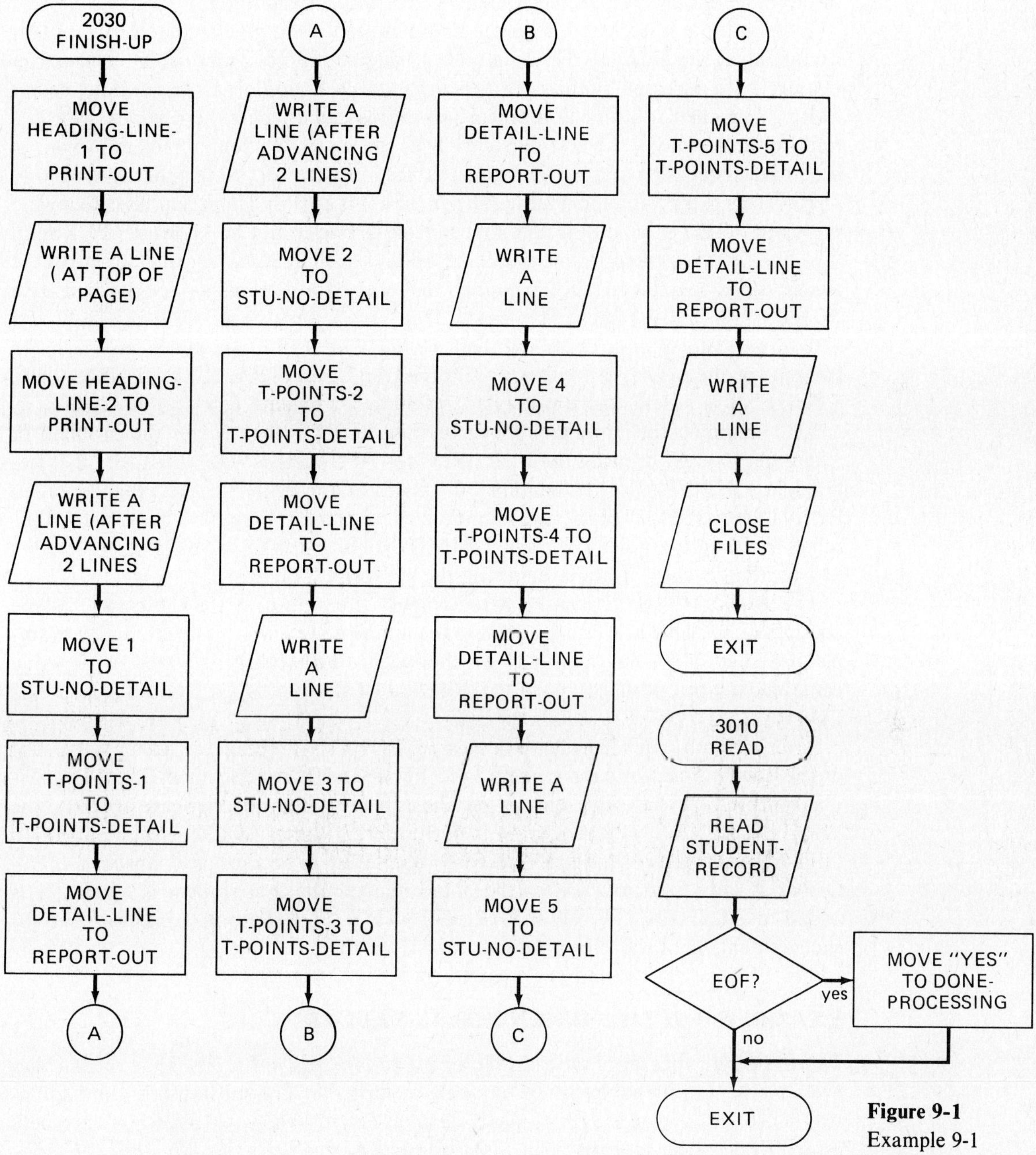

Figure 9-1
Example 9-1
(continued on next page)

Each entry in the table can be initialized to zero, and as each record is read from the input file, the contents of the points field will be added to the appropriate entry in the table. At end of file, the contents of the table are printed.

When a table is accessed, separate field names are not given to each entry. (This would defeat the purpose of using a table.) Instead of field names being used, entries in a table are accessed by their position in the table. Consider, as an example, people waiting in a check-out line at a grocery store. Instead of using their names, we could refer to the people as the first person in line, the second person in line, and so on. In both data processing and mathematics, tables are accessed using subscripts. A *subscript* refers to a position in a table. The subscript is enclosed in parentheses following the name of the table entry. The first person in line would be known as PERSON (1). The second person in line would be known as PERSON (2), and so on. In the points table created in this example, the entry for the points for student 1 is POINTS-TABLE-ENTRY (1); for student 5 it is POINTS-TABLE-ENTRY (5); and so on. Subscripts can be numbers (1, 2, 3, . . .) or field names in which the contents of the field is a number. POINTS-TABLE-ENTRY (STUDENT), where STUDENT is a field whose value is 7, refers to the seventh entry in the table.

Let's examine the flowchart shown in Figure 9-2, which solves the problem of accumulating and printing the total points for 30 students. POINTS-TABLE is defined in GET-READY to contain 30 entries. Each entry in the table is called POINTS-TABLE-ENTRY and is initialized to zero. The name POINTS-TABLE refers to the entire table. The name POINTS-TABLE-ENTRY (STUDENT) refers to a particular entry in the table using the subscript STUDENT.

The BUILD-TABLE routine actually puts the values in the table. The points input (STU-POINTS-IN) are added to the appropriate entry in the table. For example, if STU-NO-IN has a value of 27, then STU-POINTS-IN is added to the value contained in the 27th entry of POINTS-TABLE, that is, to POINTS-TABLE-ENTRY (27).

After all the input records are processed, POINTS-TABLE will contain the sum of the points input for each student, and FINISH-UP is performed. The FINISH-UP routine lists the table entries on the report. After headings are written, the WRITE-TABLE-ENTRY routine is performed 30 times (once for each entry). In GET-READY, a field called STUDENT was set up to be used as a subscript. STUDENT is initialized to 1. After the detail line for the first student is written, 1 is added to STUDENT. WRITE-TABLE-ENTRY is performed printing a line for each student, until the subscript is greater than 30.

EXAMPLE 9-2: TWO-DIMENSIONAL TABLES

The previous problem is an example of a *one-dimensional table.* That means that every element in the table can be uniquely identified by one subscript. In some tables two subscripts are necessary to describe each entry. When two subscripts are necessary to describe an entry in a table, the table is called a *two-dimensional table.* The first subscript refers to the row, and the second subscript refers to the column. In general, the number of subscripts required to identify an entry in a table is the

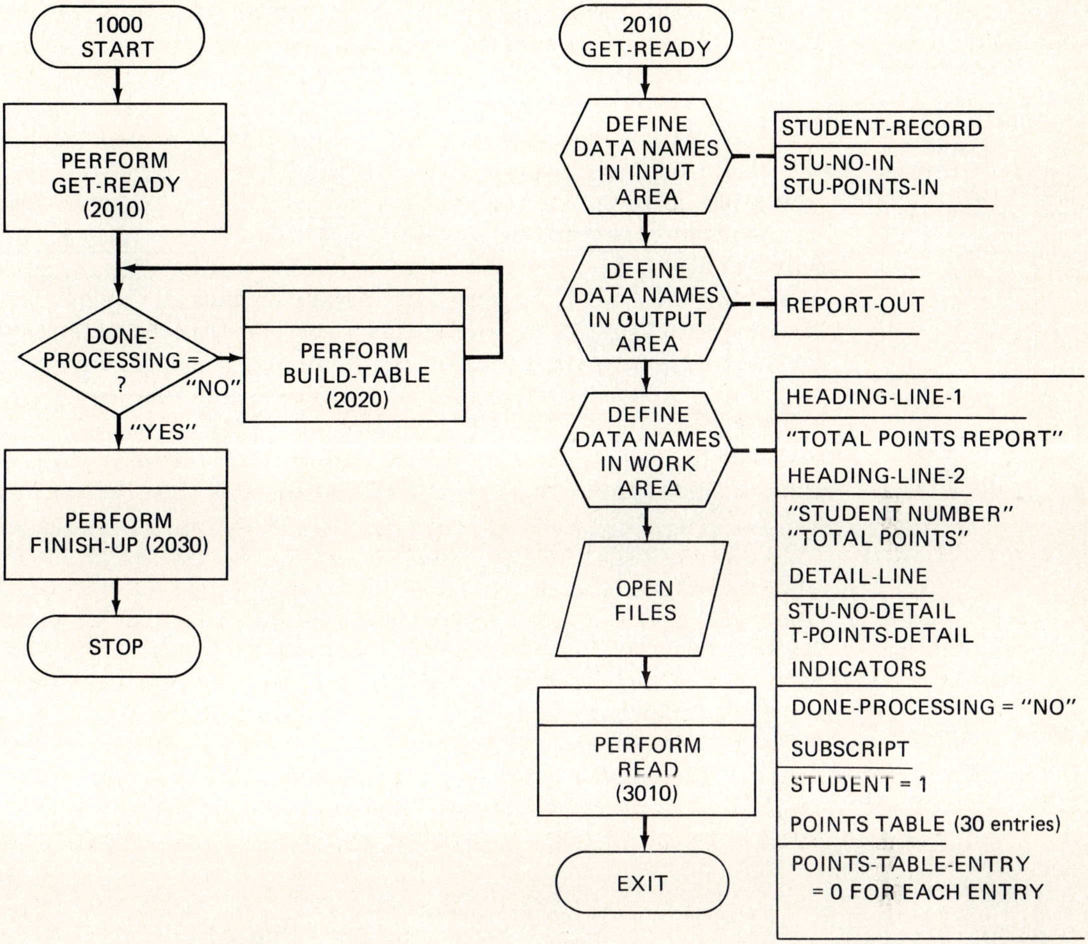

Figure 9-2
(continued on next page)

dimension of the table. The number of subscripts allowed in a program (the dimension) is determined by the computer language. For example, some versions of FORTRAN allow seven dimensions, COBOL allows three, and BASIC allows only two. When a table of more than two dimensions is used, it is difficult to physically visualize the table. For most business applications, a two-dimensional table is sufficient. This book does not discuss tables larger than two dimensions.

For this example a legal billing report is to be produced where the amount billed is equal to the rate per hour times the number of hours billed.

Table

A table is to be built right into the program to contain the billing codes and the rates for the various codes. This table appears on the next page.

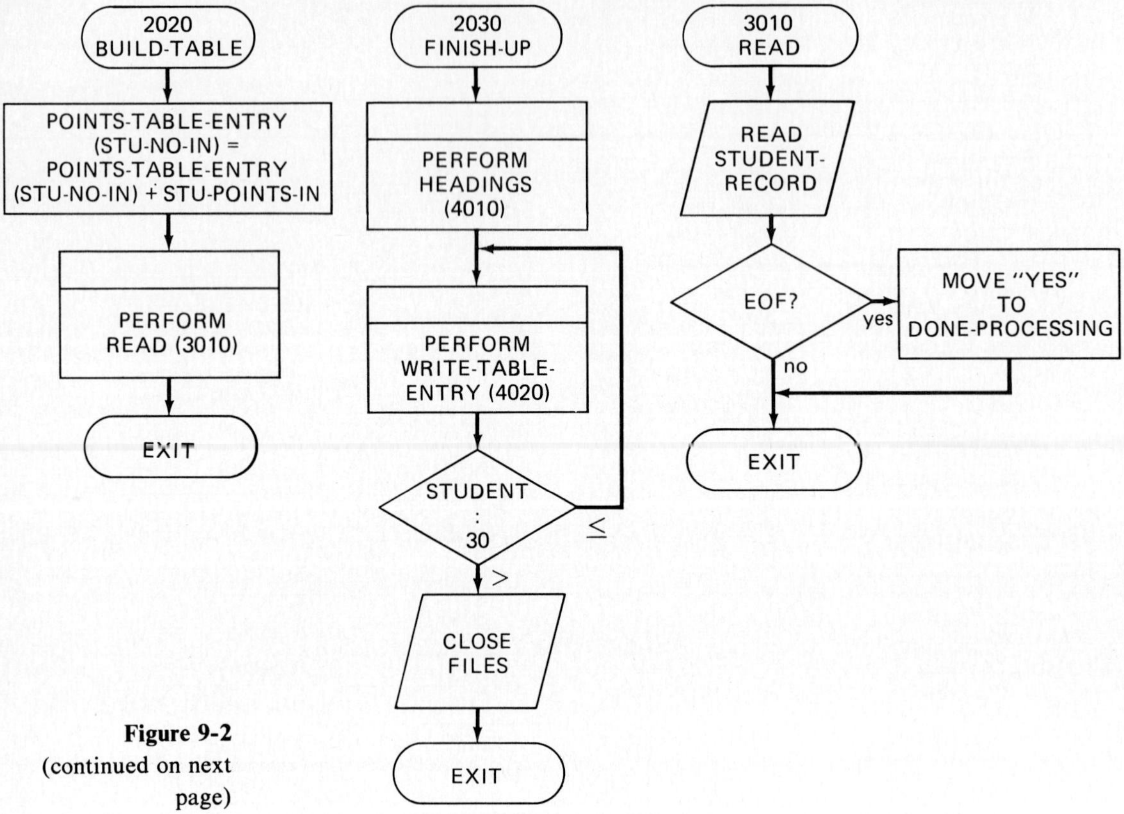

Figure 9-2
(continued on next page)

Code	*Rate/Hour*
1	\$50.00
4	\$60.00
5	\$75.00
8	\$100.00
A	\$125.00
B	\$150.00

Output

Output is to consist of a report with at most 50 detail lines per page. If the code field on the input is invalid (i.e., if the code is not in the table), print the message INVALID BILLING CODE as shown on the printer spacing chart below.

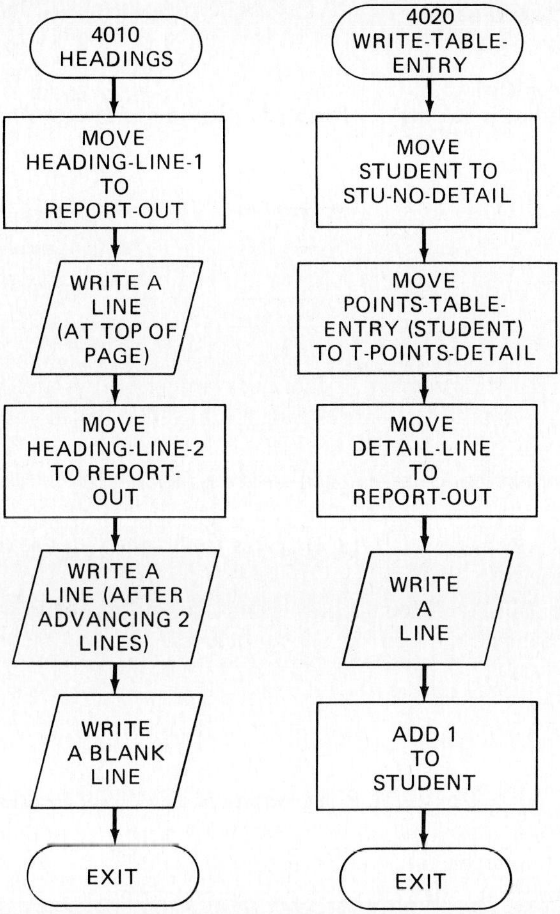

Figure 9-2
(continued)

Printer Spacing Chart

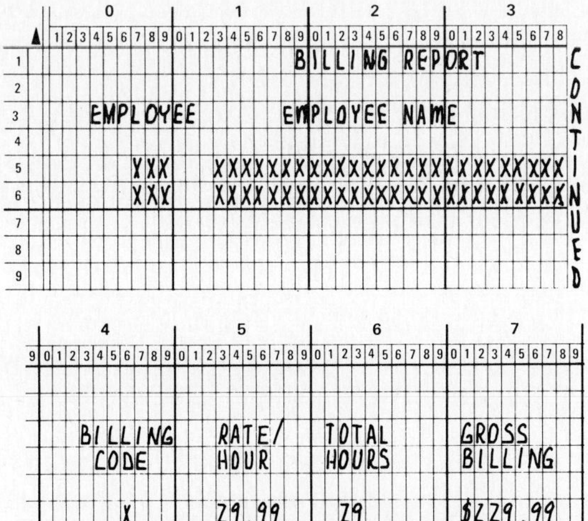

Input

Input is to consist of records with the following format:

Position	*Description*
1–3	Employee number
4–30	Employee name
31	Pay code
32–33	Total hours billed

In this program, a table containing 6 rows and 2 columns is created. This results in a total of 12 entries in the table. The first column of the table contains the code, and the second column contains the rate. Since this is a two-dimensional table, two subscripts must be used to access each entry in the table. The first subscript refers to the row, and the second subscript refers to the column. For example, RATE-TABLE-ENTRY (3,2) refers to the entry in the third row and second column, i.e., the rate 75.00.

This table could have been set up "upside-down," so to speak. We could have reversed the table as shown below.

Code	1	4	5	8	A	B
Rate/Hour	$50.00	$60.00	$75.00	$100.00	$125.00	$150.00

In this case the first row would refer to the code, and the second row would refer to the rate. The program would have to be modified to reflect the correct subscripts. It is important, therefore, to set up a table so that the rows and columns are the way you want them to appear in your program.

In this example, both the codes and the rates must be put in the table. In the student points example, only the points were contained in the table; the student numbers were not. The student numbers did not need to be included because they started at 1 and continued in sequence, resulting in the student numbers and the subscripts being identical. In this example, the pay codes are not in numerical sequence and cannot be used as subscripts (it is meaningless to speak of the Ath row), therefore, the pay codes must be included in the table.

The hierarchy chart for this example is on the top of the next page.

Construction of the pseudocode is left as an exercise. The flowchart solution is shown in Figure 9-3.

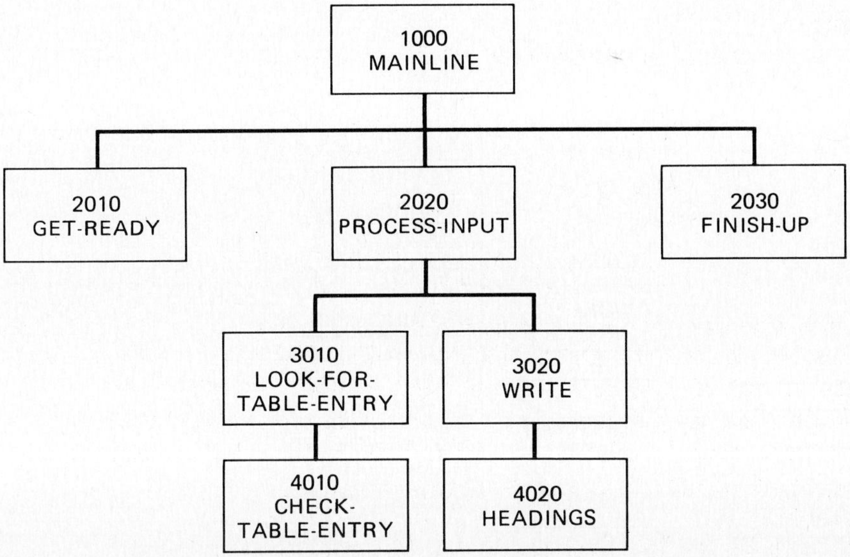

For every record read as input, we perform PROCESS-INPUT to format the detail line. After the number, name, and code are moved to the detail line, LOOK-FOR-TABLE-ENTRY is performed to find the pay rate corresponding to the code entered. After returning from LOOK-FOR-TABLE-ENTRY, we will either have found the entry in the table or have discovered that the code on the input record is not in the table.

If TABLE-ENTRY-FOUND has a value of "NO", then no entry was found and an error message is written on the report. If TABLE-ENTRY-FOUND is "YES", then the row number of the entry we want is contained in a field called TABLE-SUB. For example, if the code on the input record is 4, when we return from the LOOK-FOR-TABLE ENTRY routine, TABLE-ENTRY-FOUND will have a value of "YES" and TABLE-SUB will be 2. The instruction

MOVE RATE-TABLE-ENTRY (TABLE-SUB, 2) TO RATE-DETAIL

will then move the entry in the second row and second column of the table (that is, 60.00) to RATE-DETAIL. The number of hours specified on the input record is moved to the detail line, and the billing is calculated based on the hours input and the rate from the table.

Now look at the LOOK-FOR-TABLE-ENTRY and CHECK-TABLE-ENTRY routines to determine exactly how the table is searched for a particular code. Suppose, as an example, that the code on the input record is a 5. When the LOOK-FOR-TABLE-ENTRY routine is entered, two fields are initialized as follows:

TABLE-SUB = 1
SEARCH-FINISHED = "NO"

We then perform CHECK-TABLE-ENTRY until SEARCH-FINISHED = "YES". There must be a way in the CHECK-TABLE-ENTRY routine for

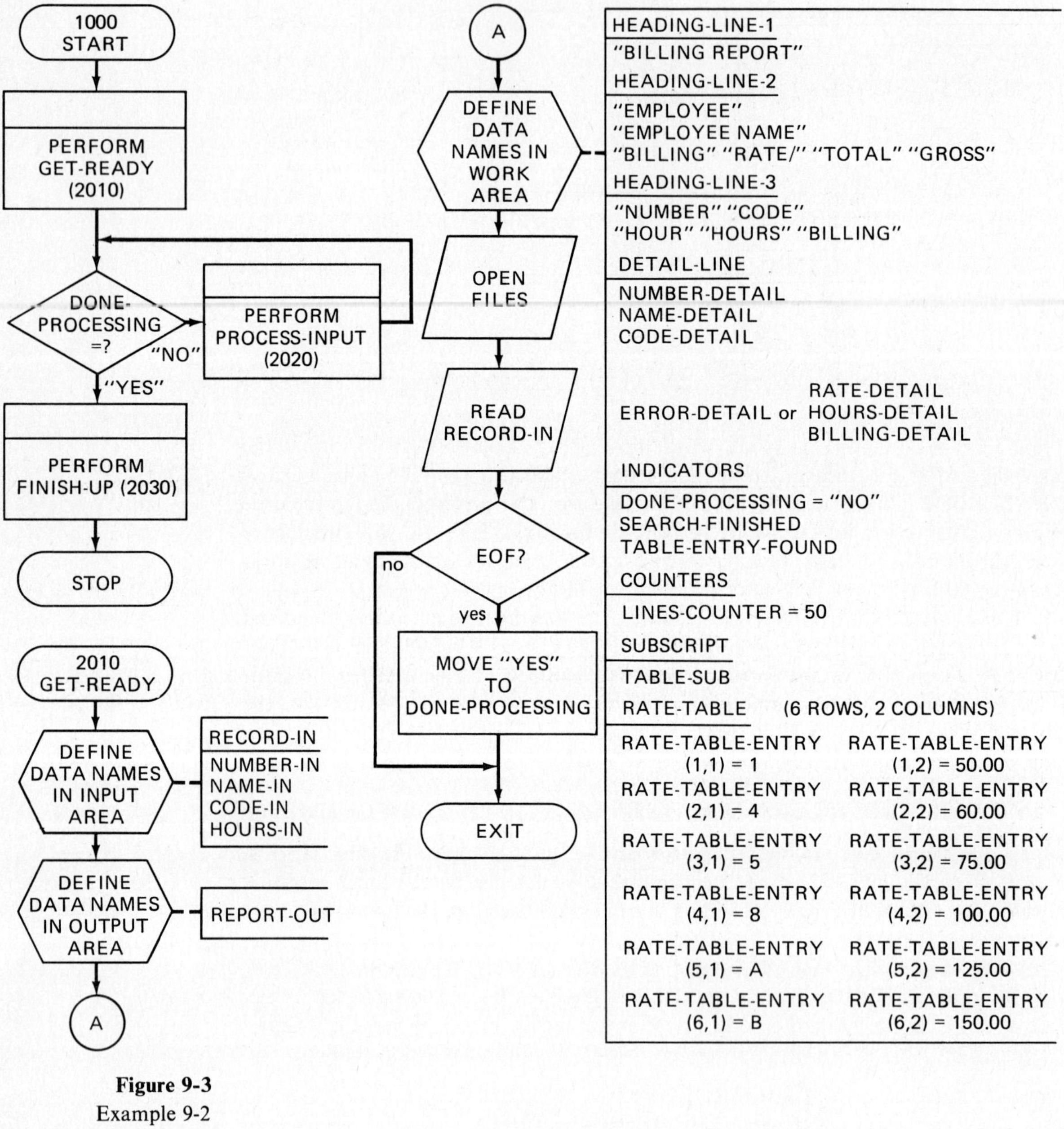

Figure 9-3
Example 9-2
(continued on next page)

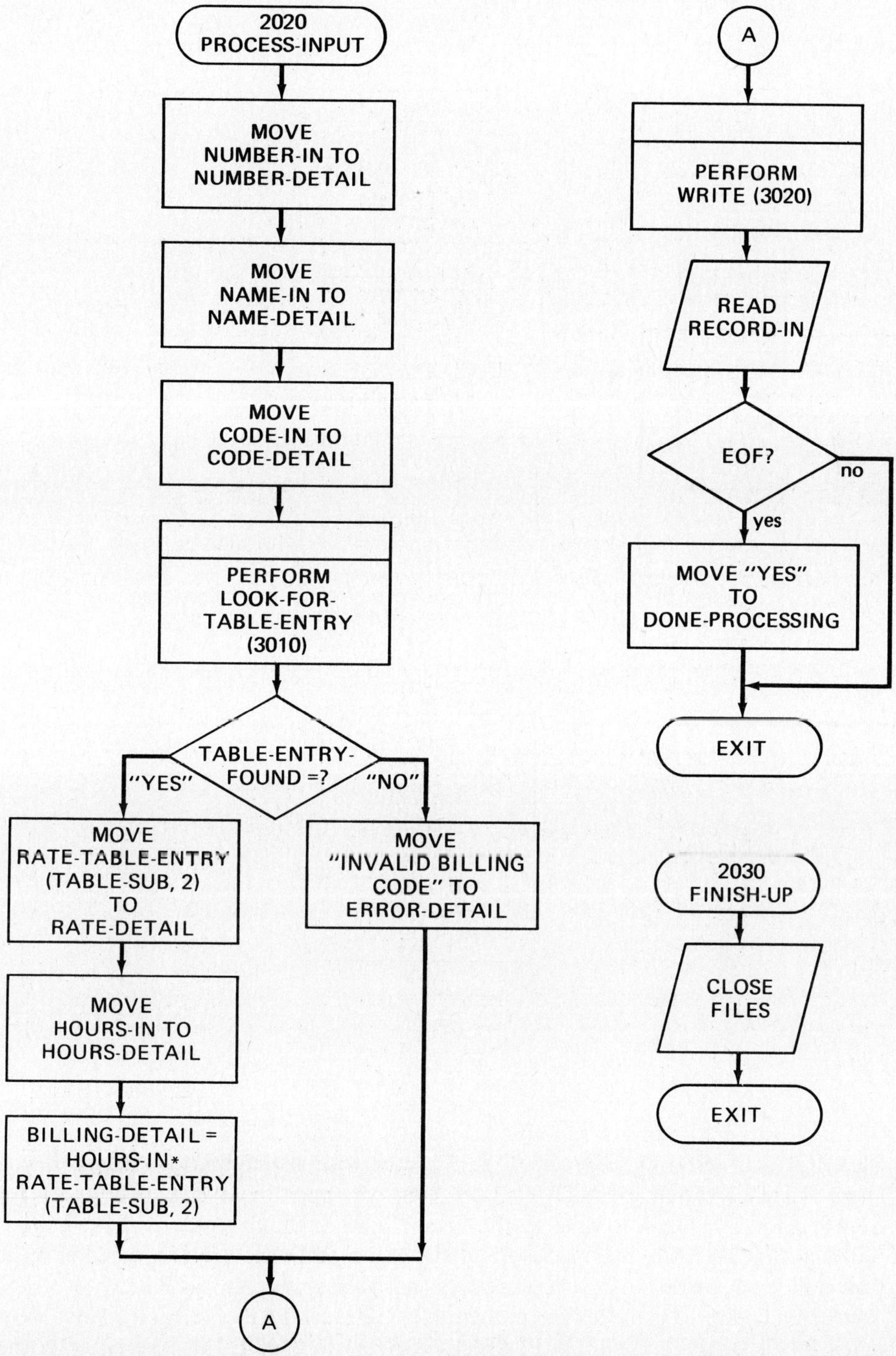

Figure 9-3
Example 9-2
(continued on next page)

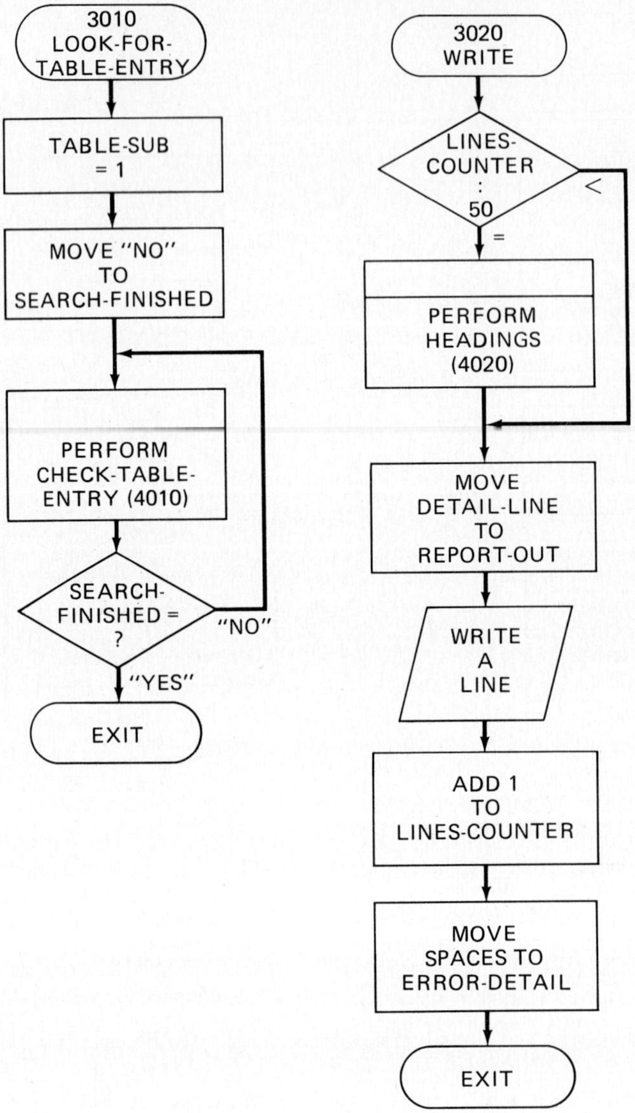

Figure 9-3
Example 9-2
(continued on next page)

SEARCH-FINISHED to become "YES"; otherwise an infinite loop exists. If you study CHECK-TABLE-ENTRY, you can see that there are two ways for SEARCH-FINISHED to take on the value "YES". The first way is if the code is found in the table. The second way is if the entire table has been searched and the code still is not found.

When a code of 5 is looked for in the table, CHECK-TABLE-ENTRY first compares RATE-TABLE-ENTRY (TABLE-SUB, 1) to CODE-IN. The entry in the first row and first column of the table is compared to 5. RATE-TABLE-ENTRY

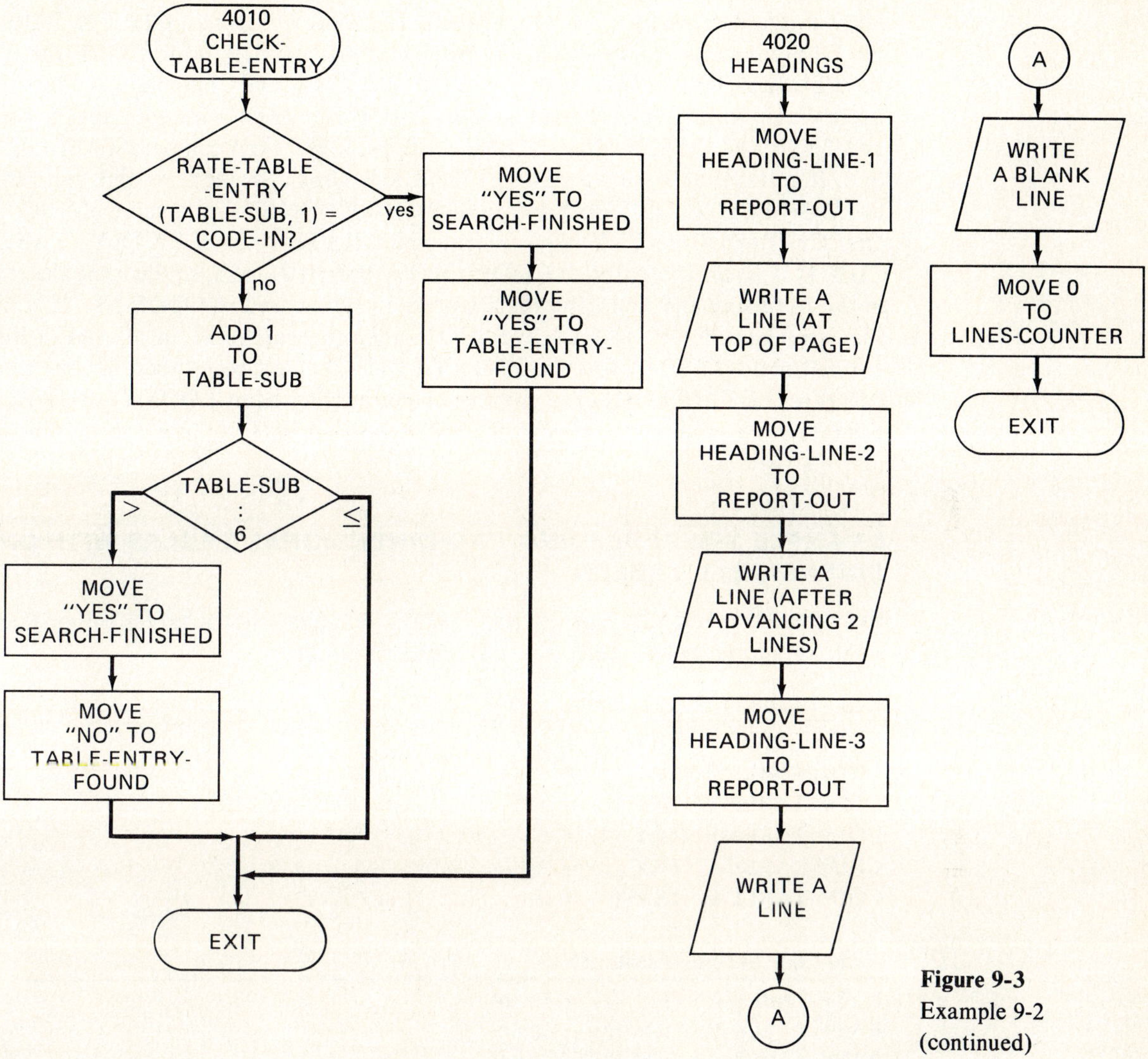

Figure 9-3
Example 9-2
(continued)

(1,1) does not have a value of 5, so we add 1 to TABLE-SUB. Now TABLE-SUB = 2. The next instruction compares TABLE-SUB to 6. If TABLE-SUB is greater than 6, it means that the entire table has been searched and the code has not been found. We would then indicate that the search is finished by moving "YES" to SEARCH-FINISHED and that the entry in the table was not found by moving "NO" to TABLE-ENTRY-FOUND.

Since TABLE-SUB is less than or equal to 6, we exit the routine and return to the LOOK-FOR-TABLE-ENTRY routine. SEARCH-FINISHED has a value of

"NO", so we perform CHECK-TABLE-ENTRY again. CHECK-TABLE-ENTRY compares RATE-TABLE-ENTRY (TABLE-SUB, 1) to CODE-IN. This time TABLE-SUB is 2, so the entry in the *second* row and first column of the table is compared to CODE-IN. RATE-TABLE-ENTRY (2,2) does not equal 5, so we add 1 to TABLE-SUB. Now TABLE-SUB = 3. We then compare TABLE-SUB to 6. It is less than 6, so we exit the CHECK-TABLE-ENTRY routine and return to LOOK-FOR-TABLE-ENTRY. SEARCH-FINISHED has a value of "NO", so CHECK-TABLE-ENTRY is performed again. RATE-TABLE-ENTRY (TABLE-SUB, 1) is again compared to CODE-IN. TABLE-SUB = 3, so this time the entry in the *third* row and first column of the table is compared to CODE-IN. This time they are equal. CHECK-TABLE-ENTRY then moves "YES" to SEARCH-FINISHED and "YES" to TABLE-ENTRY-FOUND. Processing then returns to the LOOK-FOR-TABLE-ENTRY routine. Upon exiting from LOOK-FOR-TABLE-ENTRY, the program returns to the PROCESS-INPUT routine and finishes formatting the detail line.

EXAMPLE 9-3: REPLACING TWO-DIMENSIONAL TABLES WITH ONE-DIMENSIONAL TABLES

Example 9-2 could have been written using 2 one-dimensional tables rather than a single two-dimensional table. The two tables would be:

Code-Table (6 rows, 1 column)

CODE-TABLE-ENTRY (1) = 1
CODE-TABLE-ENTRY (2) = 4
CODE-TABLE-ENTRY (3) = 5
CODE-TABLE-ENTRY (4) = 8
CODE-TABLE-ENTRY (5) = A
CODE-TABLE-ENTRY (6) = B

Rate-Table (6 rows, 1 column)

RATE-TABLE-ENTRY (1) = 50.00
RATE-TABLE-ENTRY (2) = 60.00
RATE-TABLE-ENTRY (3) = 75.00
RATE-TABLE-ENTRY (4) = 100.00
RATE-TABLE-ENTRY (5) = 125.00
RATE-TABLE-ENTRY (6) = 150.00

The logic would be changed to search for the code in CODE-TABLE. The row in which the code is found would then correspond to the row in the RATE-TABLE for the rate being used.

The pseudocode solution is:

```
1000
MAINLINE
START
DO Get-Ready (2010) routine
```

```
DO Process-Input (2020) routine UNTIL Done-Processing is equal to "Yes"
ENDDO
DO Finish-Up (2030) routine
STOP

2010
GET-READY
DEFINE data names in input, output, and work areas
OPEN files
READ a record from Record-In
   ATEND of file MOVE "Yes" to Done-Processing
ENDGET-READY

2020
PROCESS-INPUT
MOVE Number-In to Number-Detail
MOVE Name-In to Name-Detail
MOVE Code-In to Code-Detail
DO Look-For-Table-Entry (3010) routine
IF Table-Entry-Found = "Yes" THEN
   MOVE Rate-Table-Entry (Table-Sub) to Rate-Detail
   MOVE Hours-In to Hours-Detail
   MOVE Hours-In *Rate-Table-Entry (Table-Sub) to Billing-Detail
ELSE MOVE "Invalid Billing Code" to Error-Detail
ENDIF
DO Write(3020) routine
READ a record from Record-In
   ATEND of file MOVE "Yes" to Done-Processing
ENDPROCESS-INPUT

2030
FINISH-UP
CLOSE files
ENDFINISH-UP

3010
LOOK-FOR-TABLE-ENTRY
MOVE 1 to Table-Sub
MOVE "No" to Search-Finished
DO Check-Table-Entry (4010) routine UNTIL Search-Finished = "Yes"
ENDDO
ENDLOOK-FOR-TABLE-ENTRY

3020
WRITE
IF Lines-Counter = 50 THEN
   DO Headings (4020) routine
ENDIF
MOVE Detail-Line to output area
```

```
WRITE a line
ADD 1 to Lines-Counter
MOVE spaces to Error-Detail
ENDWRITE

4010
CHECK-TABLE-ENTRY
IF Code-Table-Entry (Table-Sub) = Code-In THEN
   MOVE "Yes" to Search-Finished
   MOVE "Yes" to Table-Entry-Found
ELSE ADD 1 to Table-Sub
      IF Table-Sub is greater than 6 THEN
         MOVE "Yes" to Search-Finished
         MOVE "No" to Table-Entry-Found
      ENDIF
ENDIF
ENDCHECK-TABLE-ENTRY

4020
HEADINGS
MOVE Heading-Line-1 to output area
WRITE a line at top of page
MOVE Heading-Line-2 to output area
WRITE a line after advancing 2 lines
MOVE Heading-Line-3 to output area
WRITE a line
WRITE a blank line
RESET Lines-Counter to 0
ENDHEADINGS
```

EXAMPLE 9-4: TWO-DIMENSIONAL TABLES AND TABLE VALUES INPUT FROM OUTSIDE OF PROGRAM

This program combines both an edit and the writing of a report in a program that uses tables. Store X maintains employee statistics in punched card form. The cards are periodically loaded into a table in computer memory, and calculations are done on the values stored. The table shows the number of employees within department by sex.

	Males	*Females*
Dept. 1	100	1
Dept. 2	57	130
Dept. 3	2	3
⋮		
Dept. 20	10	10

There are 20 departments.

Output

If there are no errors on the input, a statistics report is to be produced. If there are errors on the input, an error report is to be produced. If an error occurs when the input file is processed, continue processing the first 20 cards to be sure all errors on the file are listed on the report.

Printer Spacing Chart for Error Report

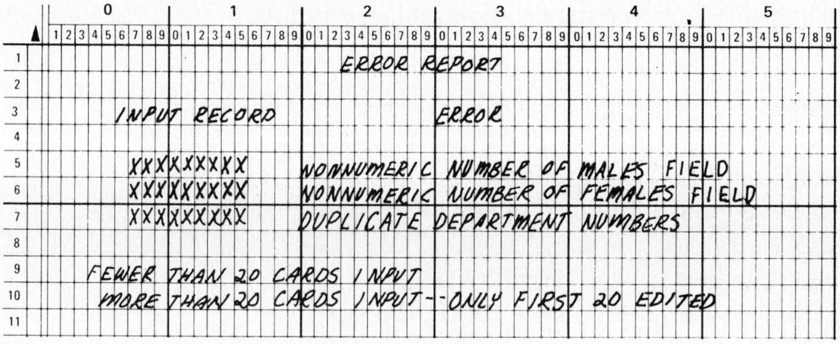

Printer Spacing Chart for Statistics Report

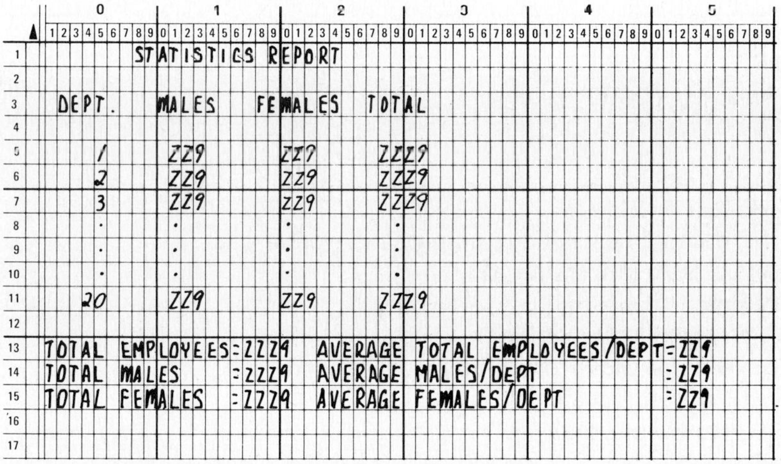

Input Card Format:

Column	*Description*
1–2	Department number
3–5	Number of males
6–8	Number of females

The cards are to be read, and the table is to be loaded into storage. When the table is loaded, the following error conditions are to be checked for:

1. Fewer than 20 cards input
2. More than 20 cards input
3. Duplicate department numbers
4. Nonnumeric number of males field
5. Nonnumeric number of females field

Only the first 20 cards are to be checked for errors.

The hierarchy chart for the solution is shown in Figure 9-4. The pseudocode for this example is:

```
MAINLINE
START
DO Get-Ready (2010) routine
DO Process-Input (2020) routine UNTIL Input-Finished = "Yes"
ENDDO
IF No-Of-Cards is greater than 20 THEN
     DO Too-Many-Records (2030) routine
ELSE IF No-of-Cards is less than 20 THEN
          DO Too-Few-Records (2040) routine
     ELSE IF Error-Indicator = "NO" THEN
               DO Stat-Report (2050) routine
          ENDIF
     ENDIF
ENDIF
DO Finish-Up (2060) routine
STOP

2010
GET-READY
DEFINE data names in input, output, and work areas
  (Set up table in work area)
OPEN files
READ a record from Card-In
  ATEND of file Move "Yes" to Input-Finished
IF Input-Finished equals "No" THEN
  ADD 1 to No-of-Cards
ENDIF
ENDGET-READY

2020
PROCESS-INPUT
IF No-Of-Cards is greater than 20 THEN
  MOVE "YES" to Input-Finished
```

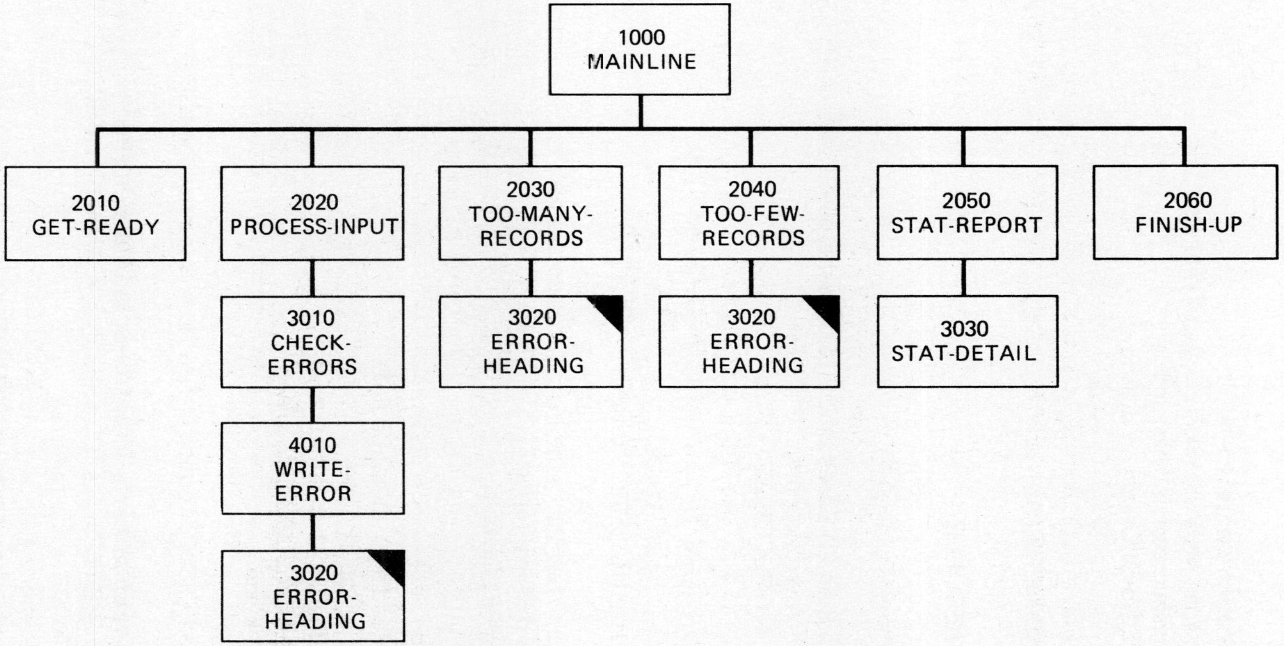

Figure 9-4
Example 9-4

```
ELSE MOVE "NO" to Errors-Finished
  MOVE 1 to Row
  DO Check-Errors (3010) routine UNTIL Errors-Finished = "Yes"
  ENDDO
  READ a record from CARD-IN
    ATEND of file MOVE "Yes" to Input-Finished
  IF Input-Finished equals "No" THEN
    ADD 1 to No-Of-Cards
  ENDIF
ENDIF
ENDPROCESS-INPUT
```

2030
<u>TOO-MANY-RECORDS</u>

```
IF First-Error = "Yes" THEN
  DO Error-Heading (3020) routine
ENDIF
MOVE "More than 20 Cards Input" to output area
WRITE a line on error report
ENDTOO-MANY-RECORDS
```

2040
<u>TOO-FEW-RECORDS</u>

```
IF First-Error = "Yes" THEN
  DO Error-Heading (3020) routine
ENDIF
MOVE "Fewer Than 20 Cards Input" to output area
WRITE a line on error report
ENDTOO-FEW-RECORDS
```

2050
<u>STAT-REPORT</u>

```
MOVE Stat-Heading-1 to output area
WRITE a line at top of page
MOVE Stat-Heading-2 to output area
WRITE a line after advancing 2 lines
WRITE a blank line
SET Row = 1
DO Stat-Detail (3030) routine UNTIL Row is greater than 20
ENDDO
COMPUTE Tot-Emp-Out = Total-Males + Total-Females
COMPUTE Ave-Emp-Out = (Total-Males + Total-Females)/20
MOVE Stat-Total-1 to output area
WRITE a line after advancing 2 lines.
MOVE Total-Males to Tot-Males-Out
COMPUTE Ave-Males-Out = Total-Males/20
MOVE Stat-Total-2 to output area
WRITE a line
```

```
MOVE Total-Females to Tot-Females-Out
COMPUTE Ave-Females-Out = Total-Females/20
MOVE Stat-Total-3 to output area
WRITE a line
ENDSTAT-REPORT

2060
FINISH-UP
CLOSE files
ENDFINISH-UP

3010
CHECK-ERRORS
IF Dept-Table-Entry (Row,1) = Blank THEN
   MOVE Dept-In to Dept-Table-Entry (Row,2)
   IF Males-In is not numeric THEN
      MOVE "Nonumeric Number of Males Field"
        to Message-Detail
      DO Write-Error (4010) routine
   ELSE MOVE Males-In to Dept-Table-Entry (Row,2)
   ENDIF
   IF Females-In is not numeric THEN
      MOVE "Nonumeric Number of Females Field"
        to Message-Detail
      DO Write-Error (4010) routine
   ELSE MOVE Females-In to Dept-Table-Entry (Row, 3)
   ENDIF
   MOVE "Yes" to Errors-Finished
ELSE IF Dept-Table Entry (Row,1) = Dept-In THEN
          MOVE "Duplicate Department Numbers" to Message-Detail
          DO Write-Error (4010) routine
          MOVE "Yes" to Errors-Finished
      ELSE ADD 1 to Row
      ENDIF
ENDIF
ENDCHECK-ERRORS

3020
ERROR-HEADING
MOVE "No" to First-Error
MOVE Error-Heading-1 to output area
WRITE a line at top of page
MOVE Error-Heading-2 to output area
WRITE a line after advancing 2 lines
WRITE a blank line
MOVE "Yes" to Error-Indicator
ENDERROR-HEADING
```

```
3030
STAT-DETAIL
MOVE Dept-Table-Entry (Row, 1) to Dept-Detail
MOVE Dept-Table-Entry (Row, 2) To Males-Detail
MOVE Dept-Table-Entry (Row, 3) to Females-Detail
COMPUTE Total-Detail = Dept-Table-Entry (Row, 2) +
        Dept-Table-Entry (Row, 3)
ADD Dept-Table-Entry (Row, 2) to Total-Males
ADD Dept-Table-Entry (Row, 3) to Total-Females
MOVE Stat-Detail to output area
WRITE a line
ADD 1 to Row
ENDSTAT-DETAIL

4010
WRITE-ERROR
IF First-Error = "Yes" THEN
   DO Error-Heading (3020) routine
ENDIF
MOVE Card-In to Input-Detail
MOVE Error-Detail output area
WRITE a line on error report
ENDWRITE-ERROR
```

The flowchart solution is in Figure 9-5.

MAINLINE routine first performs GET-READY to set up areas, open files, and read the first record from the input file. For every record read, a counter NO-OF-CARDS is incremented by 1. This counter is used to keep track of the number of input records that have been processed. After GET-READY, PROCESS-INPUT is performed until INPUT-FINISHED has a value of "YES". INPUT-FINISHED is initialized to "NO" and becomes "YES" either at EOF or at the time that the 21st record is input, whichever occurs first. (Remember that we only want to process the first 20 records.) When INPUT-FINISHED becomes "YES", NO-OF-CARDS is checked to see how many records have been input. If more than 20 records have been input, TOO-MANY-RECORDS is performed to write a message on the error report. If fewer than 20 records have been input, TOO-FEW-RECORDS is performed to write a message on the error report. If exactly 20 records have been input, ERROR-INDICATOR is checked. If ERROR-INDICATOR has a value of "YES", it means that a line has been written on the error report and no statistics report should be produced. (ERROR-INDICATOR is set to "YES" at the time that the headings are written on the error report.) If ERROR-INDICATOR has a value of "NO", then STAT-REPORT is performed to produce the statistics report.

There is no lines counter used in this flowchart. No more than 60 messages can be written on the error report, and they will all fit on one page. (The maximum number of errors would occur if there were 19 duplicates, 20 nonnumeric males, 20 nonnumeric females, and more than 20 records input.) The statistics report contains 24 lines (excluding headings) and will also fit on one page.

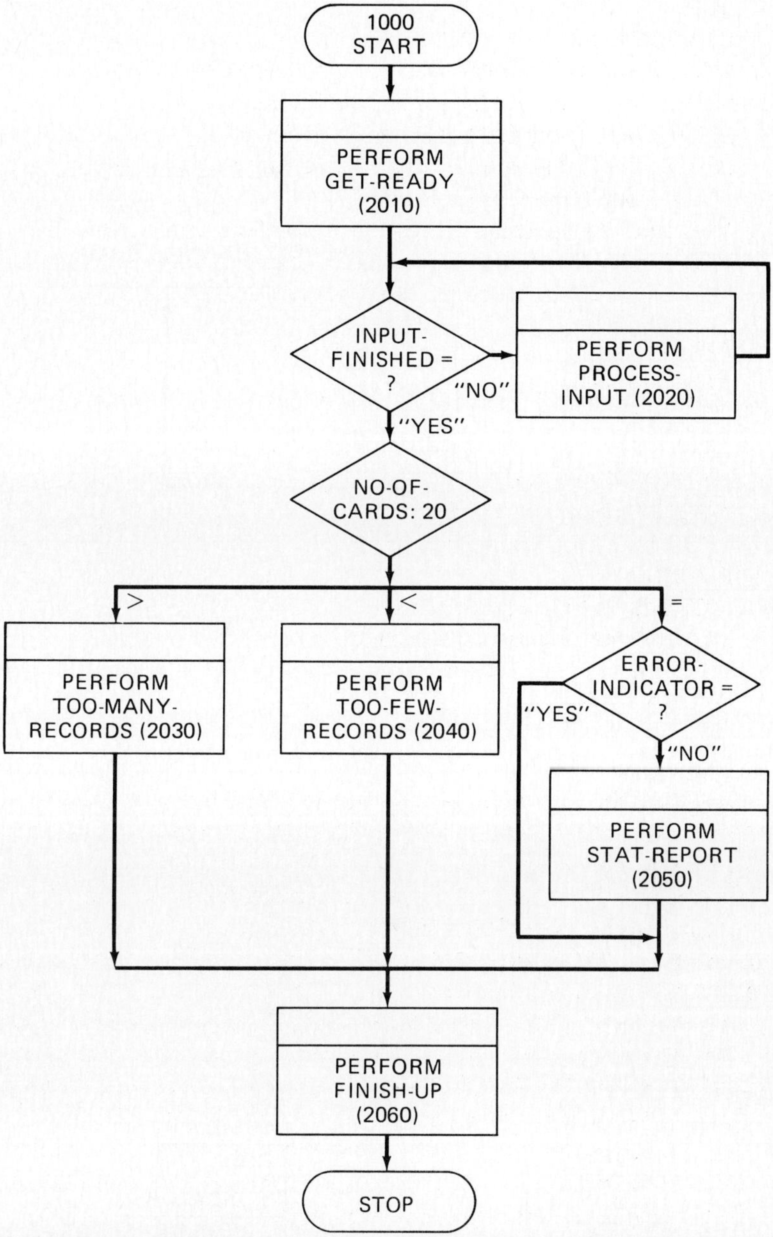

Figure 9-5
Example 9-4
(continued on next page)

PROCESS-INPUT is the routine used to enter data into the table. Values will only be entered if the number of cards is fewer than or equal to 20. For each record processed, "NO" is moved to ERRORS-FINISHED and 1 is moved to ROW. CHECK-ERRORS is then performed until ERRORS-FINISHED has a value of "YES" for the input record. After a record is processed, the next input record is read and the procedure begins again.

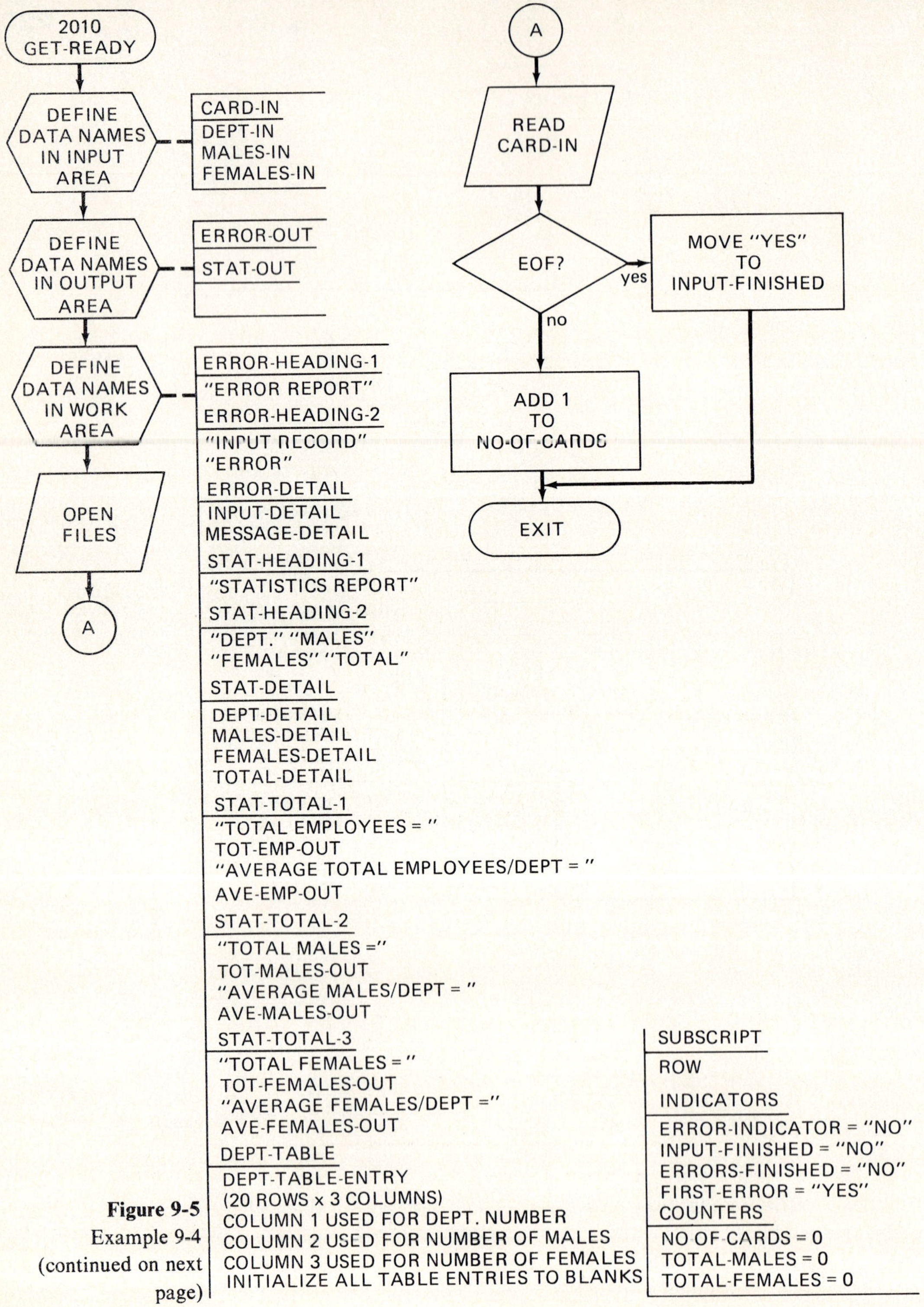

Figure 9-5
Example 9-4
(continued on next page)

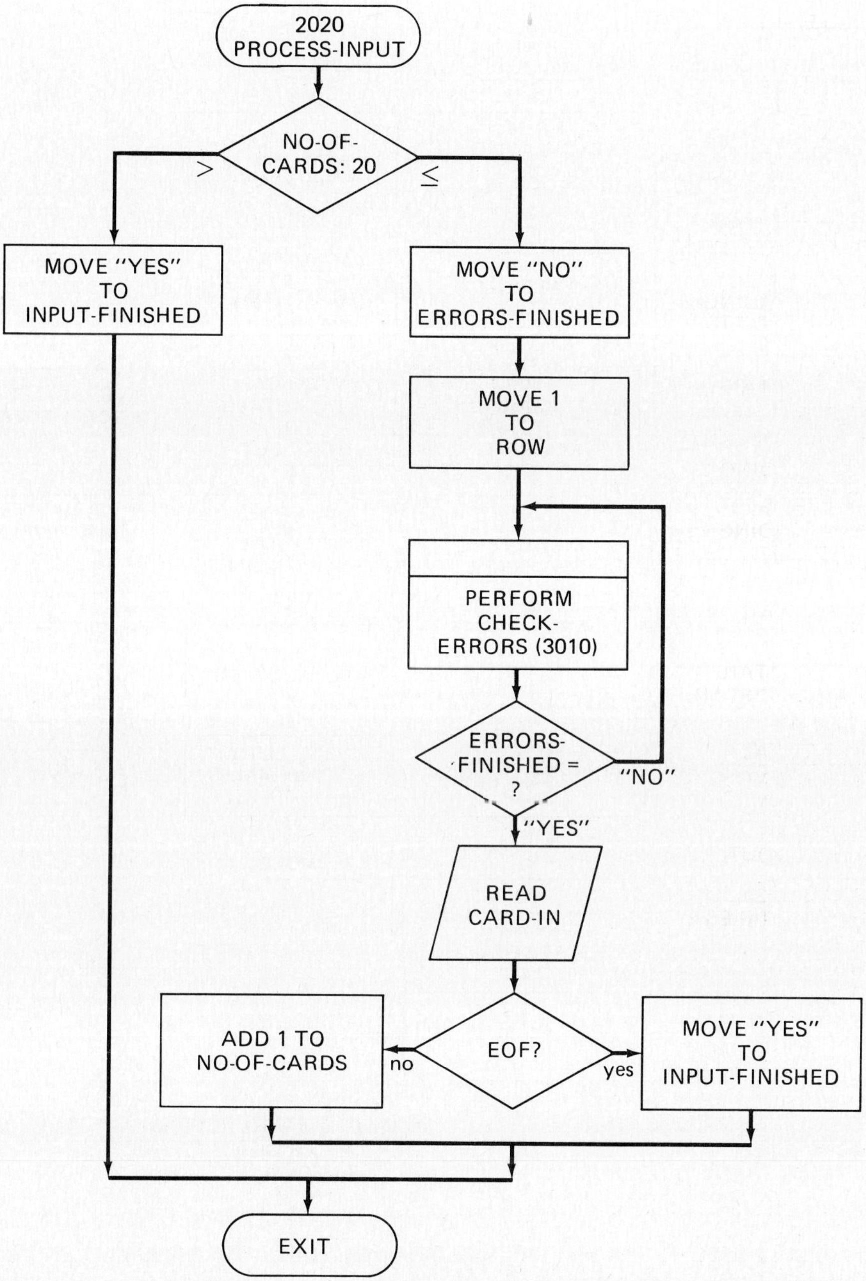

Figure 9-5
Example 9-4
(continued on next page)

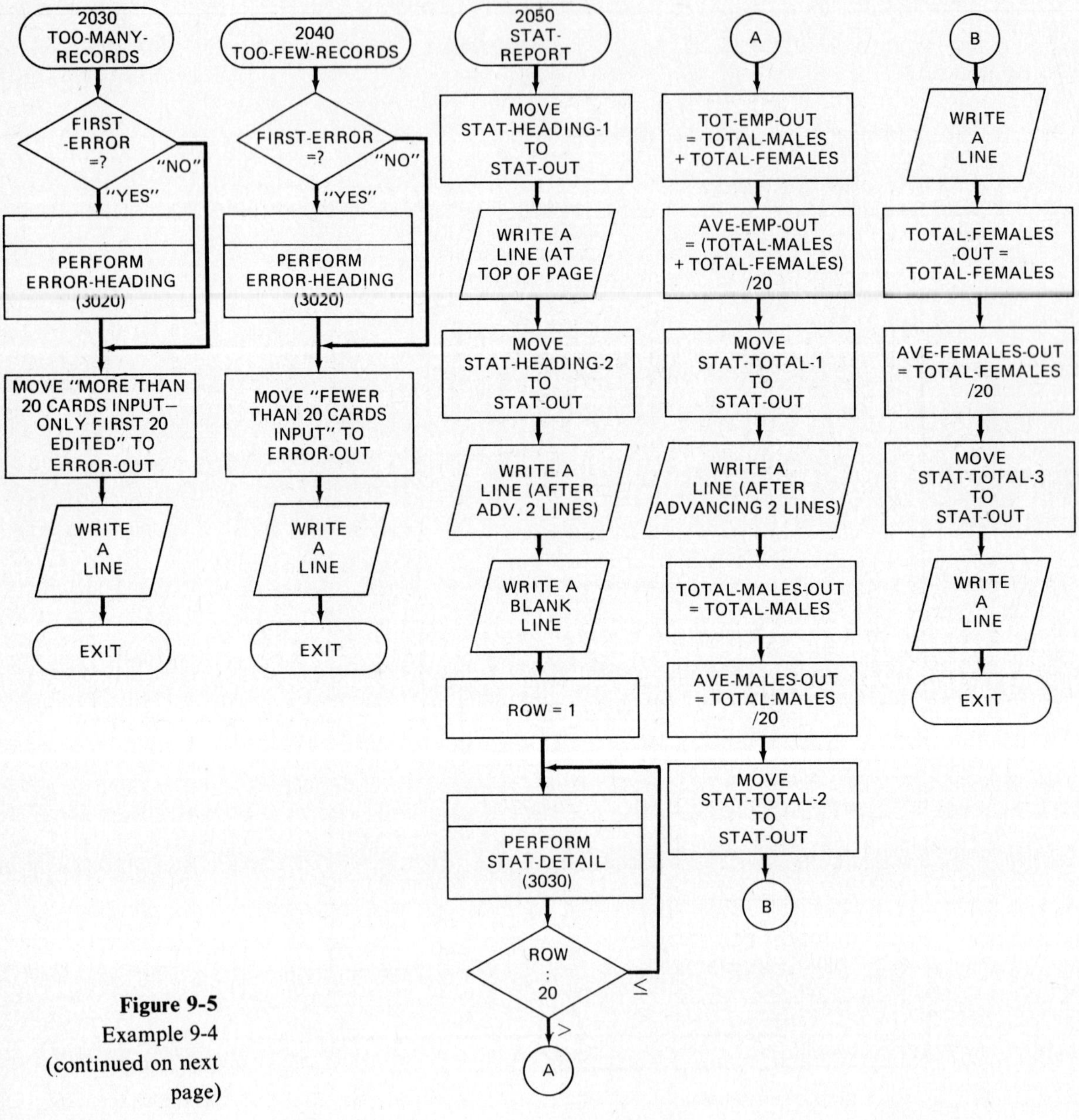

Figure 9-5
Example 9-4
(continued on next page)

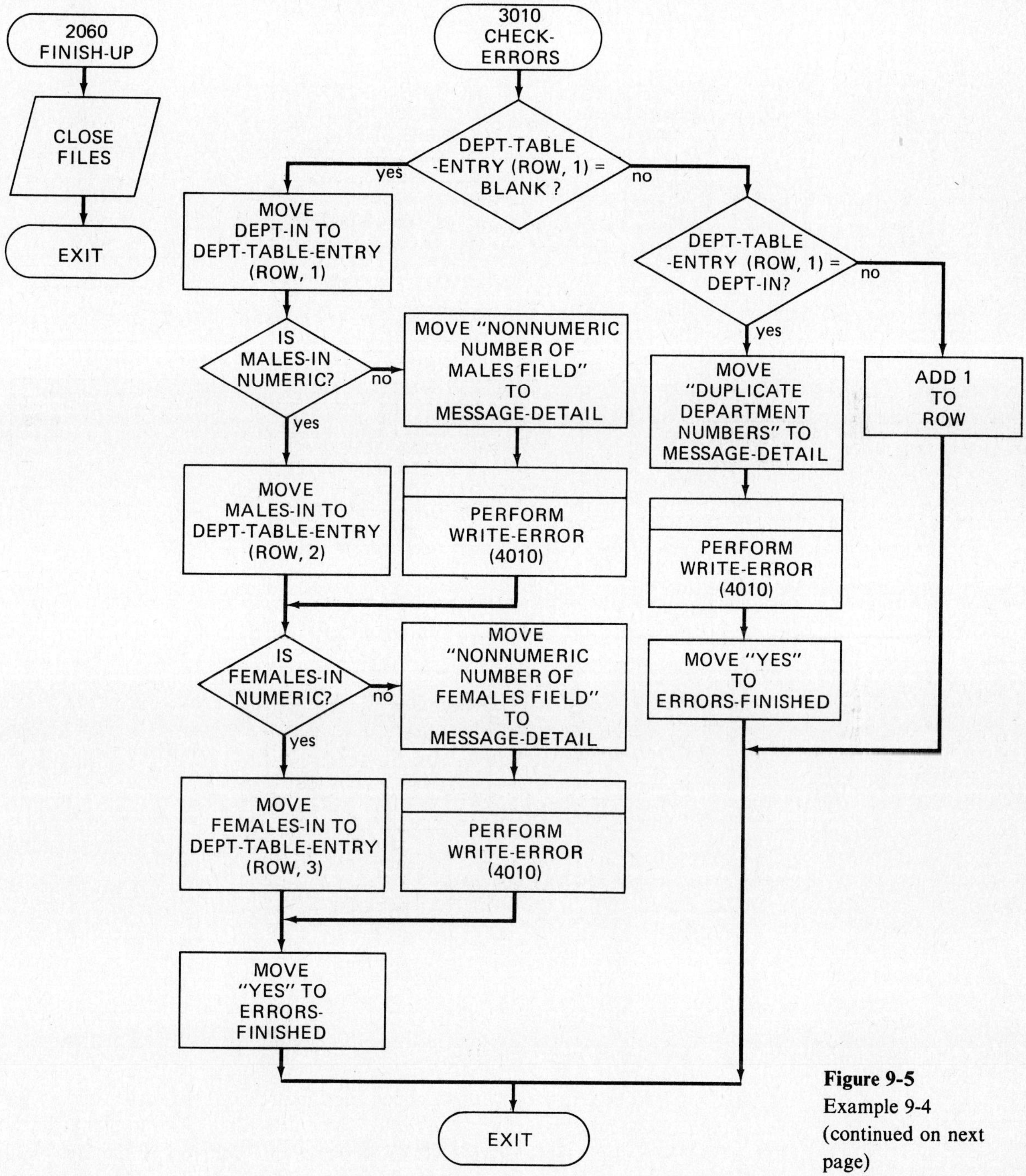

Figure 9-5
Example 9-4
(continued on next page)

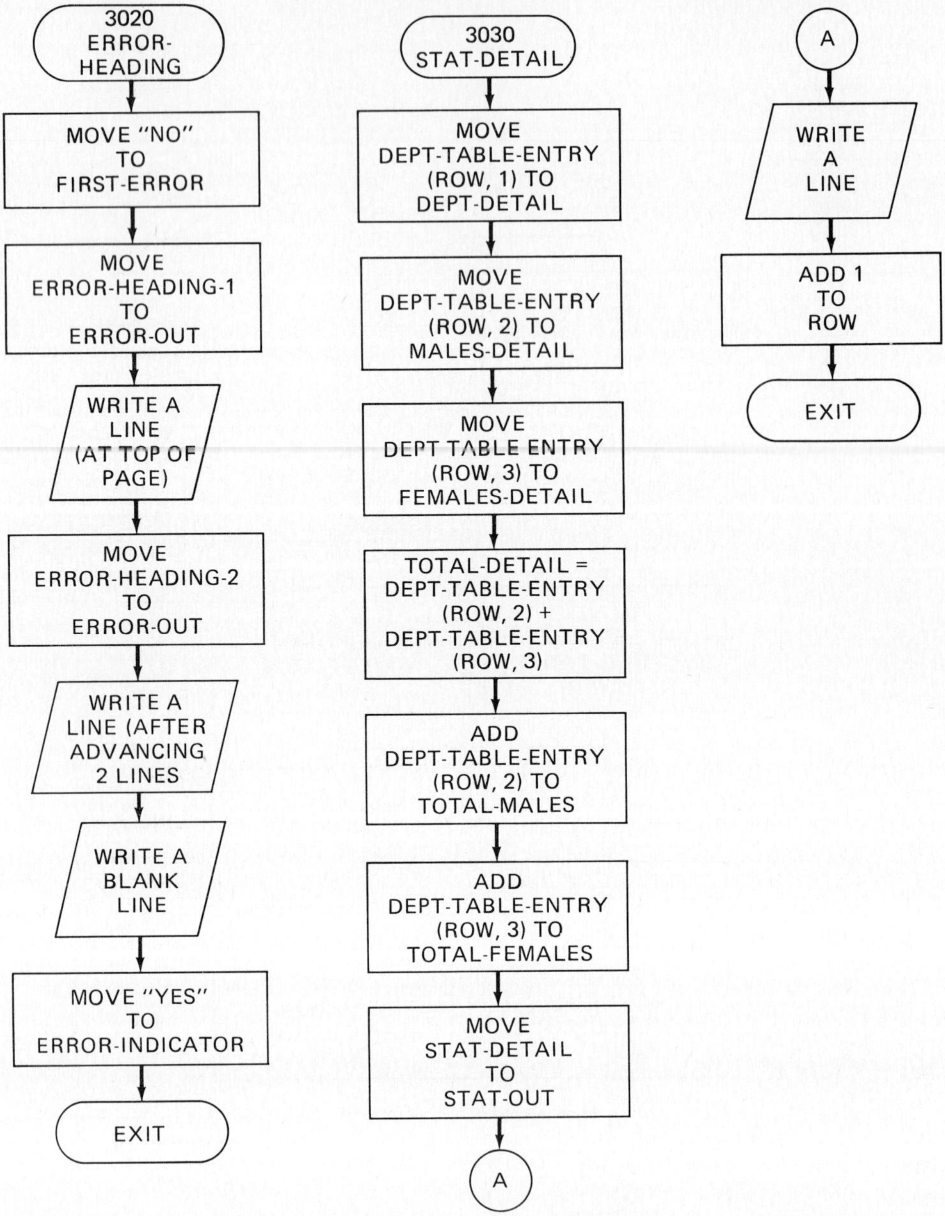

Figure 9-5
Example 9-4
(continued on next page)

CHECK-ERRORS is used both to check the input record for errors and to put the contents of the input fields into the table. The entire table is set to blanks in the GET-READY routine. CHECK-ERRORS searches the table to find the first blank entry in which to put the contents of the input record. After a "blank spot" in the table is found, the input record is moved to the table entry and checked to be sure

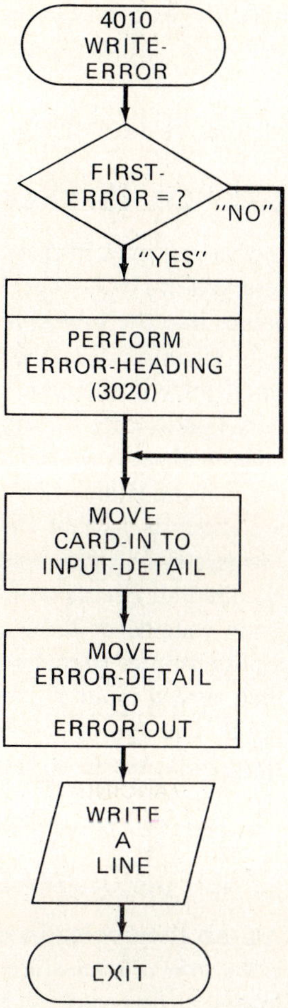

Figure 9-5
Example 9-4
(continued)

that MALES-IN and FEMALES-IN are numeric. The department number from the input record is put in the first column of the table. The number of males listed on the input record is put in the second column of the table. The number of females listed on the input record is put in the third column of the table. Finally, "YES" is moved to ERRORS-FINISHED.

For every record input, processing starts at the beginning of the table (ROW = 1). If the table entry is not blank, a duplicate is checked for by comparing the non-blank entry in the table with the department number on the input record. If they are not equal, 1 is added to ROW and the routine is exited. Processing returns to PROCESS-INPUT, and ERRORS-FINISHED is checked. IF ERRORS-FINISHED is still equal to "NO", we return to CHECK-ERRORS and look at the next row of the table. Since we are only allowing 20 records to be input, a blank entry will be found in the table before we run out of table entries.

After the table is built, if no errors occurred, STAT-REPORT is performed to write the statistics report. STAT-REPORT writes headings and performs STAT-DETAIL to write the table entries and compute the totals needed for the report. Finally, the total lines are printed on the report.

COMPILE: VS. EXECUTION-TIME TABLES

In the examples in this chapter, the space needed in the computer for the tables was reserved in GET-READY by defining the table. The methods used for getting data values into the tables, however, varied substantially.

In Example 9-1, the values in the table were determined based on calculations. Each entry in the table was initialized to zero, and as records were input, the entries in the table were incremented by the points in the input record. In Example 9-2, the codes and rates were put in the table at the time the program was written. In Example 9-4, the values were read into the program as input. When the values for a table are input as part of the coding when the program is written, the table is called a *compile-time table.* When the values are input during program execution, the table is called an *execution-time table.* For a compile-time table to be modified, the program code needs to be changed and the program must be recompiled. This requires a programmer to make and test the changes. For an execution-time table to be modified, a new input file needs to be created. No changes need to be made to the program. The second method is generally preferred for tables that need to be modified frequently, because the user can make the changes without involving a programmer.

TABLE ORGANIZATION AND SEQUENTIAL AND BINARY SEARCH

All table searching in this chapter has been sequential searching. This means that every time a value stored in the table had to be found, the first entry of the table was looked at first and the entire table was searched in sequence until the desired entry was found. To minimize the number of comparisons required to find an entry in a table, the table should be organized so that the first entry in it contains the value that will be needed most often. The last entry in the table should contain the value that will need to be found least often, and so on.

Another technique for table searching (not discussed in this book) is called binary search. A binary search is not frequently used, because it puts many constraints on the table and on the programmer. When the technique can be used, however, it can cut by more than half the number of comparisons required to find an entry in a table.

TABLE RESTRICTIONS

The following restrictions apply when processing tables:

1. When a field name is used as a subscript, it is imperative that the contents of the field be within the range of the table. If the table has 12 entries, for example, the subscript must be between 1 and 12 inclusive.

2. For most computer languages, the maximum size of the table must be specified in your program prior to execution. If you want to build a table which will have one entry for each input record, and sometimes the input file will contain 20 records, sometimes 10, sometimes 100, you must create the table to contain the maximum number of entries (in this case, 100) even though all of them may not be used. When one is working with very large tables, a lot of storage space may be wasted in the computer by this restriction.

QUESTIONS AND EXERCISES FOR REVIEW

1. Define each of the following:
   a. Subscript
   b. Table
   c. Dimension
   d. Compile-time table
   e. Execution-time table
2. What is the purpose of using tables for processing?
3. How many subscripts are required to access a table entry?
4. If X is a field containing the number 10, what does TABLE-ENTRY (X) refer to?
5. Consider the following table:

EXERCISE-5-TABLE

1	24	3
2	9	80
7	12	90
8	14	100

   Answer the following questions.
   a. What is the dimension of the table?
   b. How many rows does the table have?
   c. How many columns does the table have?
   d. What is the value of EXERCISE-5-TABLE (3, 2)?
   e. What is the value of EXERCISE-5-TABLE (1, 4)?
   f. Write an instruction to add the entry in the fourth row and second column to the entry in the first row and third column.
6. How do you modify a compile-time table?
7. How do you modify an execution-time table?
8. How should tables be organized to minimize the number of comparisons required in a sequential table search?
9. When can a field contained on an input record be used as a table subscript?
10. Draw a hierarchy chart for a program to print voter statistics after an election.

Output

Output is to consist of a report. The report is to be generated after creating the table.

Printer Spacing Chart

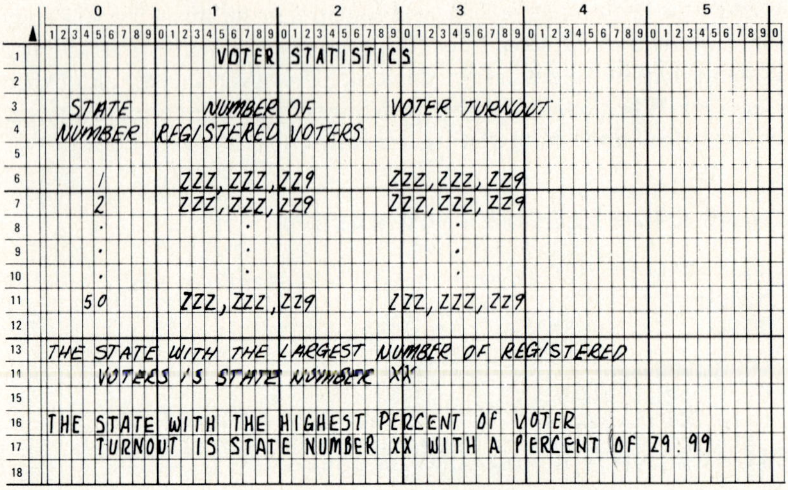

Input

Input consists of an unsorted file containing one record for each precinct in the country. The format of the record is:

Position	*Description*
1–2	State number (a number between 1 and 50). The numbers refer to the states in alphabetical order (1 refers to Alabama, 2 refers to Alaska, etc.).
3–6	Precinct number.
7–13	Number of registered voters.
14–20	Number of actual voters.

Table

A table is to be created containing one row for each state. As each record is read, accumulate the number of registered voters and actual voters in appropriate columns by state.

Calculations

Voter turnout is to be computed by dividing total actual voters by total registered voters and multiplying the result by 100. You may assume that no two states will have exactly the same percent.

11. Draw a flowchart for Exercise 10 above.
12. Construct the pseudocode for Exercise 10 above.
13. Draw a hierarchy chart for a program to produce a weekly sales report.

Output

Output is to consist of a report. Each line of the report is to contain the item number, description, quantity sold for each of the days, and the total for the week.

The item description is to be extracted from a table which is to be built into the program at compile time as follows:

Item Number	*Item Description*
100010	Desk
110011	Chair
120987	Table
129879	Sofa
878890	Bookcase
888954	Cabinet
901265	Bed
910658	Dresser
986523	Lamp

When the description for a particular item input cannot be found in the table, print INVALID ITEM under the item description on the report and continue to process the item.

Printer Spacing Chart

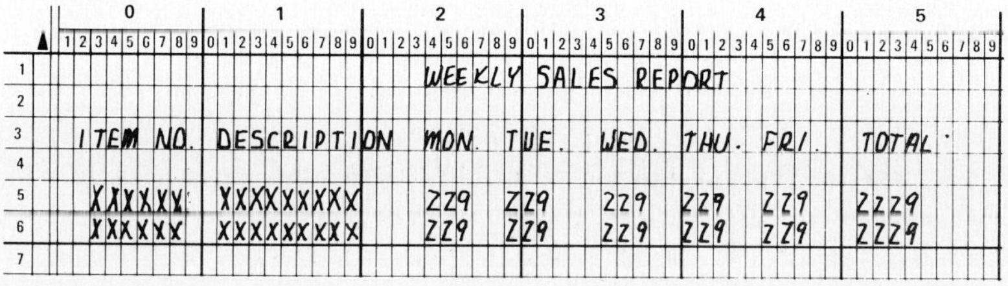

Input

Input consists of records with the following format:

Position	*Description*
1–6	Item number
7–9	Number of items sold on Monday
10–12	Number of items sold on Tuesday
13–15	Number of items sold on Wednesday
16–18	Number of Items sold on Thursday
19–21	Number of items sold on Friday

Input is sorted by item number. One line is to appear on the report per item. If there are multiple input records for a particular item, the amounts for each day are to be summed and one line is to be printed reflecting the totals.

All fields on the input record have been edited in a previous program and are numeric.

14. Draw a flowchart for Exercise 13 above.
15. Construct the pseudocode for Exercise 13 above.
16. Modify Example 5-4 (in Chapter 5) to use a table for the commission rates and selling prices. Show changes using a flowchart.

CHAPTER 10

Programs with Multiple Input Files—Sequential File Matching and Updating

SEQUENTIAL FILES

Sequential files are the most common type of file organization. In a sequential file, records are stored one after the other in a sequence based on a key field (e.g., name, account number, part number) contained within each individual record. Sequential files can be stored on many storage media, including punched cards, magnetic tape, and magnetic disk. In fact, when one is using punched cards or magnetic tape, sequential files are the only method of file organization that can be used.

The main disadvantage of sequential file processing can best be illustrated by an example. If we want to access only the 858th record on a file, the 857 records which precede it on the file must first be accessed. Therefore, sequential file processing can be very time-consuming. It is an efficient method for processing only when most of the records on the file need to be accessed at any given time. Sequential file processing is very inefficient when the records to be processed must be accessed in some sequence other than the one in which the file is organized. In a bank, for example, the teller needs to be able to access the records for individual customers as they come into the bank even though the file may be stored in account number order. It would be extremely time-consuming to search for the appropriate customer record by starting the file at the beginning and accessing records in sequence until the appropriate account is found for every customer who comes into the bank.

MASTER AND TRANSACTION FILES

Files to be processed normally fall into two categories: master files and transaction files. *Master files* contain the current information relating to the status of a given system. The phone company, for example, keeps a master file of customers to be used by the operators giving directory assistance. Each record on the file contains the customer's name, address, and phone number. *Transaction files* contain the day-to-day information used to update or process the master file. A transaction file containing phone number changes would be used to update the phone company master file described above.

There are two types of programs which are written when processing master and transaction files sequentially: the sequential file matching program and the sequential file update program. *Sequential file matching programs* are written when information from the master file is needed to process the transaction file. An example would be a program which produces invoices. The transaction file would contain the customer number and the amount of purchases. The billing address, however, would be obtained from the master file.

A *sequential file update program* is written to enable the master file to be modified in some way. The updates to be made include additions, changes, and deletions. An *addition* occurs when a new record is to be added to a master file. For example, in a payroll system, when a new employee is hired, a record for the new employee must be added to the master file. A *change* occurs whenever a record on the master file no longer contains accurate, up-to-date information. For example, in a payroll system, when the pay rate of an employee changes, the master record for that employee must be changed to reflect the new rate. A *deletion* becomes necessary when a record currently stored on the master file must be removed. For example, when an employee quits, his or her record must be removed from the payroll master file. Every system must contain an update program for its master file or the file cannot be changed without starting over and recreating the entire file.

EXAMPLE 10-1: SEQUENTIAL FILE MATCHING

A report is to be created for a company showing the amount due for each customer.

Output

Output is to consist of a report. A maximum of 45 detail lines are to appear per page. The report is to show the customer number, name, address, amount of purchases, and the billing amount (billing amount = amount of purchases − discount).

If there is a match between transaction and master, the report is to include the customer number, name, and address from the master record, the amount of purchases from the transaction record, and the billing amount based on the customer discount.

If there is a master record and no transaction record, the report is to include the customer number, name, and address from the master record. Under the amount of purchases and billing amount fields the words NO PURCHASES are to appear.

If there is a transaction record and no master record, the report is to include the customer number from the transaction record, the customer name and address fields are to be left blank, and under the amount of purchases and billing amount fields the words MASTER RECORD MISSING are to appear.

Printer Spacing Chart

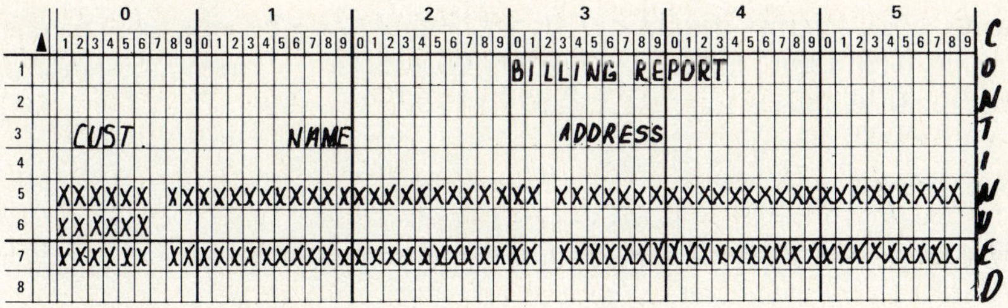

Input

Input consists of a master file and a transaction file. The formats for the records in the master file and transaction file are described below.

Master File	
Position	*Description*
1–6	Customer number
7–30	Customer name
31–56	Customer address
57	Type of customer discount (1 = no discount, 2 = 5% discount on all purchases, 3 = 10% discount on all purchases, 4 = 5% discount on first $100 purchased and 10% on remainder)
Transaction File	
1–6	Customer number
7–12	Amount of purchases

Notes about Input Files

1. Both files are in increasing order by customer number. It is important that both files be sorted in the same sequence when sequential files are processed.
2. Both files have been edited in previous programs so that all fields that are supposed to contain numbers do, in fact, contain numbers.
3. There is only one transaction record input per master. If multiple transaction records were allowed per master, the processing would change somewhat from what is shown in this example (as we'll see in Example 10-3).
4. There may be no master record for a transaction record *or* there may be no transaction record for a master record *or* there may be a match, i.e., one transaction record for a matching master record. (Note: The match is to occur on customer number.)

Calculations

1. If type of customer discount = 1, there is no discount.

   Billing amount = amount of purchases

2. If type of customer discount = 2, there is a 5 percent discount.

   Billing amount = amount of purchases − (.05 * amount of purchases)
   = .95 * amount of purchases

3. If type of customer discount = 3, there is a 10 percent discount.

   Billing amount = amount of purchases − (.10 * amount of purchases)
   = .90 * amount of purchases

4. If type of customer discount = 4, there is a 5 percent discount on the first $100 and a 10 percent discount on the remainder purchased. If the amount of pur-

chases is less than or equal to $100, then

$$\text{Billing amount} = .95 * \text{amount of purchases}$$

If the amount of purchases is greater than $100, then

$$\begin{aligned}\text{Billing amount} &= .95\,(100) + .90\,(\text{amount of purchases} - 100)\\ &= 95 + .90\,(\text{amount of purchases} - 100)\end{aligned}$$

A hierarchy chart for the solution to this problem is shown in Figure 10-1. Construction of pseudocode is left as an exercise. The flowchart is in Figure 10-2. Before looking at the flowchart, however, let's manually work through some sample data.

Suppose you were given the following input files with the customer numbers as shown:

Customer Numbers on Master File	*Customer Numbers on Transaction File*
1	1
2	4
4	5
6	

Further suppose that you were told to process these files manually. To force you to process them in the way that the computer would, the following rules must be followed:

1. Since you are processing two input files, you can have two input areas. That is, at any given time, you can access or make available for use one master file record and one transaction file record.
2. Every READ instruction accesses the next record on the file that you have read.
3. You can only use the records in the input areas. That is, you cannot look back at records you have already processed. You also cannot look ahead at records that have not yet been read.

The first thing to do would be to read or access the first record on each file.

```
CUSTOMER NUMBER ON MASTER RECORD READ = 1
CUSTOMER NUMBER ON TRANSACTION RECORD READ = 1
```

When you look at the customer numbers, it is apparent that they are equal. This would then be processed as a match.

The billing amount would be calculated, and you would print the customer number, name, address, amount of purchases, and the billing amount.

After processing the match, you would read the next record on each file.

```
CUSTOMER NUMBER ON MASTER RECORD READ = 2
CUSTOMER NUMBER ON TRANSACTION RECORD READ = 4
```

No match has occurred. In fact, we could keep reading transaction records, and there would never be a match. This is because the files are sorted. By reading a transaction

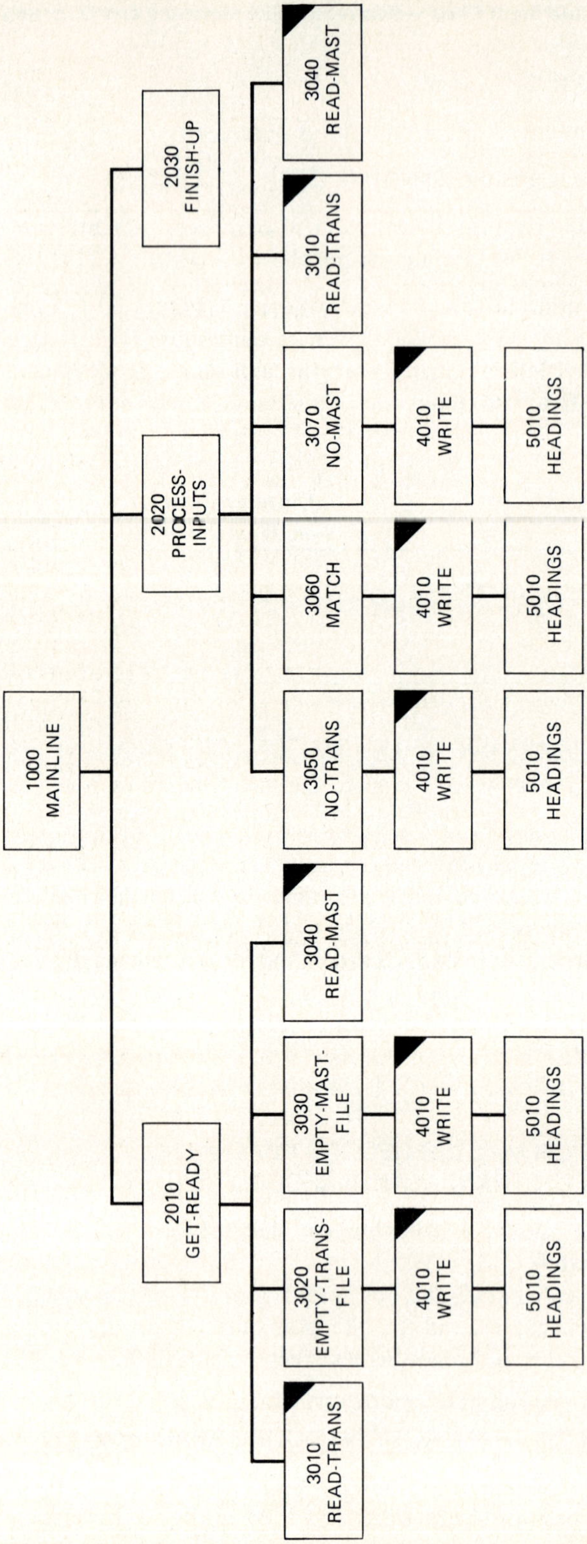

Figure 10-1
Example 10-1

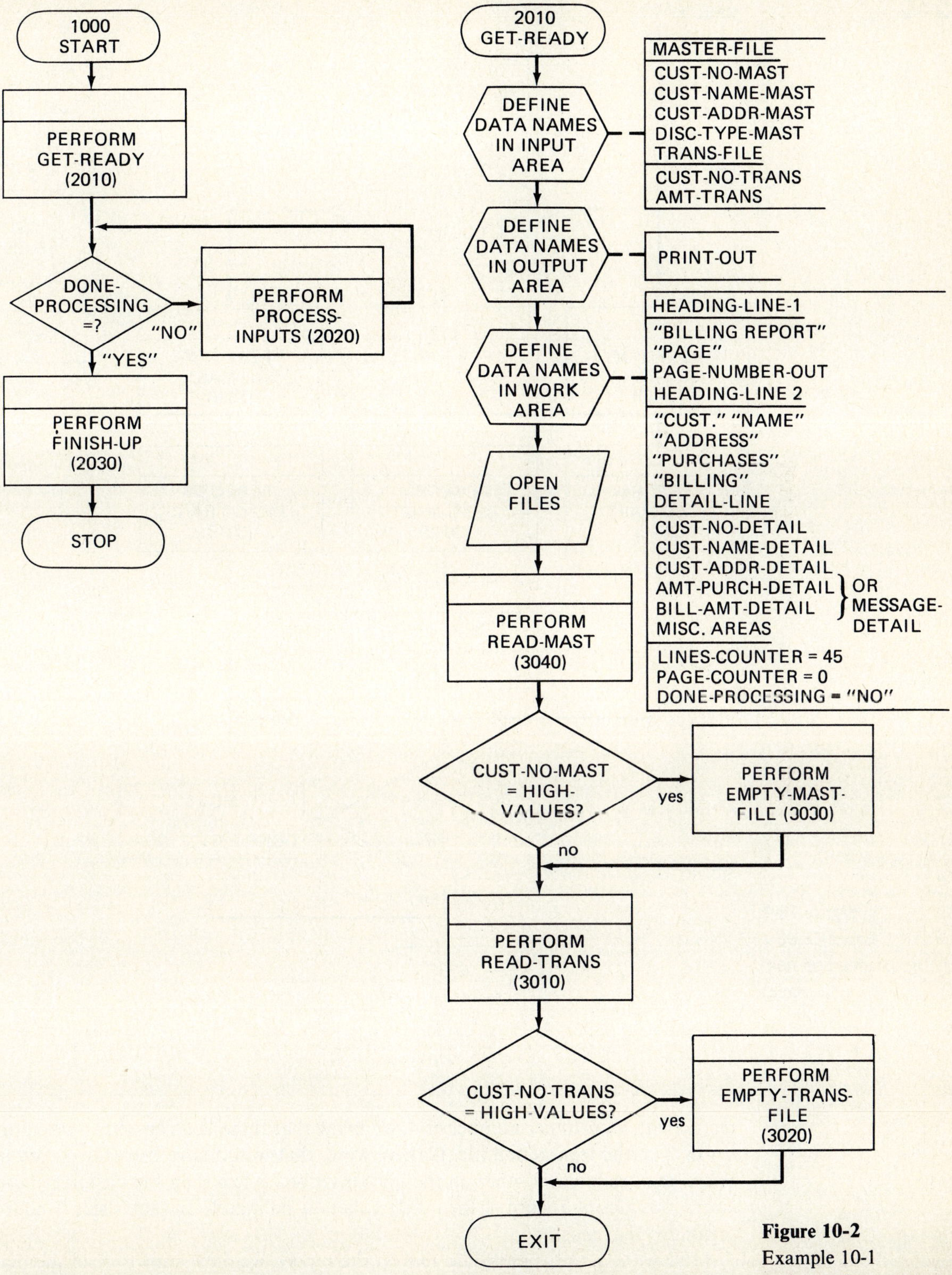

Figure 10-2
Example 10-1
(continued on next page)

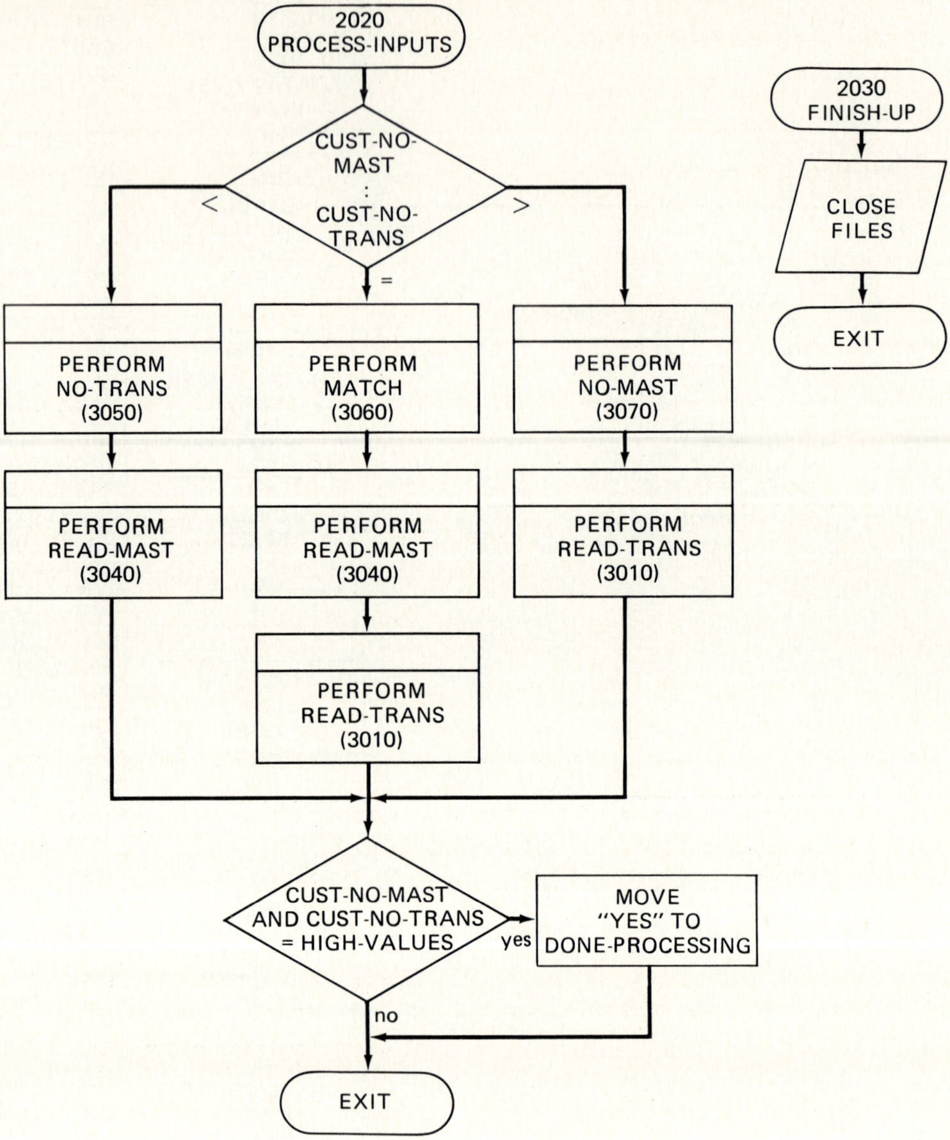

Figure 10-2
Example 10-1
(continued on next page)

record with a customer number of 4, we know that there is no customer with a number of 2 on the transaction file. If there were, that would have been the record read. When the customer number on the master record is less than the customer number on the transaction record, it means that there is no match. In fact, there is no transaction for that master.

After writing the appropriate line on the report, we only want to read the master

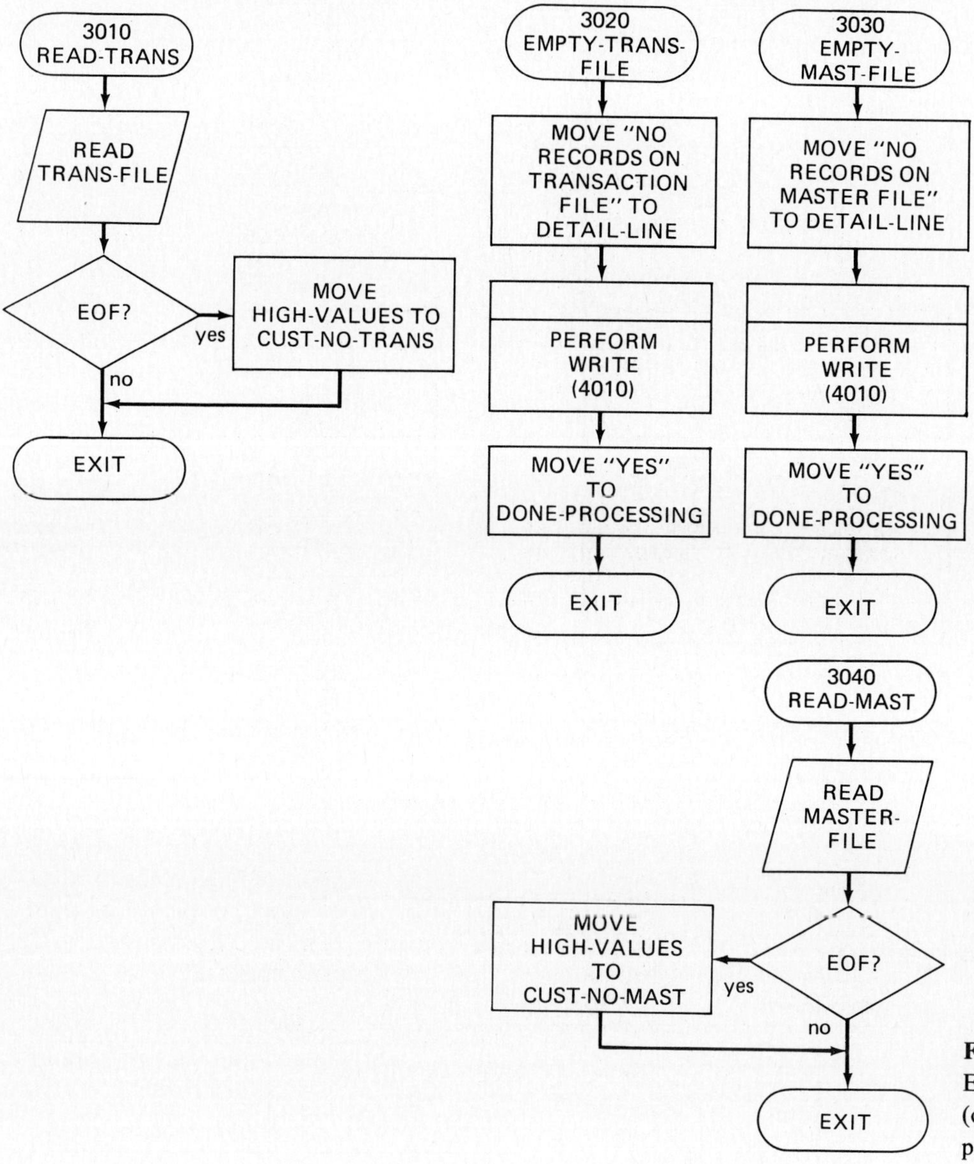

Figure 10-2
Example 10-1
(continued on next page)

file. We don't want to read the transaction file, because there may be a customer with number 4 on the master file. After the master file is read, the input areas would contain the following records:

CUSTOMER NUMBER ON MASTER RECORD = 4
CUSTOMER NUMBER ON TRANSACTION RECORD = 4

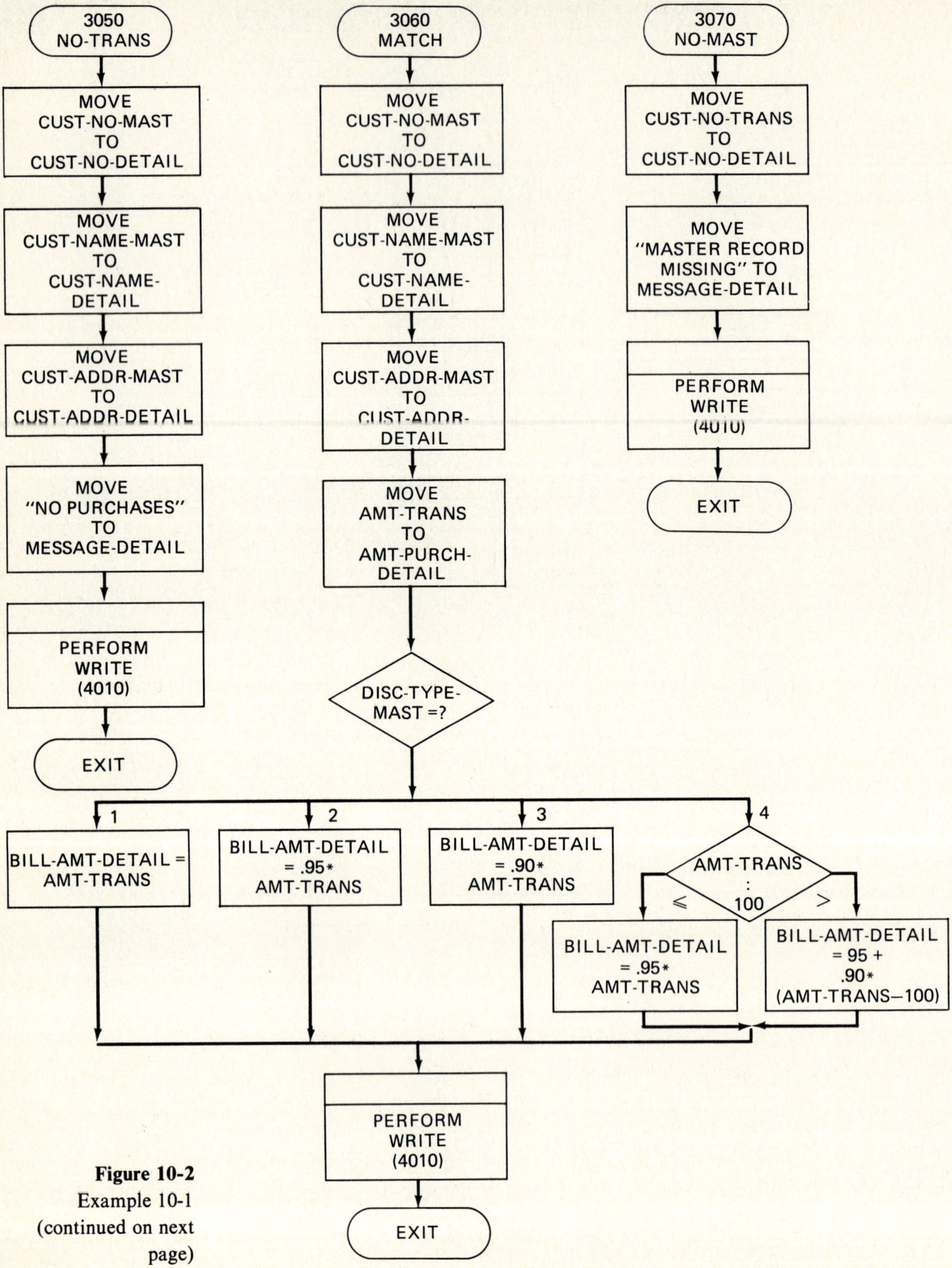

Figure 10-2
Example 10-1
(continued on next page)

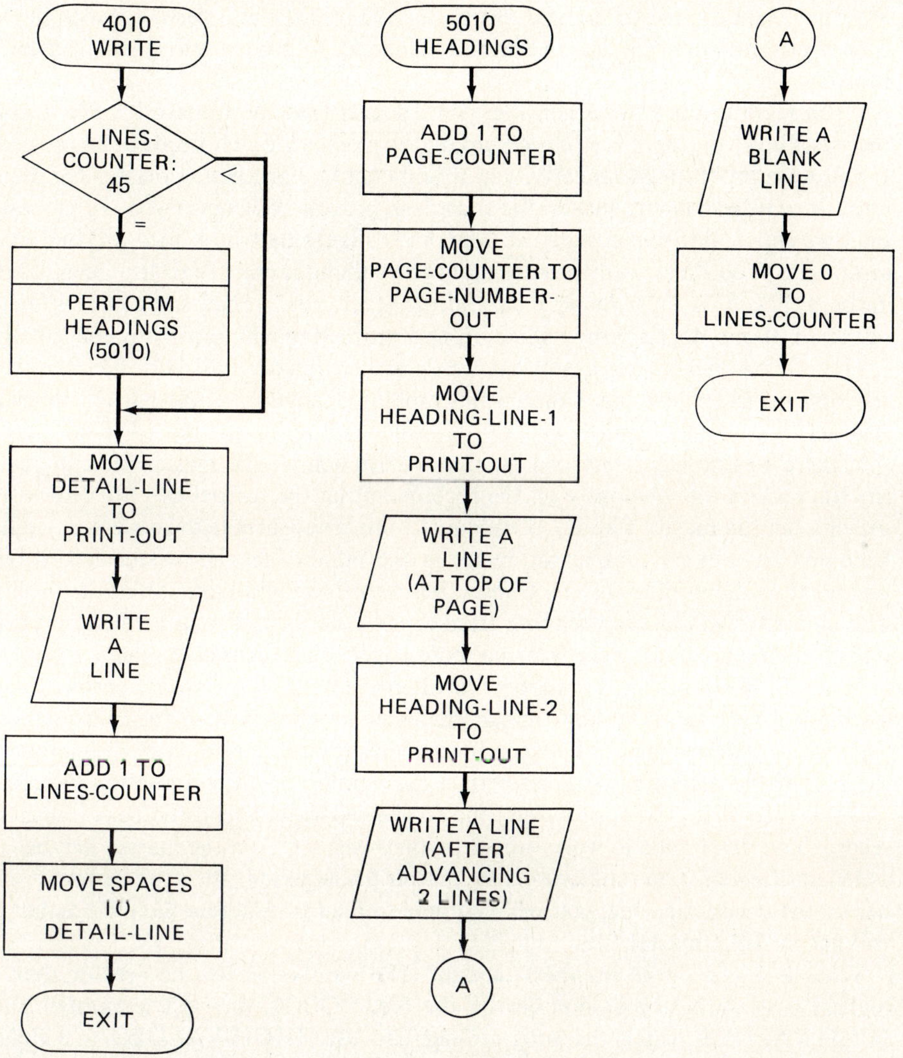

Figure 10-2
Example 10-1
(continued)

Again we have a match, so we process it and read the next record from each file.

CUSTOMER NUMBER ON MASTER RECORD READ = 6
CUSTOMER NUMBER ON TRANSACTION RECORD READ = 5

No match occurs. This time, the customer number on the master record is greater than the customer number on the transaction record. This means that there is no master record with a customer number of 5 on the master file. If there were such a record, that would have been the record read.

After writing a line on the report indicating that there is no master record for the transaction record, we only want to read the next record from the transaction file.

We don't want to read the master file, because there may be a customer with number 6 on the transaction file that we would still want to process using that master file record.

Upon reading the transaction file, you discover that the transaction file is out of records. However, there is still a record on the master file that needs to be processed. If you were processing manually, you would continue processing master file records until there were no more master file records to process. Whenever you are processing multiple input files sequentially, it is highly unlikely that both files will end at the same time. You don't want processing to stop, though, until EOF has been reached on both files. You must be very careful, however, not to read a file once EOF has occurred. If you do, an error will result and processing will terminate abnormally.

How do we make sure, then, that we do not terminate until both files are out of records? Consider how you handled this problem manually. If the master file record read had a customer number greater than the transaction file record read, it meant that there was no master record for that transaction. If the master file ends before the transaction file, obviously all the records left on the transaction file do not have matches on the master file. So, if we could somehow continue to process as we have been and have every comparison result in the number on the master record being greater than the number on the transaction record, we will have solved the problem. The computer would keep reading transaction records and writing the appropriate line on the report until there were no more transaction records to read.

When EOF occurs on the master file when there are still transaction file records, we move a very large number to the customer number field in the master record. This forces the comparison between master and transaction to show the number on the master file record being greater than the number on the transaction file record, and you then write the appropriate line on the report and read the next transaction record. You don't have to worry about reading past EOF on the master file, because as long as the customer number on the master file is greater than the customer number on the transaction file, you will continue to read transaction file records but you will not read the master file.

What is a very large number, though? The number has to be greater than the highest possible customer number on the file. COBOL provides a number called HIGH-VALUES which the programmer can use. HIGH-VALUES is a field in which all the bits are set equal to one. In other words, it is the largest value which can be contained in a field. Anything compared to HIGH-VALUES will be less. In other programming languages, you would use a field containing all 9s and make sure that no customer number on the input file is that large.

Similarly, if the transaction file ends before the master file, that is, if there are still master file records to be processed, you move HIGH-VALUES to the customer number field on the transaction file. Every time you compare the customer numbers on the master and transaction files, the master will be less than the transaction and you will write the appropriate line on the report and read the next master file record.

When you run out of records on both files, both the customer number field on the master and the customer number field on the transaction will have been set equal to HIGH-VALUES and you can terminate processing.

Now let's examine the flowchart in Figure 10-2 in more detail.

Note in GET-READY that two input areas are defined. One input area is used for the master file and one input area is used for the transaction file. Note also that when the detail line is defined, the field called MESSAGE-DETAIL, which will contain the appropriate message when no match occurs, uses the same area in storage as the amount fields that will be used when a match does occur. In order to make sure that parts of the message are not left in the space between the amount fields in the output (see the printer spacing chart in the description of this problem), it is necessary to clear or move spaces to the detail line each time the line has been moved to the output area and has been written.

After the storage areas are defined and the files are opened, the first record is read from each of the files. If either file is empty, an error message is written on the report by performing the EMPTY-MAST-FILE or EMPTY-TRANS-FILE routine. The order in which the files are read does not matter as long as one record is read from each file.

Now look at the PROCESS-INPUTS routine. Every time we enter this routine, we have a master file record, a transaction file record or HIGH-VALUES in the input areas. First, the customer numbers are compared. If they are equal, we perform the MATCH routine and then read the next record from each of the files. If the customer number on the master file record is less than the customer number on the transaction file record, it means that there is no transaction for the master, so we perform the NO-TRANS routine and read the next master file record. If the transaction file reaches EOF before the master file reaches EOF, HIGH-VALUES is moved to CUST-NO-TRANS in the READ routine so that every time the PROCESS-INPUTS routine is performed, CUST-NO-MAST is less than CUST-NO-TRANS.

If, in the PROCESS-INPUTS routine, the CUST-NO-MAST is greater than the customer number on the transaction record, it means that there is no master for the transaction, so we perform the NO-MAST routine and read the next transaction file record. If the master file reaches EOF before the transaction file reaches EOF, then HIGH-VALUES is moved to CUST-NO-MAST in the READ routine so that every time the PROCESS-INPUTS routine is performed, CUST-NO-MAST is greater than CUST-NO-TRANS.

At the end of the PROCESS-INPUTS routine, if both customer number fields are HIGH-VALUES, the value "yes" is moved to DONE-PROCESSING and PROCESS-INPUTS is not performed again.

EXAMPLE 10-2: SEQUENTIAL FILE MATCHING WITH MULTIPLE OUTPUT FILES

For this example, we want to modify Example 10-1 to produce a second output file. This file is on magnetic tape and is to contain one record for each match between master and transaction. Each record is to show the customer number, customer name, customer address, type of customer discount, amount of purchases, discount amount, and billing amount. This file will be used in a later program for producing the bills for the system.

The pseudocode solution for this example is:

```
1000
MAINLINE
START
DO Get-Ready (2010) routine
IF Done-Processing = "No" THEN
   DO Process-Inputs (2020) routine UNTIL Done-Processing = "Yes"
   ENDDO
ENDIF
DO Finish-Up (2030) routine
STOP

2010
GET-READY
DEFINE data names in input, output, and work areas
OPEN files
DO Read-Mast (3040) routine
IF Cust-No-Mast = HIGH-VALUES THEN
   DO Empty-Mast-File (3030) routine
   ENDDO
ENDIF
DO Read-Trans (3010) routine
IF Cust-No-Trans = HIGH-VALUES THEN
   DO Empty-Trans-File (3020) routine
   ENDDO
ENDIF
ENDGET-READY

2020
PROCESS-INPUTS
IF Cust-No-Mast is less than Cust-No-Trans THEN
   DO No-Trans (3050) routine
   DO Read-Mast (3040) routine
ELSE IF Cust-No-Mast is greater than Cust-No-Trans THEN
            DO No-Mast (3070) routine
            DO Read-Trans (3010) routine
        ELSE DO Match (3060) routine
                DO Read-Mast (3040) Routine
                DO Read-Trans (3010) routine
        ENDIF
ENDIF
IF Cust-No-Mast and Cust-No-Trans = HIGH-VALUES THEN
   MOVE "Yes" to Done-Processing
ENDIF
ENDPROCESS-INPUTS
```

2030
<u>FINISH-UP</u>
CLOSE Files
ENDFINISH-UP

3010
<u>READ-TRANS</u>
READ a record from Trans-File
  ATEND of file MOVE HIGH-VALUES to Cust-No-Trans
ENDREAD-TRANS

3020
<u>EMPTY-TRANS-FILE</u>
MOVE "No Records on Transaction File" to Detail-Line
DO Write (4010) routine
MOVE "Yes" to Done-Processing
ENDEMPTY-TRANS-FILE

3030
<u>EMPTY-MAST-FILE</u>
MOVE "No Records on Master File" to Detail-Line
DO Write (4010) routine
MOVE "Yes" to Done-Processing
ENDEMPTY-MAST-FILE

3040
<u>READ-MAST</u>
READ a record from Master-File
  ATEND of file MOVE HIGH-VALUES to Cust-No-Mast
ENDREAD-MAST

3050
<u>NO-TRANS</u>
MOVE Cust-No-Mast to Cust-No-Detail
MOVE Cust-Name-Mast to Cust-Name-Detail
MOVE Cust-Addr-Mast to Cust-Addr-Detail
MOVE "No Purchases" to Message-Detail
DO Write (4010) routine
ENDNO-TRANS

3060
<u>MATCH</u>
MOVE Cust-No-Mast to Cust-No-Detail and Cust-No-Tape
MOVE Cust-Name-Mast to Cust-Name-Detail and Cust-Name-Tape
MOVE Cust-Addr-Mast to Cust-Addr-Detail and Cust-Addr-Tape
MOVE Amt-Trans to Amt-Purch-Detail and Amt-Purch-Tape
MOVE Disc-Type-Mast to Disc-Type-Tape

```
IF Disc-Type-Mast = 1 THEN
     MOVE 0 to Disc-Amt-Tape
     MOVE Amt-Trans to Bill-Amt-Detail and Bill-Amt-Tape
ELSE IF Disc-Type-Mast = 2 THEN
          MOVE .05 * Amt-Trans to Disc-Amt-Tape
          MOVE .95 * Amt-Trans to Bill-Amt-Detail and Bill-Amt-Tape
      ELSE IF Disc-Type-Mast = 3 THEN
               MOVE .10 * Amt-Trans to Disc-Amt-Tape
               MOVE .90 * Amt-Trans to Bill-Amt-Detail and Bill-Amt-Tape
           ELSE IF Amt-Trans is less than or equal to 100 THEN
                     MOVE .05 * Amt-Trans to Disc-Amt-Tape
                     MOVE .95 * Amt-Trans to Bill-Amt-Detail and Bill-Amt-Tape
                ELSE MOVE 5 + .10 ** (Amt-Trans - 100) to
                            Disc-Amt-Tape
                MOVE 95 + .90 * (Amt-Trans - 100) to
                               Bill-Amt-Detail and Bill-Amt-Tape
                ENDIF
           ENDIF
      ENDIF
ENDIF
WRITE a record on tape file
DO Write (4010) routine
ENDMATCH

3070
NO-MAST
MOVE Cust-No-Trans to Cust-No-Detail
MOVE "Master Record Missing" to Message-Detail
DO Write (4010) routine
ENDNO-MAST

4010
WRITE
IF Lines-Counter = 45 THEN
  DO Headings (5010) routine
ENDIF
MOVE Detail-Line to output Area
WRITE a line
ADD 1 to Lines-Counter
CLEAR Detail-Line with spaces
ENDWRITE

5010
HEADINGS
ADD 1 to Page-Counter
MOVE Page-Counter to Heading-Line-1 (Page-Number-Out)
MOVE Heading-Line-1 to output area
```

WRITE a line at top of page
MOVE Heading-Line-2 to output area
WRITE a line after advancing 2 lines
WRITE a blank line
RESET Lines-Counter to 0
ENDHEADINGS

The differences between this example and Example 10-1 are:

1. In GET-READY we need to describe an output area to be used for the tape. The program will then have two input areas and two output areas.
2. The MATCH routine must be changed to write a record both on the report and on the tape.

EXAMPLE 10-3: MULTIPLE TRANSACTION RECORDS PER MASTER FILE RECORD

This example is a modification of Example 10-1. In Example 10-1, only one transaction record could be entered for a customer. In this example we are allowing multiple transaction records with the same customer number to be entered. However, only one line is to be written on the report per customer.

In order to allow for multiple transaction records per master file record, we need to modify the PROCESS-INPUTS, MATCH, and NO-MAST routines shown in Figure 10-1. Figure 10-3 shows the changes. In addition, the CALCULATIONS routine shown in Figure 10-3 must be added, and the following work areas must be added in the GET-READY routine:

AMT-TRANS-WORK
BILL-AMT-WORK
CUST-NO-WORK

If there is no transaction file record for a master file record (CUST-NO-MAST is less than CUST-NO-TRANS), the processing remains the same as it was in Example 10-1.

If there is no master file record for a particular transaction file record (CUST-NO-MAST is greater than CUST-NO-TRANS), then the NO-MAST routine is performed. NO-MAST saves the current customer number in CUST-NO-WORK. Then a detail line is written on the report. Finally, the next transaction record is read. This is the major difference between the routine in this example and the NO-MAST routine in Example 10-1. If the CUST-NO-TRANS has not changed from the number on the record just processed, we want to bypass the record. Otherwise, we would write two detail lines on the report for transactions with the same customer number. When we exit the NO-MAST routine and return to PROCESS-INPUTS, we do not want to read the transaction file again, because at the time the NO-MAST routine is exited, the next transaction record to be processed is in the input area.

If a match occurs (CUST-NO-MAST is equal to CUST-NO-TRANS), we do the MATCH routine. The CALCULATIONS routine accumulates the total billing

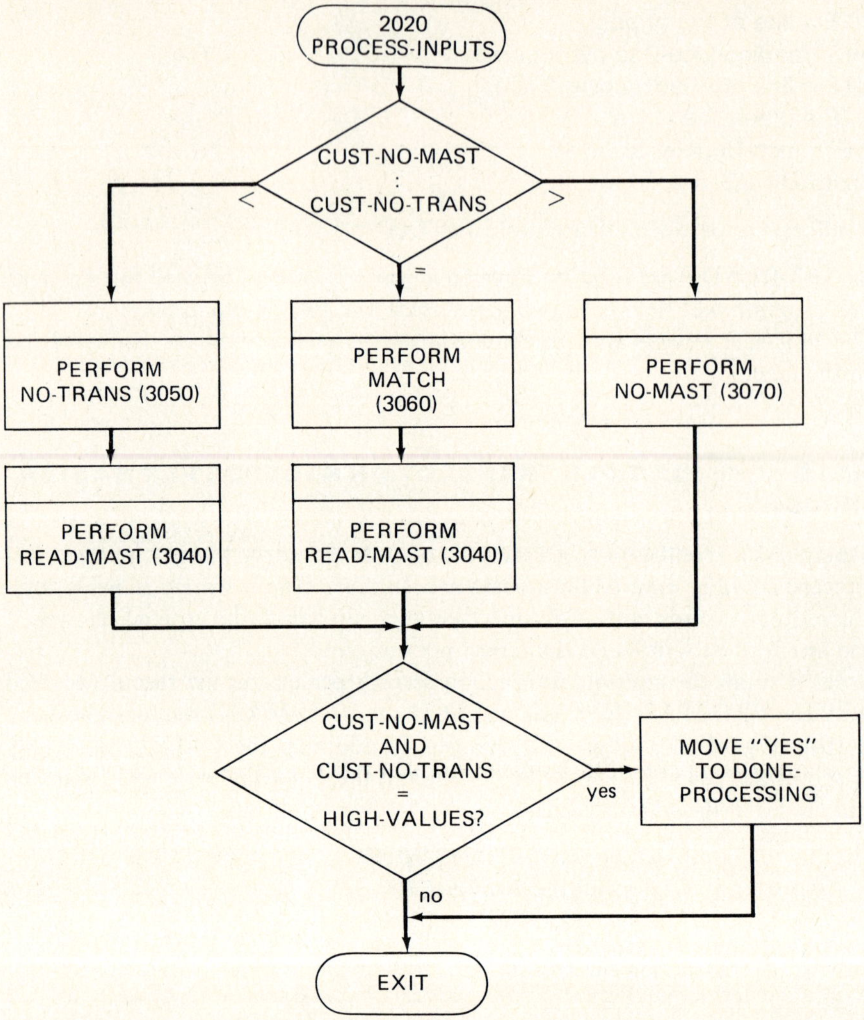

Figure 10-3
Example 10-3
(continued on next page)

amount and the total amount of the transactions for all transaction records with the same customer number. When the customer number changes, a detail line is written showing the accumulated amounts, and we return to the PROCESS-INPUTS routine. Again, we don't have to read a transaction file record, because we have read the transaction record in the CALCULATIONS routine.

SEQUENTIAL FILE UPDATE

A sequential file update program is a simple extension of a matching program. In an update program, the records on the transaction file are used to add records to the master file, change records on the master file, and delete records from the master file.

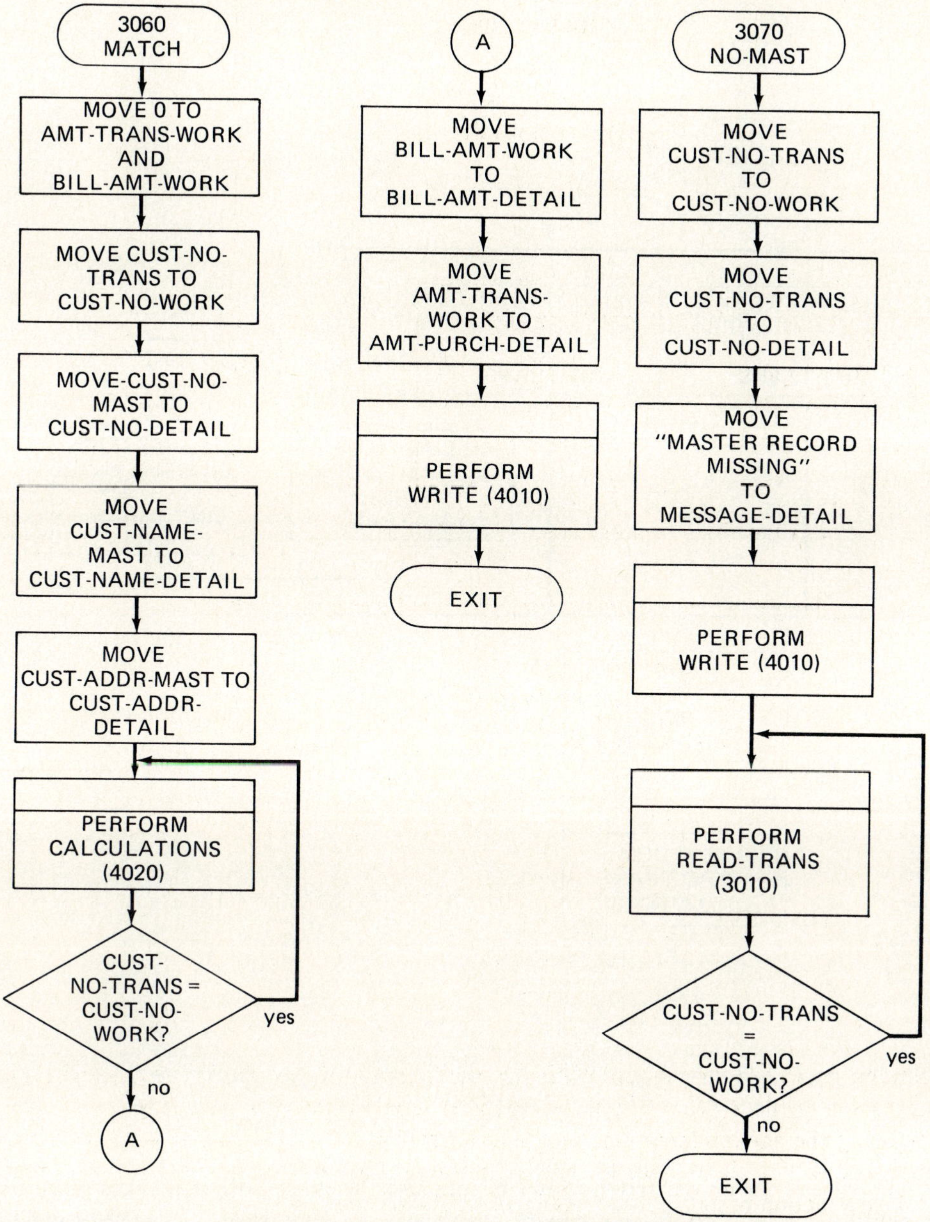

Figure 10-3
Example 10-3
(continued on next page)

In a sequential update, an entirely new master file is created from the old master and transaction files. Input to a sequential update program consists of the old master file and the transaction file. Output consists of a new master file and one or more reports describing the updates and any errors that occurred during processing. After processing, the old master file is saved for a period of time to be used as backup in case the new master file is destroyed for some reason.

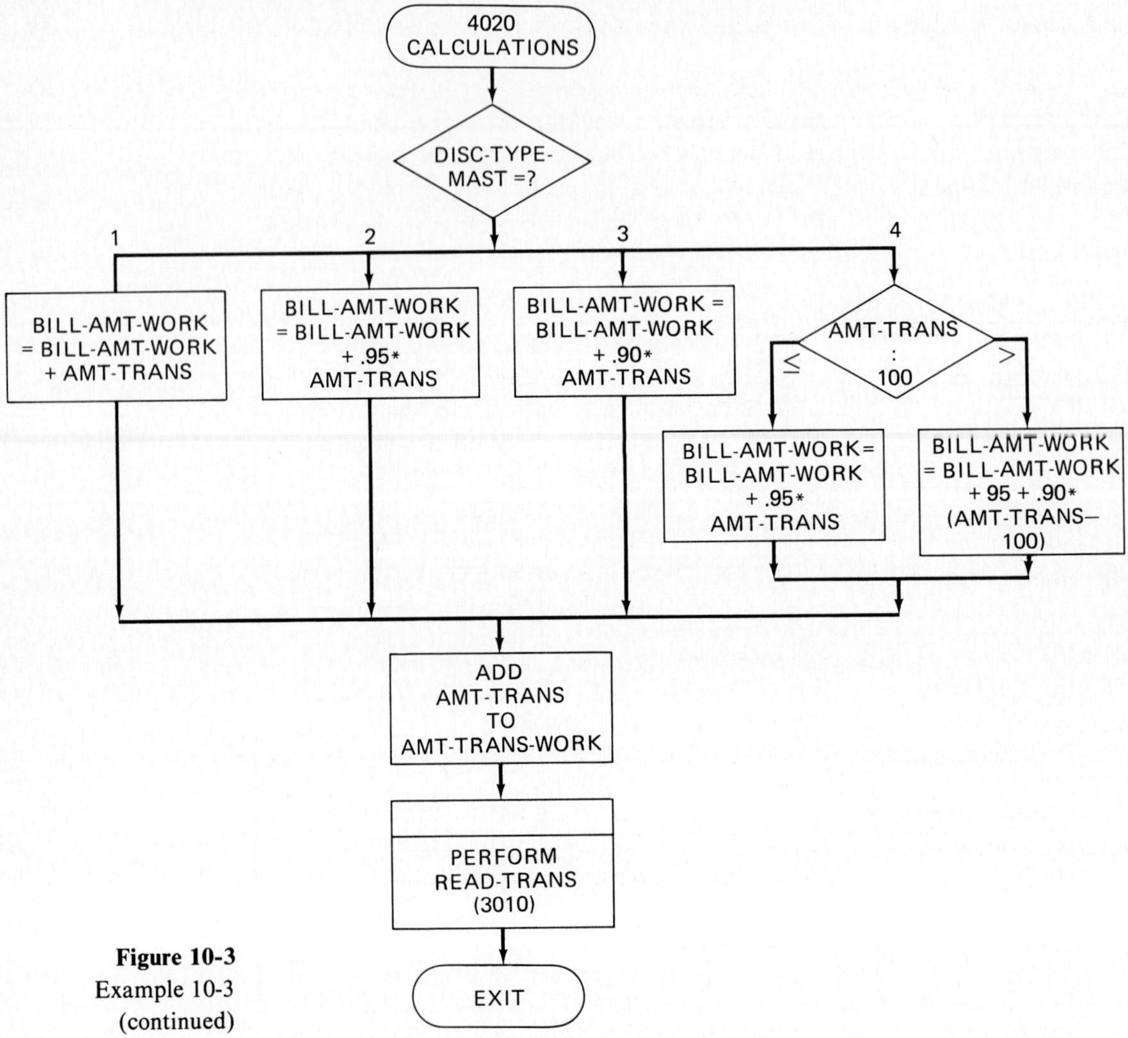

Figure 10-3
Example 10-3
(continued)

The need for an entirely new master file and the processing that takes place can be better understood if you compare it with making changes on a cassette or reel-to-reel tape on which you have previously recorded songs. In order to delete a record (song) from an old master file (old tape), we find the record (song) on the old master file (old tape), and simply do not copy it onto the new master file (new tape). We copy everything until the start of the record (song) to be deleted, bypass the record (song) to be deleted, and continue copying after the record (song) which we want to delete. To change a record (song) on an old master file (tape), we find the record (song) on the old master file (tape), make the changes, and copy the changed record (song) onto the new master file (tape). To add a record (song) onto a new master file (tape), we find where it should be and write (record) it on the new master file (tape).

In an update program, the only field on the master file record that cannot be changed is the key field. Since the *key field* identifies the record and determines its relative order on the file, changing a key field would mess up the order of the file. If it is necessary to change the key field, first delete the record using the old key. Then add the record using the new key. The new record will then be put in its proper place on the file.

EXAMPLE 10-4: SEQUENTIAL FILE UPDATE

For this example we are told to create and/or update a checking account balance master file for a bank. The format of the master file is illustrated below.

Position	*Description*
1–7	Account number
8–23	Customer name
24–50	Customer address
51–60	Current balance

The master file is in sorted order by account number.

Output Reports

In addition to the master file, two reports are to be created as output: an exception report and an update report. A maximum of 50 detail lines are to appear per page on each of the reports. Reports are to contain page numbers and the current date. The exception report is to show all records in which an error occurred. The update report is to show all records in which a successful update occurred.

Printer Spacing Chart for Exception Report

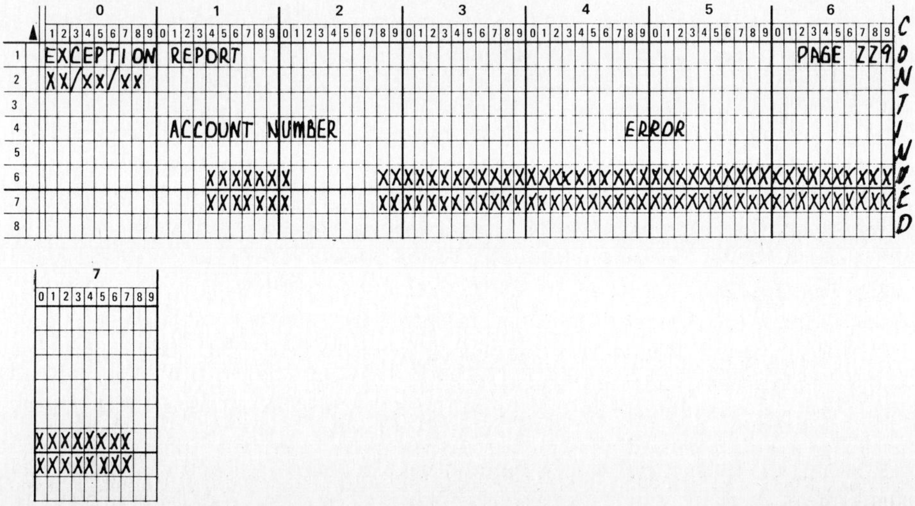

Printer Spacing Chart for Update Report

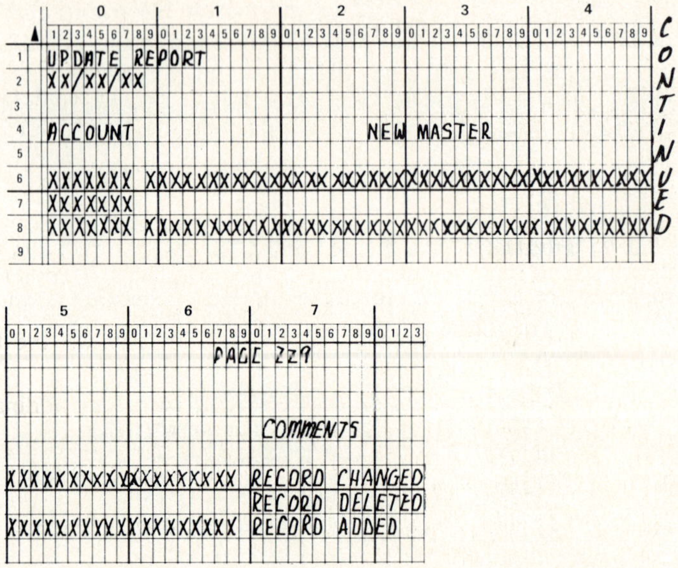

Input

In addition to the master file described above, a transaction file is input. The format of the transaction file is:

Position	*Description*
1–7	Account number
8–23	Customer name
24–50	Customer address
51–60	Additions to current balance
61–70	Subtractions from current balance
80	Code (A = addition, i.e., new record; D = deletion, i.e., terminated customer; C = change)

The transaction file is also in sorted order by account number. It has been edited in a previous program to ensure that the code field is valid and that the account numbers are unique (only one transaction record per master). In addition, the edit program ensures that columns 51 to 70 are numeric.

Rules for Updates

1. CODE = A: This is an addition (i.e., a new customer). A new master file record needs to be created with the data from the transaction record. If a record already exists on the master file for the customer, an error is generated. Use the message CANNOT ADD RECORD—MASTER ALREADY EXISTS. To create a new master file, all transaction records entered have a code of A, and an "empty" old master file is used.

2. CODE = D: This is a deletion (i.e., a customer has closed an account). The record is to be deleted from the master file. If a record with that account number does not exist on the master file, an error is generated. Use the message CANNOT DELETE RECORD—MASTER DOES NOT EXIST.

3. CODE = C: This is a change to a record on the master file. If a record with that account number doesn't exist on the master file, an error is generated. Use the message CANNOT CHANGE RECORD—MASTER DOES NOT EXIST.

Changes to Be Made

1. If the customer name field on the transaction record is not blank, replace the name field on the master record with the name field on the transaction record.
2. If the customer address field on the transaction record is not blank, replace the address field on the master record with the address field on the transaction record.
3. Always modify the current balance on the master record by adding the additions to current balance from the transaction record and subtracting the subtractions from current balance from the transaction record.

A hierarchy chart for this example is given in Figure 10-4. The pseudocode solution for this example is:

```
1000
MAINLINE
DO Get-Ready (2010) routine
DO Update-File (2020) routine UNTIL Done-Processing is equal to "yes"
ENDDO
DO Finish-Up (2030) routine
STOP

2010
GET-READY
DEFINE data names in input, output, and work areas
OPEN files
GET current date for reports
DO Read-Mast (3020) routine
DO Read-Trans (3030) routine
IF T-Account-No = HIGH VALUES THEN
   DO No-Trans (3010) routine
ENDIF
ENDGET-READY

2020
UPDATE-FILE
IF OM-Account-No is less than T-Account-No THEN
        DO No-Trans-For-Mast (3050) routine
ELSE IF OM-Account-No = T-Account-No THEN
             DO Match (3040) routine
```

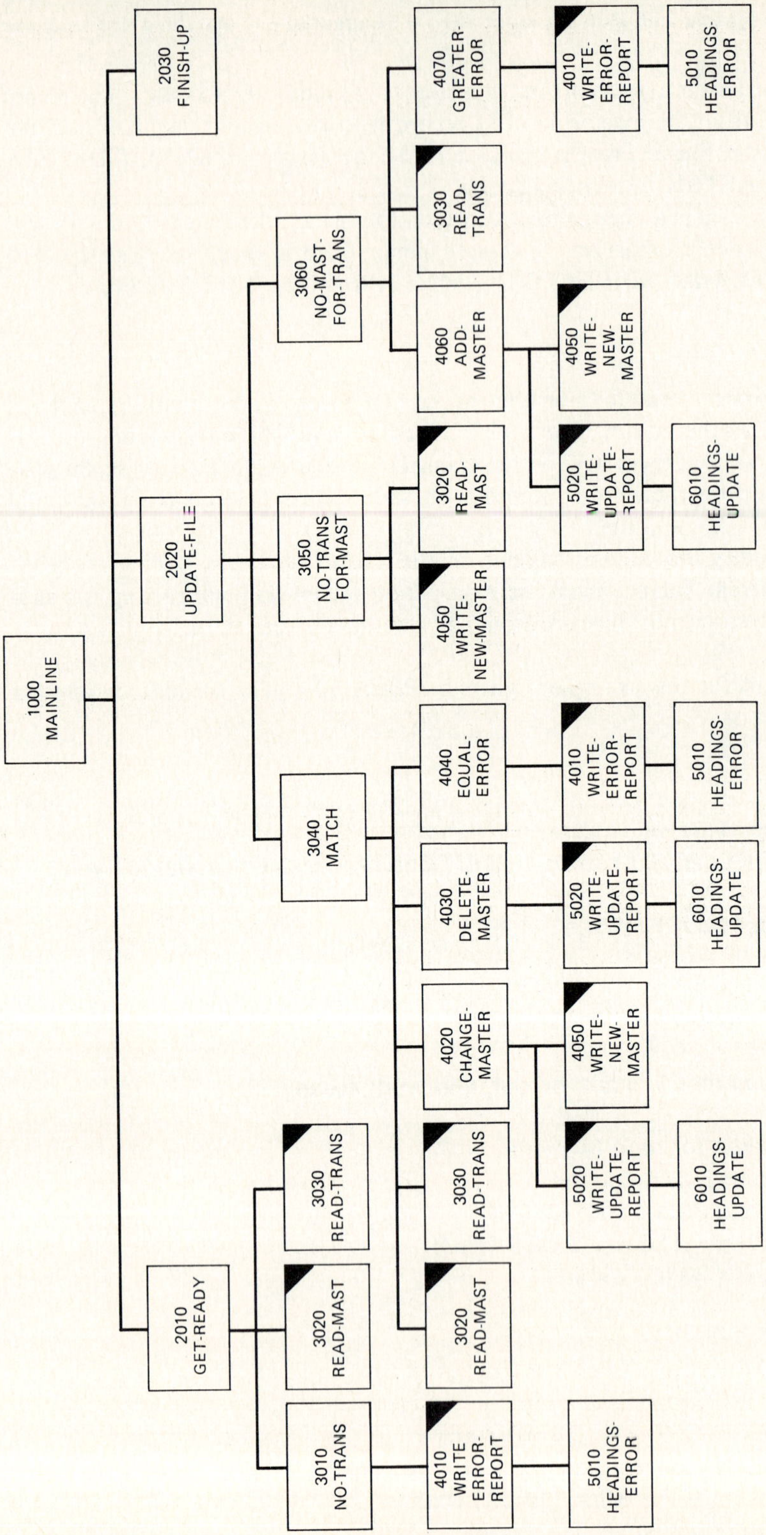

Figure 10-4
Example 10-4

```
        ELSE DO No-Mast-For-Trans (3060) routine
        ENDIF
 ENDIF
 IF OM-Account-No and T-Account-No = HIGH VALUES THEN
        MOVE "Yes" to Done-Processing
 ENDIF
 ENDUPDATE-FILE

 2030
 FINISH-UP
 CLOSE files
 ENDFINISH-UP

 3010
 NO-TRANS
 MOVE "No Records on Transaction File" to ER-Detail-Line
 DO Write-Error-Report (4010) routine
 MOVE "Yes" to Done-Processing
 ENDNO-TRANS

 3020
 READ-MAST
 READ a record from Master File
   ATEND of file MOVE HIGH-VALUES to OM-Account-No
 ENDREAD-MAST

 3030
 READ-TRANS
 READ a record from Transaction File
   ATEND of file MOVE HIGH-VALUES to T-Account-No
 ENDREAD-TRANS

 3040
 MATCH
 IF T-Code = "C" THEN
      DO Change-Master (4020) routine
      DO Read-Mast (3020) routine
      DO Read-trans (3030) routine
 ELSE IF T-Code = "D" THEN
              DO Delete-Master (4030) routine
              DO Read-Mast (3020) routine
              DO Read-Trans (3030) routine
         ELSE DO Equal-Error (4040) routine
             DO Read-Trans (3030) routine
         ENDIF
 ENDIF
 ENDMATCH
```

```
3050
NO-TRANS-FOR-MAST
MOVE Old-Master-Rec to New-Master-Rec (output area)
DO Write-New-Master (4050) routine
DO Read-Mast (3020) routine
ENDNO-TRANS-FOR-MAST

3060
NO-MAST-FOR-TRANS
IF T-Code = "A" THEN
   DO Add-Master (4060) routine
ELSE Do Greater-Error (4070) routine
ENDIF
DO Read-Trans (3030) routine
ENDNO-MAST-FOR-TRANS

4010
WRITE-ERROR-REPORT
IF ER-Lines-Counter = 50 THEN
   DO Headings-Error (5010) routine
ENDIF
MOVE ER-Detail-Line to output area
WRITE a line
ADD 1 to ER-Lines-Counter
ENDWRITE-ERROR-REPORT

4020
CHANGE-MASTER
IF T-Cust-Name is blank THEN
   MOVE OM-Cust-Name to NM-Cust-Name
ELSE MOVE T-Cust-Name to NM-Cust-Name
ENDIF
IF T-Address is blank THEN
   MOVE OM-Address to NM-Address
ELSE MOVE T-Address to NM-Address
ENDIF
MOVE T-Account-No to NM-Account-No
COMPUTE NM-Balance =OM-Balance + T-Additions -
                              T-Subtractions
DO Write-New-Master (4050) routine
MOVE OM-Account-No to UR-OM-Detail
MOVE New-Master-Rec to UR-NM-Detail
MOVE "Record Changed" to UR-Comments-Detail
DO Write-Update-Report (5020) routine
ENDCHANGE-MASTER
```

```
4030
DELETE-MASTER
MOVE OM-Account-No to UR-OM-Detail
MOVE spaces to UR-NM-Detail
MOVE "Record Deleted" to UR-Comments-Detail
DO Write-Update-Report (5020) routine
ENDDELETE-MASTER

4040
EQUAL-ERROR
MOVE "Cannot Add Record—Master Already Exists" to
  ER-Error-Detail
MOVE T-Account-No to ER-Account-No-Detail
DO Write-Error-Report (4010) routine
ENDEQUAL-ERROR

4050
WRITE-NEW-MASTER
WRITE New-Master-Rec
ENDWRITE-NEW-MASTER

4060
ADD-MASTER
MOVE T-Account-No, T-Cust-Name, and T-Address
  to New-Master-Rec
COMPUTE NM-Balance = T-Additions − T-Subtractions
DO Write-New-Master (4050) routine
MOVE New-Master-Rec to UR-NM-Detail
MOVE T-Account-No to UR-OM-Detail
MOVE "Record Added" to UR-Comments-Detail
DO Write-Update-Report (5020) routine
ENDADD-MASTER

4070
GREATER-ERROR
IF T-Code = "D" THEN
   MOVE "Cannot Delete Record—Master Does Not Exist"
     to ER-Error-Detail
ELSE MOVE "Cannot Change Record—Master Does Not Exist"
     to ER-Error-Detail
ENDIF
MOVE T-Account-No to ER-Account-No-Detail
DO Write-Error-Report (4010) routine
ENDGREATER-ERROR

5010
HEADINGS-ERROR
ADD 1 to ER-Page-Counter
```

```
MOVE ER-Page-Counter to Heading-Line-1
MOVE ER-Heading-Line-1 to output area
WRITE a line at top of page
MOVE ER-Heading-Line-2 to output area
WRITE a line
MOVE ER-Heading-Line-3 to output area
WRITE a line after advancing 2 lines
WRITE a blank line
RESET ER-Lines-Counter to 0
ENDHEADINGS-ERROR

5020
WRITE-UPDATE-REPORT
IF UR-Lines-Counter = 50 THEN
   DO Headings-Update (6010) routine
ENDIF
MOVE UR-Detail-Line to output area
WRITE a line
ADD 1 to UR-Lines-Counter
ENDWRITE-UPDATE-REPORT

6010
HEADINGS-UPDATE
ADD 1 to UR-Page-Counter
MOVE UR-Page-Counter to Heading-Line-1
MOVE UR-Heading-Line-1 to output area
WRITE a line at top of page
MOVE UR-Heading-Line-2 to output area
WRITE a line
MOVE UR-Heading-Line-3 to output area
WRITE a line after advancing 2 lines
WRITE a blank line
RESET UR-Lines-Counter to 0
ENDHEADINGS-UPDATE
```

The flowchart solution is shown in Figure 10-5.

The GET-READY routine defines two input areas and three output areas. Notice that each report has its own output area and is considered to be a separate file. In GET-READY, when the first record is read from each of the files, no error results if the master file has no records on it, but an error does result if the transaction file is empty. If the transaction file is empty, it doesn't make sense to use an update program, because you cannot update a file if there is nothing to update it with. An update program can be used, however, to initially create a master file. To do that, you would use an "empty" master file and a transaction file that contains only records to be added. Therefore, it is not incorrect to use an "empty" master file as input.

In the UPDATE FILE routine, if the account number on the master file (OM-ACCOUNT-NO) is less than the account number on the transaction file (T-

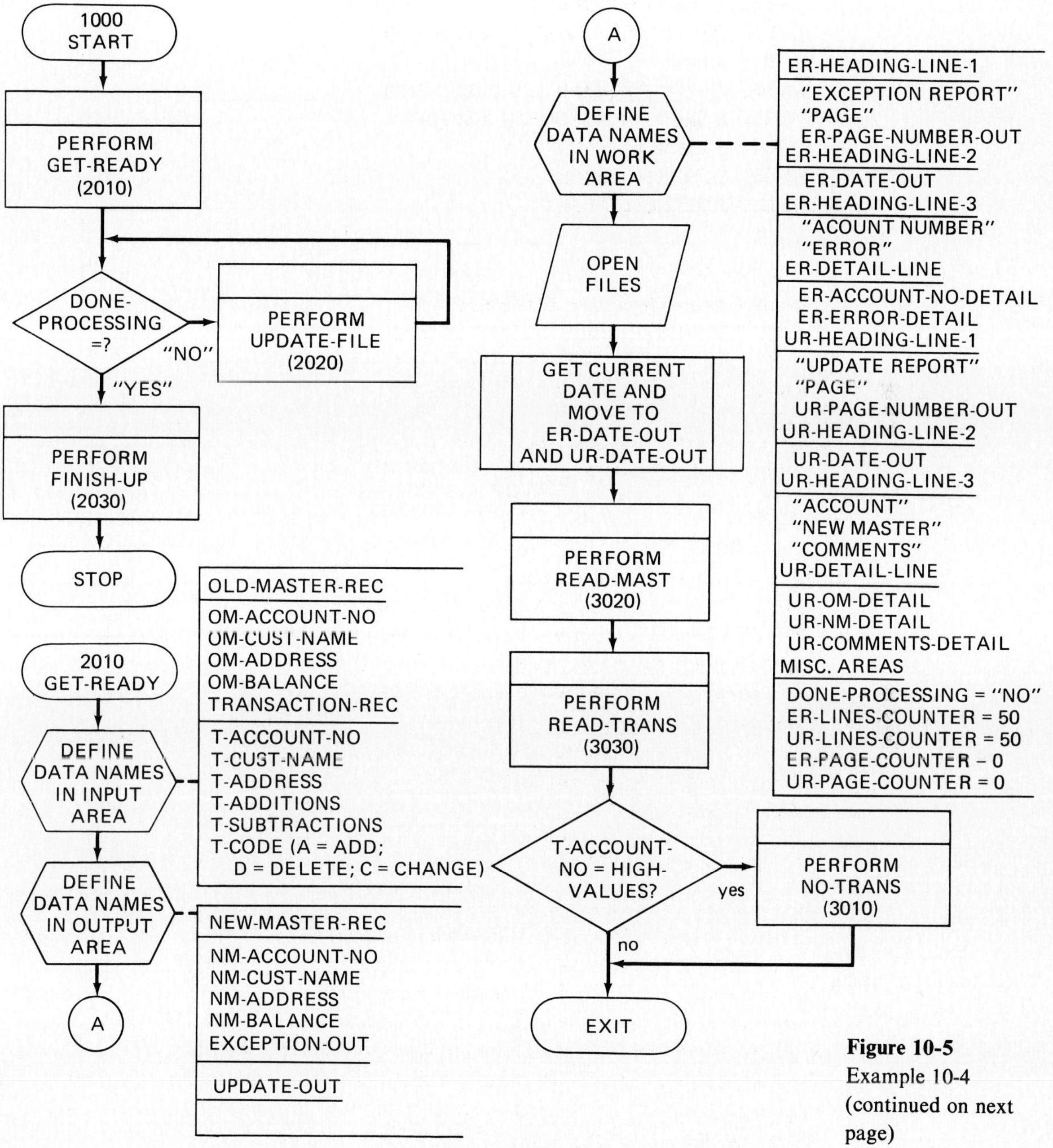

Figure 10-5
Example 10-4
(continued on next page)

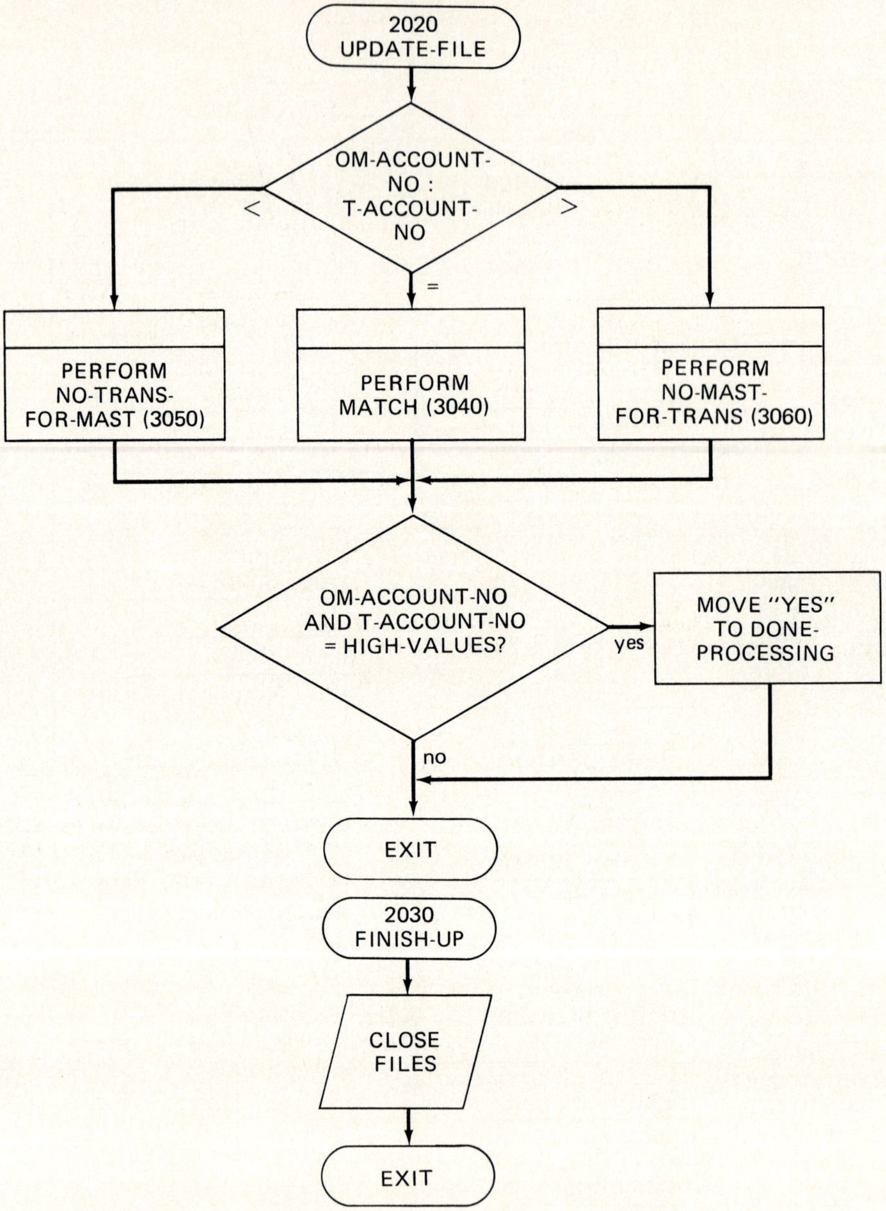

Figure 10-5
Example 10-4
(continued on next page)

ACCOUNT-NO), you have a master record for which no change is to take place. You must, however, copy the record from the old master file to the new master file. This is done in the NO-TRANS-FOR-MAST routine. A very common programming error is to forget to copy "unchanged" master file records onto the new master file. After the old master record is copied onto the new master file, the next old master file record is read.

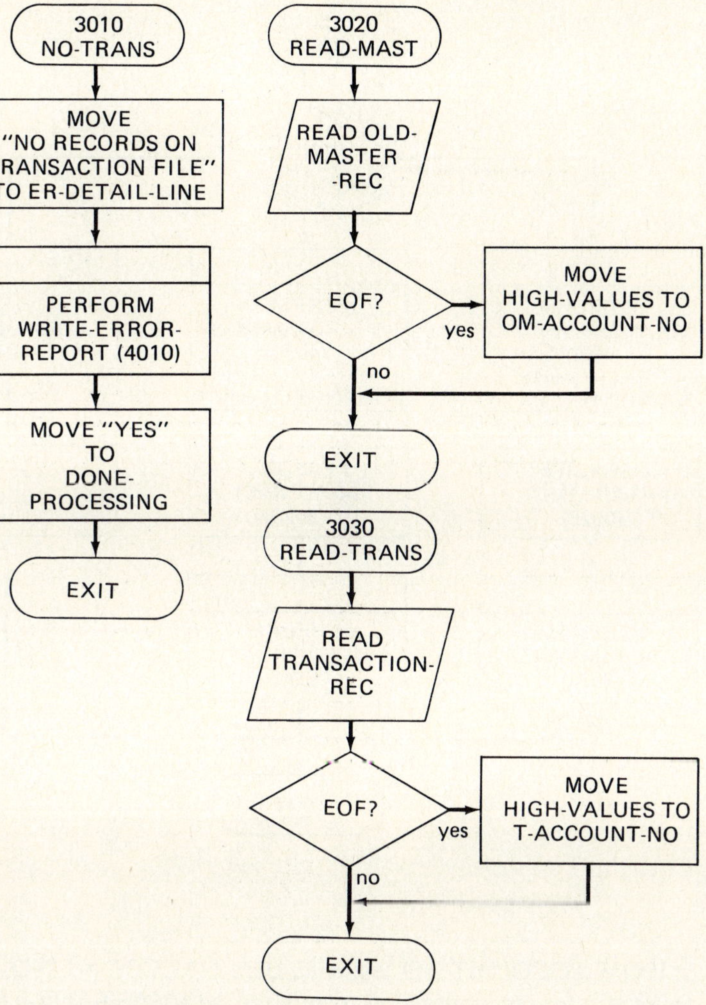

Figure 10 5
Example 10-4
(continued on next page)

If OM-ACCOUNT-NO is equal to T-ACCOUNT-NO, then a match occurs and the MATCH routine is performed. When a match occurs, the update must involve a change to the old master record (code = C) or a record to be deleted from the old master file (code = D). If the transaction record indicates that a record is to be added (code = A) to the master file and a match occurs between master and transaction, i.e., the master record already exists on the file, then an error results. A record cannot be added if it already exists on the master file. After a match is processed, both the master file and transaction file are read.

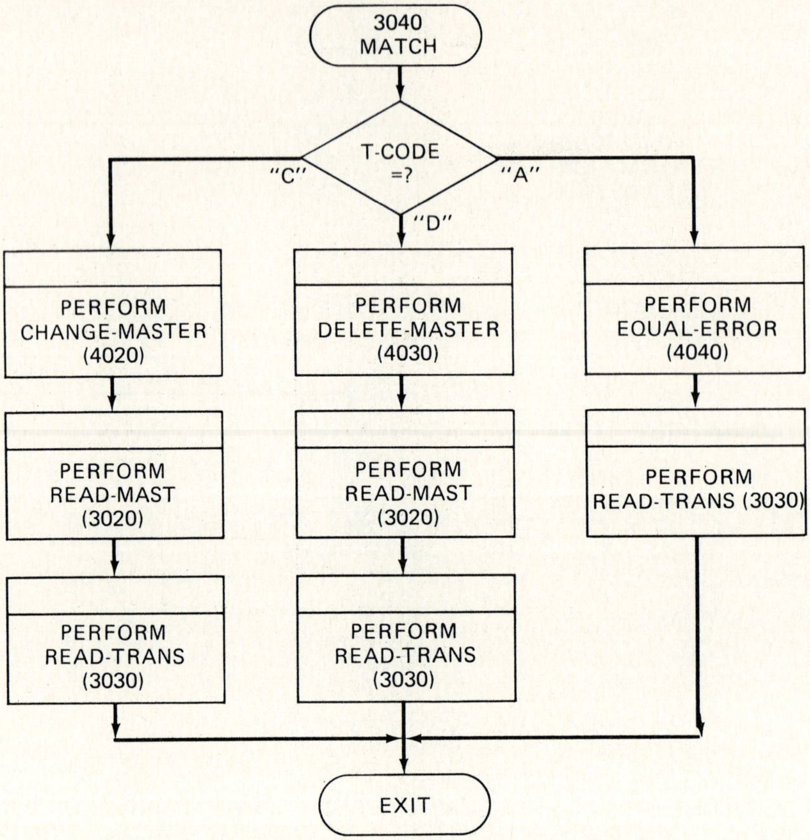

Figure 10-5
Example 10-4
(continued on next page)

If OM-ACCOUNT-NO is greater than T-ACCOUNT-NO, then there is no master record for the transaction record and NO-MAST-FOR-TRANS is performed. If the transaction record indicates that a record is to be deleted or changed, an error results, because you cannot delete or change a record that does not exist. The only valid code on the transaction, therefore, is an A, indicating that a record is to be added. After the record is added to the new master file or an error is written on the exception report, the next transaction file record is read.

If multiple updates are allowed for a master, i.e., more than one transaction record is allowed with the same account number, the processing is slightly more complicated. Processing multiple transactions with the same account number is left as an exercise for the reader.

QUESTIONS AND EXERCISES FOR REVIEW

1. Define each of the following terms:
   a. Sequential file
   b. Master file

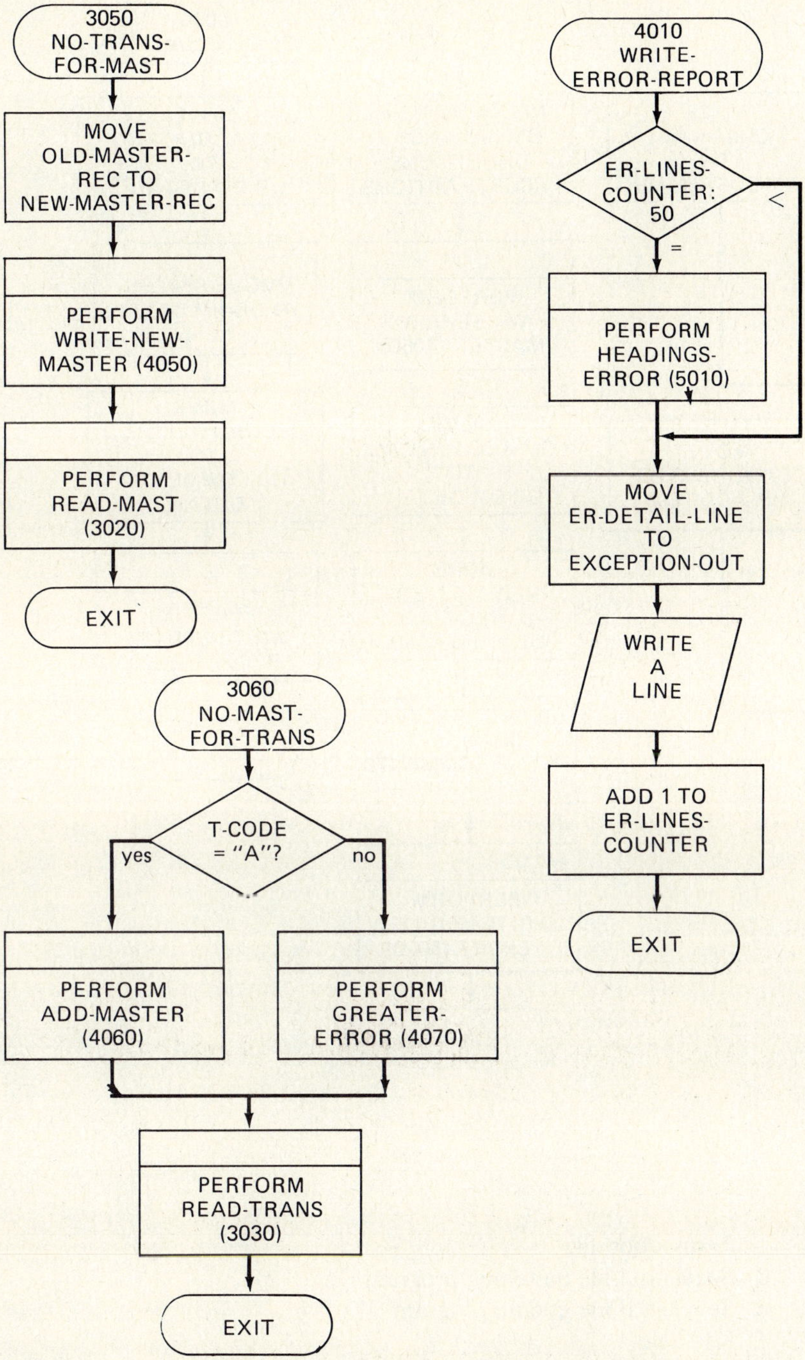

Figure 10-5
Example 10-4
(continued on next page)

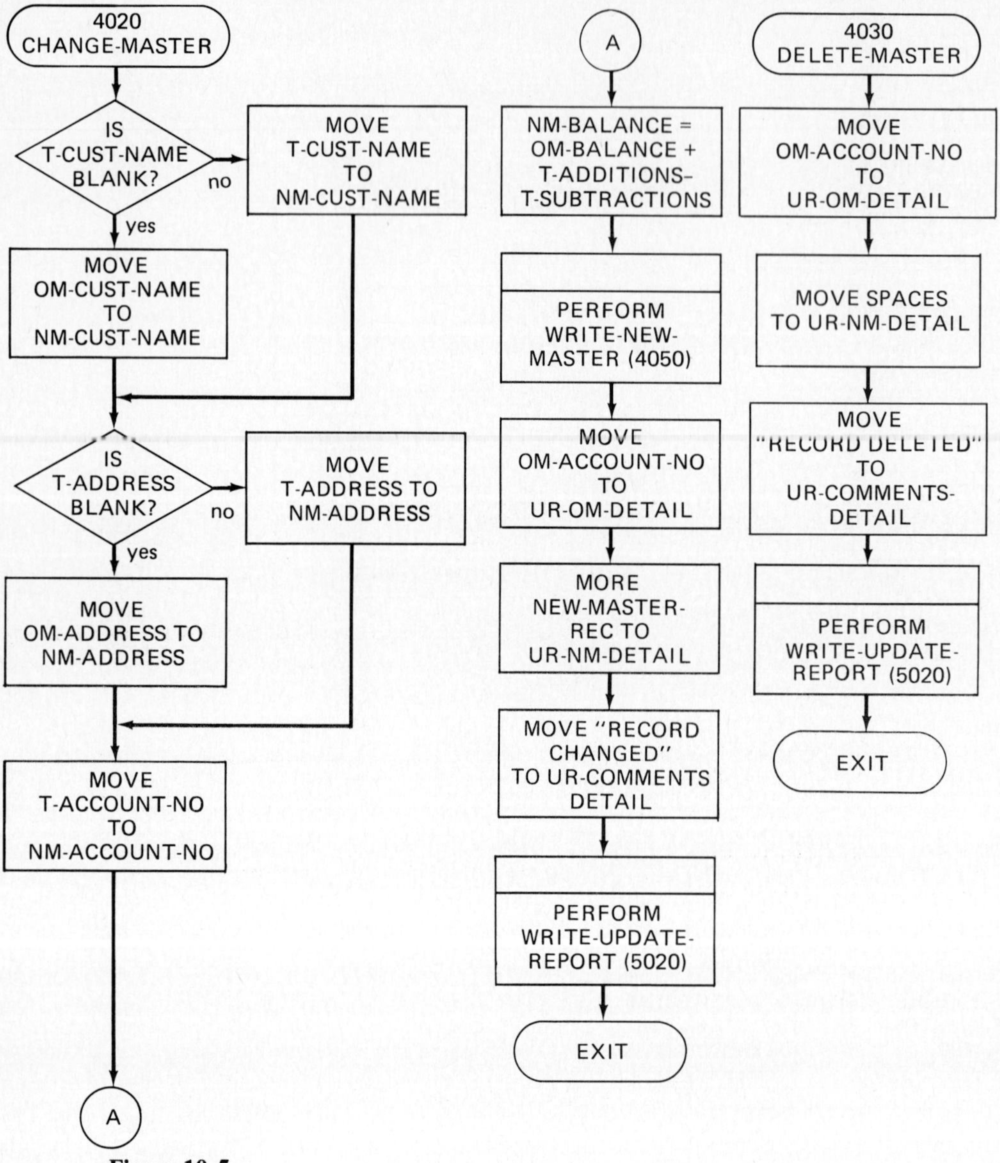

Figure 10-5
Example 10-4
(continued on next page)

c. Transaction file
d. Sequential file matching program
e. Sequential file update program
f. Key field
g. HIGH-VALUES

2. When is sequential file processing inefficient?
3. Why must every system contain an update program for its master file?

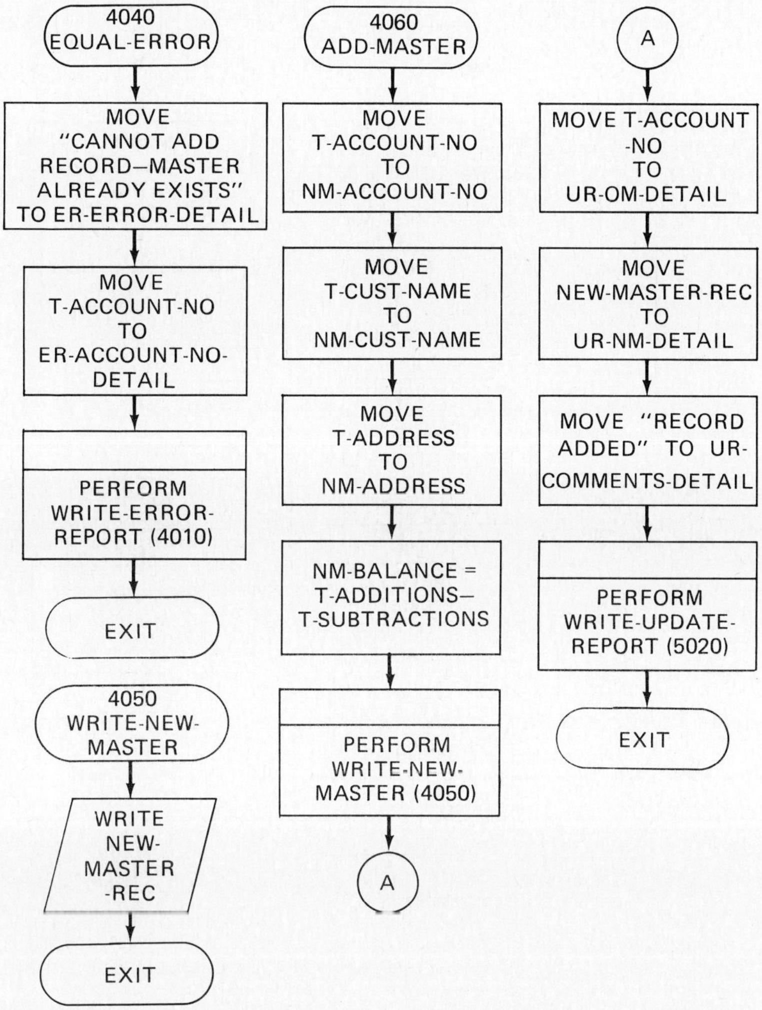

Figure 10-5
Example 10-4
(continued on next page)

4. Why must both master and transaction files be in the same sorted order prior to processing?
5. What does it mean when the key field on the master record is greater than the key field on the transaction record?
6. What does it mean when the key field on the master record is less than the key field on the transaction record?
7. At what point should processing terminate when doing sequential file matching or updating?
8. In the GET-READY routine, should the master file or the transaction file be read first? Why?
9. In sequential updates, why is an entirely new master file created? What is done with the old master file?

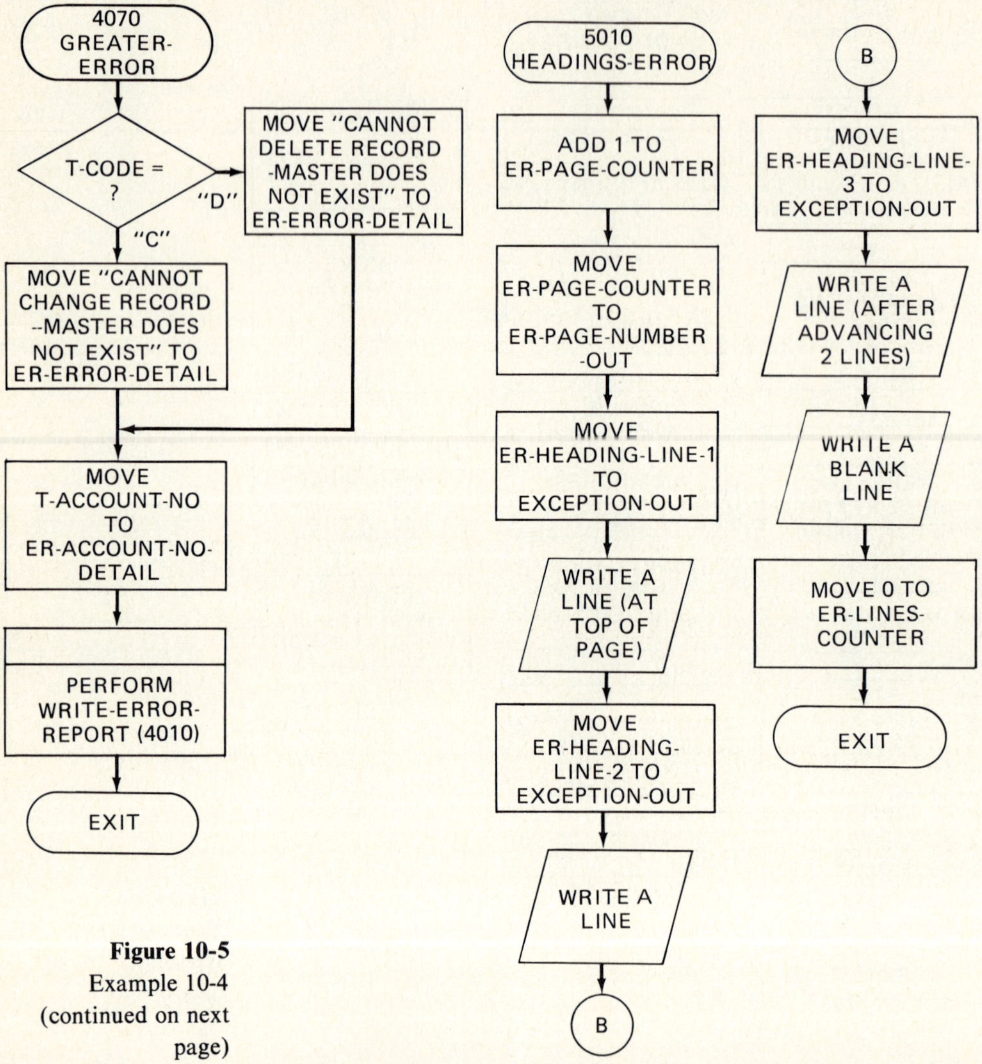

Figure 10-5
Example 10-4
(continued on next page)

10. Why is it forbidden to change the key field?
11. If it is necessary to change the key field, what must you do?
12. How can an update program be used to create a master file?
13. When the transaction file indicates an "add," what would cause an error to occur?
14. When the transaction file indicates a "change" or "delete," what would cause an error to occur?
15. Draw a hierarchy chart for a program to solve the following problem: A report is to be created for a utility company showing the average bill for each customer over the last year. This report is going to be used to help customers arrange for

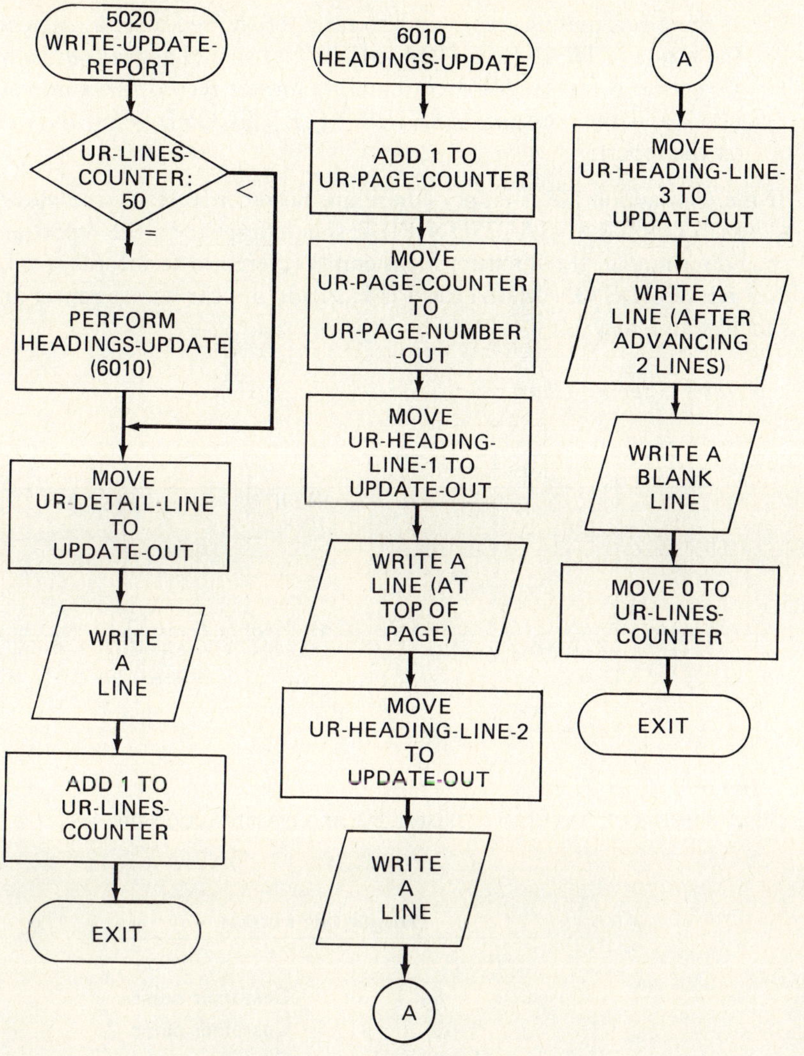

Figure 10-5
Example 10-4
(continued)

a budget payment plan, where customers pay equal installments every month rather than receive bills that vary erratically from month to month.

Output

Output is to consist of a report. A maximum of 35 detail lines are to appear per page. The report is to show the customer number, name, and average amount for the year. The average amount field is to show the following:

a. If there is a match between transaction and master, the average of the 12 monthly amounts (add the amounts and divide by 12) is to appear on the report.

b. If there is a master record and no transaction record for a particular customer, the message TRANSACTION MISSING should appear on the report.
c. If there is a transaction record and no master record, the name field should be blank and the message MASTER FILE RECORD MISSING should appear on the report.

If the transaction file is empty (there are no records on it), the message NO RECORDS ON TRANSACTION FILE should appear on the report and processing should terminate. If the master file is empty (there are no records on it), the message NO RECORDS ON MASTER FILE should appear on the report and processing should terminate.

Printer Spacing Chart

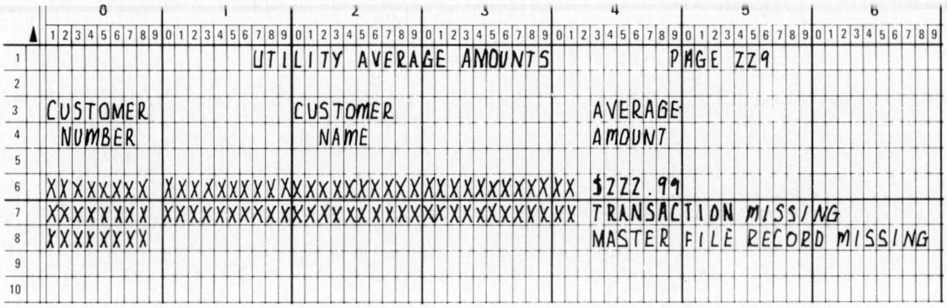

Input

Input consists of two files: a master file and a transaction file.

Master File Format

Position	*Description*
1–8	Customer number
9–40	Customer name
41–90	Customer address

Transaction File Format

Position	*Description*
1–8	Customer number
10–14	January amount
15–19	February amount
20–24	March amount
25–29	April amount
30–34	May amount
35–39	June amount
40–44	July amount
45–49	August amount
50–54	September amount

55–59	October amount
60–64	November amount
65–69	December amount

Both files are in increasing order by customer number. There is at most one record on each file per customer. There may be no transaction record for a master record, or there may be no master record for a transaction record, or there may be a match—i.e., one transaction record for a matching master record. The match is to occur on customer number.

16. Draw a program flowchart for Exercise 15 above.
17. Construct the pseudocode for Exercise 15 above.
18. Draw a hierarchy chart for a program to solve the following problem: The owner of a baseball team keeps a master file of his players during spring training. A program is to be written to initially create the file and update the file after every preseason game.

Output

Output is to consist of an updated master file (with the same format as the old master file) and two reports. The exception report is to show all records in which an error occurred. The update report is to show all records for which a successful update occurred. A maximum of 30 detail lines are to appear on a page for each of the reports. Reports are to contain page numbers and the current date.

If no transaction file is entered (i.e., it is empty), print an appropriate message on the exception report and terminate processing.

Totals are to be included on the update report. The totals should show the total number of records added to the master file, the total number of records deleted from the master file, and the total number or records changed on the master file.

Printer Spacing Charts

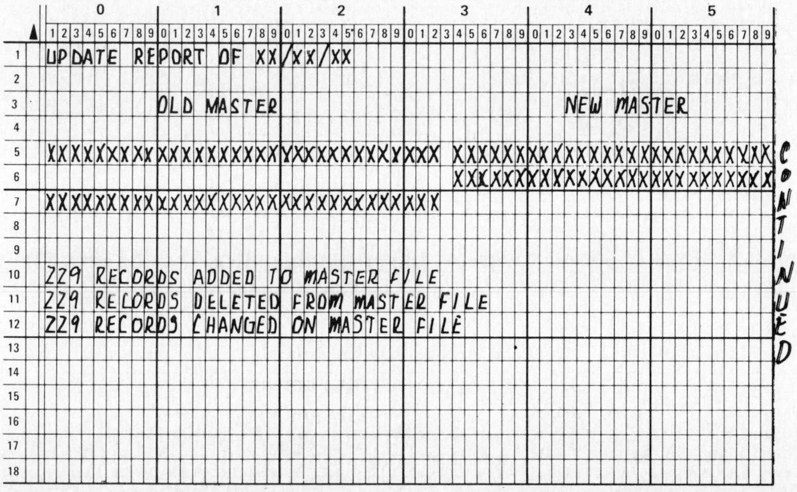

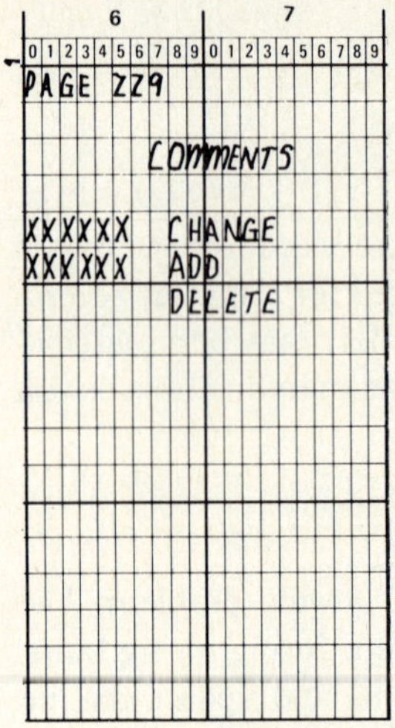

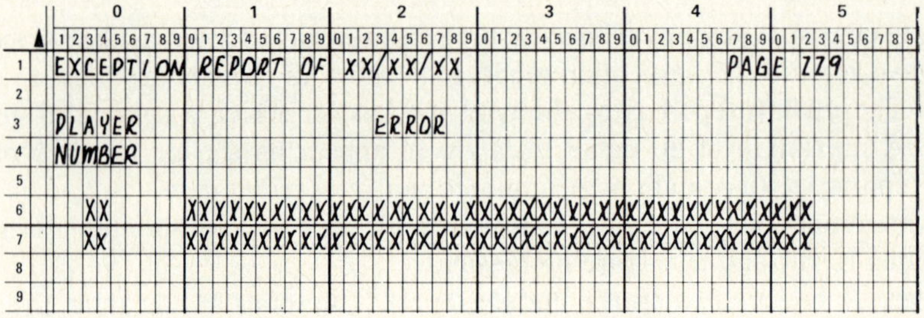

Input

Input consists of two files.

Master File Format

Position	*Description*
1–20	Player's name
21–22	Player's number
23–26	Total hits
27–30	Total at-bats
31–34	Total home runs

The master file is in sorted order by player number. It is created or updated by transaction records.

Transaction File Format

Position	*Description*
1–20	Player's name (this field is present on the record for adds only and cannot be changed)

21–22	Player's number
23–26	Hits during the game
27–30	At-bats during the game
31–34	Home runs during the game
35	Code (A = addition, i.e., new player; D = deletion, i.e., player being dropped from the team; C = change)

The transaction file is in sorted order by player number. It has been edited to ensure that the code field is valid and that all fields that should be numeric are, in fact, numeric. In addition, the edit program ensures that the player numbers are unique.

Rules for Updates

1. CODE = A: This is an addition (a new player). A new master file record is to be created with the data from the transaction record. If a record already exists on the master file for the player, an error condition results. Use the message CANNOT ADD RECORD—MASTER ALREADY EXISTS.

2. CODE = D: This is a deletion (a player being dropped from the team). The record is to be removed from the master file. If a record with that player number doesn't exist on the master file, an error condition results. Use message CANNOT DELETE RECORD—MASTER DOES NOT EXIST.

3. CODE = C: This is a change to a record on the master file. If a record with that number doesn't exist on the master file, an error condition results. Use the message CANNOT CHANGE RECORD—MASTER DOES NOT EXIST. If a match exists between master and transaction, the master record is to be updated by adding the fields for hits, at-bats, and home runs from the transaction record to the corresponding master record fields.

19. Draw a flowchart for Exercise 18 above.
20. Construct the pseudocode for Exercise 18 above.

CHAPTER 11

Nonsequential Processing

BACKGROUND

A large percentage of today's data processing is done in a nonsequential manner. Recall from Chapter 10 that when a file is processed sequentially, the records are read one after another in sequence. In order to access the 75th record on a sequential file, the 74 records that precede it must be read first. This type of processing works well for payroll systems, for example, where every record on the file needs to accessed to produce pay checks. Sequential processing, however, would not work well for an online banking system in which very few records need to be accessed from the file at any given time. In general, most online systems require the use of nonsequential processing.

Files which are to be processed in a nonsequential manner must be created on a direct-access storage device. Magnetic disk is the most popular direct-access device. Cards and magnetic tape can only be used for sequential file processing. Magnetic disk, however, can be used for both sequential and nonsequential processing.

Each record to be stored on a direct-access device is assigned a location on the disk. Each of the locations on a disk has an *address*. Just as you can find a house on a block by knowing its address, you can find a record on a disk by knowing its address. Unlike sequential processing, nonsequential processing allows the program to access a record directly by using its address without having to read all the preceding records on the file.

The advantages of using nonsequential processing include the following:

1. You can find a particular record on a file without accessing all the records which precede it on the file.
2. The transaction records don't have to be sorted prior to processing. You can process the transactions in the order that they happen to occur.
3. Updating does not require the creation of an entirely new master file. Since there is no need to insert additional records in sequence, new records can be placed anywhere on the master file.

There are many ways to organize a file in a nonsequential manner. The two most common are direct file organization and indexed sequential file organization.

DIRECT FILE ORGANIZATION AND PROCESSING

When using direct file organization, the address on the device assigned to a particular record is derived from the *key* of the record which is stored on the file. For example, an inventory file may use the item's part number as the key field; a student file may use the student's social security number. The key field must be designated by the programmer as a unique field within the record. This means that if the key field is a part number, for example, then each record must have its own part number and no duplicate part numbers are allowed. It is not necessary that the key field be numeric.

The trick with direct file organization is having the program translate the key contained on the record into an address on the disk. The routine used to compute an address from the key of a record is called a *randomizing routine*. Randomizing usually involves a mathematical computation done on the key field. The method chosen for randomizing depends on such things as the specific key being used, the size of the file, the type of direct-access device being used and its manufacturer, and the record itself.

There are three major disadvantages in using the direct file organization:

1. It is difficult to create a good randomizing routine. Quite often the randomizing routine will assign multiple records to the same address. Since two records cannot be stored in the same location, additional space needs to be allocated on the disk for the "duplicates." Substantial programming effort results, therefore, in knowing where to put the duplicates on the disk and in retrieving them.
2. Direct files waste considerable space on the device. Because there is little control over the values of the keys, there must be enough space allocated on the device so that all addresses which can be computed from a particular key are allocated to the file.
3. It is not possible to process a direct file sequentially. This means that if you want to generate a report in sequential order, you must presort the direct file into a sequential order.

INDEXED FILE ORGANIZATION AND PROCESSING

One type of nonsequential processing that is very popular is called indexed sequential or indexed processing. Indexed sequential processing provides for both sequential and direct processing of the same file. It does this by using indexes which contain the addresses of records stored on the file.

An indexed sequential file is created on a direct-access device using three areas on the device. These areas are called the *prime data area,* the *overflow data area,* and the *index area.*

The index area contains the record key and address for each record on the file. The key field, such as a part number, employee number, etc., must be designated by the programmer as a unique field within the record. The index is organized and stored in sequential order based on the key. When a specific record is required for processing, the computer can find the record by checking the index to determine the address of the record on the file. This is done much like using an index in a book. You look up the topic in the index, determine the page the desired topic is on, and go directly to that page. If, on the other hand, the book was "processed" sequentially, you would start on page 1 of the book and read until you found the desired topic.

When the indexed sequential file is initially established, all the data records are loaded into the prime data area and the keys are loaded into the index area. After the file is established, records can be added without reorganizing the entire file. All new records are placed into an overflow area on the device, and the indexes are updated. The indexed sequential access method links all records together sequentially, so that even though a record may be located in an overflow area, as far as the user is concerned, it appears to be in sequence.

When a record is deleted from an indexed sequential file, it is not physically removed from the file *(physically deleted).* The record remains on the file, but it is said to be *logically deleted.* A field within the record is used to indicate that the record has been deleted. At some point in time you end up with a very cumbersome file that has a lot of records that have been added in the overflow area and a lot of space being used by records that have been logically deleted but are still physically on the file. In order to make the file more manageable again, it must be reorganized. That is, the file must be read sequentially, copying all the records onto a new device and omitting those records that have been deleted.

The primary advantage of indexed sequential is that it allows both sequential and direct processing of the same file. There are two major disadvantages of the method, however:

1. Processing of the files is relatively inefficient compared to both sequential and direct file processing. This is because every time a record needs to be retrieved from the device, one or more indexes must be read in addition to the record being read.
2. The more records that are added to the file after its initial creation, the more inefficient the processing becomes because of the difficulty of searching for records in the overflow area. Periodically, indexed sequential files must be reorganized to take the data from the overflow areas and put it in the prime area to increase the efficiency of the programs.

Various computer systems have different methods for creating and working with indexed files. The concepts described above and in the examples which follow are fairly standard. As you go from system to system, however, the method for creating the index, checking for error conditions, and so on may vary. It is important, therefore, that you consult the manual for your computer when working with indexed files.

EXAMPLE 11-1: CREATING AN INDEXED SEQUENTIAL FILE

Suppose that Company X maintains its customer accounts in an indexed sequential file using account numbers for record keys. We are to create the customer master file from the input file described below.

Output

Master File to Be Created

Position	*Description*
1	Delete code (D = record is deleted; A = record is available)
2–6	Account number (key)
7–20	Customer name
21–60	Customer address
61–65	Credit limit
66–70	Unpaid balance

An error report is to be generated listing the errors that occur when creating the master file. If no errors occur during processing, the message NO ERRORS—FILE

CREATED AS INPUT is to be printed on the report. The heading on the report is to read MASTER FILE CREATE—ERRORS. Page numbers are to appear on the report. A maximum of 60 detail lines are to appear per page. Detail lines are to contain the Account Number and the error message.

Printer Spacing Chart

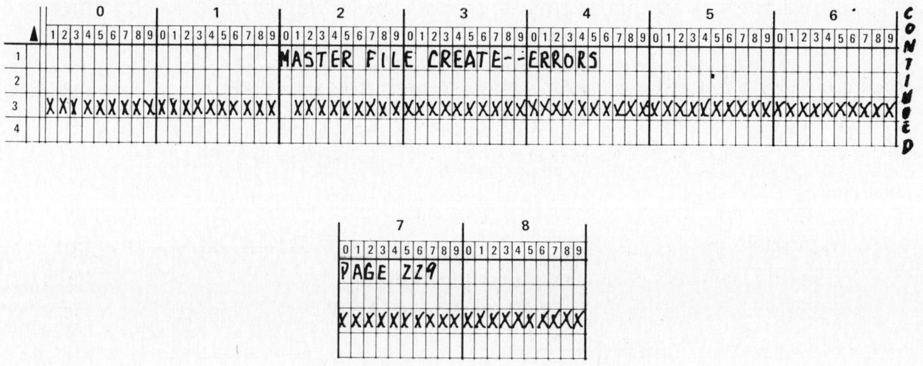

Input

The input file consists of records with the following format:

Position	*Description*
1–5	Account number
6–19	Customer name
20–59	Customer address
60–64	Credit limit
65–69	Unpaid balance

Before we look at the flowchart solution shown in Figure 11-1, the following points need to be made about the input file and the master file:

1. Some indexed systems require that the input be sorted by the key before the master file is created. For this problem, the key is the account number. Let's assume that the input file has already been sorted by account number in a previous program.
2. The master file contains a field called DELETE-CODE. This is the field that is used to determine whether the record has been logically deleted from the file. When creating the file, we will move an A to this field for every record.

Now examine the solution shown in Figure 11-1. First consider how we determine whether the NO ERRORS message should be written on the report. In GET-READY, an indicator called ERROR-IND is used. The purpose of this field is to keep track of whether any lines have been written on the error report. At the time

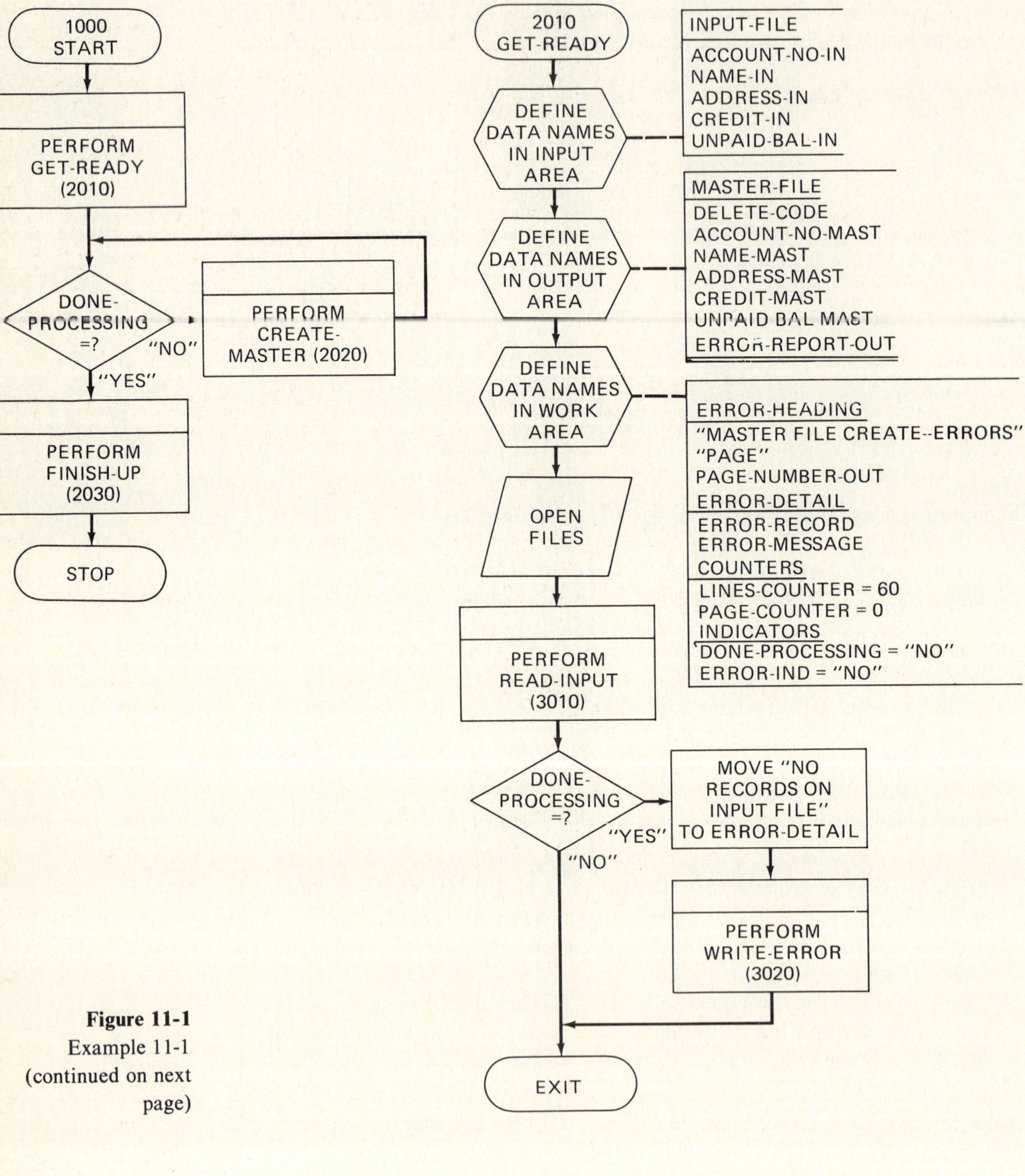

Figure 11-1
Example 11-1
(continued on next page)

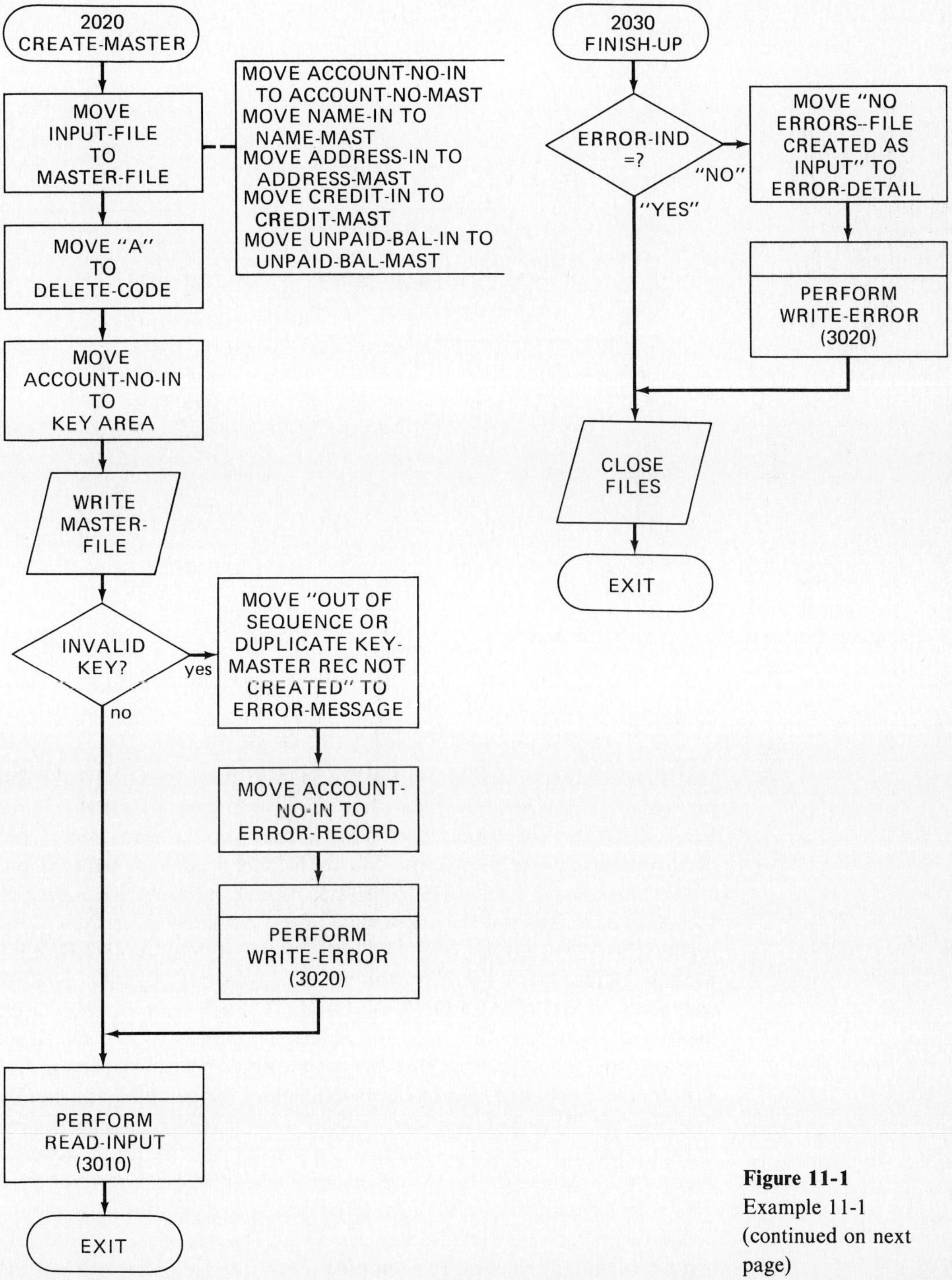

Figure 11-1
Example 11-1
(continued on next page)

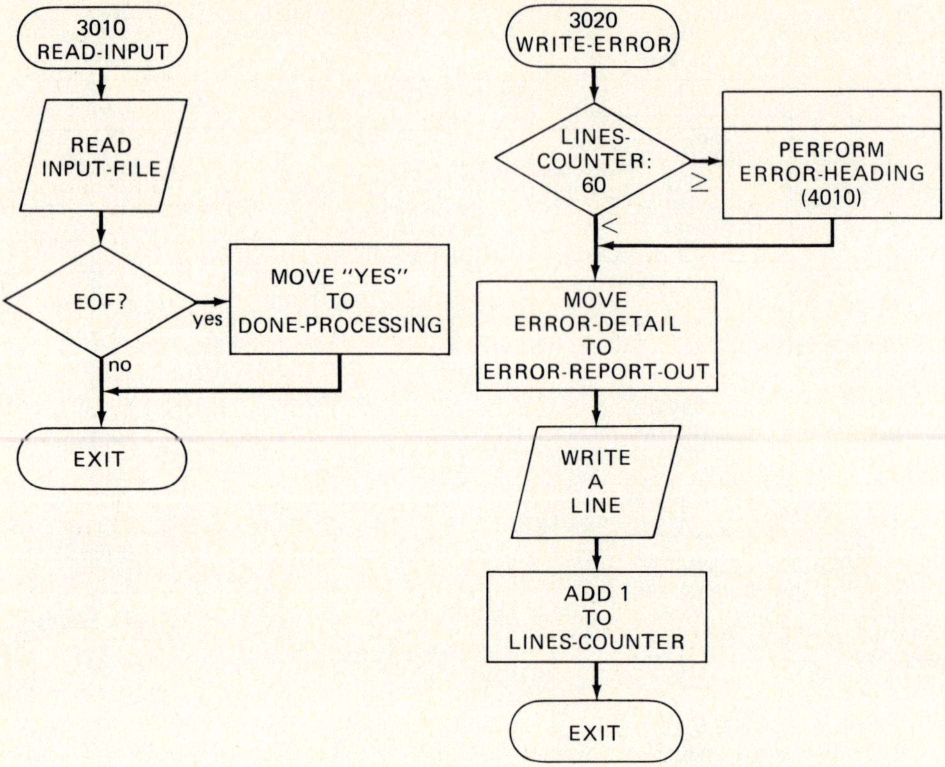

Figure 11-1
Example 11-1
(continued on next page)

that the first line is written on the report, and the ERROR-HEADING routine is performed, ERROR-IND receives a value of 1. The FINISH-UP routine checks ERROR-IND. If no lines have been written on the error report (i.e., no errors occurred during processing), the NO ERRORS message is written on the report.

Next look at the CREATE-MASTER routine. This routine is performed for each record to be written on the master file. The first thing the routine does is move the input fields to the output area. The instruction MOVE "A" TO DELETE-CODE is used to indicate that the record is not being deleted, i.e., it's available. The next instruction is MOVE ACCOUNT-NO-IN TO KEY AREA. The *key area* is an area used by the computer to create and access the index for the indexed sequential file. The key area is not an area that the programmer needs to define in GET-READY. It is an area in storage that has been defined by the compiler and can be used by the programmer. Whenever you read or write a record on an indexed sequential file, you tell the computer the key by putting it in the key area. After the record is written on the indexed sequential file, it is necessary to check whether an error occurred. (Note: This error checking does not have to be done when processing sequential files.) The computer indicates an invalid key error when the keys are entered out of sequence and/or when a duplicate key is entered.

The remaining routines are similar to what we have done in the past and will not be explained further.

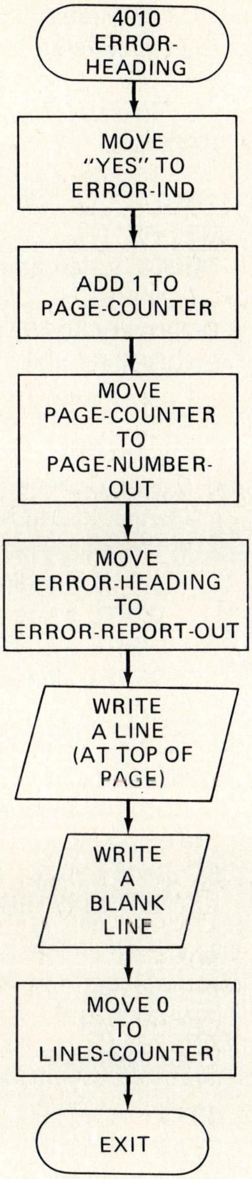

Figure 11-1
Example 11-1
(continued on next page)

EXAMPLE 11-2: PROCESSING AN INDEXED SEQUENTIAL FILE SEQUENTIALLY

For this example, we are told to list the indexed sequential file created in Example 11-1. The solution is shown in the pseudocode below.

1000
<u>MAINLINE</u>
START

```
DO Get-Ready (2010) routine
DO List-Master (2020) routine UNTIL Done-Processing is equal to "yes"
ENDDO
DO Finish-Up (2030) routine
STOP

2010
GET-READY
DEFINE data names in input, output, and work areas
OPEN files
DO Read (3010) routine
ENDGET-READY

2020
LIST-MASTER
IF Delete-Code = "A" THEN
   MOVE Rest-of-Master (Master record excluding delete code) to Detail-Line
   IF Lines-Counter = 60 THEN
      MOVE Heading-Line to Report-Out
      WRITE a line at top of page
      WRITE a blank line
      RESET Lines-Counter to 0
   ENDIF
   MOVE Detail-Line to Report-Out
   WRITE a line
   ADD 1 to Lines-Counter
ENDIF
DO Read (3010) routine
ENDLIST-MASTER

2030
FINISH-UP
CLOSE files
ENDFINISH-UP

3010
READ
READ a record from master file
   ATEND of file MOVE "yes" to Done-Processing
ENDREAD
```

The only thing different between this program and a program that would list a sequential file is in the LIST-MASTER routine. Every record that is read in this program must have its delete code checked, because we don't want to list records that have been logically deleted and still physically exist on the file. When a sequential file is listed, all records physically on the file will be listed.

EXAMPLE 11-3: UPDATING AN INDEXED SEQUENTIAL FILE

For this example we want to construct a hierarchy chart, pseudocode, and flowchart for a program which will update the file created in Example 11-1.

Output

In addition to the updated master file, a report is to be generated as output. The report is to show the updates that have taken place. A maximum of 60 detail lines are to appear per page, including the blank lines shown between detail lines. If an entire transaction will not fit on a page, go to a new page.

Printer Spacing Chart

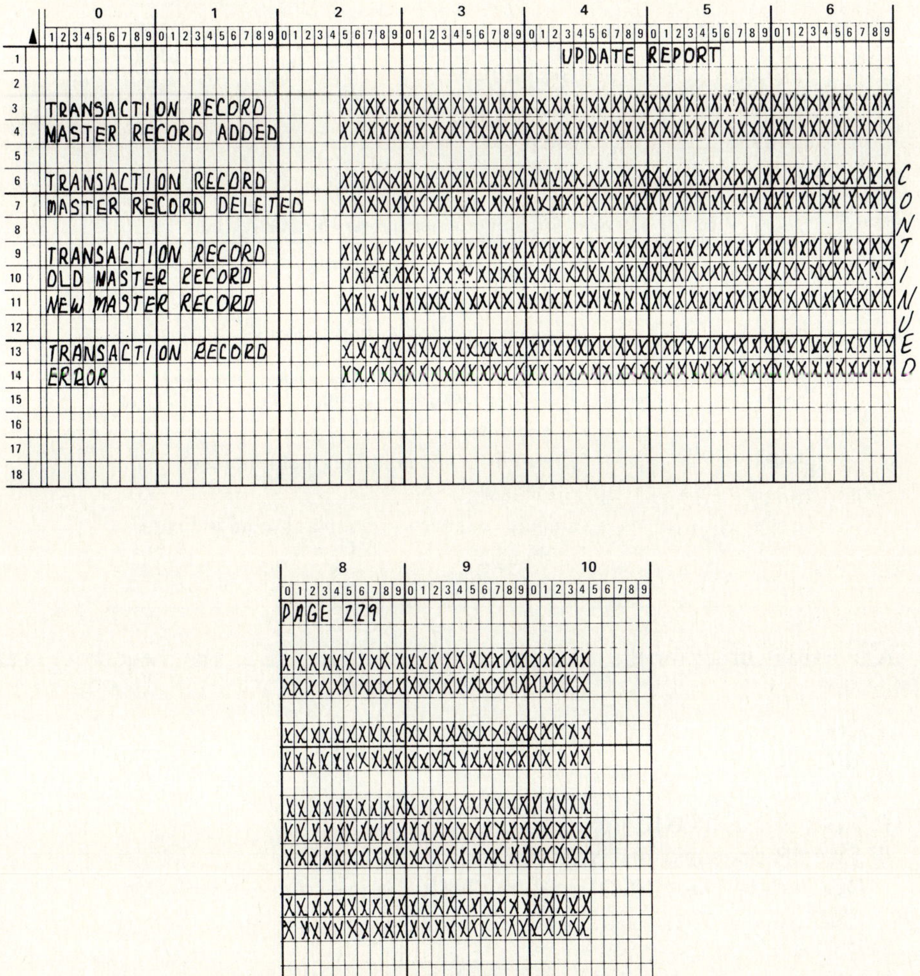

Input

Input consists of the master file created in Example 11-1 and a transaction file that contains three types of records, as follows:

Add Record (to add a record to the master file)

Position	*Description*
1–5	Account number
6–19	Customer name
20–59	Customer address
60–64	Credit limit
65–69	Unpaid balance
70	Code = A

Delete Record (to delete a record from the master file)

Position	*Description*
1–5	Account number
6–69	Blank
70	Code = D

Change Record (to change a record on the master file)

Position	*Description*
1–5	Account number
6–19	Customer name—a nonblank field indicates a change
20–59	Customer address—a nonblank field indicates a change
60–64	Credit limit—a nonblank field indicates a change
65–69	Unpaid balance—a nonblank field indicates a change
70	Code = C

A hierarchy chart for the solution is shown in Figure 11-2. The pseudocode is as follows:

```
1000
MAINLINE
START
DO Get-Ready (2010) routine
IF Done-Processing = "No" THEN
  DO Update-File (2020) routine UNTIL Done-Processing = "Yes"
  ENDDO
ENDIF
DO Finish-Up (2030) routine
STOP
```

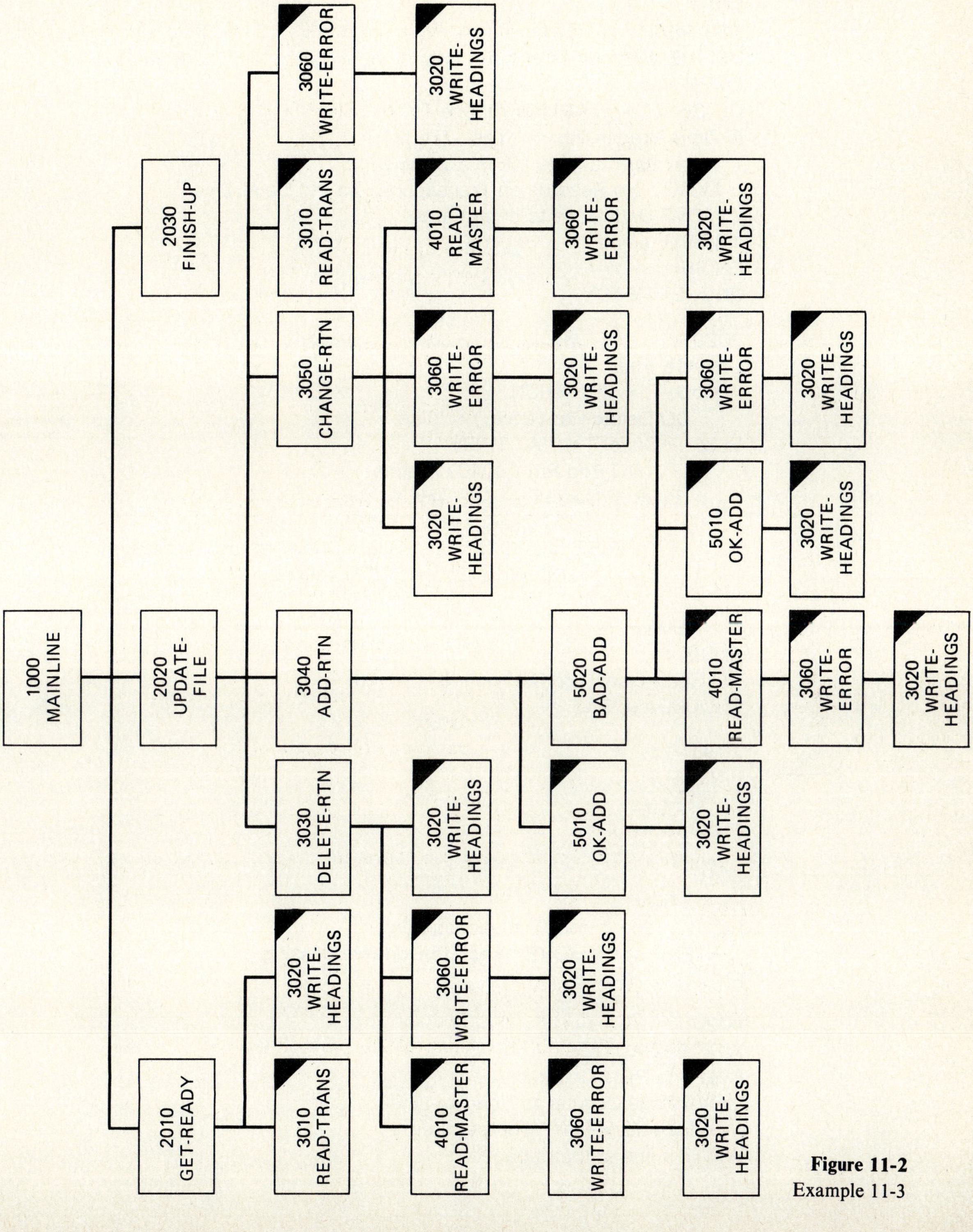

Figure 11-2
Example 11-3

```
2010
GET-READY
DEFINE data names in input, output, input-output, and work areas
OPEN files
DO Read-Trans (3010) routine
IF Done-Processing = "Yes" THEN
   DO Write-Headings (3020) routine
   MOVE "No Records on Transaction File" to Detail-Line
   MOVE Detail-Line to output area
   WRITE a line
ENDIF
ENDGET-READY

2020
UPDATE-FILE
IF Code-T = "D" THEN
       DO Delete-Rtn (3030) routine
ELSE IF Code-T = "A" THEN
              DO Add-Rtn (3040) routine
        ELSE IF Code-T = "C" THEN
                        DO Change-Rtn (3050) routine
                ELSE MOVE "Invalid Update Code" to Error-Message
                         DO Write-Error (3060) routine
               ENDIF
       ENDIF
ENDIF
DO Read-Trans (3010) routine
ENDUPDATE-FILE

2030
FINISH-UP
CLOSE files
ENDFINISH-UP

3010
READ-TRANS
READ a record from Transaction-File
   ATEND of file MOVE "Yes" to Done-Processing
ENDREAD-TRANS

3020
WRITE-HEADINGS
ADD 1 to Page-Counter
MOVE Page-Counter to Heading-Line
MOVE Heading-Line to output area
WRITE a line at top of page
```

```
WRITE a blank line
MOVE 0 to Lines-Counter
ENDWRITE-HEADINGS


3030
DELETE-RTN
DO Read-Master (4010) routine
IF Master-Read-Error = "No" THEN
  IF Delete-Code = "D" THEN
        MOVE "Record Already Deleted" to Error-Message
        DO Write-Error (3060) routine
  ELSE MOVE "D" to Delete-Code
        REWRITE record
        IF Error THEN
           MOVE "Cannot Rewrite Deleted Master" to
              Error-Message
           DO Write-Error (3060) routine
        ELSE IF Lines-Counter is greater than or equal to 58 THEN
                 DO Write-Headings (3020) routine
           ENDIF
           FORMAT Detail-Line
           MOVE Detail-Line to Report-Out
           WRITE a line after advancing 2 lines
           FORMAT 2d Detail-Line
           MOVE Detail-Line to Report-Out
           WRITE a line
           ADD 3 to Lines-Counter
        ENDIF
  ENDIF
ENDDELETE-RTN


3040
ADD-RTN
MOVE Account-No-T to key area
MOVE Account-No-T, Name-T, Address-T, Credit-T, and Unpaid-Bal-T to
  Master-File record
MOVE "A" to Delete-Code
MOVE Master-File to Master-Save
WRITE Master-File
IF Error THEN
  DO Bad-Add (5020) routine
ELSE DO OK-Add (5010) routine
ENDIF
ENDADD-RTN
```

```
3050
CHANGE-RTN
DO Read-Master (4010) routine
IF Master-Read-Error = "No" THEN
  IF Delete-Code = "A" THEN
       MOVE Master-File to Master-Save
       IF Name-T is not blank THEN
            MOVE Name-T to Name-M
       ENDIF
       IF Address-T is not blank THEN
           MOVE Address-T to Address-M
       ENDIF
       IF Credit-T is not blank THEN
           MOVE Credit-T to Credit-M
       ENDIF
       IF Unpaid-Bal-T is not blank THEN
           MOVE Unpaid-Bal-T to Unpaid-Bal-M
       ENDIF
       REWRITE record
       IF Error THEN
          MOVE "Cannot Rewrite Record" to Error-Message
          DO Write-Error (3060) routine
       ELSE IF Lines-Counter is greater than or equal to 57 THEN
                DO Write-Headings (3020) routine
          ENDIF
          FORMAT Detail-Line
          MOVE Detail-Line to output area
          WRITE a line after advancing 2 lines
          FORMAT 2nd Detail-Line
          MOVE Detail-Line to output area
          WRITE a line
          FORMAT 3rd Detail-Line
          MOVE Detail-Line to output area
          WRITE a line
          ADD 4 to Lines-Counter
  ELSE MOVE "Can't Change Deleted Record" to Error-Message
     DO Write-Error (3060) routine
  ENDIF
ENDIF
ENDCHANGE-RTN

3060
WRITE-ERROR
IF Lines-Counter is greater than or equal to 58 THEN
  DO Write-Headings (3020) routine
```

```
ENDIF
FORMAT Detail-Line
MOVE Detail-Line to output area
WRITE a line after advancing 2 lines
FORMAT 2nd Detail-Line
MOVE Detail-Line to output area
WRITE a line
ADD 3 to Lines-Counter
ENDWRITE-ERROR
4010
READ-MASTER
MOVE Account-No-T to key area
READ Master-File
IF Error THEN
   MOVE "Cannot Retrieve Master" to Error-Message
   DO Write-Error (3060) routine
   MOVE "Yes" to Master-Read-Error
ELSE MOVE "No" to Master-Read-Error
ENDIF
ENDREAD-MASTER
5010
OK-ADD
IF Lines-Counter is greater than or equal to 58 THEN
   DO Write-Headings (3020) routine
ENDIF
FORMAT Detail-Line
MOVE Detail-Line to output area
WRITE a line after advancing 2 lines
FORMAT 2d Detail-Line
MOVE Detail-Line to output area
WRITE a line
ADD 3 to Lines-Counter
ENDOK-ADD
5020
BAD-ADD
DO Read-Master (4010) routine
IF Master-Read-Error = "No" THEN
      IF Delete-Code = "A" THEN
            MOVE "Can't Add Record—Duplicate" to Error-Message
            DO Write-Error (3060) routine
      ELSE MOVE Master-Save to Master-File
            REWRITE record
            IF Error THEN
                  MOVE "Cannot Rewrite Record" to Error-Message
                  DO Write-Error (3060) routine
```

```
      ELSE DO OK-Add (5010) routine
      ENDIF
    ENDIF
  ENDIF
  ENDBAD-ADD
```

The flowchart is shown in Figure 11-3.

Notice that the master file is defined in the GET-READY routine as an input-output area. This means that the same file will have records read from it and records written on it. It is not necessary to use both an old master file and a new master file when doing indexed sequential updates. All the updates to the master file are written right on the file that is to be changed.

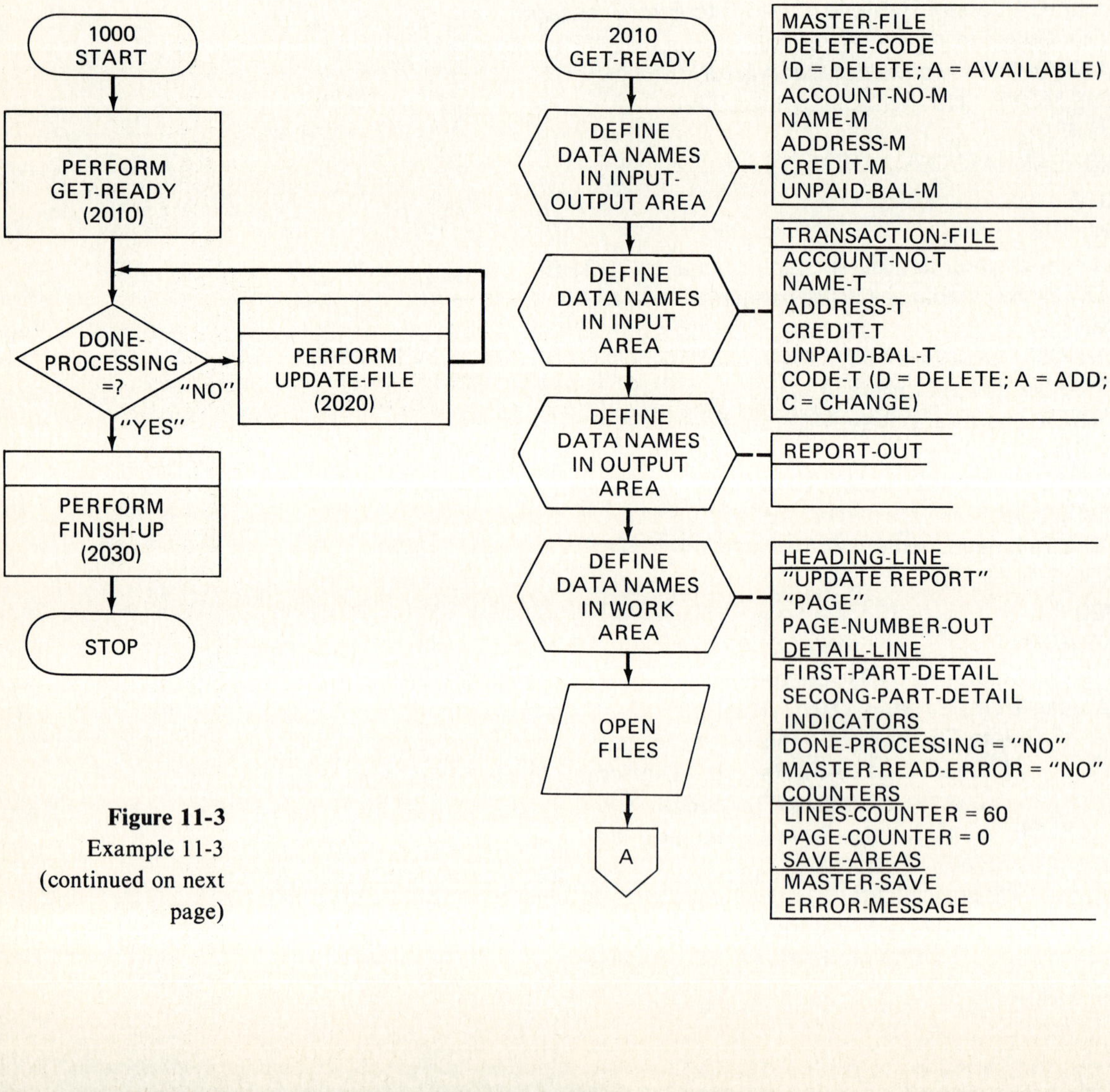

Figure 11-3
Example 11-3
(continued on next page)

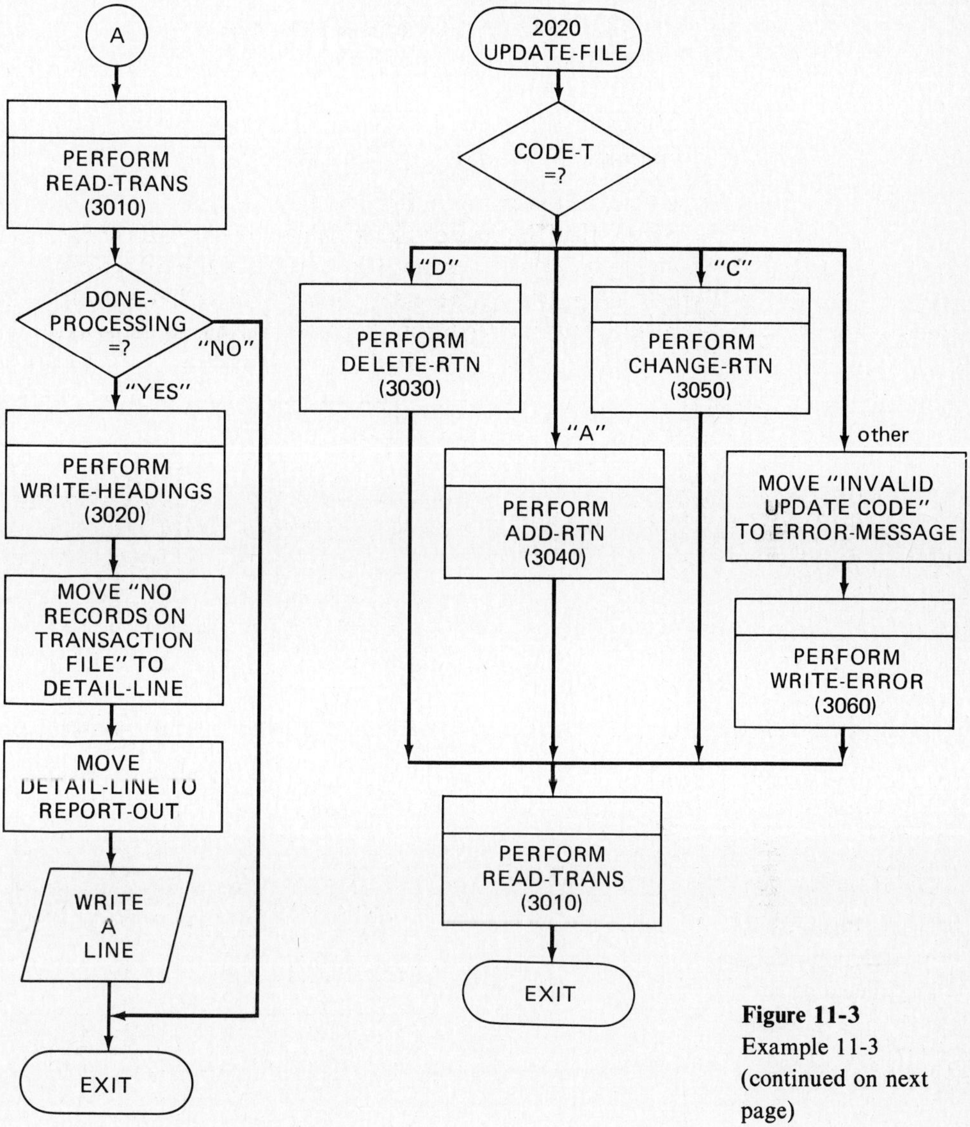

Figure 11-3
Example 11-3
(continued on next page)

It is important to notice that unlike the sequential update program which reads both the transaction and master files and determines if there is a match, the indexed sequential update reads only the transaction file and then looks for the appropriate master file record. Because no sequential matching on the files occurs, it is not necessary to sort the transaction records prior to processing. The transaction records can be entered in any sequence.

The UPDATE-FILE routine is performed for every transaction record. If the code

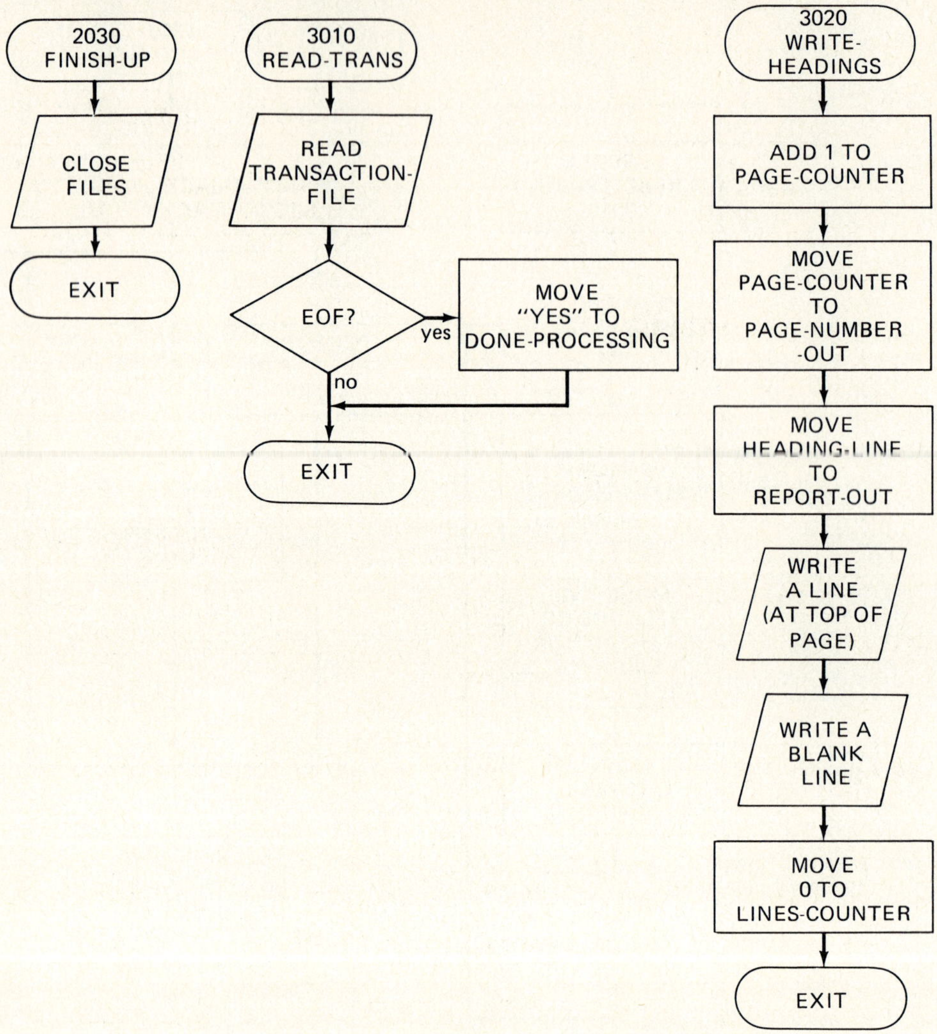

Figure 11-3
Example 11-3
(continued on next page)

on the transaction record is a D, the DELETE-RTN routine is performed. If the code on the transaction record is an A, the ADD-RTN routine is performed. If the code on the transaction record is a C, the CHANGE-RTN routine is performed. If the code is not D, A, or C, then the error routine is called to write a message on the report.

The DELETE-RTN routine is performed to delete a record from the master file. The master file is read first thing in the routine. The READ-MASTER routine moves the key to the key area and attempts to retrieve the master record from the indexed sequential file. Every time you try to access the indexed sequential file, you must check to see if there was an error. In this case, if there was an error, an error

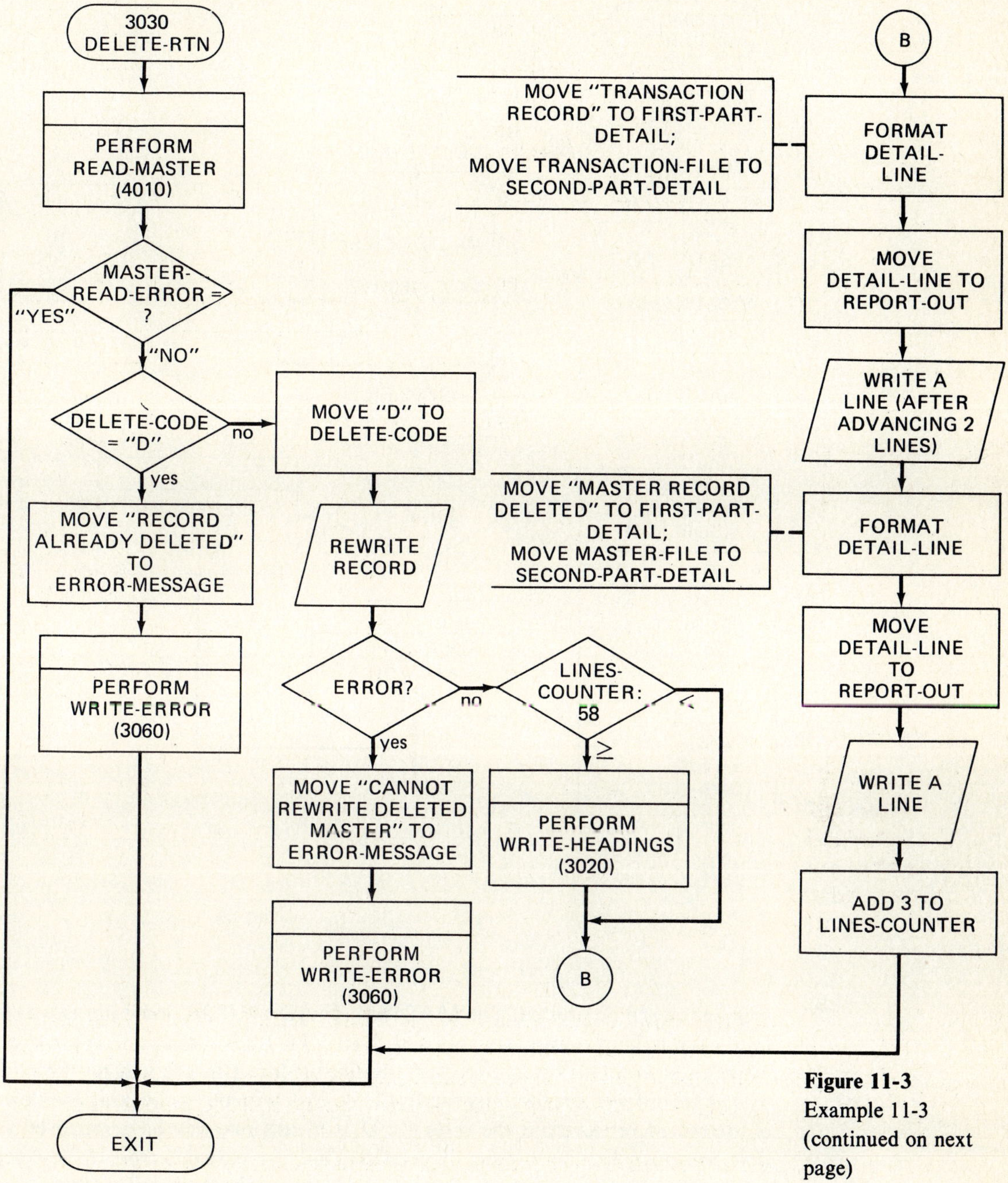

Figure 11-3
Example 11-3
(continued on next page)

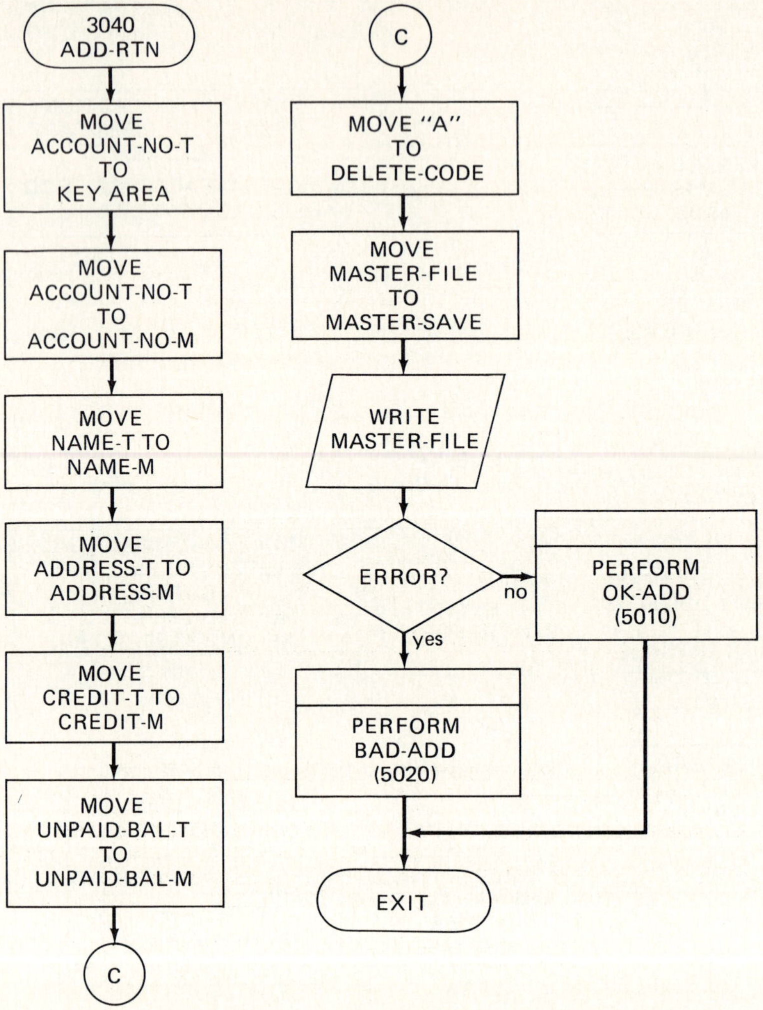

Figure 11-3 Example 11-3 (continued on next page)

message would be printed. The MASTER-READ-ERROR indicator is what is used to tell the calling routine (in this case DELETE-RTN) whether an error occurred when an attempt was made to read the master file. If there was no error (i.e., the master record was successfully read), the next step involves checking the delete code of the record retrieved. If the code is a D, it means that you have retrieved a record that previously had been logically deleted. This results in an error. If the delete code on the record retrieved is not a D, we want to delete the record. This is accomplished by moving a D to the delete code field and rewriting the record.

Some explanation is needed regarding the rewrite instruction. When a new record (i.e., a record not previously on the file) is written on an indexed sequential file, the

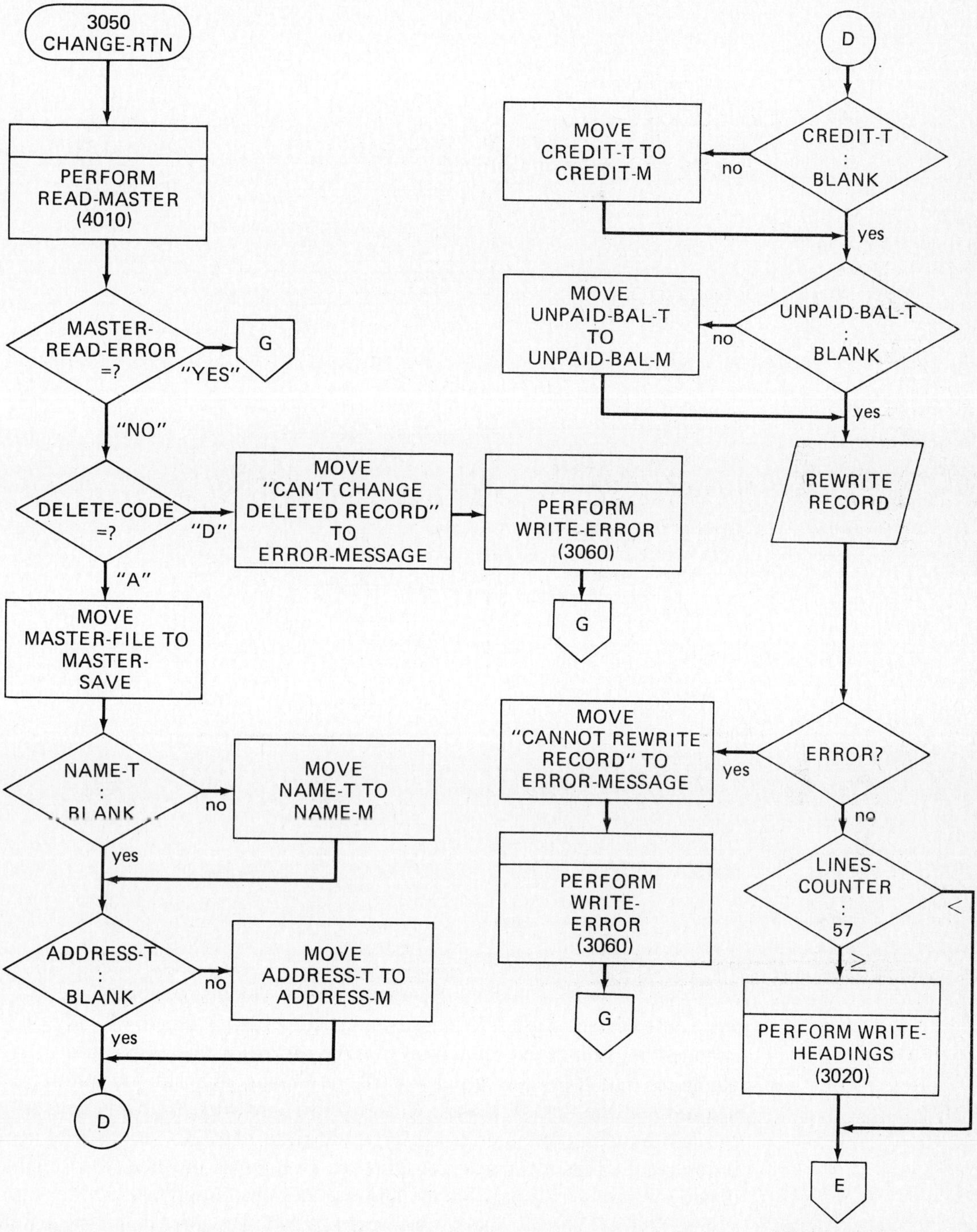

Figure 11-3
Example 11-3
(continued on next page)

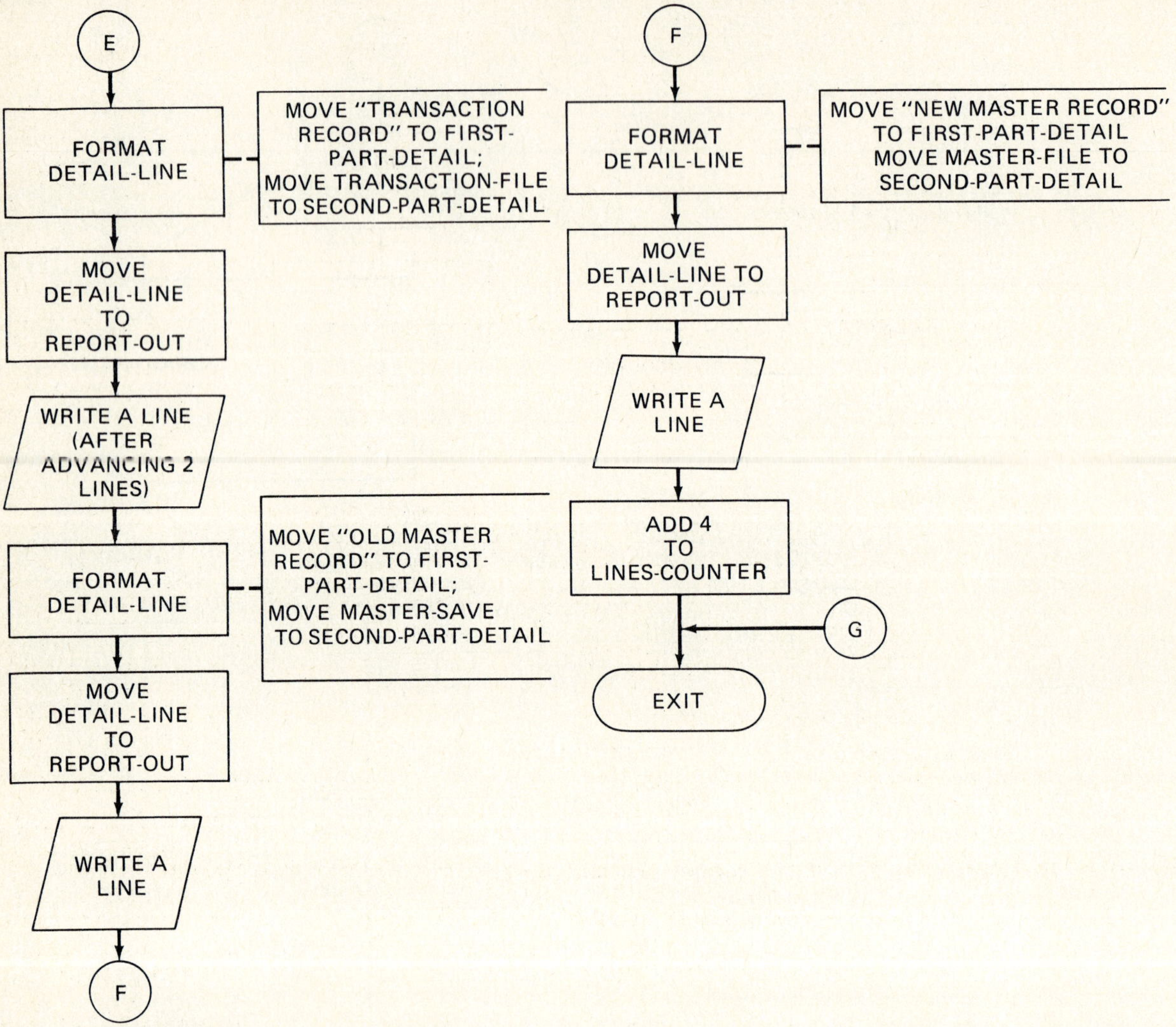

Figure 11-3
Example 11-3
(continued on next page)

write instruction is used. When an old record (i.e., a record already on the file) is changed on an indexed sequential file, the rewrite instruction is used. This tells the computer that the record already exists on the file and that you want to use its storage area on the device to write a changed record with the same key. After a write or rewrite instruction is used, the program must check to see whether an error condition resulted from the access to the file. If no error resulted, the remainder of the delete routine is used to print the desired lines on the report.

The ADD-RTN routine is performed to add a record to the master file. ADD-RTN formats the record, saves it in a field called MASTER-SAVE (the reason for

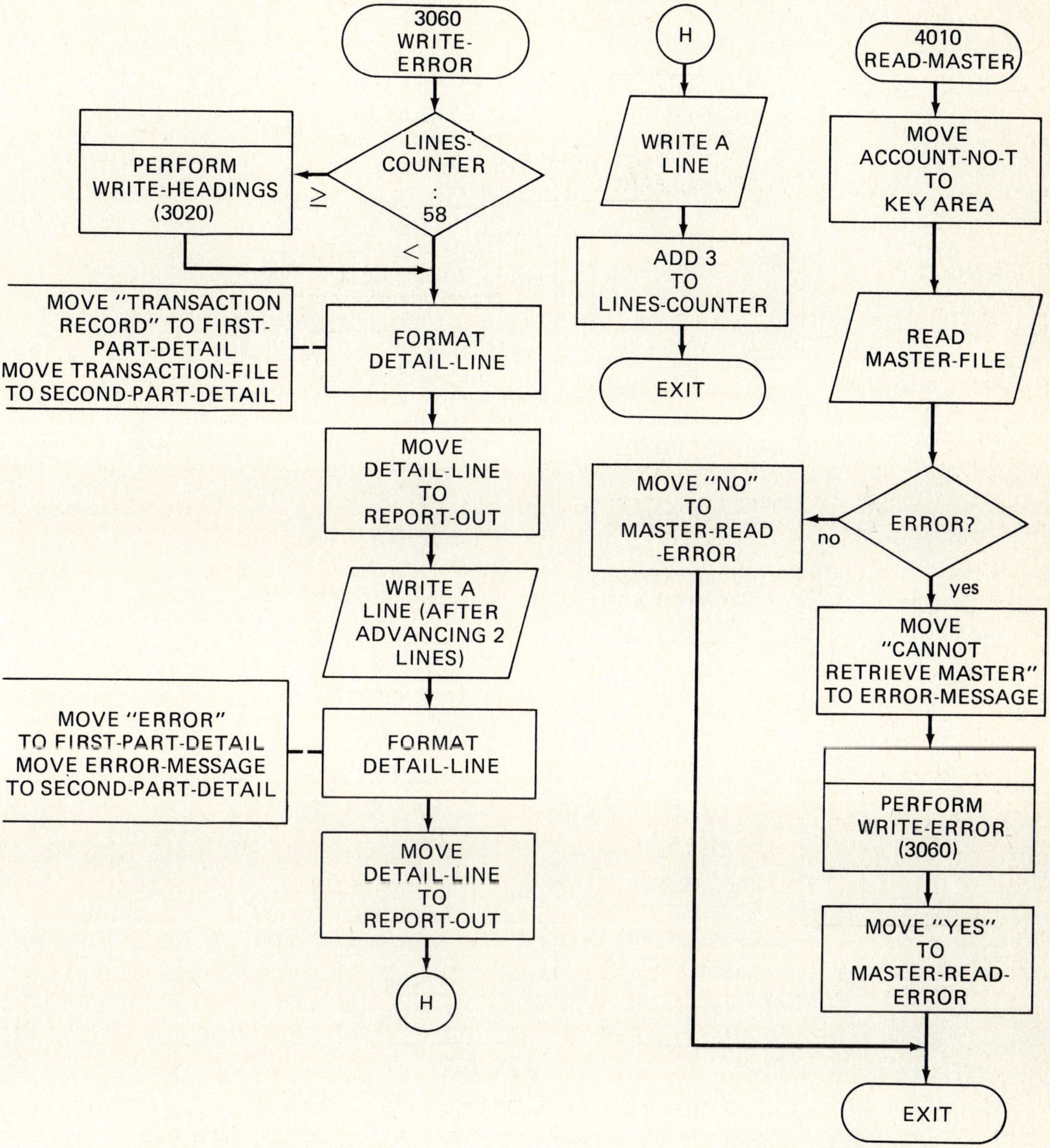

Figure 11-3
Example 11-3
(continued on next page)

this will be explained later), writes the record on the master file, and then checks to see if an error resulted when the record was written on the file. If no error resulted, the OK-ADD routine is performed to print the desired lines on the report.

If there was an error when the record was written on the indexed sequential file, it probably means that the record already exists on the file (a duplicate key). The

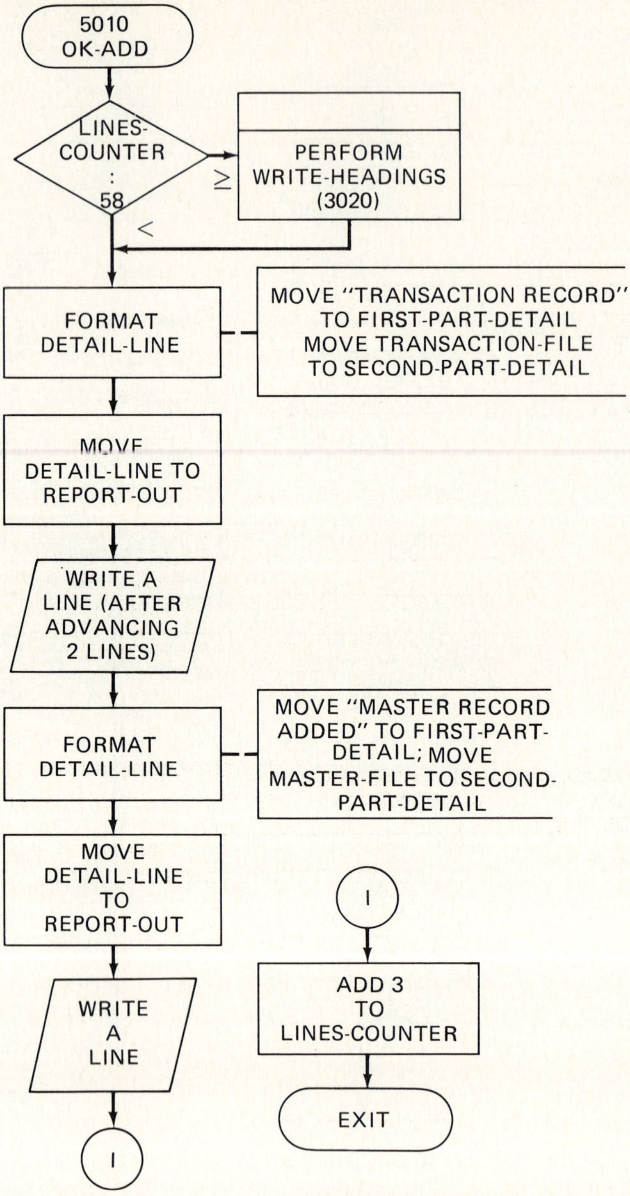

Figure 11-3
Example 11-3
(continued on next page)

BAD-ADD routine is used to check whether the error was caused by an attempt to write a record with a duplicate key on the file. If, in fact, the error was caused by a duplicate key, the BAD-ADD routine checks to see if the duplicate key resulted from a record that had been logically deleted but still physically exists on the file. If that is the case, we simply rewrite the desired record. Note that when the READ-MASTER routine is performed in the BAD-ADD routine, the record read is placed in the

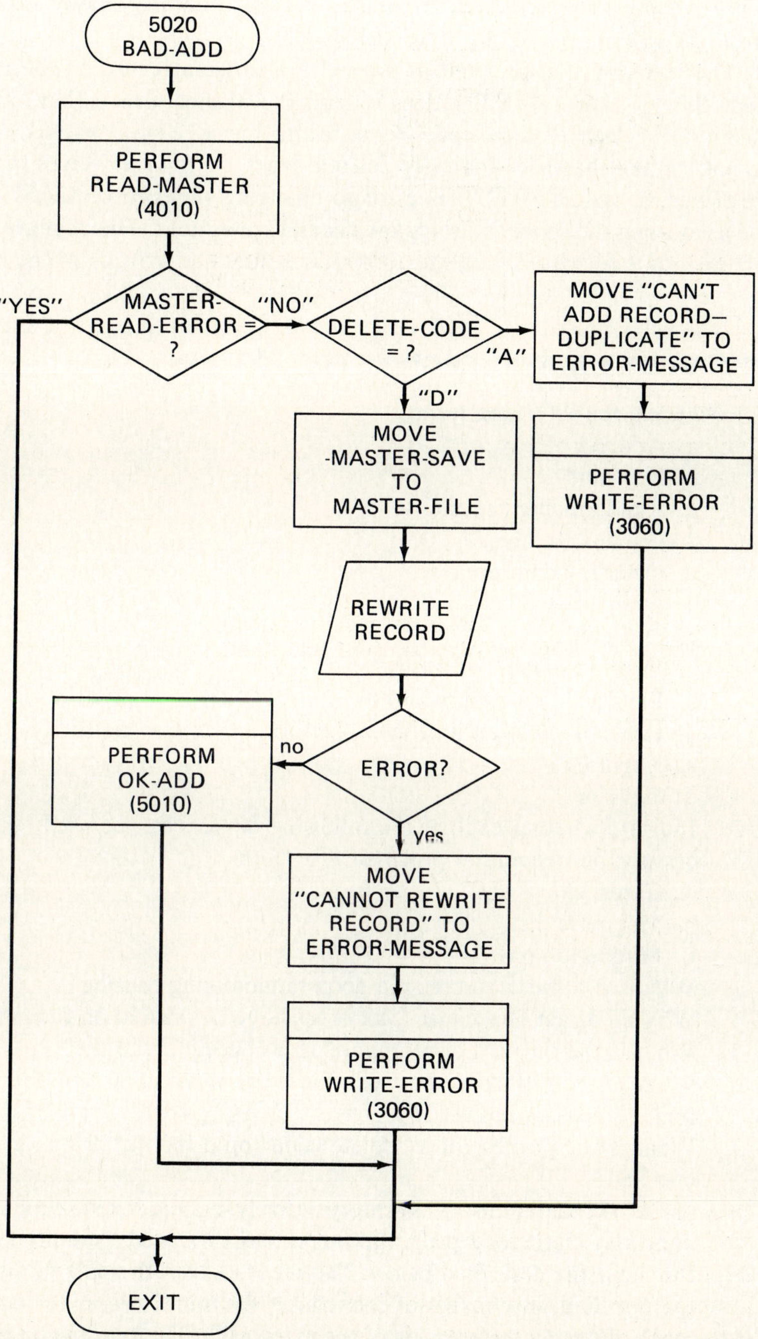

Figure 11-3
Example 11-3
(continued)

input-output area overlaying the master record that was formatted during the ADD-RTN routine. If it turns out that the write error was due to a duplicate key, we want an easy way to reconstruct the master record. This is done by moving the record from MASTER-SAVE to MASTER-FILE.

The CHANGE-RTN routine is used to change a record on the master file. The first thing CHANGE-RTN does is read the master record that is to be changed. Then it checks the delete code of the record to make sure that the record retrieved is not one that has been logically deleted. Next the program saves the master record retrieved in MASTER-SAVE prior to changing the record. MASTER-SAVE will be used when the report lines for the change are written. The changes are then made, the record is rewritten, and the appropriate lines are written on the report.

QUESTIONS AND EXERCISES FOR REVIEW

1. Define the following terms:
   a. Address of a record
   b. Key field
   c. Randomizing routine
   d. Prime data area
   e. Overflow data area
   f. Index area
   g. Direct file
   h. Indexed sequential file
   i. Physically deleted record
   j. Logically deleted record
   k. Key area
   l. Rewrite
2. Indicate whether each of the following devices can be used for sequential processing, nonsequential processing, or both.
   a. Cards
   b. Magnetic disk
   c. Magnetic tape
3. Why is it difficult to create a good randomizing routine?
4. Why do direct files cause a lot of space to be wasted on the device?
5. What is the purpose of reorganizing a nonsequential file?
6. What is the difference between the write instruction and the rewrite instruction? When is each used?
7. What is the purpose of a "delete code" on a record? When does it need to be checked?
8. XYZ Inc. maintains its inventory records in an indexed sequential file. Draw a hierarchy chart for a program to create the indexed sequential master file from the input file described below. The record key is the part number.

   Output: Output consists of the master file and a report listing the errors that resulted during the creation of the master file. The heading on the report should read INVENTORY FILE CREATE OF MM/DD/YY—ERRORS. The current date taken from the system should be used in the heading line. A maximum of 50 detail lines are to appear per page. If no errors occur during processing, the message NO ERRORS should be printed on the report.

Each master file record should contain the following fields. Note that the first position of the record is to contain the delete indicator or switch.

Position	*Description*
1	Delete code (1 = available; 0 = deleted)
2–10	Part number
11–30	Part name
31–35	Price/unit
36–39	Amount on hand

Input

Input consists of a file sorted by part number. The format of each record is:

Position	*Description*
1–9	Part number
10–29	Part name
30–34	Price/unit (has been edited and is numeric)
35–38	Amount on hand (has been edited and is numeric)

9. Draw a flowchart to solve Exercise 8 above.
10. Construct the pseudocode to solve Exercise 8 above.
11. Draw a flowchart to sequentially list the master file described in Exercise 8 above. The heading on the report should read INVENTORY FILE AS OF MM/DD/YY   PAGE XXX. The current date taken from the system and the page number are to appear in the heading line. A maximum of 40 detail lines are to appear per page.
12. Construct the pseudocode for Exercise 11 above.
13. Draw a flowchart to update the master file created in Exercise 8 above.

Input-Output

Use the master file described in Exercise 8 above.

Output

Use as output the report format described in Example 11-3.

Input

The transaction file used to update the master consists of five types of records, as follows:

a. *Add record* (to add a record to the master file)

Position	*Description*
1–9	Part number
10–29	Part name
30–34	Price/unit
35–38	Amount on hand
39	Code = 1

When an "Add" is processed, the program must check to be sure that the part name field is not blank and that the price/unit and amount on hand are numeric. If the above conditions are not met, print an appropriate error message on the report and do not update the master file with the transaction record.

b. *Delete Record* (to delete a record from the master file)

Position	*Description*
1–9	Part number
10–38	Blank
39	Code = 2

c. *Change Part Name* (to change the part name field on the master file)

Position	*Description*
1–9	Part number
10–29	Part name
30–38	Blank
39	Code = 3

When a "part name change" is processed, the program must check to be sure that the part name field on the transaction record is not blank. If it is, print an appropriate error message on the report and do not update the master file with the transaction record.

d. *Change Price/Unit* (to change the price/unit field on the master file)

Position	*Description*
1–9	Part number
10–29	Blank
30–34	Price/Unit
35–38	Blank
39	Code = 4

When a "price/unit change" is processed, the program must check to be sure that the price/unit field on the transaction record is numeric. If it is not, print an appropriate error message on the report and do not update the master file with the transaction record.

e. *Change Amount on Hand* (to change the amount on hand field on the master file)

Position	*Description*
1–9	Part number
10	This field will contain an A, S, or R. If it does not contain an A, S, or R, print an appropriate error message on the report and do not update the master file with the transaction record. If the field contains an A, the program should *add* the amount on the transaction record to the amount on the master file record. If the field contains an S, the program should *subtract* the amount on the transaction record from the amount on the master file record. If the field contains an R, the program should *replace* the amount on the master file record with the amount on the transaction record.
11–34	Blank
35–38	Amount on hand
39	Code = 5

When an "amount on hand change" is processed, the program must check to be sure that the amount on hand field on the transaction record is numeric. If it is not, print an appropriate error message on the report and do not update the master file with the transaction record.

14. Draw a hierarchy chart for Exercise 13 above.
15. Construct the pseudocode for Exercise 13 above.

Index